# Public School Law

*Teachers' and Students' Rights*

**Martha M. McCarthy**
*Indiana University*

**Nelda H. Cambron**
*Miami University*

ALLYN AND BACON, INC.
Boston   London   Sydney   Toronto

To our families—
without their patience and encouragement
this book could not have been written

**Library of Congress Cataloging in Publication Data**

McCarthy, Martha M.
　Public school law.

　Includes bibliographical references and index.
　1. Teachers—Legal status, laws, etc.—United States. 2. Students—Legal status, laws, etc.—United States. I. Cambron, Nelda H. II. Title.
KF4119.M38　　　　344.73'078　　　　81-1304
ISBN 0-205-07278-X　　347.30478　　　　AACR2

Printed in the United States of America

Printing number and year (last digits):
10　9　8　7　6　5　4　3　2　1　　86　85　84　83　82　81

# Contents

*Foreword* by Kern Alexander   viii
*Preface*   x

1 **Introduction: The Legal Foundation of Public Education**   1
·STATE CONTROL OF EDUCATION   1
   Legislative Power   2
   State Agencies   3
   Local School Boards   5
FEDERAL ROLE IN EDUCATION   7
   United States Constitution   7
   Federal Legislation   10
FUNCTION AND STRUCTURE OF THE JUDICIAL
SYSTEM   12
   State Courts   14
   Federal Courts   14
CONCLUSION   16


**PART I   Teachers and the Law   19**

2 **Terms and Conditions of Employment**   21
CERTIFICATION   21
EMPLOYMENT BY LOCAL SCHOOL BOARDS   24
CONTRACTS   26
TENURE   28
REDUCTION IN FORCE   30
OTHER REQUIREMENTS   32
CONCLUSION   34

3 **Constitutional Rights of Teachers**   39
FREEDOM OF EXPRESSION   39
ACADEMIC FREEDOM   44
FREEDOM OF ASSOCIATION   49

POLITICAL ACTIVITY  52
FREEDOM OF RELIGION  56
RIGHT TO PRIVACY  60
PERSONAL APPEARANCE  62
REMEDIES UNDER CIVIL RIGHTS LEGISLATION  64
CONCLUSION  68

**4  Discrimination in Employment**  75
RACE DISCRIMINATION  75
  Selection and Hiring Practices  76
  Staff Reductions  79
  Reverse Discrimination  83
SEX DISCRIMINATION  86
  Pregnancy-Related Policies  87
  Retirement Programs  90
  Employment Opportunities  91
  Title IX and Employment Discrimination  93
AGE DISCRIMINATION  94
DISCRIMINATION BASED ON HANDICAPS  97
CONCLUSION  99

**5  Teacher Dismissal**  107
DUE PROCESS  108
  What Is Due Process of Law?  108
  Procedural Requirements  109
  Summary of Procedural Rights  114
PROCEDURAL RIGHTS OF THE NONTENURED
TEACHER  114
DISMISSAL FOR CAUSE  118
  Incompetency  121
  Immorality  122
  Insubordination  126
  Other Causes  129
  Reduction in Force  132
  Summary of Dismissal Grounds  133
REMEDIES FOR WRONGFUL DISMISSALS  133
  Damages  133
  Reinstatement  134
  Attorneys' Fees  134
CONCLUSION  135

**6  Collective Bargaining**  145
PRIVATE AND PUBLIC SECTOR BARGAINING  145
  Historical Development of Bargaining Rights in the Private
  Sector  146
  Organizational Rights of Public Employees  147

EMPLOYEES' RIGHTS IN THE BARGAINING
PROCESS    147
   Diversity in Bargaining Practices    148
   Bargaining Statutes    149
   Nonunion Teachers' Rights    152
SCOPE OF NEGOTIATIONS    154
   Governmental Policy    155
   Mandatory, Permissive, or Prohibited Items    156
STRIKES    159
CONCLUSION    161


7    Tort Liability    167
ELEMENTS OF NEGLIGENCE    168
   Breach of Duty to Protect Others from Harm    168
   Failure to Exercise Reasonable Care    171
DEFENSES AGAINST NEGLIGENCE    173
   Governmental Immunity    174
   Contributory Negligence    176
   Intervening Act    176
   Notice of Claim    177
ASSAULT AND BATTERY    178
WORKERS' COMPENSATION    179
DEFAMATION    180
LIABILITY INSURANCE    181
CONCLUSION    182


PART II    Students and the Law    187


8    School Attendance: Requirements and Rights    189
COMPULSORY ATTENDANCE    189
   Exceptions to Compulsory Attendance    190
   Attempts to Evade Compulsory Attendance Laws    191
   Required Immunization    192
REQUIREMENTS PERTAINING TO THE INSTRUCTIONAL
PROGRAM    193
   Curricular Requirements and Prohibitions    193
   Prescribed Books    195
   Required Fees for Textbooks and Courses    197
STUDENT ACHIEVEMENT: RIGHT OR
RESPONSIBILITY?    199
   Educational Malpractice    199
   Competency Testing    201

EXTRACURRICULAR ACTIVITIES   203
Training Regulations   203
Transfer Policies   204
Other Conditions   205
STUDENT RECORDS   207
CONCLUSION   209


9   Equal Educational Opportunity: Pupil Classification Practices   217
EQUAL PROTECTION GUARANTEES   217
RACIAL CLASSIFICATIONS   219
CLASSIFICATIONS BASED ON SEX   221
High School Athletics   222
Academic Programs   225
Unresolved Questions   227
CLASSIFICATIONS BASED ON MARRIAGE AND
PREGNANCY 227
Married Students   228
Pregnant Students   228
CLASSIFICATIONS BASED ON AGE   229
CLASSIFICATIONS BASED ON ABILITY OR
ACHIEVEMENT   231
Tracking Schemes   231
Special Education Placements   232
Gifted and Talented Students   234
CLASSIFICATIONS BASED ON HANDICAPS   235
Constitutional Protections   235
Statutory Protections   237
CLASSIFICATIONS BASED ON ETHNIC
BACKGROUND/NATIVE LANGUAGE   241
CONCLUSION   244


10   Students' First Amendment Rights   255
RELIGIOUS GUARANTEES   255
Prohibitions Against Religious Indoctrination by the State   256
Religious Challenges to Secular Activities   259
FREEDOM OF SPEECH AND EXPRESSION   261
Application of the *Tinker* Principle   261
Expression Considered Disruptive   263
FREEDOM OF PRESS: STUDENT PUBLICATIONS   264
Prior Review Regulations   265
Permissible and Impermissible Content   266
School-Sponsored Publications   269
Time, Place, and Manner Regulations   270

FREEDOM OF ASSEMBLY AND ASSOCIATION  271
    Student Clubs  271
    Speakers and Assemblies  272
CONCLUSION  273

11  **Student Discipline**  283
PUNISHMENT IN GENERAL  284
EXPULSIONS AND SUSPENSIONS  287
    Expulsions  287
    Suspensions  288
    Remedies for Unlawful Suspensions or Expulsions  290
DISCIPLINARY TRANSFERS  292
CORPORAL PUNISHMENT  293
    Federal Constitutional Issues  293
    State Laws and School Board Policies  294
ACADEMIC SANCTIONS  296
REGULATION OF STUDENT APPEARANCE  298
    Pupil Hairstyle  298
    Pupil Attire  300
SEARCH AND SEIZURE  301
    Locker searches  303
    Personal Searches  303
    Suggestions for School Personnel  307
CONCLUSION  308

12  **Conclusion: Summary of Legal Generalizations**  317
GENERALIZATIONS  318
CONCLUSION  323

*Glossary*  325
*Index*  329

# Foreword

Upon reading any book, one looks for at least three attributes: scholarship, relevance, and readability. This book clearly has all three. An examination of the references reveals that the authors not only are authorities in the field, but also have very carefully researched and documented each point of law that they address. Law, of course, is not created by authors; nonetheless, their interpretations of the rules laid down by courts and legislatures require a consummate knowledge of the subject matter so as to convey accurately the intent of lawmakers. The authors of this book have carefully delved into hundreds of cases as well as statutory materials, and with scholarly precision have restated the law in a way that is understandable to a broad audience.

A book must be relevant to the state of affairs in the particular field of study, and *Public School Law: Teachers' and Students' Rights* definitely meets this requirement. As those involved in the public schools will testify, the recent upheavals in the law have had a profound impact on the operation of every classroom in the nation. Legal concerns of education two decades ago, which generally revolved around rather mundane issues of administrative law, have been expanded by the innovative application of constitutional principles which have broadened the legal rights and prerogatives of both students and teachers. Today, as never before, the legal fulcrum on which the student-teacher-school relationship balances requires constant reevaluation and attention so as to protect basic human rights and, at the same time, permit public schools to progress in their appropriate pursuits. In this regard, the book presents an even and unemotional view of the law. For example, each chapter provides the reader with positive legal guideposts for educational practice which neither attenuate nor overextend the true meaning of current legal issues.

While some books may survive only on their substance, most will rise or fall on their presentation and readability as well. Fortunately, the content of this book is both substantive and readable. The book's presentation is characterized by good organization, and the authors have a pleasant and uncomplicated writing style that enables the least versed person to glean meaning from the material. Because of its style, the book may be used either as a textbook for aspiring educators or as a general reference for practitioners and others interested in public schools. Either way, the book is an important contribution to the literature of public education and will be widely studied and referenced in the future.

Kern Alexander
Professor of Education
University of Florida

# Preface

This book provides basic information on the current status of the law as it applies to teachers and students in public education. The tension between governmental controls and the exercise of protected rights is examined within the public school context. Specific school situations are analyzed in connection with applicable constitutional and statutory law and the rationale for judicial interpretations of legal mandates. This information should help alleviate concerns voiced by educators who feel that the scales of justice have been tipped against them.

During the past three decades, lawmakers have reshaped a great deal of educational policy. Most school personnel are aware of the burgeoning litigation and legislation, and some are familiar with the names of a few landmark Supreme Court cases. Nonetheless, many teachers and administrators harbor misunderstandings regarding the basic legal concepts that are being applied to educational questions. As a result, they are uncertain about the legality of daily decisions they must make in the operation of schools.

*Public School Law: Teachers' and Students' Rights* differs from other law materials currently available to educators in that legal principles applicable to practitioners are addressed in a succinct but comprehensive manner. Legal aspects of topics that tend to be more relevant to educational policymakers than to practitioners, such as school property and finance, are not covered. Rather, topics with a direct impact on teachers and students are explored. Rights and responsibilities are delineated in areas such as student discipline, teacher dismissal, teachers' constitutional rights, and student classification practices. Implications of legal mandates are discussed, and guidelines are provided for school personnel.

We have attempted to present the material in a nontechnical manner for the novice legal scholar. However, the topics are thoroughly documented, should the reader choose to explore specific cases or points of law in greater detail. Because the use of some legal language cannot be avoided, a glossary of basic terms is provided at the end of the book.

A few comments about the nature of the law might assist the reader in using this book. Laws are not created in a vacuum; they reflect the social and philosophical attitudes of society. Moreover, laws are made by human beings who have personal opinions and biases. While we may prefer to think that the law is always objective, personal considerations do have an impact on the development and interpretation of legal principles.

Also, the law is not static, but rather is continually evolving as courts reinterpret constitutional provisions and legislatures enact new laws. As this book goes to press, judicial decisions are being rendered and statutes are being proposed that may alter the complexion of the law vis-à-vis teachers and students. In addition, some questions confronting school personnel have not yet been addressed by the Supreme Court and have generated conflicting decisions among lower courts. It may be frustrating to a reader, searching for concrete answers, to learn that in some areas the law is far from clear.

In spite of unresolved issues, certain legal principles have been established and can be relied on for direction in many school situations. It is important for educators to become familiar with these principles and to use them as guides to action. With knowledge of the logic underlying the law, school personnel can be more confident in making decisions involving legal questions that have not received judicial or legislative clarification.

Throughout this book, much of the discussion of the law focuses on court cases, because the judiciary plays an important role in interpreting constitutional and legislative provisions. Decisions are emphasized that are illustrative of points of law or indicative of legal trends. A few cases are pursued in some depth to provide the reader with an understanding of the rationale behind the decisions. Reviewing the factual situations that have generated these controversies should make it easier for educators to identify potential legal problems in their own school situations.

For organizational purposes, Part I of this book contains chapters dealing with teachers and the law, and Part II includes chapters focusing on students and the law. An introductory chapter establishes the legal context for the subsequent examination of teachers' and students' rights, and a concluding chapter provides a summary of the major legal principles. Subheadings appear within chapters to facilitate the use of this book for reference if a specific topic is of immediate interest. The reader is encouraged, however, to read the entire text, because some topics are addressed in several chapters from different perspectives, and many of the principles of law apply across chapter divisions. For example, litigation involving various aspects of teachers' rights has relied on precedents established in students' rights cases; the converse also has been true. Taken together, the chapters provide an overall picture of the relationships among issues and the applicable legal principles.

Although the content is oriented toward teachers, much if not most of the material should be of equal interest to administrators and school board members, because many of the legal generalizations pertain to all educational personnel. In addition, this book should serve as a useful guide for parents who are interested in the law governing their children in public schools. With the comprehensive coverage of students' and teachers' rights, this book also is appropriate for use as a basic text for in-service sessions or university units or courses.

While this material should assist school personnel in understanding the current application of the law, it is not meant to serve as a substitute for legal counsel. Educators confronting legal problems should always seek the advice of a competent attorney. Also, there is no attempt here to predict the future course of courts and legislatures. Given the dynamic nature of the law, no single text can serve to keep school personnel abreast of current legal developments. If we can provide an awareness of rights and responsibilities, motivate educators to translate the basic concepts into actual practice, and generate an interest in further study of the law, our purposes in writing this book will have been achieved.

These prefatory remarks would not be complete without mention of the people who assisted in making this book possible. We both are indebted to Kern Alexander, who has influenced the direction of our professional careers and has provided continual support for this project. We also owe a great deal to our students, practicing or aspiring teachers and administrators, who motivated us to write this book and provided reactions to drafts of the material. Amy Zent, Martha Eger, Robert Cabello, and Harry McCabe, in particular, deserve recognition for the time they spent checking case citations. Gratitude also is extended to Nita Coyle and Jan Fulton, who tirelessly typed the numerous drafts of this manuscript.

The contribution of our parents to this book and to all our professional endeavors cannot be measured. They not only provided encouragement and support but also spent thankless hours proofreading the material. George, Kari, and Kristian Kuh deserve special acknowledgment, because without their patience and understanding this book could not have been completed. George made many sacrifices during the past two years so his wife, Martha, could devote long hours to this project. In addition, he provided valuable editorial suggestions and much encouragement throughout this undertaking. To all these individuals, we extend our heartfelt thanks.

Martha M. McCarthy
Nelda H. Cambron

# 1

# Introduction: The Legal Foundation of Public Education

The authority for the establishment and the control of American public education is grounded in law. State and federal constitutional and statutory provisions furnish the framework within which daily operational school decisions are made. There must be a legal basis for all school practices, and policies established at any level of the complex educational enterprise must be consistent with legal mandates from higher authorities. The overlapping jurisdictions of federal and state constitutions, Congress and state legislatures, federal and state courts, and various governmental agencies (including local school boards) often confuse educators as they attempt to follow the law in their respective roles. In an effort to untangle the maze of legal relationships, this chapter provides a description of the major sources of law and how they interact to form the legal basis for public education. This overview establishes a context for the subsequent chapters in which the various legal principles are discussed more fully as they apply to specific school situations involving teachers and students.

## STATE CONTROL OF EDUCATION

The tenth amendment to the United States Constitution stipulates that "the powers not delegated to the United States by the Constitution, nor prohibited by it to the states, are reserved to the states respectively, or to the people." In 1941, the Supreme Court recognized that this amendment was intended "to allay fears that the new national government might seek to exercise powers not granted, and that the states might not be able to exercise fully their reserved powers." [1] Since the Federal Constitution does not authorize Congress to provide for education, the legal control of public education resides with the state as one of its sovereign powers. The Supreme Court repeatedly has affirmed the comprehensive authority of "the states and of school officials to prescribe and control conduct in the schools" as long as actions are consistent with fundamental federal constitutional safeguards.[2] The state's authority over education has been considered comparable to its powers to tax and to provide for the general welfare of its residents.

Most state constitutions specifically mention the legislative responsibility for establishing public schools. For example, the Illinois Constitution stipulates that "the General Assembly shall provide a thorough and efficient system of free schools, whereby all children of this State may receive a good common school education." [3] While each state's educational system is unique in some respects, there are striking similarities among states regarding the basic features of public education.

## LEGISLATIVE POWER

The state legislature has plenary, or absolute, power to make laws governing education. In an early case, the Supreme Court of Virginia recognized the breadth of this power:

> The legislature . . . has the power to enact any legislation in regard to the conduct, control, and regulation of the public free schools, which does not deny to the citizen the constitutional right to enjoy life and liberty, to pursue happiness and to acquire property.[4]

In contrast to the federal government, which has only those powers stipulated in the United States Constitution, state legislatures retain all powers not expressly forbidden by state or federal constitutional provisions. Courts have affirmed the state legislature's authority to create and redesign school districts, raise revenue and distribute educational funds, control teacher certification, prescribe curricular offerings, and regulate other specific aspects of public school operations. Moreover, states can mandate school attendance in the interest of creating an educated citizenry. Presently, all fifty states require students between specified ages (usually six to sixteen) to attend a public or private school or to receive equivalent instruction that must be approved by the state agency.

In some instances, state laws are subject to several interpretations, and courts are called upon to clarify the legislative intent. Also, a state's attorney general may be asked to interpret a law and to advise school boards on the legality of their actions. The official opinion of an attorney general should be followed by school personnel, unless challenged and overruled in court.

Although the state legislature cannot delegate its law-making powers, it can delegate to subordinate agencies the authority to make rules and regulations that are necessary to implement the law. These administrative functions must be carried out within the guidelines established by the legislature. State laws are either mandatory (pertaining to essential state interests in providing education) or permissive (allowing local discretion in providing programs and services).[5] Some states are quite liberal in delegating administrative authority,[6] while other states stipulate detailed standards that must be followed by subordinate agencies.[7] Although it is a widely held misconception that local school boards control public education within this nation, local boards have only those powers conferred by the state. Courts consistently have reiterated that the authority for education is not a local one, but is a central power residing in the state legislature.[8] School buildings are considered state property, and local school board members are state officials.

## STATE AGENCIES

Since it has not been feasible or desirable to include in statutes every minor detail governing public schools, all states have established some type of state board of education. This board often supplies the structural details necessary to carry out broad legislative mandates. In most states, members of the state board of education are elected by the citizenry or appointed by the governor, and the board usually functions immediately below the legislature in the hierarchy of educational governance.

Courts generally have upheld decisions made by state boards of education, unless the decisions have violated legislative or constitutional mandates.[9] In 1973, the Kansas Constitution was interpreted as authorizing the state board of education to require local school districts to develop regulations pertaining to student and employee conduct. The Kansas Supreme Court held that the constitutional grant of general supervisory power to the state board was self-executing in that it required no supplemental legislation to make it effective. The Court noted that the state board's authority to supervise public schools and adopt regulations for that purpose could not be thwarted by the legislature's failure to adopt enabling legislation.[10]

In 1978, the Supreme Court of Pennsylvania recognized the state board of education's authority to issue and enforce uniform student disciplinary regulations governing all schools within the state.[11] Even though local school districts asserted that uniform guidelines were impractical and that local boards were entitled under state law to apply their own disciplinary codes, the Pennsylvania high court held that "far reaching and unequivocal powers" were granted by the legislature to the state board. The court reasoned that the board's authority to establish standards governing all educational programs included the right to enact statewide disciplinary policies.

The following year, the Sixth Circuit Appeals Court upheld the Ohio State Board of Education's authority to compel a school district to be annexed to a neighboring district because it failed to meet minimum standards under state law.[12] Annexation was ordered pursuant to a statutory mandate that any school district not offering educational programs for students in grades one through twelve would be dissolved as of a specified date. The district in question did not have enough students to establish a high school under state board of education regulations. Subsequently, the state board requirement that school districts had to have 240 students to establish a high school was changed to require a minimum number of course offerings instead of a minimum number of pupils. Residents asserted that the revised regulation could be satisfied by the school district, but the Ohio Supreme Court upheld the state board's denial of the request for a second postponement of annexation. Residents then brought suit in federal court, alleging that the school district's constitutional rights to remain in existence were abridged by the state action. Rejecting the claim, the federal district court ruled that fourteenth amendment equal protection and due process rights were not impaired. The Sixth Circuit Appellate Court affirmed the lower court holding and reiterated that the state board of education has authority to enact and enforce reasonable rules and regulations pursuant to state law. The court further emphasized that the federal judiciary would not relitigate state issues under the guise of unsubstantiated federal constitutional violations.

In addition to the state board, generally considered a policy-making body, all states have designated a chief state school officer (often known as the superintendent of public instruction or commissioner of education) to function in an executive capacity. Traditionally, the duties of the chief state school officer have been regulatory in nature. However, other activities, such as research and long-range planning, recently have been added to this role. In some states, the chief school officer is charged with adjudicating educational controversies, and citizens cannot evoke judicial remedies for a grievance pertaining to the internal operations of schools until such administrative appeals have been exhausted. For example, in New York, the commissioner of education is given the final administrative authority to settle educational grievances. Courts have held that when considering an appeal from a state superintendent's decision, they will not judge the wisdom of the decision or overrule such a decision unless it is clearly arbitrary or against the preponderance of evidence.[13]

Each state also has established a state department of education, consisting of educational specialists who provide consultation to the state board, chief state school officer, and local school boards. State department personnel often collect data from school districts to ensure that legislative enactments and state board policies are properly implemented. Most state departments also engage in research and development activities to improve educational practices within the state.

## LOCAL SCHOOL BOARDS

Although education is state controlled in this nation, it is mainly locally administered. All states except one have created local school boards in addition to state education agencies and have delegated certain administrative authority over schools to these local boards. There are approximately 16,000 school districts in this country, some with only a few students and others with several hundred thousand pupils. Many operational decisions governing the day-to-day activities of schools are made by local boards of education.

As with the delegation of authority to state agencies, this delegation to local agencies is handled very differently among the states. In some states with a deeply rooted tradition of local control over education (e.g., Colorado), local school boards are given a great deal of latitude in making operational decisions about schools. In other states that tend toward centralized control of education (e.g., Florida), local boards must function within the framework of detailed legislative directives. Only Hawaii has totally eliminated any local delegation of administrative authority so that all decisions concerning public schools are made at the state level.

Local school board members usually are elected by the citizenry within the school district. Board members are considered to be school officers and to possess a delegation of sovereign power, in contrast to school employees, who are hired to implement directives. Public officers cannot hold two offices if one is subordinate to the other, and in some states they cannot occupy two lucrative offices.[14] Public officers also are prohibited from having an interest in contracts made with their agencies.[15] Generally, statutes stipulate procedures that must be followed in removing public officers from their positions. Typical causes for removal include neglect of duty, illegal performance of duty, breach of good faith, negligence, and incapacity.

Local school boards hold powers specified in state law, powers implied by law, and other powers reasonably necessary to achieve the purposes of the granted powers.[16] These delegated powers usually encompass the authority to determine the specifics of the curriculum offered within the school district, to raise revenue to build and maintain schools, to select personnel, and to enact other policies necessary to implement the educational program pursuant to law. Courts have ruled that the rights to alter attendance zones and close schools are properly within a local school board's delegated discretionary authority.[17] Courts also have upheld the implied rights of local boards to establish and support secondary schools, kindergartens, nongraded schools, and various school-related programs, without specific legislation granting such authority.[18]

Decisions made by local boards of education often have been challenged on the grounds that the board has acted beyond its lawful scope of authority. In 1976, the New York Court of Appeals upheld action by the New York City Board of Education which shortened the school instructional period by two forty-five-minute periods each week.[19] The court reasoned that in the absence of any state regulations specifying a minimum length of instructional time for schools, the local board acted within its legal powers. In a 1978 case, the Virginia Supreme Court also addressed the scope of authority of local school boards. The court interpreted Virginia law as prohibiting the state board of education from requiring local school boards to submit to binding arbitration in disputes between the boards and nonsupervisory personnel.[20] The court concluded that the power of "general supervision," vested by the legislature in the state board, did not include the authority to "supervise schools," which was clearly delegated to local boards. The court reasoned that supervision of schools encompassed the handling of disputes involving employees.

State legislatures have not, however, relinquished their legal responsibility for education. The state can restrict the administrative authority of local boards by enacting legislation to that effect. School boards cannot exercise powers that are not at least implied in state law. For example, the Supreme Court of Washington ruled that a school board could not maintain a clinic offering medical, surgical, and dental treatment for needy pupils because there was no implied statutory authority for such an activity.[21]

Furthermore, local school boards cannot delegate their decision-making authority to other agencies or associations. In an illustrative case, a New Jersey court ruled that a school board could not relinquish responsibility for determining courses of study or settling classroom controversies to the teachers' association.[22] Also, the Iowa Supreme Court held that a school board could not delegate its rule-making authority to a state high school athletic association.[23]

A local school board must act as a body; individual board members are not empowered to make policies or perform official acts on behalf of the board. Also, board meetings and records must be open to the public. Local boards have some latitude in adopting operational procedures, but they are legally bound to adhere to such procedures once they are established. While courts are reluctant to interfere with decisions made by boards of education and will not rule on the wisdom of such decisions, they will invalidate any board action that is arbitrary, capricious, or outside the board's legal authority (*ultra vires*).

Local boards are authorized to perform discretionary duties (i.e., involving judgment), while school employees, such as superintendents, principals, and teachers, can perform only ministerial duties that are necessary to carry out policies. Hence, a superintendent can recommend personnel to be hired and propose a budget to the board, but the board must actually make the personnel decisions and adopt the budget. Although it might appear that school administrators and teachers are left little decision-making authority, this is not actually the case. Administrators as well as classroom teachers can enact rules and regulations, consistent with board policy and law, to ensure the efficient operation of the school or class under their supervision.

## FEDERAL ROLE IN EDUCATION

In contrast to state constitutions, the Federal Constitution is silent regarding education; hence, individuals do not have an inherent right to an education simply because of United States citizenship.[24] The United States differs from most countries in that the national government does not directly control public education. The Federal Constitution does, however, confer basic rights on individuals, and these rights must be respected by school personnel. Furthermore, Congress exerts control over the use of federal funds provided to schools under authority of the general welfare clause and regulates certain aspects of schools under provisions of the commerce clause.

### UNITED STATES CONSTITUTION

A constitution, by definition, is a body of precepts providing the system of fundamental laws of a nation, state, or society. The United States Constitution establishes a separation of powers among the executive, judicial, and legislative branches of government. These three branches form a system of checks and balances to ensure that the intent of the Constitution is respected. The Federal Constitution also provides a systematic process for altering the document, if this is deemed necessary. Article V stipulates that amendments may be proposed by a two-thirds vote of each house of Congress, or by a special convention called by Congress upon request of two-thirds of the state legislatures. Proposed amendments must then be ratified by three-fourths of the states in order to become part of the Constitution.

Since the Federal Constitution is the supreme law of this nation, state authority over education must be exercised in a manner consistent with its provisions. In 1958, the Supreme Court declared:

> It is, of course, quite true that the responsibility for public education is primarily the concern of the States, but it is equally true that such responsibilities, like all other state activity, must be exercised consistently with federal constitutional requirements as they apply to state action.[25]

The federal government has greatly influenced public schools through its judicial branch. The Supreme Court has interpreted various constitutional guarantees as they apply to educational matters. While all federal constitutional mandates affect public education to some degree, the following provisions have had the greatest impact on public school policies and practices.

**General Welfare Clause.** Under Article I, Section 8 of the Constitution, Congress has the power "to lay and collect Taxes, Duties, Imposts and Excises, to pay the Debts and provide for the Common Defense and General Welfare of the United States. . . ." Although historically this clause has been the subject of much debate, the Supreme Court has interpreted the provision as allowing Congress to tax and spend public monies for a variety of purposes related to the general welfare.[26] The Court has stated that it will not interfere with the discretion of Congress in this domain, unless Congress exhibits a clear display of arbitrary power.[27]

Using the general welfare rationale, Congress has enacted legislation providing substantial federal support for research and instructional programs in areas such as science, mathematics, reading, special education, vocational education, career education, and bilingual education. Also, in the interest of the general welfare of the nation, Congress has provided financial assistance for the school lunch program and for services to meet the special needs of various groups of students, such as the culturally disadvantaged.

**Commerce Clause.** Congress is empowered to "regulate Commerce with foreign Nations, and among the several States, and with Indian tribes" under Article I, Section 8, Clause 3 of the Constitution. Safety, transportation, and labor regulations enacted pursuant to this clause have affected the operation of public schools. Traditionally, courts have favored a broad interpretation of "commerce" and an expanded federal role in regulating commerce activities to ensure the prosperity of the country. In 1976, however, the Supreme Court interpreted the tenth amendment as limiting the power of Congress to regulate state governmental activities under the commerce clause. The Court invalidated amendments to the Fair Labor Standards Act that extended wage and hour standards to most public employees, including school personnel.[28] The Court held that the state's power to determine employee wages is an "undoubted attribute of state sovereignty." [29] This restricted view of the federal government's authority to regulate state functions under the commerce clause may deter enactment of other national legislation pertaining to schools, such as a federal collective bargaining law for public employees.

**Obligation of Contracts Clause.** Article I, Section 10 of the Constitution stipulates that states cannot pass any law impairing the obligation of contracts. Administrators, teachers, and noncertified personnel are protected from arbitrary dismissals by contractual agreements. School boards also enter into numerous contracts with individuals and companies in carrying out the daily business activities of schools. The judiciary often is called upon to evaluate the validity of a given contract, or to assess whether one party has breached its contractual obligations.

**First Amendment.** The first amendment affords the following pervasive personal freedoms to citizens:

> Congress shall make no law respecting an establishment of religion, or prohibiting the free exercise thereof; or abridging the freedom of speech, or of the press; or the right of the people peaceably to assemble, and to petition the Government for a redress of grievances.

The religious freedoms contained in this amendment have evoked lawsuits challenging the use of public funds to aid nonpublic school students and contesting school policies and practices as abridging the wall of separation between church and state. Cases involving students' rights to express themselves freely and to distribute student literature have been initiated under first amendment guarantees of freedom of speech and press. Also, teachers' rights to academic freedom, as well as to speak out on matters of public concern, have generated numerous legal challenges. The right of assembly has been the focus of litigation involving student clubs and employees' rights to organize and engage in collective bargaining.

**Fourth Amendment.** The fourth amendment guarantees the right of citizens "to be secure in their persons, houses, papers, and effects against unreasonable searches and seizures." Since the late 1960s, this amendment has frequently appeared in educational cases involving searches of students' lockers and personal belongings.

**Fifth Amendment.** The fifth amendment provides in part that no person shall be "compelled in any criminal case to be a witness against himself, nor be deprived of life, liberty, or property without due process of law; nor shall private property be taken for public use, without just compensation." Several cases have addressed the application of the self-incrimination clause in instances where teachers have been questioned by superiors about their activities outside the classroom. The last clause of the fifth amendment has been used in educational litigation to protect citizens' rights to appropriate compensation for property acquired for school purposes. Due process litigation concerning schools usually has been initiated under the fourteenth amendment, which pertains directly to state action. However, many cases in the District of Columbia (involving topics such as desegregation and the rights of handicapped children) have relied on the due process guarantees of the fifth amendment, because the fourteenth amendment does not apply in this jurisdiction.[30]

**Eighth Amendment.** The eighth amendment prohibits excessive bail and fines and protects citizens against cruel and unusual punishment by governmental agents. While this amendment has appeared more often in suits challenging the treatment of prisoners or other persons involuntarily institutionalized, it has been used in a few cases challenging the administration of corporal punishment in public schools.

**Ninth Amendment.** The ninth amendment stipulates that "the enumeration in the Constitution, of certain rights, shall not be construed to deny or disparage others retained by the people." This amendment has appeared in educational litigation in which teachers have asserted that their right to personal privacy outside the classroom is protected as an unenumerated right. Also, grooming regulations applied to teachers and students have been challenged as impairing personal rights retained by the people under this amendment.

**Fourteenth Amendment.** The fourteenth amendment is the most widely used in school litigation because it pertains specifically to actions of the states. In part, the fourteenth amendment provides that no state shall "deny to any person within its jurisdiction the equal protection of the laws." This clause has been particularly significant in school cases involving alleged discrimination based on race, sex, ethnic background, and handicaps. In addition, school finance litigation often has been grounded in the equal protection clause.

The due process clause of the fourteenth amendment, which prohibits states from depriving citizens of life, liberty, or property without due process of law, also has played an important role in school litigation. Students have asserted their state-created property right to an education in cases challenging the adequacy of procedures followed in making instructional assignments and in administering punishment for misconduct. Teachers also have used the due process clause to contest dismissal and disciplinary actions involving alleged infringements of protected liberty and property rights. The Supreme Court has interpreted fourteenth amendment liberties as including the personal freedoms contained in the Bill of Rights. Thus, the first ten amendments, originally directed toward the federal government, have been applied to state action as well.

FEDERAL LEGISLATION

Congress is empowered to enact laws in order to translate the intent of the Federal Constitution into actual practices. Laws reflect the will of the legislative branch of government, which, in this nation, represents the citizenry.

Since the states have sovereign power regarding education, the federal government's involvement in public schools has been one of indirect support, not direct control.

Federal legislation affecting public education actually was enacted prior to ratification of the Federal Constitution. The Ordinances of 1785 and 1787, providing land grants to states for the maintenance of public schools, encouraged the establishment of public education in many states. While these grants reflected a federal interest in general education for all citizens, the federal government did not attempt to exercise control over education as a prerequisite to receipt of the grants. Later, the Morrill Act of 1862 provided for the establishment of land-grant colleges. The Smith-Lever Act (1914) provided grants for county extension services for agriculture and homemaking, in addition to teacher training in these areas. In 1917, the initial federal legislation supporting vocational education in public secondary schools was enacted. The National School Lunch Act, affecting nonpublic as well as public schools, was passed in 1946 in order to improve the quality of food services available in schools.

The first major attempt by Congress to stimulate educational reform through its powers under the general welfare clause was the National Defense Education Act (1958), which provided financial assistance to institutions and students in areas such as mathematics, science, and foreign languages. Later, the Vocational Education Act of 1963 provided funds to expand occupational and technical training in public schools. The most comprehensive law offering financial assistance to schools, the Elementary and Secondary Education Act of 1965 (ESEA), supplied funds for compensatory education programs for economically disadvantaged students and for demonstration and innovative programs. The Act also provided financial assistance to improve supplementary educational services and libraries and to strengthen state departments of education. Other ESEA provisions, including various amendments, have provided fiscal support for services for special categories of students, such as handicapped, gifted, and non-English-speaking children.

Congress has exerted considerable influence in shaping public school policies by establishing guidelines that must be followed in order for schools to be eligible to receive federal funds. Individual states or school districts have the option of accepting or rejecting federal assistance under such categorical aid legislation. If funds are accepted, however, the federal government has the authority to prescribe guidelines for their use and to monitor state and local agencies to ensure fiscal accountability. Since most federal aid is categorical in nature, it cannot be spent at the discretion of local school boards. The one major exception to this rule is assistance to school districts that are "impacted" by nontaxable federal property. Such districts are entitled to federal funds to compensate for the tax revenues lost due to the tax-exempt governmental property. This "impact aid" can be used to address the general needs of the school district.

In addition to laws providing financial assistance to public schools, Congress has enacted legislation designed to clarify the scope of individuals' civil rights. In the latter part of the nineteenth century, several acts were passed primarily to protect the rights of black citizens. Some of these, particularly the Civil Rights Act of 1871, have been revived in recent years and used by students and teachers to gain relief in instances where their constitutional rights have been impaired by school policies and practices. Section 1983 of the Civil Rights Act of 1871 states:

> Every person who, under color of any statute, ordinance, regulation, custom, or usage of any State or Territory, subjects or causes to be subjected any citizen of the United States or other person within the jurisdiction thereof to the deprivation of any rights, privileges or immunities secured by the Constitution and laws, shall be liable to the party injured in an action at law, suit in equity, or other proper proceeding for redress.[31]

Subsequent civil rights legislation enacted during the 1960s and early 1970s has further defined the rights of citizens to remain free from discrimination. The vindication of individual rights in school settings has generated substantial litigation involving Title VI of the Civil Rights Act of 1964 (prohibiting discrimination on the basis of race, color, or national origin in federally assisted programs or activities), Title VII of the Civil Rights Act of 1964 (prohibiting employment discrimination on the basis of race, color, religion, national origin, or sex), Title IX of the Education Amendments of 1972 (prohibiting sex discrimination against participants in educational programs receiving federal funds), and the Rehabilitation Act of 1973 (prohibiting discrimination against handicapped persons in federally assisted programs or activities).

Other federal legislation has established funding sources to assist school districts in attaining equity. For example, the Bilingual Education Act of 1968 and the Education for All Handicapped Children Act of 1975 have provided federal funds to assist education agencies in offering services for students with special needs. Several federal agencies have developed regulations to ensure the proper implementation of these laws. If these regulations are not followed by public schools, the federal funds can be withdrawn. Often, courts have been called upon to interpret these acts and their regulations as they apply to teachers and students.

## FUNCTION AND STRUCTURE
## OF THE JUDICIAL SYSTEM

Judicial mandates are often cited in conjunction with statutory and constitutional provisions as a major source of educational law. Alexis de Toqueville noted in 1945 that "scarcely any political question arises in the United States that is not resolved sooner or later into a judicial question." [32] Courts, however, do not initiate laws as legislative bodies do; courts establish legal principles by exercising their powers of judicial review. Courts apply appropriate principles of law to settle disputes and do not intervene unless an actual controversy exists. Although most constitutional provisions and statutory enactments never become the source of litigation, some provisions must be clarified by the judiciary. Since federal and state constitutions set forth broad policy statements rather than specific guides to action, courts serve an important function in interpreting such mandates and determining the legality of various laws and administrative regulations. It has been firmly established that the United States Supreme Court has the ultimate authority in interpreting federal constitutional guarantees.[33] Consequently, the Supreme Court occupies a powerful position as the "final arbiter of the nature and limits of state power under the Constitution." [34]

The United States Supreme Court has articulated specific guidelines that it follows in exercising its powers of judicial review. It does not anticipate a constitutional question in advance of the necessity of deciding it, and does not rule on the constitutionality of legislation in a nonadversary proceeding. It does not decide a case on constitutional grounds if there is some other ground upon which the case may be decided. Furthermore, when an act of Congress is questioned, the Court always attempts to "ascertain whether a construction of the statute is fairly possible by which the question may be avoided." [35] In applying appropriate principles of law to specific cases, the Court tries to follow the doctrine of *stare decisis* (abide by decided cases), and thus relies on precedents established in previous decisions.

Courts have assumed an increasingly significant role in determining educational policy since the landmark desegregation decision, *Brown v. Board of Education of Topeka,*[36] was delivered. Much of this judicial intervention has involved the protection of individual rights and the attainment of equity for minority groups.[37] During the past decade, courts have addressed nearly every facet of the educational enterprise, including students' rights to free expression, compulsory attendance and mandatory curriculum offerings, school finance reform, employment practices, student discipline, educational malpractice, sex discrimination, collective bargaining, employees' rights to privacy, desegregation, and the rights of handicapped and non-English-speaking students.

Courts, however, will not intervene in a school-related controversy if the dispute can be settled in a legislative or administrative forum. In 1973, the Supreme Court emphasized that in situations involving "persistent and difficult questions of educational policies," the judiciary's "lack of specialized knowledge and experience counsels against premature interference with the informed judgments made at the state and local levels." [38]

In evaluating the impact of case law, it is important to keep in mind that a judicial ruling applies as precedent within the geographical jurisdiction of the court delivering the opinion. It is possible for two state supreme courts or two federal courts to render conflicting decisions on an issue, and such decisions are binding in their respective jurisdictions until the United States Supreme Court rules on the issue. Only Federal Supreme Court opinions have national application.

## STATE COURTS

All state educational systems provide some type of administrative appeals procedure for aggrieved individuals to use in disputes involving the internal operations of schools. Many school-related controversies never reach the courts because they are settled in these administrative forums. Courts require that administrative appeals be pursued before court action is brought, so that the judiciary does not become involved in disputes that can be settled through administrative channels.[39] When administrative appeals are exhausted without relief, however, court action can be initiated.

State courts are established pursuant to state constitutional provisions, and the structure of judicial systems varies among states. In contrast to federal courts, which have only those powers granted in the United States Constitution, state courts have the authority to settle most types of controversies, unless restricted by state law. State judicial systems usually include trial courts of general jurisdiction, courts of special jurisdiction such as probate or juvenile courts, and appellate courts. All states have a court of last resort in the state appeals process[40]; decisions rendered by state high courts can be appealed to the United States Supreme Court.

## FEDERAL COURTS

Article III, Section I of the Federal Constitution establishes the United States Supreme Court and authorizes Congress to create other federal courts as necessary. Traditionally, the federal judiciary did not address educational concerns; less than three hundred cases involving education had been initiated in federal courts prior to 1954.[41] Today, however, hundreds of school cases are initiated in federal courts each year. During the past two decades, the federal judiciary has shed its laissez-faire posture toward schools, and has exhibited a reformation attitude in protecting individual rights in educational settings.

The federal court system is comprised of three levels—district courts, circuit courts of appeal, and the United States Supreme Court. Each state has at least one federal district court. Many states have two or three, and California, New York, and Texas have four each. Judgments at the district court level are usually presided over by one judge.

On the federal appeals level, the nation is divided into eleven geographic circuits, and each circuit has a federal circuit court of appeals.[42] Federal circuit courts have from three to fifteen judges, depending on the workload of the circuit. Federal circuit courts follow established rules in exercising appellate review. They will not overturn district court rulings unless the lower court decisions represent clearly erroneous applications of the law.

Decisions rendered at the federal circuit level are extremely important, particularly if the Supreme Court has not addressed the issue involved in a specific case. Although a federal circuit court decision is binding only in the states within that circuit, such decisions often influence other appellate courts when they deal with similar questions. The jurisdiction of the federal circuits is as follows.

First Circuit: Maine, New Hampshire, Massachusetts, Rhode Island, and Puerto Rico.

Second Circuit: Vermont, New York, and Connecticut.

Third Circuit: Pennsylvania, New Jersey, Delaware, and the Virgin Islands.

Fourth Circuit: Maryland, Virginia, West Virginia, North Carolina, and South Carolina.

Fifth Circuit: Georgia, Florida, Alabama, Mississippi, Louisiana, Texas, and the Canal Zone.

Sixth Circuit: Michigan, Ohio, Kentucky, and Tennessee.

Seventh Circuit: Indiana, Illinois, and Wisconsin.

Eighth Circuit: Minnesota, Iowa, Missouri, Arkansas, North Dakota, South Dakota, and Nebraska.

Ninth Circuit: Washington, Oregon, California, Nevada, Arizona, Idaho, Montana, Alaska, Hawaii, and Guam.

Tenth Circuit: Wyoming, Utah, Colorado, New Mexico, Kansas, and Oklahoma.

D.C. Circuit: Washington, D.C.[43]

The United States Supreme Court is the highest court in the nation, beyond which there is no appeal. It disposes of approximately 5,000 cases a year, but renders a written opinion on the merits in less than five percent of these cases.[44] The Court often concludes that the topic of a case is not appropriate or of sufficient significance to warrant Supreme Court review. Since the Supreme Court has authority to determine which cases it will hear, many issues are left for resolution by lower courts. Accordingly, precedents regarding some school controversies must be gleaned from federal circuit courts or state supreme courts and may vary from one jurisdiction to another.

Suits are initiated in a federal court instead of a state court if they involve an interpretation of the United States Constitution or federal laws or if they entail disputes between parties residing in different states. Individuals need not exhaust administrative remedies before initiating a suit in federal court if the abridgment of a federally protected right is involved.

## CONCLUSION

American public schools are governed by a complex body of regulations that are grounded in constitutional provisions, statutory enactments, agency regulations, and court decisions. During recent years, legislation and litigation pertaining to schools have increased dramatically in both volume and complexity. Although rules made at any level must be consistent with those of higher authorities, administrators and classroom teachers retain considerable latitude in establishing rules and procedures within their specific jurisdictions. As long as educators act reasonably and do not impair protected rights of others, their actions will be upheld if challenged in court.

School personnel, however, cannot plead "ignorance of the law" as a valid defense for illegal actions.[45] Therefore, educators should be aware of the constraints placed on their rule making prerogatives by school board policies and federal and state constitutional and statutory provisions. In the subsequent chapters, an attempt is made to explicate the major legal principles that affect teachers and students in their daily school activities.

## NOTES

1. United States v. Darby, 312 U.S. 100, 124 (1941).
2. Tinker v. Des Moines Independent School Dist., 393 U.S. 503, 507 (1969).
3. Ill. Const., art. 10, § 1.
4. Flory v. Smith, 134 S.E. 360, 362 (Va. 1926). *See also* Board of Educ. of Aberdeen-Huntington Local School Dist. v. State Bd. of Educ., 116 Ohio App. 515, 189 N.E.2d 81 (1962); State Tax Comm'n v. Board of Educ. of Jefferson County, 235 Ala. 388, 179 So. 197 (1938).
5. *See* William Hazard, *Education and the Law* (New York: The Free Press, 1971), p. 3.
6. *See* School Dist. No. 3, Town of Adams v. Callahan, 297 N.W. 407 (Wis. 1941); Sunnywood Common School Dist. v. County Bd. of Educ., 131 N.W.2d 105 (S.D. 1964).
7. *See* State *ex rel.* Donaldson v. Hines, 182 P.2d 865 (Kan. 1947).
8. *See* State *ex rel.* Clark v. Haworth, 122 Ind. 462, 23 N.E. 946 (1890).
9. *See* Bell v. Board of Educ., 215 S.W.2d 1007 (Ky. 1948); Board of Educ. v. Rogers, 15 N.E.2d 401 (N.Y. 1938); Wiley v. Alleghany County School Comm'rs, 51 Md. 401 (1879).
10. State *ex rel.* Miller v. Board of Educ. of Unified School Dist. No. 398, Marion County, 511 P.2d 705 (Kan. 1973).
11. Girard School Dist. v. Pittenger, 392 A.2d 261, 264 (Pa. 1978).
12. Wilt v. State Bd. of Educ., 608 F.2d 1126 (6th Cir. 1979), *cert. denied*, 100 S. Ct. 1654 (1980). *See also* Board of Educ. of Bratenahl Local School Dist. v. State Bd. of Educ., 373 N.E.2d 1238 (Ohio 1978).

13. *See* Craig v. Board of Educ., 19 N.Y.S.2d 293 (1940), *aff'd* 27 N.Y.S.2d 993 (App. Div. 1941).
14. *See* Ind. Const., art. 2, § 9.
15. *See* People v. Becker, 246 P.2d 103 (Cal. App. 1952).
16. *See* Hazard, *Education and the Law*, p. 4.
17. *See* Beegle v. Greencastle-Antrim School Dist., 401 A.2d 374 (Pa. 1979).
18. *See* Schwan v. Board of Educ. of Lansing School Dist., 27 Mich. App. 391, 183 N.W.2d 594 (1971); Sinnott v. Colombet, 40 P. 329 (Cal. 1895); Stuart v. School Dist. No. 1 of the Village of Kalamazoo, 30 Mich. 69 (1874).
19. New York City School Bds. Ass'n v. Board of Educ. of City School Dist. of City of New York, 39 N.Y.2d 111, 383 N.Y.S.2d 208, 347 N.E.2d 568 (1976). *See also* Welling v. Board of Educ., 382 Mich. 620, 171 N.W.2d 545 (1969).
20. School Bd. of City of Richmond v. Parham, 243 S.E.2d 468 (Va. 1978).
21. McGilvra v. Seattle School Dist. No. 1, 194 P. 817 (Wash. 1921).
22. Board of Educ. v. Rockaway Township Educ. Ass'n, 295 A.2d 380 (N.J. Super. 1972).
23. Bunger v. Iowa High School Athletic Ass'n, 197 N.W.2d 555 (Iowa 1972). *See* text with note 76, Chapter 8.
24. *See* San Antonio Independent School Dist. v. Rodriguez, 411 U.S. 1 (1973).
25. Cooper v. Aaron, 358 U.S. 1, 19 (1958).
26. *See* United States v. Gettysburg Electric Ry., 160 U.S. 668 (1896); United States v. Butler, 297 U.S. 1 (1936); Helvering v. Davis, 301 U.S. 619 (1937).
27. Helvering v. Davis, *id.* at 644–45.
28. National League of Cities v. Usery, 426 U.S. 833 (1976).
29. *Id.* at 845.
30. *See* note 43, *infra*.
31. 42 U.S.C. § 1983 (1976).
32. Alexis de Toqueville, *Democracy in Education*, ed. rev. (New York: Alfred A. Knopf, 1945), p. 280.
33. *See* Marbury v. Madison, 5 U.S. (1 Cranch) 137 (1803).
34. John Coons, William Clune, and Stephen Sugarman, *Private Wealth and Public Education* (Cambridge, Mass.: Harvard University Press, 1970), p. 287.
35. Crowell v. Benson, 285 U.S. 22, 62 (1932). *See also* Ashwander v. Tennessee Valley Authority, 297 U.S. 288, 348 (1936) (Brandeis, J., concurring).
36. 347 U.S. 483 (1954).
37. *See* Betsy Levin, *The Courts as Educational Policy Makers and Their Impact on Federal Programs* (Santa Monica, Cal.: Rand, Inc., 1977), pp. 4–6.
38. San Antonio Independent School Dist. v. Rodriguez, 411 U.S. 1, 42 (1973).
39. *See* Phillips County v. Hughes, 552 P.2d 328 (Mont. 1976).
40. In most states, the high court is called the supreme court. In New York, however, this court is called the New York State Court of Appeals.

41. John Hogan, *The Schools, the Courts, and the Public Interest* (Lexington, Mass.: D. C. Heath & Co., 1974), p. 7.

42. Under constitutional authority, Congress also has established federal courts of special jurisdiction such as the Court of Claims, Tax Court, and Customs Court.

43. Washington, D.C., has its own federal district court and circuit court of appeals because of the fact that only federal laws apply in this jurisdiction.

44. Arval Morris, *The Constitution and American Education* (St. Paul, Minn.: West Publishing Co., 1980), p. 25.

45. *See* Wood v. Strickland, 420 U.S. 308 (1975); text with note 41, Chapter 11.

# PART I

# Teachers and the Law

Legal mandates affecting all aspects of public education have increased significantly in recent years. In this dynamic legal environment, it is essential for educators to be cognizant of the parameters of their protected rights, as well as the legal principles governing their professional roles. The current status of the law in relation to public school teachers is depicted in this section.

The initial four chapters of this part address the balancing of interests between the teacher's freedom to exercise personal rights and governmental authority to restrict these rights for the welfare of the schools. Chapter 2 deals with various terms and conditions of teacher employment, including certification, contractual obligations, and tenure protections. This analysis covers the legality of prerequisites to employment (e.g., competency examinations, citizenship requirements) and conditions attached to maintaining employment (e.g., continuing education requirements, residency stipulations). The next two chapters focus on the teacher's protected rights and the remedies available when such rights are impaired by employment practices. In Chapter 3, teachers' freedoms of speech, association, religion, and privacy are discussed. Chapter 4 addresses constitutional and statutory protections against discrimination in employment. Alleged discriminatory practices based on race, sex, age, and handicap are explored in connection with selection and hiring practices, termination decisions, working conditions, and employee benefits. Chapter 5 provides an overview of the law pertaining to teacher dismissals. Procedural due process guarantees are delineated as they apply to the tenured and nontenured teacher. Statutory grounds for dismissal are identified with specific illustrations from a number of states.

The last two chapters in this section focus on topics of substantial concern to teachers—collective bargaining and tort liability. In Chapter 6, the evolution of collective bargaining in public education, and its impact on teacher employment, is explored in relation to bargaining rights, impasse procedures, agency shop provisions, negotiable items, and strikes. Chapter 7 includes a general treatment of tort law, with major emphasis on the elements of negligence and defenses that can be used to protect educators from liability for pupil injuries.

These chapters provide a legal framework for understanding teachers' rights and responsibilities in public school systems. With an increased awareness of the impact of the law on the many facets of school operations, teachers can more effectively and responsibly perform their duties in the classroom.

# 2

# Terms and Conditions of Employment

As noted in Chapter 1, the control of public education resides with the states. This control is exclusive as long as the constitutional rights of individuals are respected. The judiciary has clearly recognized the plenary power of the state legislature in establishing, conducting, and regulating all public education functions. The legislature, through statutory law, establishes the parameters within which the educational system operates; the actual administration of the school systems is delegated to state boards of education, state departments of education, and local boards of education. These agencies promulgate rules and regulations pursuant to legislative policy for the operation of the public schools.

Among the areas affected by these state statutory and regulatory provisions are the terms and conditions of a teacher's employment. In this chapter, state requirements for teacher certification, employment, contracts, tenure, and related conditions of employment are discussed.

## CERTIFICATION

To qualify for a teaching position in public schools, all prospective teachers must acquire a valid certificate or license. Certification is a state responsibility, and certificates are issued according to the statutory provisions of each state. Although the responsibility for licensing resides with the legislature, administration of the process has been delegated to state boards of education and state departments of education. It is recognized that states have not only the right but also the duty to establish certain minimum qualifications and to ensure that teachers meet these standards.[1]

Certificates are granted primarily on the basis of professional preparation. In most states, educational requirements include a college degree, with minimum credit hours or courses identified in various curricular areas. In addition to professional preparation, other prerequisites to certification may include good personal character, a specified age, United States citizenship, signing of a loyalty oath, and passage of an academic examination. The following is a representative statutory requirement.

> The Department of Public Instruction shall have the power, and its duty shall be—
>
> (a) To provide for and to regulate the certificates and the registration of persons qualified to teach in such schools;
>
> (b) To certify as qualified to practice the art of teaching in such schools any applicant eighteen (18) years of age, of good moral character, not addicted to the use of intoxicating liquor or narcotic drugs and who has graduated from a college, university or institution of learning approved as herein provided, and who has completed such professional preparation for teaching as may be prescribed by the State Board of Education, and to register such person upon such proof as the State Board of Education may require that such applicant possess such qualifications.[2]

As noted in the above statutory requirement, an applicant for teacher certification may be required to possess "good moral character." The definition of what constitutes good character is often elusive, with a number of factors entering into the determination. The Supreme Court of Oregon found that evidence of burglary eight years prior to application for a teaching certificate was pertinent in assessing character for certification purposes.[3] The Oregon court noted that character embraced all "qualities and deficiencies regarding traits of personality, behavior, integrity, temperament, consideration, sportsmanship, altruism, etc." [4] Courts generally will not rule on the wisdom of a certifying agency's assessment of character; they will intervene only if statutory or constitutional rights are abridged.

Certification of teachers by examination was common prior to the expansion of teacher education programs in colleges and universities. However, until recently only a few states (Mississippi, North Carolina, South Carolina, and West Virginia) required passage of an exam for certification. These states have employed the National Teachers Examination, and its use has been upheld by the United States Supreme Court as constitutionally permissible even though the test has been shown to disproportionately disqualify black applicants.[5] With the recent advent of teacher competency tests in six additional states, there seems to be a trend toward the reinstatement of examinations as a prerequisite to certification.[6]

The signing of a loyalty oath often is included as a condition of obtaining a teaching certificate, but such oaths cannot be used to restrict associational rights guaranteed under the Constitution. The Supreme Court has invalidated oaths that require teacher applicants to swear that they are not members of subversive organizations[7]; however, teachers can be required to sign an oath pledging support for the United States Constitution and an individual state's constitution.[8]

As a condition of certification, a teacher may be required to be a citizen of the United States. In 1979, the Supreme Court addressed the question of whether use of such a requirement in New York violated the equal protection clause of the fourteenth amendment.[9] Under the New York education laws, a teacher who is eligible for citizenship but refuses to apply for naturalization cannot be certified. Although the Supreme Court has placed restrictions on the states' ability to exclude aliens from governmental employment, it has recognized that certain functions are "so bound up with the operation of the state as a governmental entity as to permit the exclusion from those functions of all persons who have not become part of the process of self-government." [10] Following this principle, the Court held that teaching is an integral "governmental function"; thus, a state must show only a rational relationship between a citizenship requirement and a legitimate state interest. Accordingly, the Court concluded that New York's interest in furthering its educational goals justified the citizenship stipulation for teachers.

A teacher who has met all of the legal qualifications for certification must be issued a certificate. This certificate to teach is a license, and not an absolute right to acquire a position. Hence, the legislature may impose new or additional burdens on the teacher.[11] The certifying agency, however, may not place restrictions on licensing that violate statutory provisions. A New York appellate court held that the denial of a teaching license to one classified as legally blind was "arbitrary, capricious, and contrary" to law.[12]

Certification indicates only that a teacher has met minimum qualification requirements of the state. It does not entitle an individual to employment in a particular district or guarantee employment in the state,[13] nor does it prevent a local school board from requiring additional qualifications or conditions for employment.[14] However, if a local board imposes minimum standards for employment, such as the completion of a master's degree, the requirements must be uniformly applied to all teachers in the district.[15]

Teaching credentials must be in proper order to ensure full employment rights. Where a state law required a teacher's certificate to be on file in the district of employment, the failure to file the certificate rendered the teacher's contract voidable.[16] Similarly, lack of proper credentials can invalidate a claim for compensation.[17] Teaching services provided without certification are viewed by courts as voluntary and, as such, require no compensation.

The state is empowered not only to certify teachers but also to revoke certification. Although a local board may initiate charges against a teacher, only the state can revoke a teacher's certificate. Revocation of a certificate is an extreme action. In most states, it must be based on statutory cause, with full procedural rights provided to the teacher.[18] The most frequently cited causes for revoking certification are immorality (31 states), incompetency (24 states), contract violation (22 states), and neglect of duty (21 states).[19]

When revocation of a certificate is being considered, determination of a teacher's competency encompasses not only classroom performance but also actions outside of the school setting that may impair the teacher's effectiveness. The California Supreme Court found that a teacher's participation in a "swingers" club and disguised appearance on television discussing nonconventional sexual behavior justified revocation of certification on grounds of unfitness to teach.[20] In an earlier case, however, the California Supreme Court held that an isolated incident of private homosexuality did not justify license revocation; no relationship was shown between the teacher's activity and effectiveness to teach.[21] Similarly, a California appellate court concluded that arrest and conviction for possession of marijuana was insufficient to justify revocation of a teacher's certificate, because there was no evidence that the incident had an adverse effect on students or teachers.[22]

## EMPLOYMENT BY LOCAL SCHOOL BOARDS

As noted, certification does not guarantee employment in a state; it attests only to the fact that the teacher has met minimum state requirements. The decision to employ or not to employ a certified teacher is among the discretionary powers of local school boards. While such powers are broad, school board actions cannot be arbitrary or capricious, or in violation of an individual's statutory or constitutional rights.[23] Employment decisions must be neutral as to race, religion, national origin, and sex.[24] Unless individually protected rights are abridged, courts will not review the wisdom of a local school board's judgment in employment decisions if the board has acted in good faith.[25]

The duty to appoint teachers is vested in the school board and cannot be delegated.[26] Employment decisions cannot be made by the superintendent or board members individually but must be made by the board as a collective body. In most states, binding employment agreements between a teacher and school board must be approved at legally scheduled board meetings. Procedurally, a number of state laws specify that the superintendent must make employment recommendations to the board [27]; however, the board is not compelled to follow these recommendations unless mandated to do so by law.

Although the state prescribes the minimum certification standards for teachers, this does not preclude the local school board from requiring higher professional or academic standards as long as they are applied in a uniform and nondiscriminatory manner. For example, school boards often establish continuing education requirements for teachers. The right of a board to dismiss teachers for failure to satisfy such requirements has been upheld by the Supreme Court.[28] The Court concluded that school officials merely had to establish that the requirement was rationally related to a legitimate state objective, which in this case was to provide competent, well-trained teachers.

School boards can adopt reasonable health and physical standards for teachers. However, regulations must not contravene various state and federal laws designed to protect the rights of the handicapped. For example, the Third Circuit Court of Appeals ruled in a Pennsylvania case that school officials cannot refuse to consider blind individuals as teachers for sighted students.[29] A New York trial court similarly held that blindness cannot disqualify one as a teacher.[30] School board standards for physical fitness generally are upheld by courts as long as they are rationally related to ability to perform teaching duties. A New York appellate court found that obesity *per se* was not reasonably related to ability to teach or to maintain discipline.[31]

The authority to assign teachers to schools within the district resides with the board of education. As with employment in general, the decisions can be challenged only if arbitrary or made in bad faith.[32] Within the limits of certification, a teacher can be assigned to teach in any school at any grade level. However, assignments designated within the teacher's contract cannot be changed during a contractual period without the consent of the teacher. That is, a board cannot move a teacher to a first-grade class if the contract specifies a fifth-grade assignment. If the contract designates only a teaching assignment within the district, the assignment still must be in the teacher's area of certification. Additionally, objective, nondiscriminatory standards must be used in any employment or assignment decision pertaining to teachers.[33]

The school board also retains the authority to reassign or transfer teachers. Such transfers often are challenged as constituting demotion. Although the majority of the cases have involved transfers from administrative or supervisory positions, actions also have been initiated by teachers. A Pennsylvania teacher contested a transfer from a ninth-grade class to a sixth-grade class as a demotion.[34] The court, noting the equivalency of the positions, stated that "there is no less importance, dignity, responsibility, authority, prestige, or compensation in the elementary grades than in secondary." [35] However, in another instance the reassignment of a Montana band instructor to a teaching position in an ungraded rural school without a band was held to be a demotion.[36] Similarly, the reassignment of an Ohio regular classroom teacher as a permanent substitute or floating teacher was found to be a demotion in contravention of the state tenure law.[37] The court recognized the pervasive authority of the superintendent and board to make teaching assignments, but noted that this power may be limited by other statutory provisions, such as the tenure law. This reduction in status without a notice and hearing deprived the teacher of due process guarantees.

The transfer of a teacher from one position to another does not require due process unless the action violates constitutional rights.[38] The Supreme Court of California held that a transfer in assignment based on a teacher's criticism of school policies impaired the teacher's right to freedom of expression, and thus necessitated a hearing.[39] However, routine transfers would not invoke such constitutional protections.

The assignment of extracurricular duties often is defined in a teacher's contract; in the absence of such specification, it is generally held that boards can make reasonable and appropriate extracurricular assignments. A California teacher claimed that being required to supervise six athletic events during the school year was both beyond the scope of his duties and unprofessional.[40] The court determined that the assignment was within the scope of the contract and reasonable, since it was impartially distributed and did not place an onerous burden on the teacher in terms of time. Assignments are usually restricted by the courts to activities that are an integral part of the school program[41] and, in some situations, to duties that are related to the employee's teaching responsibilities.[42] A New Jersey appellate court stated that reasonableness of assignment should be evaluated in terms of time involvement, teachers' interests and abilities, benefits to students, and the professional nature of the duty.[43]

## CONTRACTS

The general principles of contract law apply to the teacher's contract. Like all other legal contracts, it must contain the basic elements of (1) offer and acceptance, (2) competent parties, (3) consideration, (4) legal subject matter, and (5) proper form.[44] Beyond these basic elements, it also must meet the requirements specified in state law.

The authority to contract with teachers is an exclusive right of the board. The school board's offer of a position to a teacher, including (1) designated salary, (2) specified period of time, and (3) identified duties and responsibilities, creates a binding contract when accepted by the teacher. In most states, only the board can make an offer, and this action must be approved by a majority of the board members in a properly called meeting. The failure to provide adequate notice of a meeting to all board members can invalidate contractual actions taken by the board at the meeting.[45]

Contracts also can be invalidated for lack of competent parties. To form a valid, binding contract, both parties must have the legal capacity to enter into an agreement. The school board has been recognized as a legally competent party with the capacity to contract.[46] A teacher who lacks certification or is under the statutorily required age for certification is not a competent party for contractual purposes. Consequently, a contract formed with such an individual is not enforceable.[47]

Consideration is another essential element of a valid contract. Consideration is something of value that one party pays in return for the performance of the other party. Also, the contract must pertain to a legal subject matter and follow the proper form required by law. Most states prescribe that a teacher's contract must be in writing to be enforceable. If there is no statutory specification, an oral agreement is legally binding on both parties.

A teacher's contract cannot be unilaterally abrogated by the school board. Termination of the contract must be based on cause, which generally is identified in state law. Prior to dismissal, the teacher must be provided with notice of the charges and a hearing.[48] At the end of the contract period, renewal of the contract is at the discretion of the board, and nonrenewal requires no explanation, unless one is statutorily mandated.

The contract cannot be used as a means of waiving a teacher's statutory rights. In Iowa, by law, teachers are classified as probationary and nonprobationary. The first two years of employment are designated as probationary, and renewal of the contract is at the school board's discretion. However, after the teacher is classified as nonprobationary, employment can be terminated only if cause is established. A local school district incorporated the following clause into a nonprobationary teacher's contract:

> It is mutually agreed that this contract shall be for one year only and shall not continue beyond the 2nd day of June, 1978. On said date this contract shall terminate without notice, hearing, or any other action by the Board.[49]

At the end of the school year, the teacher was terminated by the board pursuant to the contract clause. The Supreme Court of Iowa declared the clause invalid. In overturning the board's action, the court noted that the statutory procedural protections are a part of the teacher's contract, and thus negate the waiver of rights. Since the board did not establish cause for dismissal, the teacher's contract was automatically renewed.

The teacher's legal rights of employment are derived from the contract.[50] Additional rights accrue from any collective bargaining agreement in effect at the time of employment. Also, statutory provisions and rules and regulations of the school board may be considered as part of the terms and conditions of the contract. If not included directly, the provisions existing at the time of the contract may be implied.[51] For example, a valid school board maternity leave policy that is not incorporated into the teacher's contract cannot be evaded on grounds that it is beyond the scope of the contractual relationship.

## TENURE

Since the first state enacted tenure legislation for teachers in the early 1900s, the concept has been extended to forty-seven of the fifty states.[52] Although financial exigency, declining enrollment, and public demand for accountability have subjected tenure to close scrutiny by policy makers, tenure systems appear to be firmly entrenched in American public education. Modifications or reforms in the system may occur, but the actual dissolution of the practice is unlikely.

Many purposes have been advanced for the tenure system. The basic and fundamental purpose, of course, is job security for the teacher. An examination of judicial decisions reveals that a number of purposes have been ascribed to tenure laws by courts. These reasons have included ensuring permanency in the teaching force, improving the teaching force, protecting the capable and experienced teacher, and eliminating employment uncertainty.

Tenure is a contractual relationship with a school district which ensures the teacher that employment will be terminated only for adequate cause and that procedural due process will be provided. Since tenure is a statutory right rather than a constitutional right, specific procedures and protections vary among the states. Most tenure statutes specify requirements and procedures for obtaining tenure and identify causes and procedures for dismissal of a tenured teacher. In interpreting tenure laws, courts have attempted to protect teachers' rights while simultaneously maintaining flexibility for school officials in personnel management.[53]

Employment contracts can be classified into three categories: term contracts, continuing contracts, and tenure contracts.[54] Term contracts are valid for a fixed length of time and must be renegotiated at the expiration date; no responsibility is placed on either party beyond the contract period. In practice, the words "continuing contract" and "tenure contract" are used interchangeably, but they convey significantly different legal rights.[55] Under a continuing contract, a teacher's employment continues from year to year unless terminated in accordance with state law. A continuing contract usually requires notification of termination by a specified date, with no requirement for statement of cause or other aspects of due process. In contrast, a tenure contract guarantees continued employment unless terminated for cause. Dismissal under a tenure contract necessitates at least minimum due process procedures.

The authority to grant tenure is a discretionary power of the local school board which cannot be delegated. Although the school board confers tenure, it cannot alter the tenure terms established by the legislature.[56] Revisions in the tenure law must be accomplished through the legislative process. A teacher may acquire tenure only in the manner prescribed by law.[57] Thus, if the statute requires a probationary period, this term of service must be completed prior to acquisition of tenure. Statutes also identify areas in which school personnel may accrue tenure. A number of states limit tenure to teaching positions, thereby excluding administrative and supervisory positions.[58] It must be noted that tenure granted by the school board does not guarantee permanent employment, nor does it convey the right to teach in a particular school or grade.[59] Teachers may be dismissed for the causes specified in the tenure law, and may be reassigned to positions for which they are certified.

Supplementary service contracts usually are considered to be outside of the scope of tenure protections. For example, a Florida appellate court concluded that tenure rights applied only to employment as a teacher in the area of certification and did not cover employment as a coach.[60] The Minnesota Supreme Court also found the position of coach to be outside the statutory protections provided to teaching positions.[61] Similarly, the Supreme Court of Nebraska held that supplementary contracts for coaches were not identified in the tenure statute and, therefore, were not afforded the procedural and substantive protections of continuing employment contracts.[62]

Prior to the awarding of tenure to a teacher, most states require a probationary period of approximately three years. This period is established to allow school boards to assess a teacher's ability and competencies. During this period, there is no guarantee of employment beyond each annual contract. At the completion of the probationary service, the board must determine whether to grant tenure or to terminate employment. If the board decides to terminate a probationary teacher, this action may be accomplished without citing cause or providing a hearing unless such provisions are mandated by statute. Successful completion of the probationary period with satisfactory or outstanding ratings does not restrict the decision of the board; however, state law may afford protections to teachers with satisfactory records during the probationary period. For example, in Michigan, the tenure law provides that a teacher who satisfactorily completes the probationary period is entitled to tenure. Where a school district notified a teacher of nonrenewal of contract but did not indicate that performance was unsatisfactory, a Michigan appeals court held that the teacher was entitled to tenure.[63]

Most tenure statutes require regular and continuous teaching service to complete the probationary period. For example, the Massachusetts tenure statute requires teaching service of three consecutive school years immediately prior to the award of tenure.[64] Interpreting this mandate, a Massachusetts appellate court held that a teacher who taught for approximately three-fourths of a school term could not count such teaching service toward tenure because it was less than a school year.[65] On the other hand, part-time employment of a continuous and regular nature was interpreted as meeting probationary requirements under the Massachusetts statute, because the law required only continuous service and did not designate a separate classification for part-time service.[66]

In most states, a probationary teacher who is not provided proper notice that the contract will not be renewed is entitled to an additional year of employment. However, a question frequently litigated is whether the teacher also is entitled to tenure if the improper notice occurs at the completion of the probationary period. New York courts consistently have held that tenure is not conveyed unless there is actual service beyond the probationary period.[67] In contrast, under the Michigan tenure law, which confers tenure upon satisfactory completion of the probationary period, the lack of proper notice entitles the teacher to tenure.[68] Generally, the lack of notice results only in an additional year of employment rather than tenure.[69]

The United States Constitution, Article I, Section 10, provides that the obligation of a contract may not be impaired. In establishing tenure, a legislature may create a contractual relationship that cannot be altered without violating constitutional guarantees. The United States Supreme Court found such a contractual relationship in the 1927 Indiana Teacher Tenure Act, which prevented the state legislature from subsequently depriving teachers of rights conveyed under the act.[70] However, a statutory relationship that does not have the elements of a contract can be altered or repealed at the legislature's discretion.[71] Some state tenure laws are clearly noncontractual, containing provisos that the law may be altered, while other state laws are silent on revisions. If a tenure law is asserted to be contractual, the language of the act is critical in judicial interpretation of legislative intent.

## REDUCTION IN FORCE

As noted in the preceding section, tenure laws ensure that teachers will not be dismissed except for cause. Cause may include a number of factors, such as incompetency, immorality, neglect of duty, or unfitness to teach.[72] These causes deal directly with the teacher's abilities and competencies. However, school districts may be faced with conditions beyond their control that necessitate staff reductions. Effective management of a school system requires flexibility in tenure laws to enable school officials to make appropriate cutbacks or reductions in force (RIF). Consequently, such a necessary reduction can constitute sufficient "cause" for the dismissal of a tenured teacher.

During the past decade, reduction in force has become an increasing concern of all teachers. Pupil enrollments have declined steadily since 1971, with a projected decline of six million pupils by 1983.[73] On the average, schools will experience a drop of approximately 13 percent in enrollments during this period; however, the impact is far from uniform. To illustrate, between 1970 and 1975 the national average decline in public school population was 2.3 percent, but a number of large urban areas experienced drastic losses: St. Louis, 22.6 percent; San Francisco, 22.2 percent; Cleveland, 15 percent; Detroit, 14.3 percent; and Baltimore, 13.7 percent.[74] Of the fifty largest school systems, all experienced at least a 10 percent decrease in enrollment.[75]

The problem of declining enrollment is further exacerbated by reduced revenue, taxpayer resistance to increased taxes, and inflation. Since most state aid is distributed on a per pupil basis, a decline in enrollment results in a commensurate decline in state revenue to support the schools. The Ohio school aid formula illustrates the double-edged effect of this phenomenon. State aid is distributed inversely to district wealth, which is determined by dividing average daily membership into the total assessed value of property. Thus, as enrollment declines, the district appears wealthier on a per pupil basis and receives less aid. The district not only reports fewer pupils for aid purposes, but also, because of the wealth measure, receives less aid on those reported. From the revenue dimension, schools also are caught in the Proposition 13/tax limitation syndrome. Taxpayers are unwilling to pass tax levies for additional school revenue. The magnitude of this problem has been demonstrated by voter approval of spending or tax limitation measures in numerous states. Declining enrollment, the taxpayer revolt, and inflation have created an untenable position for school districts, resulting in the necessity to reduce personnel.

Most state statutes provide for teacher dismissals because of declining enrollment or financial difficulties; however, a number of states have gone further and adopted reduction-in-force legislation, which specifies the basis for selection of teachers, procedures to be followed, and oftentimes provisions for reinstatement. Examples of specific statutory provisions are shown below.

*Illinois.* If the removal or dismissal results from the decision of the board to decrease the number of teachers employed by the board or discontinue some particular type of teaching service, written notice shall be given the teacher by registered mail at least 60 days before the end of the school term, together with a statement of honorable dismissal and the reason therefor, and in all such cases the board shall first remove or dismiss all teachers who have not entered upon contractual continued service before such board shall remove or dismiss any teacher who has entered upon contractual continued service and who is legally qualified to hold a position currently held by a teacher who has not entered upon contractual continued service; and if the board within one calendar year thereafter increases the number of teachers or reinstates the positions so discontinued, the positions thereby becoming available shall be tendered to the teachers so removed or dismissed so far as they are legally qualified to hold such positions.[76]

*Ohio.* When by reason of decreased enrollment of pupils, . . . a board of education decides that it will be necessary to reduce the number of teachers, it may make a reasonable reduction. In making such reduction, the board shall proceed to suspend contracts in accordance with the recommendation of the superintendent of schools who shall, within each teaching field affected, give preference to teachers on continuing contracts and to teachers who have greater seniority. Teachers, whose continuing contracts are suspended, shall have the right of restoration to continuing service status in the order of seniority of service in the district if and when teaching positions become vacant or are created for which any of such teachers are or become qualified.[77]

The Illinois statute is comprehensive, providing for all aspects of the termination—notice, statement of reasons, selection of teachers, and call back—while the Ohio law requires only that preference be granted on the basis of contract status and seniority.

In the absence of controlling legislation, teacher contracts or collective bargaining agreements may dictate procedures. Considerable pressure is exerted on school boards to negotiate reduction policies or, at a minimum, to adopt formal procedures. To accurately assess teachers' legal rights in personnel reduction, a number of sources must be consulted, including state statutes, board policies, collective bargaining legislation and agreements, teacher contracts, and court decisions. As enrollments continue to decline, courts seem destined to play an important role in interpreting the legality of such RIF provisions.[78]

## OTHER REQUIREMENTS

As noted previously, school districts may place additional conditions on employment beyond the state requirements. For example, school boards often require teachers to live within the district in which they teach. These residency requirements have been challenged as interfering with interstate and intrastate travel and impairing equal protection rights. Generally, as long as the board has a rational basis for adopting the rule, courts will uphold a residency requirement as constitutionally acceptable.

A Sixth Circuit Court of Appeals case is illustrative of this genre of cases and provides an example of a well-defined school board rationale.[79] The case involved a Cincinnati board policy that required all new employees to establish residency in the district within ninety days of employment. The plaintiff teacher questioned the rule as an infringement of his constitutional right to travel. Declining to extend constitutional protection to intrastate travel, the court required the district to show only a rational basis for the regulation. The superintendent enumerated the following reasons for establishing the residency requirement:

(1) such a requirement aids in hiring teachers who are highly motivated and deeply committed to an urban educational system, (2) teachers who

live in the district are more likely to vote for district taxes, less likely to engage in illegal strikes, and more likely to help obtain passage of school tax levies, (3) teachers living in the district are more likely to be involved in school and community activities bringing them in contact with parents and community leaders and are more likely to be committed to the future of the district and its schools, (4) teachers who live in the district are more likely to gain sympathy and understanding for the racial, social, economic, and urban problems of the children they teach and are thus less likely to be considered isolated from the communities in which they teach, (5) the requirement is in keeping with the goal of encouraging integration in society and in the schools.[80]

Within one month of the Sixth Circuit Appellate Court decision, the United States Supreme Court upheld a municipal regulation requiring all employees in the city of Philadelphia to be residents of the city.[81] The requirement was challenged as a violation of interstate travel by a fire department employee who was terminated when he moved to New Jersey. In upholding the regulation, the Court distinguished a requirement of residency of a given duration *prior to employment* (which violates the right to interstate travel) from a continuing residency requirement applied *after employment*. The Court concluded that a continuing residency requirement, if "appropriately defined and uniformly applied," does not violate an individual's constitutional rights.[82]

Although residency requirements have been upheld at the federal level, individual states may have statutory provisions prohibiting such requirements. For example, Indiana school boards, by statute, are not permitted to adopt any requirements pertaining to employee residence.[83] In states with such statutory provisions, the laws would have to be repealed or amended to enable school boards to establish residency regulations.

In addition to sanctioning residency requirements, courts have applied a similar rationale in upholding school board policies prohibiting school employees from engaging in outside employment during the school year. The Fifth Circuit Court of Appeals reviewed the constitutionality of a board policy, incorporated into employment contracts, which provided that employees "shall not engage in any other business or profession directly or indirectly, for full time or part time, but shall devote his or her entire working time to the performance of . . . duties under this contract." [84] In this case, the school board relied on the outside employment policy in declining to renew the contracts of a principal and his wife, an elementary teacher, after they purchased a dry goods store. Prior to that time the couple had operated a substantial cattle ranch, but the school board based its decision entirely on the purchase of the dry goods store. The couple challenged the board's action as a violation of their substantive due process rights because the policy was not related to a legitimate state interest. Additionally, they claimed that their rights to equal protection of the laws were impaired because of the arbitrary and selective enforcement of the policy. The court upheld the school board policy, finding that it was related to a legitimate state purpose—"assuring that public school employees devote their professional energies to the education of children." [85] However, the court concluded that the rule was arbitrarily and discriminatorily applied to the plaintiffs. Although a number of employees in the district were involved in outside employment, the policy had never been applied to anyone else. The court held that a restriction must be applied equally to all who are similarly situated. The appellate court noted the "wide latitude" the school board has in adopting policies necessary for effective administration of the schools but emphasized that such policies must be uniformly applied.

## CONCLUSION

Except for certain constitutional limitations, the employment of teachers is governed by state laws. The state prescribes general requirements for certification, contracts, tenure, and employment. Local school boards must follow state mandates and, in addition, may impose other requirements. In general, the following terms and conditions of employment exist for teachers.

1. The state establishes minimum qualifications for certification, which may include professional preparation, a specified age, United States citizenship, good moral character, signing of a loyalty oath, and passage of an academic examination.
2. A teacher must acquire a valid certificate to teach in any public school system.
3. Certification does not assure employment in a state.
4. Certification may be revoked for cause.
5. Employment appointments of teachers must be made by the local school board as a body at an officially scheduled board meeting.
6. A teacher may be assigned or transferred to any school or grade at the board's discretion, as long as the assignment is within the teacher's certification area and not circumscribed by contract terms.
7. Contracts of teachers must satisfy the conditions of offer and acceptance, competent parties, consideration, legal subject matter, and proper form; and they must conform to any additional specifications contained in state laws.
8. Tenure is a statutory right which ensures that dismissal must be based on adequate cause and accompanied by procedural due process.

9. Tenure must be conferred in accordance with statutory provisions.
10. All states with tenure laws stipulate that teachers must fulfill a probationary period of employment prior to the award of tenure.
11. Personnel reductions are permissible under state law when financial and/or other conditions warrant such action.
12. Courts generally have upheld school board residency requirements and prohibitions against outside employment if formulated on a reasonable basis.

## NOTES

1. *See* Georgia Ass'n of Educators v. Nix, 407 F. Supp. 1102 (D. Ga. 1976).
2. Pa. Stat. Ann. 24 § 1225.
3. Bay v. State Bd. of Educ., 378 P.2d 558 (Ore. 1963).
4. *Id.* at 561.
5. *See* United States v. South Carolina, National Educ. Ass'n v. South Carolina, 445 F. Supp. 1094 (D. S.C. 1977), *aff'd*, 434 U.S. 1026 (1978), text with note 10, Chapter 4.
6. *ASCD News Exchange*, Vol. 21, No. 5, September 1979, p. 8. States with competency tests for teachers include Louisiana, Florida, Virginia, Georgia, Tennessee, and Arkansas.
7. Keyishian v. Board of Educ., 385 U.S. 589 (1967). *See* text with note 65, Chapter 3.
8. *See* Ohlson v. Phillips, 397 U.S. 317 (1970).
9. Ambach v. Norwick, 441 U.S. 68 (1979).
10. *Id.* at 73–74.
11. *See* Hodge v. Stegall, 242 P.2d 720 (Okla. 1952).
12. Chavich v. Board of Examiners of Bd. of Educ., 252 N.Y.S.2d 718, 723 (Sup. Ct., Kings County, 1964). *See* text with note 111, Chapter 4.
13. *See* Richards v. Board of Educ. of Township High School Dist. No. 201, 171 N.E.2d 37 (Ill. 1960).
14. *See* Wardwell v. Board of Educ. of the City School Dist. of Cincinnati, 529 F.2d 625 (6th Cir. 1976).
15. *See* Moore v. Board of Educ. of Chidester School Dist. No. 59, 448 F.2d 709 (8th Cir. 1971).
16. Johnson v. School Dist. No. 3 Clay County, 96 N.W.2d 623 (Neb. 1959).
17. *See* Floyd County Bd. of Educ. v. Slone, 307 S.W.2d 912 (Ky. 1957).
18. *See* Greenwald v. Community School Bd. No. 27, 329 N.Y.S.2d 203 (Sup. Ct., Queens County, 1972); Stone v. Fritts, 82 N.E. 792 (Ind. 1907). *See* text with note 7, Chapter 5, for details of procedural due process.
19. Floyd G. Delon, *Legal Controls on Teacher Conduct: Teacher Discipline* (Topeka, Kan.: National Organization on Legal Problems in Education, 1977), p. 8.

20. Pettit v. State Bd. of Educ., 513 P.2d 889 (Cal. 1973).
21. Morrison v. State Bd. of Educ., 461 P.2d 375 (Cal. 1969).
22. Comings v. State Bd. of Educ., 100 Cal. Rptr. 73 (Cal. App. 1972).
23. *See* Williams v. Summer School Dist. No. 2, 255 F. Supp. 397 (D. S.C. 1966).
24. *See* Chapter 4 for a discussion of discriminatory employment practices.
25. *See* Yaffe v. Board of Educ. of City of Meriden, 380 A.2d 1 (Conn. C.P. 1977); Anderson v. Board of Educ. of City of Yonkers, 354 N.Y.S.2d 521 (Sup. Ct., Westchester County, 1974).
26. *See* Hilf v. Evergetis, 385 N.Y.S.2d 204 (App. Div. 1976); Illinois Educ. Ass'n Local Community High School Dist. 218 v. Board of Educ., Cook County, 340 N.E.2d 7 (Ill. 1975); Long v. Board of Educ., Ontario Local School Dist., 340 N.E.2d 439 (Ohio C.P. 1975).
27. *See* Bonar v. City of Boston, 341 N.E.2d 684 (Mass. 1976); Armstead v. Starkville Municipal Separate School Dist., 331 F. Supp. 567 (D. Miss. 1971).
28. Harrah Independent School Dist. v. Martin, 440 U.S. 194 (1979). The policy required teachers to earn an additional five semester hours of college credit every three years while employed.
29. Gurmankin v. Costanzo, 556 F.2d 184 (3d Cir. 1977).
30. Bevan v. New York State Teachers' Retirement System, 345 N.Y.S.2d 921 (Sup. Ct., Albany County, 1973).
31. Parolisi v. Board of Examiners of City of New York, 285 N.Y.S.2d 936 (Sup. Ct., Kings County, 1967).
32. *See* State *ex rel.* State Bd. of Educ. v. Montoya, 386 P.2d 252 (N.M. 1963).
33. *See* Moore v. Board of Educ. of Chidester School Dist. No. 59, 448 F.2d 709 (8th Cir. 1971); Singleton v. Jackson Municipal Separate School Dist., 419 F.2d 1211 (5th Cir. 1969).
34. *In re* Santee Appeal, 156 A.2d 830 (Pa. 1959).
35. *Id.* at 832.
36. Smith v. School Dist. No. 18, Pondera County, 139 P.2d 518 (Mont. 1943).
37. Mroczek v. Board of Educ. of the Beachwood City School Dist., 400 N.E.2d 1362 (Ohio C.P. 1979).
38. *See* State *ex rel.* Withers v. Board of Educ., 172 S.E.2d 796 (W.Va. 1970). *See also* text with note 9, Chapter 3.
39. Adcock v. Board of Educ. of San Diego Unified School Dist., 513 P.2d 900 (Cal. 1973).
40. McGrath v. Burkhard, 280 P.2d 864 (Cal. App. 1955).
41. *See* Pease v. Millcreek Township School Dist., 195 A.2d 104 (Pa. 1963).
42. *See* Parrish v. Moss, 106 N.Y.S.2d 577 (Sup. Ct., Kings County, 1951).
43. Board of Educ. v. Asbury Park Educ. Ass'n, 368 A.2d 396 (N.J. Super. 1976).
44. *See* Kern Alexander, Ray Corns, and Walter McCann, *Public School Law* (St. Paul, Minn.: West Publishing Co., 1969), pp. 389–92, for a discussion of contract elements.
45. *See* Green v. Jones, 108 S.E.2d 1 (W.Va. 1959).

46. *See* School Bd. of Leon County v. Goodson 335 So. 2d 308 (Fla. App. 1976); Allen v. Town of Sterling, 329 N.E.2d 756 (Mass. 1975); Detroit Federation of Teachers, Local 231 v. Board of Educ. of School Dist. of City of Detroit, 213 N.W.2d 839 (Mich. App. 1973).

47. *See* Floyd County Bd. of Educ. v. Slone, 307 S.W.2d 912 (Ky. 1957).

48. *See* text with note 7, Chapter 5, for a discussion of procedural due process requirements.

49. *See* DeLong v. Board of Educ. of Southwest School Dist., 306 N.E.2d 774 (Ohio App. 1973).

50. Bruton v. Ames Community School Dist., 291 N.W.2d 351 (Iowa 1980).

51. *See* Romeike v. Houston Independent School Dist., 368 S.W.2d 895 (Tex. Civ. App. 1963); Board of Educ. of Richmond School Dist. v. Mathews, 308 P.2d 449 (Cal. App. 1957).

52. William R. Hazard, *Education and the Law* (New York: The Free Press, 1978), p. 370.

53. Virginia Nordin, "Employees," *The Yearbook of School Law 1977*, edited by Philip Piele (Topeka, Kan.: National Organization on Legal Problems in Education, 1977), p. 177.

54. Hazard, *Education and the Law*, p. 359.

55. *Id.*

56. *See* Brown v. Board of School Trustees of Nettle Creek, 398 N.E.2d 1359 (Ind. App. 1980); Boyd v. Collins, 182 N.E.2d 610 (N.Y. 1962).

57. *See* Branson v. Board of Trustees of Yreka Union High School Dist., 23 Cal. Rptr. 288 (Cal. App. 1962); Zimmerman v. Board of Educ. of City of Newark, 183 A.2d 25 (N.J. 1962).

58. *See* Council of Directors and Supervisors of Los Angeles City Schools v. Los Angeles Unified School Dist., 110 Cal. Rptr. 624 (Cal. App. 1973); Moresh v. Board of Educ. of City of Bayonne in County of Hudson, 144 A.2d 897 (N.J. Super. 1958).

59. *See* Adelt v. Richmond School Dist., 58 Cal. Rptr. 151 (Cal. App. 1967); Board of Educ., Tucson High School Dist. No. 1 v. Williams, 403 P.2d 324 (Ariz. App. 1965).

60. State v. Smith, 142 So. 2d 767 (Fla. App. 1962).

61. Rochester Educ. Ass'n v. Independent School Dist., 271 N.W.2d 311 (Minn. 1978).

62. Neal v. School Dist. of York, 288 N.W.2d 725 (Neb. 1980).

63. Morse v. Wozniak, 398 F. Supp. 597 (E.D. Mich. 1975).

64. Brodie v. School Community of Easton, 324 N.E.2d 922 (Mass. App. 1975).

65. *Id.*

66. Frye v. School Committee of Leicester, 16 N.E.2d 41 (Mass. 1938).

67. *See* Matthews v. Nyquist, 412 N.Y.S.2d 501 (App. Div. 1979); Mugavin v. Nyquist, 367 N.Y.S.2d 604 (App. Div. 1975).

68. *See* Morse v. Wozniak, 398 F. Supp. 597 (E.D. Mich. 1975).

69. *See* Snell v. Brothers, 527 S.W.2d 114 (Tenn. 1975).

70. Indiana *ex rel.* Anderson v. Brand, 303 U.S. 95 (1938). Under such legislation, the status of teachers who have received tenure cannot be

altered, but the legislature is not prohibited from changing the law for future employees.

71. *See* Gullett v. Sparks, 444 S.W.2d 901 (Ky. 1969).

72. *See* text with note 70, Chapter 5, for an overview of causes for dismissal.

73. Shirley B. Neill and Jerry Curtis, *Staff Dismissals: Problems and Solutions* (Sacramento, Cal.: American Association of School Administrators, 1978), p. 5.

74. William A. Spenda, Garry M. Whalen, and Cathleen Otto, "The Role of Negotiations in the Equation 'Declining Enrollment = Layoffs': A Management Perspective," *Journal of Law and Education*, Vol. 7, No. 2, 1978, p. 244.

75. Neill and Curtis, *Staff Dismissals*, p. 59.

76. Ill. Ann. Stat. § 122.24-12.

77. Ohio Rev. Code Ann. § 3319.17.

78. *See* text with note 168, Chapter 5, for discussion of procedural issues related to reduction in force.

79. Wardwell v. Board of Educ. of the City School Dist. of Cincinnati, 529 F.2d 625 (6th Cir. 1976).

80. *Id.* at 628.

81. McCarthy v. Philadelphia Civil Service Comm'n, 424 U.S. 645 (1976).

82. *Id.* at 647. In 1978, the Supreme Court of New Hampshire refused to uphold a residency requirement of the Manchester school system. The court did not find "a public interest which is important enough to justify the restriction on the private right." Angwin v. City of Manchester, 386 A.2d 1272, 1273 (N.H. 1978).

83. Ind. Code Ann. 20 § 6.1–6.12.

84. Gosney v. Sonora Independent School Dist., 603 F.2d 522, 523 (5th Cir. 1979).

85. *Id.* at 526.

# 3

# Constitutional Rights
of Teachers

Statutory law is prominent in defining specific rights and responsibilities of public school teachers. As indicated in the previous chapter, states have the power to establish a uniform system of public schools, and have enacted laws delineating requirements for certification, contracts, tenure, and many other aspects of teaching. Beyond these statutory provisions for employment, significant substantive rights are conferred through the Federal Constitution. These guaranteed rights cannot be infringed by state or local action without an overriding governmental interest, nor can employment be conditioned on their relinquishment. The exercise of these protected rights often results in a conflict of interests between school officials and teachers. In arriving at a "balance of interests," courts have cautiously guarded teachers' rights against undue governmental encroachment. This chapter provides an overview of the scope of teachers' constitutional rights as defined by the judiciary. When applicable, federal and state laws supplementing these rights are discussed.

## FREEDOM OF EXPRESSION

The first amendment to the United States Constitution guarantees every citizen the right to freely express opinions, including the right to criticize governmental policies and actions. Although the right to free expression is protected, courts have recognized, at the same time, that there must be a balancing of the interests of employers and employees. Until the 1968 Supreme Court decision *Pickering v. Board of Education,* a teacher's freedom of expression was an ill-defined right.[1] The Supreme Court in *Pickering* did not establish strict criteria for weighing the public interest in regulating schools against the individual interest in freely expressing ideas. It did, however, identify general guidelines that have been followed in subsequent cases arising from teachers' exercise of freedom of expression.

The controversy in *Pickering* revolved around a letter the teacher wrote to a local newspaper criticizing the school board's expenditure of funds, especially the allocation of funds between the educational and athletic programs. The school board dismissed Pickering based on this letter, which included false statements, damaging to the reputation of the school board members and district administrators. The Illinois courts upheld the dismissal, finding the letter "detrimental to the best interests of the schools." [2]

In balancing the interest of the teacher in expressing views on public issues and the interest of the board in efficiently operating the school district, the Supreme Court advanced two tests: (1) Was a question of "maintaining either discipline by immediate superiors or harmony among co-workers" presented? [3] and (2) Did the statements impede the teacher's classroom performance or the normal operation of the school? [4] Responding to the first test, the Court found that the statements were directed at no one with whom Pickering would have daily contact; thus, there was no indication that school discipline or harmony was impaired. The lack of interference with the operation of the school and the teacher's performance led the Court to conclude that "the interest of the school administration in limiting teachers' opportunities to contribute to public debate is not significantly greater than its interest in limiting a similar contribution by any member of the general public." [5] In fact, the Court noted that a teacher's role provides a special vantage point from which to formulate an "informed and definite opinion" on allocation of funds, thus making it essential for teachers to be able to speak freely without fear of reprisal.

It is noteworthy that the Court did not conclude that false statements *per se* were damaging to the operation of the school system. Although finding the statements to be incorrect, the Court did not allow this to invalidate the teacher's constitutional claim. Rather, the Court declared that "absent proof of false statements knowingly or recklessly made," a teacher's views on public issues cannot form the basis for dismissal.[6]

The "balancing of interests" test has been dominant in subsequent cases that further define a teacher's right to freedom of speech. The Eighth Circuit Court of Appeals upheld the dismissal of a teacher who encouraged students to oppose R.O.T.C. visitation on the school campus.[7] The teacher, speaking to his algebra class, indicated that the student body was large enough to "get the military off the campus." Based on these remarks, the school board dismissed the teacher for inciting the students and for disrupting normal school operations. The court, in balancing the interests of the teacher and of the school administrators, applied the *Pickering* criteria and found that the teacher's remarks (1) interfered with the operation of the school, (2) were unrelated to his class, and (3) created a potentially disruptive situation. Viewed in relation to the *Pickering* guidelines, the teacher's speech was not constitutionally protected in this situation.

However, if expression does not interfere with an employer-employee relationship or threaten normal school operations, it is unlikely that a teacher's opinion can be silenced simply because it is unpopular with school authorities. Lack of any potential disruption led the Second Circuit Court of Appeals to conclude that a teacher's dismissal for wearing a black armband as a symbolic protest against the Vietnam War was an unconstitutional interference with freedom of expression.[8]

Pending or actual dismissal is not necessary to invoke first amendment protections. A transfer from one school to another, or a transfer that might constitute a demotion, can be viewed as violating a teacher's rights if instigated as a retaliatory measure for the exercise of expression protected by the first amendment. The California Supreme Court invalidated the transfer of a teacher for criticism of school policies in a school-sponsored open forum.[9] The court noted that *some* disharmony and friction may result from a teacher's remarks, but this alone is not a sufficient ground to curtail expression. The court recognized that the magnitude of the adverse impact of a teacher's comments must be assessed. Similarly, the Seventh Circuit Court of Appeals invalidated the transfer of a teacher who had made public comments favoring a master collective bargaining contract. The court reasoned that the expression did not interfere with the teacher's classroom duties or with the normal operation of the school.[10] In the absence of disruption, the court concluded that a retaliatory transfer for protected speech was as impermissible as a retaliatory dismissal.

When a teacher's remarks have posed a threat to the management of the school system, courts have recognized the school board's discretionary authority to implement transfers. The Supreme Court of Missouri upheld the transfer of a teacher who called two assistant principals "scabs" during a teachers' strike.[11] The court examined the transfer action to determine (1) whether it was punitive for the exercise of protected speech, or (2) whether it was necessary for the efficient operation of the school system. The court concluded that the transfer was not a disciplinary action, but that the teacher's remarks "demonstrated disrespect for the authority of plaintiff's superiors, tended to undermine and disrupt the relationship between them, interfere with the management and operation of the school, and create animosity and the possibility of physical violence between plaintiff and the assistant principals."[12] In contrast to *Pickering,* this situation involved speech affecting a close working relationship between the teacher and immediate supervisors. Because of the impact on the employment relationship, the court found the transfer to be for "legitimate managerial reasons."

Since *Pickering,* the contention that a teacher's dismissal has resulted from the exercise of first amendment rights has been advanced as a defense in many termination actions. Along with the alleged protected expression, a number of other valid causes may exist to support a board's dismissal decision. In some instances, courts have held that if speech is a "contributing" factor, termination is unconstitutional. Other courts have required that protected speech must be the "substantial" factor in order for a dismissal decision to be overturned. In *Mt. Healthy City School District Board of Education v. Doyle,* the Supreme Court provided clarification as to when protected speech would require remedial action.[13]

In *Mt. Healthy,* a nontenured teacher's telephone call to a local radio station concerning a proposed teacher dress and appearance code prompted the school board to initiate dismissal proceedings. The teacher previously had been involved in several incidents; however, in dismissing him the board cited "lack of tact in handling professional matters" with reference to only two incidents—the radio station call and obscene gestures made to female students.[14] Doyle challenged the dismissal as an invasion of his first and fourteenth amendment rights, and both the trial court and the Sixth Circuit Court of Appeals concluded that reinstatement was warranted. The courts reasoned that the telephone call was protected speech and was a substantial reason for the dismissal decision. In reversing the lower court rulings, the United States Supreme Court introduced a third test—whether the school board would have reached the same decision in the absence of the teacher's exercise of protected speech. The Court reasoned that the exercise of protected speech should place an employee in no better or no worse position with regard to continued employment.

> The constitutional principle at stake is sufficiently vindicated if such an employee is placed in no worse a position than if he had not engaged in the conduct. A borderline or marginal candidate should not have the employment question resolved against him because of constitutionally protected conduct. But the same candidate ought not to be able, by engaging in such conduct, to prevent his employer from assessing his performance record and reaching a decision not to rehire on the basis of that record, simply because the protected conduct makes the employer more certain of the correctness of its decision.[15]

The case was remanded for a determination of whether the board could show by a "preponderance of evidence" that it would have reached the same conclusion if the radio station incident had not occurred. *Mt. Healthy* provides further refinement in the "balancing of interests," indicating that the constitutional guarantee of free speech does not require remedial action in every dismissal involving free expression.

Since the Supreme Court's decision in *Mt. Healthy,* courts have examined cases involving teachers' freedom of speech to determine (1) if the teacher's speech is protected, (2) if protected speech is a motivating factor in dismissal, and (3) if the board can show by a preponderance of evidence that the teacher would have been dismissed if the protected expression had not occurred. A Virginia teacher who was dismissed for complaining about her status as a "floating" teacher was reinstated when it was shown that the board would not have reached the same dismissal decision absent the teacher's complaint.[16] Similarly, the Eighth Circuit Court of Appeals found that two letters to the editor of the local newspaper were the motivating force in the dismissal of an Iowa teacher.[17] Considering the letters' protected expression, the dismissal was invalidated. The Ninth Circuit Court of Appeals concluded that the involuntary transfer of a teacher from one school to another involved a "valuable governmental benefit" that could not be impaired simply because the teacher disagreed with certain school policies.[18] Since the teacher's criticism was shown to be the basis for the board action, the transfer was deemed unconstitutional. In a Sixth Circuit Court of Appeals case, an Ohio school board could not successfully rebut a probationary teacher's showing that her release was predicated on protected union-related activities.[19] Although her performance evaluations had declined each year, the court concluded that the evaluations were tainted by the teacher's union activities. Thus, the court ruled that she would have been retained *except for* the protected activities.

In contrast, where a nontenured teacher claimed that nonrenewal was based on a difference of opinion with the director of the school, a federal district court concluded that the board introduced sufficient evidence to substantiate that dismissal was imminent regardless of conduct protected by the first amendment.[20] Similarly, an Arkansas coach failed to establish that his comments to several outsiders about the internal operation of the athletic program were crucial in bringing about his dismissal, because the board introduced a long history of controversy between the board and the coach.[21] Accordingly, the dismissal was upheld. From these cases, it can be seen that protected speech which is a partial or even a substantial factor in dismissal does not proscribe justified board action. This in no way diminishes first amendment rights of teachers; it only ensures that these rights are not used to shield teachers when adequate cause exists to warrant dismissal.

The Supreme Court in *Pickering* firmly established the right of teachers to free public expression of their opinions. However, in subsequent cases, a distinction has been drawn between public and private comments. Relying on *Pickering,* courts have considered private communications outside the scope of first amendment protection. In a university case, a nontenured associate professor alleged that her employment was terminated because she made critical comments about the department chairperson.[22] The Court distinguished her remarks from those of Pickering, noting the private nature of the former in contrast to the public nature of the latter. This case is illustrative of the reasoning adhered to by a number of courts prior to the removal of this dichotomy in *Givhan v. Western Line Consolidated School District.*[23]

The Supreme Court in *Givhan* directly addressed the issue of constitutional protection afforded to the private expression of teachers. Givhan was dismissed primarily for her criticism of school policies, expressed in private to the school principal. The Fifth Circuit Court of Appeals, relying on *Pickering* and *Mt. Healthy,* upheld the dismissal, finding that "private expression by a public employee is not protected." [24] The Supreme Court disagreed with the appellate court's conclusion, noting rather that it was only "coincidental" that the controversial expressions in *Pickering* and *Mt. Healthy* had focused on public comments. The Court refused to afford a lesser degree of protection to private expression than to public expression. However, the Court did recognize that public expression is generally evaluated on its content and impact, whereas private expression, because of the nature of the employer-employee relationship, might involve other considerations such as manner, time, and place of the remarks.

In summary, a public employee cannot be denied freedom of expression, whether it involves public statements or private comments to a supervisor. However, this is not an unrestricted right and can be circumscribed if it interferes with the smooth operation of the school system. To justify dismissal or other disciplinary action, this interference must be more than minor friction created by the expression of a philosophy or opinion with which school officials disagree. On the other hand, proof that speech is constitutionally protected and is the motivating factor in a dismissal decision does not ensure reinstatement if the board can show by a "preponderance" of evidence that it would have arrived at the same decision if the protected expression had not occurred. The exercise of first amendment rights does not guarantee remedial action; it only ensures that the employee will be in no worse or no better position after expressing views. It must be recognized that in an assessment of whether speech is protected, a number of factors are considered—impact on the operation of the school; impact on the teacher's performance; effect on teacher-superior relationships; effect on co-workers; and appropriateness of time, place, and manner of remarks. All factors are evaluated in arriving at a "balance of interests" between the teacher's right to freedom of speech and the board's interest in ensuring the efficient operation of the school system.

## ACADEMIC FREEDOM

Academic freedom is acclaimed as integral and essential to teaching. The teacher, as a professional, desires a certain amount of control over course content, course materials, and teaching methods. Although originally applied primarily to professors in higher education, this concept has evolved to include teachers in public elementary and secondary schools. Of course, the application and definition of academic freedom have been much more restrictive in the public school setting.

It has been deemed desirable that professors should have the broadest range of freedom in their teaching and research. Historically, this notion came from German universities[25] and applied to internal, not external, activities of faculty members.[26] The concept has undergone substantial change in American universities. It has been expanded to include the rights of faculty members as citizens, encompassing conduct away from the classroom as well as freedom within the classroom.[27] The public school teacher recently has asserted a similar claim to academic freedom, and has turned to the courts for delineation of this "right."

It has been only since the 1960s that courts have become involved in the issue of academic freedom. They have refrained from establishing a general legal theory or clear standards in regard to academic rights, preferring to decide such issues on a case by case basis.[28] Because of the close nexus between the teacher's freedom in academic matters and the authority of the local education agency to control instructional decisions, courts generally have deferred to the policies of school boards. However, when a constitutionally protected right has been infringed, judicial intervention has been justified. Courts have attempted to balance the teacher's right to use discretion in performing required duties with the state's interest in safeguarding the education and welfare of pupils.

Teachers' rights to free expression outside of the classroom have been discussed in other sections; therefore, this discussion concentrates on academic freedom within the classroom setting.[29] Can the teacher determine the most appropriate materials for classroom use? Does the first amendment guarantee the teacher complete freedom in expressing personal ideas and philosophies? Is the teacher free to determine teaching methodology? What topics or issues can the teacher discuss in a course?

The United States Supreme Court has not decided a case dealing directly with teachers' academic freedom or freedom of expression in the classroom. However, the Court has discussed the issue in several opinions. Justice Stewart addressed teachers' academic rights in his concurring opinion in *Epperson v. Arkansas*.[30] He noted that if states are allowed to circumscribe the school curriculum, they may "clearly impinge" on the teacher's first amendment guarantees. Another reference to the importance of academic freedom was made in *Keyishian v. Board of Regents*.

> Our nation is deeply committed to safeguarding academic freedom, which is of transcendent value to all of us and not merely to the teachers concerned. That freedom is therefore a special concern of the first amendment, which does not tolerate laws that cast a pall of orthodoxy over the classroom.[31]

Although the Supreme Court has not provided a definitive ruling as to the academic rights of teachers, cases from the various lower federal and state courts can be relied on for direction. From these rulings, general guidelines on acceptable teacher behavior in the classroom can be ascertained.

The types of supplemental materials introduced into courses have been the subject of litigation, especially materials of an obscene or sexual nature. One of the earliest cases involved the assignment of an article from the *Atlantic Monthly* magazine by a senior high English teacher.[32] The article contained several references to "a vulgar term for an incestuous son."[33] After complaints from parents, the teacher was dismissed. The teacher brought suit, alleging that her right to academic freedom was impaired, and the First Circuit Court of Appeals ordered reinstatement. The appellate court found the article to be scholarly rather than obscene, and stated that "sensibilities of parents are not the full measure of what is proper education."[34] Even though the court acknowledged the teacher's right to academic freedom, the decision actually was based on a procedural issue—failure to notify the teacher that such conduct was forbidden.

A similar case decided a year later directly addressed the question of academic freedom. An eleventh-grade English teacher assigned the reading of a story, "Welcome to the Monkey House," by Kurt Vonnegut.[35] Several complaints were registered by students and parents. After a conference with the principal and associate superintendent, the teacher was warned not to use the story in her classes because it encouraged "the killing off of elderly people and free sex." However, feeling a "professional obligation," the teacher would not agree to discontinue its use and was subsequently dismissed. Recognizing the need to balance the teacher's interest in academic freedom against the school's interest in providing proper instruction, the court concluded that materials would not be protected if they were inappropriate for the age of the students or created "a material and substantial threat of disruption." Since neither condition was found, the court ruled that the dismissal of the teacher was "an unwarranted invasion of her first amendment right to academic freedom."[36]

In addition to the age of the students and potential for disruption, other factors, such as relevancy of the material and its general acceptance by the teaching profession, have been considered in assessing whether or not certain teaching methods and materials are afforded constitutional protection. The Seventh Circuit Court of Appeals upheld the dismissal of three teachers who had distributed a brochure on the pleasures of drug use and sex to an eighth-grade class.[37] This decision was based on the age of the pupils and the material's lack of relevance to a legitimate educational purpose. The brochure was not discussed as a topic in class, but was merely distributed in the classroom. Similarly, a Louisiana appellate court concluded that a teacher's controversial statements regarding the sexual behavior of blacks lacked instructional relevance.[38] The court ruled that the "statements made by plaintiff clearly served no serious educational purpose, and [were] therefore not entitled to protection."[39]

Although there must be some relationship between an activity and the educational objectives of the course, relevance alone may not be sufficient to justify the use of particular teaching methods and materials. In a Massachusetts case, an eleventh-grade English teacher was dismissed for the illustrative use of a slang term for sexual intercourse in a discussion of taboo words.[40] A federal district court concluded that the teaching method was relevant to the discussion; however, because the method did not have the "support of the preponderant opinion of the teaching profession," it could be the basis for dismissal.[41] This conclusion was tempered because the court also held that there must be a regulation or other notice to the teacher that such a teaching method is prohibited. In the opinion of the court, the failure to provide prior notice unduly restricts the teacher's ability to experiment with various teaching techniques. Since no regulation existed, the district court reinstated the teacher. The decision subsequently was affirmed by the First Circuit Court of Appeals.[42]

Some cases have focused on whether or not the expression of personal opinions, especially on controversial topics, can be a valid basis for dismissing a teacher. In a Texas case, a high school civics teacher was dismissed for discussing and expressing personal opinions on issues such as interracial marriages and antiwar protests in his classes.[43] In upholding the actions of the teacher, the court delineated the substantive right of teachers to select teaching methods with valid educational purposes and the procedural right not to be dismissed for using particular methods unless the methods are prohibited by the school system.[44] The court emphasized, however, that a teacher, when expressing personal opinions, must be careful to present opposing views.

Teaching methodology that offends community mores often has been the basis for a school board imposing restrictions on teachers. Community objection to a Communist speaker in a political science class resulted in an Oregon school board policy that banned all political speakers.[45] In this case, the teacher had arranged for four speakers, each representing a different political viewpoint—a Democrat, a Republican, a member of the John Birch Society, and a Communist. All speakers but the Communist had addressed the class when the board banned political speakers. Refraining from considering the issue of academic freedom, the court simply dealt with teaching methodology as a form of "freedom of expression." The court held that methodology was expression protected by the first amendment, but emphasized that such expression could be constrained if the restrictions were "reasonable in light of the special circumstances of the school environment." [46] Upholding the teacher, the court concluded that the challenged methodology was appropriate for the high school curriculum, since there was no evidence of past or potential disruptions and there was general acceptance of the method among the profession.

In a Texas case, parental complaints resulted in the school board's dismissing a nontenured teacher for the use of a controversial simulation technique.[47] The "Sunshine Simulation" was employed in history classes to teach the post–Civil War Reconstruction period and resulted in arousing student feelings on racial issues. Because of parental objections, the teacher was instructed that "nothing controversial should be discussed in the classroom," specifically the issue of blacks in American history.[48] In ordering reinstatement of the teacher, the Fifth Circuit Court of Appeals concluded that classroom discussion is a constitutionally protected activity.

In contrast to the preceding courts, the Tenth Circuit Court of Appeals has held that community standards must be considered in determining whether certain materials and methods can be used in the classroom.[49] In the Tenth Circuit case, teachers were dismissed for discussing controversial issues and using the records *Hair* and *Alice's Restaurant*. The teachers claimed that their dismissal resulted from the exercise of academic freedom, thereby violating their first amendment rights. The court declined to rule on the academic freedom issue and upheld the dismissals because of "deficiencies in teaching ability." Although recognizing the board's authority to control the activities of teachers, the court stated:

> Undoubtedly [teachers] have some freedom in the techniques to be employed, but this does not say that they have an unlimited liberty as to structure and content of the courses, at least at the secondary level. Thus in a small community . . . the board members and the principal surely have a right to emphasize a more orthodox approach.[50]

The school board's control of library materials and book selections for classroom use has been contested as infringing on the first amendment rights of teachers. From a legal standpoint, the authority to select and purchase textbooks is vested in the school board through statute. Whether this power also gives the board the right to forbid the use of certain books in the classroom and expunge selected books from the library has been the subject of much litigation. In a Sixth Circuit Court of Appeals case, an Ohio school board refused to approve teachers' recommendations to purchase Joseph Heller's *Catch 22* or Kurt Vonnegut's *God Bless You, Mr. Rosewater* and additionally ordered *Catch 22* removed from the school library along with Vonnegut's *Cat's Cradle*.[51] The appellate court affirmed the board's right under Ohio law to select textbooks for classroom use. The teachers' recommendations thus could not prevail over the board's discretionary authority to make curricular decisions. Selection of books, in the opinion of the court, did not interfere with academic freedom, since teachers were still free to refer to and discuss the controversial books. However, the court concluded that the removal of books placed a "serious burden upon freedom of classroom discussion" which was not mitigated by the availability of the books from public libraries.[52] The court reasoned that, although final approval and purchase of textbooks may reside with the board, actual removal of books because they are "distasteful" to the board cannot be allowed to abridge first amendment rights of teachers or students.

In an opposing stance on book removals, the Second Circuit Court of Appeals found no constitutional infringement in a school board's removal of a controversial book from a junior high school library.[53] The court recognized that a duly authorized body must determine the library collection. Since this authority resided with the school board under state law, the court refused to interfere by reviewing "either the wisdom or the efficacy of the determination of the board." [54]

The control of library materials as it affects the freedom of students and teachers is far from a settled issue. Most of the challenges to school board curricular decisions have been based on students' rights to know and receive information.[55] Some courts have been very protective of students' rights to be exposed to controversial materials.[56] But, in general, the cases tend to support the authority of school boards to control library and curriculum materials. A number of courts have upheld curriculum censorship even when decisions are based on the political, moral, and social beliefs of the board members.[57] Although courts may not always agree with school boards' actions, they recognize that the legal authority to select materials is vested in the boards. Thus, the judiciary is hesitant to interfere with these decisions unless there is clear abuse of discretion.

In summary, the judiciary has recognized that the first amendment does include a degree of academic freedom for public school teachers in the classroom, but has carefully balanced the rights of teachers, parents, students, and the state. Academic freedom can probably be described more accurately as a protected "interest" rather than a "right." [58] Instead of establishing standards for resolving controversies over this protected interest, courts have preferred to view each case individually. Therefore, teachers must rely on the various judicial decisions for general guidance only.

In exercising academic freedom, a teacher should be aware of the relationship between the particular materials or teaching methods employed and the course being taught. If methods or materials are completely unrelated to course objectives, their use would not be viewed as legally protected. Relevancy applies not only to the particular course, but also to the age and maturity of the pupils. A controversial topic that would be appropriate for high school students would not necessarily be appropriate for elementary and junior high students. Other factors considered include the presence of proscriptive school board regulations, acceptance of the particular activity by "experts" in the teaching profession, and the existence of any threat of material and substantial disruption. In general, courts have ruled that teachers' discretion in selecting books for their classrooms does not transcend the authority of school boards to make curricular decisions.

## FREEDOM OF ASSOCIATION

Although not specifically enumerated as a constitutional right, freedom of association is an implied guarantee under the first and fourteenth amendments. Governments attempting to protect public institutions from treasonable and seditious actions of employees frequently have adopted legislation infringing upon this associational right. The method most commonly employed to achieve this objective has been the required signing of loyalty oaths with disclaimer provisions. As in the area of protected speech, courts have been more reluctant in recent years to sustain state action limiting the teacher's right to freedom of association.

In the 1940s, concern for citizen loyalty and fear of Communism led many states to impose oaths that disqualified members of the Communist Party from public service positions. For example, the New York Feinberg Law required each employee to sign a certificate disclaiming membership in the Communist Party. In effect, the law was designed to exclude from public employment anyone who advocated the overthrow of the government by force or violence. New York courts interpreted the law as requiring more than mere membership in the Communist Party in order to disqualify one for public employment; the individual had to have prior knowledge of the organization's subversive purpose. In 1952, the Supreme Court in *Adler v. Board of Education* upheld this law as interpreted by the New York courts.[59] Thus, the Court concluded that "knowing" membership was a legitimate basis for excluding an individual from public employment. The Court stated:

> Teachers may work for the school system upon the reasonable terms laid down by the proper authorities of New York. If they do not choose to work on such terms, they are at liberty to retain their beliefs and associations and go elsewhere.[60]

In the same year that the Court upheld the New York law, it invalidated an Oklahoma oath mandated by statute.[61] Differentiating between the two laws, the Court concluded that the New York law required knowledge of organizational purposes for disqualification, while membership alone disqualified employees under the Oklahoma law. A presumption of disloyalty based on mere membership without determination of whether or not an individual was actually aware of organizational purposes was held to be unconstitutional.

Since 1952, subsequent Supreme Court decisions have mitigated the Court's earlier restrictive stance. For example, vagueness or ambiguity in construction has rendered oaths unconstitutional. The Supreme Court held that a Florida oath, compelling employees to swear they had never "knowingly lent their aid, support, advice, counsel, or influence to the Communist Party," allowed infinite interpretations of punishable actions.[62] Quoting from an earlier decision, the Court stated, "a statute which either forbids or requires the doing of an act in terms so vague that men of common intelligence must necessarily guess at its meaning and differ as to its application violates the first essential of due process of law." [63] Similarly, a Washington oath requiring individuals to subscribe to the fact that they were not "subversive" persons, or members of the Communist Party or other subversive organizations, was invalidated on vagueness and uncertainty.[64]

In early cases, the Supreme Court relied on the distinction between innocent and knowing membership in subversive organizations when it held that associational rights could be limited; censoring knowing membership was viewed as constitutionally permissible. Later, knowing membership without specific intent to further the subversive purposes of an organization came under attack. The Supreme Court found that an Arizona oath prohibiting knowing membership threatened freedom of association and, by implication, assumed "guilt by association." [65] A year later, the Supreme Court reexamined the New York Feinberg Law in *Keyishian v. Board of Regents*. Several faculty members of the State University of New York had refused to sign the "Feinberg Certificate," which required a pledge that they were not Communists and that they had notified the president of the university system regarding any prior affiliation with the Communist Party. The Supreme Court reiterated the governing standard with regard to subversive intent: "Mere *knowing* membership without specific *intent* to further the unlawful aims of an organization is not a constitutionally adequate basis for exclusion." [66] [Emphasis added.] Informed membership alone was not found to pose a threat to the government; therefore, it could not be subjected to unreasonable restraints.

However, loyalty oaths *per se* have not been invalidated. Such oaths, absent disclaimer provisions, can be required for public employment. In general, these oaths require an employee to pledge support for the United States Constitution and an individual state's constitution. The following Colorado oath is representative:

> I solemnly (swear) (affirm) that I will uphold the constitution of the United States and the constitution of the State of Colorado, and I will faithfully perform the duties of the position upon which I am about to enter.[67]

Although it was challenged as an invasion of the first amendment rights of freedom of speech and association, the Supreme Court held that the Colorado oath was within the discretion of the legislature.

Statutory provisions which may infringe on first amendment associational rights are closely scrutinized by the judiciary. A Texas statute, allowing county judges to compel certain organizations to disclose their membership lists, was challenged as an invasion of associational and privacy rights guaranteed by the first amendment.[68] This law specifically applied the disclosure requirement to organizations engaged in activities designed to disrupt public schools. The Fifth Circuit Court of Appeals noted that the United States Supreme Court had allowed such governmental action only when disclosure was "substantially related" to a compelling state interest. The appellate court recognized the legitimacy of Texas's interest in preserving the peaceful operation of schools, but concluded that the statute swept too broadly. Under this law, all members of the organization were subject to public recrimination, not just those who participated in the disruptive activities.

The fact that associational rights are ensured by the first amendment does not preclude school administrators from legitimately questioning a teacher about activities that may adversely affect classroom teaching. In *Beilan v. Board of Public Education of Philadelphia,* the Supreme Court held that refusal to answer such questions can justify dismissal.[69] Emphasizing that a teacher does not surrender belief, speech, and associational rights in employment, the Court recognized a concomitant duty to answer all questions pertaining to fitness to teach. The Court concluded that questions regarding alleged past activities in the Communist Party were relevant to classroom teaching, and that refusal to answer such inquiries could result in dismissal. Although membership in an organization *per se* is protected, if the issue of disloyalty arises, a teacher must answer questions posed by superiors—as long as the questions are related to fitness to teach.

Inclusive in the right of freedom of association is the right to form and join a union. Until the late 1960s, this was not a firmly acknowledged right, as evidenced by some state laws that prohibited union membership. More recently, however, the first amendment has been interpreted as protecting union membership.[70]

## POLITICAL ACTIVITY

Guarantees ensured under the speech and assembly provisions of the first amendment have been invoked to safeguard the political activities of teachers. As noted in *Pickering,* the teacher's right to speak out on public issues is constitutionally protected.[71] The teacher not only is entitled to speak on political issues, but also is entitled to actively campaign for political candidates and personally run for office. These activities cannot be curtailed by school officials through transfer, demotion, or dismissal of teachers.

Although the teacher is free to participate in political campaigns, restrictions can be placed on such activity within the school environment. In an early California case, a teacher was suspended for ten weeks without pay for a comment made to his high school class in support of a particular candidate for school superintendent.[72] The teacher stated:

> Many of you know Mr. Golway, what a fine man he is, and that his hopes are to be elected soon. I think he would be more helpful to our

department than a lady, and we need more men in our schools. Sometimes your parents do not know one candidate from another; so they might be glad to be informed. Of course, if any of you have relatives or friends trying for the same office, be sure and vote for them.[73]

The court found these remarks to be "wholly foreign" to the objectives and purposes of the school, and to have the potential to create strife and disruption in the operation of the school.

Certain types of political activity on school premises have been sanctioned by the courts. The Supreme Court of California upheld the constitutional right of a teachers' union to circulate a petition concerning the financing of public education.[74] The school board had refused to allow circulation of the petition, asserting that the issue involved opposing political views that would create divisiveness in the faculty, and that it would be difficult for those individuals circulating the petition to determine which teachers in the school lounge were off-duty. In rejecting the board's reasoning, the court reiterated the legal stance that speech-related activities cannot be restricted merely to avoid controversy; any constraint must be justified by evidence that the speech poses a "clear and substantial threat" to the operation of the school system.

Although teachers have not been permitted to campaign within the classroom and limitations have been placed on activities that interfere with the operation of the school, courts have invalidated policies that would restrict political activity outside of school. In addition, several state legislatures have enacted specific laws to strengthen the teacher's political rights. For example, the Kentucky legislature passed the following statute:

No teacher or employee of any district board of education shall be appointed or promoted to or dismissed from any position or in any way favored or discriminated against with respect to employment because of his political or religious opinions or affiliations or ethnic origin.[75]

The Supreme Court of Kentucky interpreted this law as broad enough to preclude transfers and demotions of employees supporting a school board candidate opposed by the superintendent.[76] In this case, the only reason the superintendent gave for demoting and transferring seven teachers and administrators was that it was "for the betterment of the schools." In holding for the plaintiffs, the court concluded that such punitive action was arbitrary and therefore void.

Throughout the history of public employment, non–civil service employees have been subject to patronage dismissals. Under patronage employment, employees who are not members of the incumbent party are replaced with party members. When control shifts from one party to another, such a practice involves a substantial turnover in employees. In 1976, the United States Supreme Court addressed patronage dismissals and their effect on freedoms of belief and association in a noneducation case, *Elrod v. Burns*.[77] In this case, Republican employees of the Cook County, Illinois, sheriff's office were replaced by individuals who were members of the sheriff's party (Democrats). The defendants offered two justifications for the patronage system: (1) to provide effectiveness and efficiency in government, and (2) to ensure representative government. The Court did not find that being a party member was necessarily an incentive to work more effectively, and further noted that the threat of replacement after each election was counterproductive to effectiveness and efficiency. The fear that opposing party members might impede representative government by subverting the new administration's policies was found to be inadequate for "wholesale" dismissals. Rather, the Court held that limiting dismissals to policy-making and confidential positions would accomplish the objectives of preserving the democratic process. In this case, the Court reaffirmed that public employers must have "interests of vital importance" in order to restrict an employee's constitutional rights.

The Supreme Court established in *Elrod* that a non-policy-making, nonconfidential employee could not be dismissed solely on the basis of political association and beliefs. In challenging such a discharge, the burden falls on the teacher to show, by a preponderance of evidence, that protected political activity was the motivating factor in the school board's action. The burden then shifts to the board to show that it would have reached the same decision had the protected activity not occurred. For example, a West Virginia district court reviewed the claims of eight school employees who asserted that their dismissals or transfers resulted from their support of an unsuccessful school board candidate.[78] Of the eight employees, only three could substantiate their claims. The court did not find that a principal's husband's active support of the unsuccessful candidate was the motivating factor in the principal's demotion to a teaching position. Rather, the board documented that she was incapable and inefficient in her role. However, an untenured bus driver was reinstated because a board member directly indicated that discharge was based on the fact that the driver's father-in-law had not "stayed out" of the campaign. As in other claims of constitutional infringement, the employee must demonstrate that protected conduct was the motivating factor in the board's action.

A teacher, as a United States citizen, has the right to run for and to hold public office. Certain statutory restrictions, however, may be placed on the types of offices a teacher may hold. Common law provides that an individual may not hold incompatible offices. Although a teaching position is not viewed as an office, courts have examined the subordinate/superordinate relationship between a teaching position and an elected office. Where one position is subordinate to another, courts generally have held that the positions are incompatible. An example of such a relationship would be the election of a teacher to the school board. The potential for conflict is significant in this instance because of the employer-employee relationship.[79] In ruling that a teacher could not be elected to the board of trustees for the school district, the Supreme Court of Wyoming reasoned that there are many instances in which a teacher's self-interest would run counter to the board's loyalty to the public. The court further noted that the teacher "as a trustee would be supervising himself and at the same time supervising other teachers and administrative personnel who in turn have some supervision or authority over [him] as a teacher." [80] Because of such factors, most courts have held that it is not in the general public interest for a teacher to serve as a member of the school board in the employing school district. This would not, of course, foreclose a teacher from serving on the board of another school district.

School boards have placed other restrictions on teachers running for office, such as requiring that they take mandatory leaves of absence while campaigning. A Kentucky appeals court addressed the constitutionality of a school board policy that required all employees seeking public office involving part-time service (e.g., state legislators) to take a one-month leave of absence prior to the election.[81] The court concluded that the requirement unduly penalized teachers for exercising their political rights, in the absence of evidence that the activity would be detrimental to the performance of their duties. Without a showing of an adverse effect on teaching, the court found the policy to be unconstitutional. This would imply that a school board must formulate leave policies so that the impact of the particular political activity on an individual teacher's duties is considered.

It is noteworthy that board policies on campaign leaves also may be restricted by certain federal statutes. Under the Voting Rights Act of 1965, a policy affecting a "standard, practice, or procedure with respect to voting" must be submitted to the Attorney General or the Federal District Court of the District of Columbia for clearance in those states that have had prior voter discrimination. The intent of this Act is to determine if new policies affecting voting rights are discriminatory in purpose or effect. In a Georgia case, the United States Supreme Court held that a county school board policy mandating a leave of absence for employees campaigning for public office came within the meaning of the Voting Rights Act.[82] The policy was announced one month after a black employee of the board of education declared his candidacy for the legislature. Considering the facts surrounding adoption of the policy, and the burden it placed on employees seeking elective office, the Court held that sufficient evidence existed to indicate potential for discrimination. The Court ruled that such a policy must receive preclearance pursuant to the Voting Rights Act.

Courts have recognized the importance of teachers' freedoms of political association and belief under the first amendment. In attempting to balance the interests of school officials and teachers, courts assess restrictions on political activity in light of their adverse impact on teaching duties.

## FREEDOM OF RELIGION

In part, the first amendment to the Federal Constitution states that "Congress shall make no law respecting an establishment of religion, or prohibiting the free exercise thereof." This basic principle of "separation of church and state" as it relates to public education has been a continual source of litigation. Constitutional challenges have revolved around such issues as financial aid to parochial schools and prayer, Bible reading, and religious instruction in public schools.[83] State action in any of these areas that would violate either the establishment clause or the free exercise clause of the first amendment is closely scrutinized by the federal courts.

Conflicts concerning teachers' free exercise of beliefs have arisen often in the school setting. Can a teacher engage in proselytization of a particular religious sect in the classroom? Is a teacher permitted to disregard the prescribed curriculum if it conflicts with avowed religious beliefs? Can a teacher be compelled to pledge allegiance to the flag in contravention of religious convictions? What actions must a school district take to accommodate teachers' religious beliefs? These issues provide the central focus for defining teachers' religious freedoms in public schools.

Proselytizing in the public schools is strictly prohibited. This is pointedly illustrated by a statement of the Iowa Supreme Court.

> If there is any one thing which is well settled in the policies and purposes of the American people as a whole, it is the fixed and unalterable determination that there shall be an absolute and unequivocal separation of church and state, and that our public school system . . . shall not be used directly or indirectly for religious instruction, and above all that it shall not be made an instrumentality of proselytizing influence in favor of any religious organization, sect, creed, or belief.[84]

Improper use of one's influence and authority to promote a religious cause or belief in the classroom can result in dismissal. For example, in a New York case a tenured teacher was dismissed for efforts to recruit students into a particular religious organization.[85] She encouraged students to attend meetings of the organization, offered transportation to meetings, used the school classroom to promote her religious beliefs, and conducted prayer sessions in her office. The court held these actions to be in violation of the establishment clause of the first amendment.

Inasmuch as a teacher cannot proselytize in the classroom, a teacher also cannot selectively disregard portions of the prescribed curriculum of the school that may conflict with religious beliefs. The Seventh Circuit

Court of Appeals addressed this issue in 1979 when a probationary kindergarten teacher was dismissed for her refusal to teach patriotic matters.[86] Relying on the Biblical prohibition against the worship of graven images, the teacher refused to teach curriculum matters concerning the flag, love of country, and observance of patriotic holidays. For example, she felt that teaching students about the role of Abraham Lincoln in American history was tantamount to idolatry. The court found that allowing individual teachers to fashion their own curriculum would create a "distorted and unbalanced view" of history. Acknowledging the teacher's freedom to believe, the court noted that "she has no constitutional right to require others to submit to her views and to forgo a portion of their education they would otherwise be entitled to enjoy." [87] By refusing to hear the teacher's appeal, the United States Supreme Court allowed the Seventh Circuit's decision to stand.

The flag salute ceremony, or Pledge of Allegiance, as a specific aspect of the curriculum, generally is viewed in a different light from the above curricular questions. Until the early 1940s, most courts found the flag salute unrelated to the issue of religious freedom and thereby sustained its required observance. However, in 1943 the Supreme Court invalidated a West Virginia statute compelling students to participate in the flag salute ceremony.[88] The Court emphatically proclaimed that public officials cannot determine what shall be orthodox in matters of religion. Although this case pertained to students' rights, subsequent courts have inferred that teachers' rights would share the same protections. The Second Circuit Court of Appeals, adopting this stance, upheld a teacher's right to refuse to participate in the Pledge of Allegiance as a matter of "personal conscience." [89] The appellate court echoed the Supreme Court in concluding that "the right to remain silent in the face of an illegitimate demand for speech is as much a part of first amendment protections as the right to speak out in the face of an illegitimate demand for silence." [90] Similarly, the Supreme Court of Massachusetts, in an opinion to the governor concerning a proposed Pledge of Allegiance Act, ruled that a forced requirement impaired the first amendment rights of teachers.[91] However, teachers cannot use their personal beliefs as a basis for denying students the opportunity to engage in the Pledge of Allegiance. Teachers can decline to participate, but they cannot eliminate this observance within their classrooms.

Another source of controversy has been the wearing of religious garb by public school teachers. Litigation has resulted when nuns have been hired to teach in public schools but have been forbidden to wear the dress of their religious order. In 1894, the Pennsylvania Supreme Court upheld the right of nuns to teach in the public schools and to wear their religious dress.[92] In reaction to this decision, the Pennsylvania legislature enacted a statute specifically prohibiting the wearing of religious dress by public school teachers. Later, the Pennsylvania Supreme Court found the statute to be constitutional, ruling that it was within the legislature's power to regulate and control appearances of sectarianism.[93] The court noted that the statute was "directed against acts, not beliefs, and only against acts of the teacher whilst engaged in the performance of his or her duties as such teacher." [94] While the Pennsylvania high court held that the regulation of religious dress was within the purview of the government, a number of other courts have rendered contrary opinions, finding dress unrelated to instruction. At the present time, judicial opinion is split on the right of public school teachers to wear religious dress.

In addition to first amendment guarantees of religious freedom, Title VII of the Civil Rights Act of 1964 protects the teacher from religious discrimination in employment.[95] One of the primary religious issues litigated under this Act has been the degree of accommodation that an employer must make in the work schedule for employees because of religious reasons. This has been a particular issue with regard to members of the Worldwide Church of God, who observe the Sabbath from sunset on Friday until sunset on Saturday. In the 1972 amendments to Title VII, Congress defined religion as including

> all aspects of religious observance and practice, as well as belief, unless an employer demonstrates that he is unable to reasonably accommodate an employee's or prospective employee's religious observance or practice without undue hardship on the conduct of the employer's business.[96]

Since neither Congress nor the Equal Employment Opportunity Commission delineated "reasonable accommodation," the Supreme Court addressed this issue and formulated general guidelines. In *Trans World Airlines (TWA) v. Hardison,* a member of the Worldwide Church of God was discharged for refusal to work on Saturdays.[97] The plaintiff was unable to avoid a Saturday work schedule because TWA's shift assignments were based on seniority in accordance with the terms of a collective bargaining agreement. He challenged TWA, claiming that individual religious rights must take precedence over a collective bargaining contract or a seniority system. The Court examined the actions of TWA to determine if, in fact, an attempt had been made to accommodate the needs of the plaintiff. Evidence showed that TWA did take appropriate action, which included several meetings with the plaintiff as well as a search to find someone to exchange shifts. The Court concluded that these attempts were adequate, and that there was no requirement for the employer to take action inconsistent with the seniority system established in a valid collective bargaining agreement. Unless a discriminatory purpose can be shown, a bona fide seniority system is not unlawful under Title VII. The Court reasoned that to require an employer to bear more than a *de minimis* cost in making religious accommodations would constitute an undue hardship.

The standard of reasonable accommodation under Title VII has been followed by several courts in construing state statutory or constitutional provisions.[98] A recent public school case dealt with a provision of the California constitution which stipulates that "a person may not be disqualified from entering or pursuing a business, profession, vocation, or employment because of sex, race, creed, color, or national or ethnic origin." [99] In this case, an elementary teacher who was a member of the Worldwide Church of God was excused from Friday evening and Saturday school activities; however, his requests for leave for certain holy days were denied. Consequently, over a period of four years the teacher accumulated thirty-one unauthorized absences. Prior to each absence, he prepared detailed lesson plans that were usually taught by the same substitute teacher. These continual unexcused absences ultimately resulted in dismissal action. The teacher challenged the dismissal and the trial court upheld the school board's decision.

On appeal, the California Supreme Court interpreted the state constitution as "forbid[ding] disqualification of employees for religious practices unless reasonable accommodation by the employer is impossible without undue hardship." [100] Since the school district was not compelled to violate a contract or pay overtime wages to a substitute teacher, the question of hardship revolved around whether the use of substitute teachers had a detrimental effect on the educational program. The court acknowledged that it was preferable to have the regular teacher in the classroom but, nonetheless, held that the use of a substitute was not "unreasonably burdensome" for the district. The court also noted that the leave requested by the teacher did not exceed the amount allowed under California law, as each teacher is permitted ten days of leave for illness or personal necessity. The court further concluded that only minimum disruption was created, since most of the teacher's absences each year were on consecutive days and he knew the dates sufficiently in advance to enable him to prepare lesson plans. Also, the fact that neighboring school districts permitted such absences strengthened the conclusion that reasonable accommodation had not been made for the teacher.

The court rejected the district's claim that the requested accommodation constituted preferential treatment based on religion, noting that "the purpose and the primary effect . . . are not to favor any religion but to promote equal employment opportunities for members of all religious faiths." [101] The court carefully noted that such accommodation was not required for secular requests. The United States Supreme Court declined to review this case, and thus left the California Supreme Court decision in place.

In general, a school district must not interfere with a teacher's free exercise of religion. However, it cannot be inferred from this constitutional right that a teacher can promote tenets of a particular belief in the classroom or selectively omit aspects of the curriculum that may conflict with beliefs. It is incumbent upon school officials to make reasonable accommodations to meet an individual's religious needs, as long as an undue hardship is not imposed on the district. The criteria for assessing reasonable accommodation have evolved from federal and state legislation barring religious discrimination in employment. Among the factors considered in determining reasonableness are the costs of the accommodation and its impact on school operations and contractual agreements.

## RIGHT TO PRIVACY

The axiom of the teacher as exemplar has provided the rationale for school administrators to curtail the conduct or activities of teachers outside the realm of the classroom. Teachers have resisted such encroachment into their private lives as a violation of their right to privacy and freedom of association. In the area of personal freedom, by far the most contested issues have involved the sexual conduct of teachers. School boards, seeking to instill conventional values in students, have viewed with disapproval teacher conduct involving homosexuality, unwed pregnancies, and other alleged sexual improprieties. Because of the dynamic nature of societal values and standards, courts have been hesitant to establish definite criteria for evaluating teacher conduct, preferring instead to decide each issue in relation to the particular circumstances. Historically, a higher standard of conduct has been demanded of educators than of citizens in general; however, an examination of the litigation of the past decade reveals a judicial tendency to support the individual teacher's right to privacy. This does not mean that boards cannot impose restrictions on unconventional behavior, but that such constraints must be based on evidence that the conduct impairs a teacher's effectiveness in the classroom.

Dismissals resulting from unacceptable private conduct are generally based on immorality or unfitness to teach.[102] In challenging such dismissals, teachers usually contend that board action violates their right to privacy. To adequately support dismissal charges, the board must show a connection between the unacceptable conduct and teaching effectiveness; that is, there must be a harmful effect on students or a detrimental impact on collegial relationships. Two cases from the Eighth Circuit Court of Appeals are illustrative of the judicial stance. The first case dealt with the dismissal of a single, female teacher who was living with her boyfriend in a mobile home near the school.[103] Although she claimed that the dismissal violated her privacy rights, the court upheld the school board's action, noting that conclusive evidence was presented to establish that the teacher's behavior outside the classroom had an adverse effect on her students.[104] In contrast, where a female teacher was dismissed because of overnight male guests in her apartment, the appellate court held that the mere "potential" for misconduct was insufficient to support dismissal.[105] Recognizing that the teacher's behavior may not have involved good judgment, the court concluded that there was no indication that the teacher's behavior had resulted in adverse reaction from either students or the community.

School boards frequently have associated pregnancies out of wedlock with immoral conduct. As in other areas of the teacher's personal life, courts are now less prone to agree that the unwed status of a pregnant employee itself is evidence of immoral character. The prevailing position of the courts is reflected in a 1974 decision in which an Alabama federal district court invalidated the dismissal of an unwed pregnant teacher for immorality.[106] In upholding the teacher's right to privacy in sexual matters, the court found that the board had not established a nexus between the charge of immorality and the competency or fitness of the teacher. Similarly, in 1977 the Supreme Court of New Mexico held that the pregnancy of an unmarried teacher did not warrant dismissal for good and just cause.[107]

Courts generally have held that mere community disapproval of an individual teacher's personal life cannot serve as the basis for dismissal or nonretention, as long as teaching performance is satisfactory. This view is exemplified in a 1979 case rendered by the Tenth Circuit Court of Appeals. In this case, the teacher was officially dismissed for lack of classroom discipline, disorderliness of the classroom, and inability to motivate students.[108] Unofficially, the actual reasons involved an alleged affair with a neighbor, lack of church attendance, card playing, and an unattractive physical appearance. Although the teacher denied the rumors concerning her personal conduct, the principal's response was that "it really doesn't matter whether it's true or not, because that was what was going around the community."[109] The court, entering judgment for the teacher, held these grounds to be wholly impermissible.

An unresolved issue that has generated considerable controversy is the homosexual teacher's right to privacy.[110] With the general lack of societal consensus on homosexuality, courts have moved cautiously in this area. Litigation from California has been the most extensive and far-reaching in modifying strict censure of all homosexual behavior. Like most courts, the California Supreme Court traditionally had viewed homosexual behavior as evidence of unfitness to teach.[111] Departing dramatically from that posture, in 1969 the California high court placed limitations on the authority of employers to interfere in an individual's private life. The court enunciated criteria for evaluating a teacher's behavior, noting that a relationship must be established between the questionable behavior and fitness to teach in order for sanctions to be imposed.[112] The one-time, isolated incident of homosexual activity in this case did not demonstrate such a connection. Subsequent decisions in the state have followed this precedent.

In contrast to the California rulings, a 1977 Washington Supreme Court decision represents the opposing viewpoint on dismissing teachers for engaging in homosexual conduct.[113] As in the above California case, the teacher's conduct had been private, receiving public notoriety only upon dismissal. However, the court found that the board's mere knowledge of the teacher's activity was sufficient to establish impairment of teaching effectiveness. Even though the teacher argued that his behavior had been private, with the publicity resulting from the school board's actions, the court admonished that the teacher subjected himself to risk of dismissal by maintaining homosexual company. The United States Supreme Court subsequently declined to review the case.

The Supreme Court's refusal to hear the Washington case may portend a possible lessening of safeguards previously conferred on the teacher's right to privacy outside the classroom. Additional support for this position is provided by the Court's refusal to review a Third Circuit Court of Appeals decision upholding the firing of two public employees for living in "open adultery." [114] Justice Marshall, strongly disagreeing with the Supreme Court's denial of review, stated that the ruling "permits a public employer to dictate the sexual conduct and family living arrangements of its employees, without a meaningful showing that these private choices have any relation to job performance." [115] Marshall objected to sanctioning the invasion of personal privacy. In his opinion, the terminations would not withstand even minimal scrutiny, since there was no proof that the employees were incompetent or that their private lives interfered with their professional duties. Although involving noneducational personnel (library workers), this decision may have implications for future cases involving teacher conduct.

In the past decade, teachers have demanded and received greater protection of individual freedoms under the first and fourteenth amendments. The courts, while recognizing the duty of school officials to maintain certain values and standards, have extended teachers' rights to privacy and have protected conduct as long as it does not detrimentally affect students and the school. The law in this area, however, is still evolving, and possibly other courts will follow the Third Circuit Court of Appeals in placing constraints on public employees' rights to privacy in their personal activities.

## PERSONAL APPEARANCE

Teachers have challenged regulations governing their appearance as violating constitutionally protected rights to privacy, free expression, and personal liberty. Many of the codes pertaining to appearance were originally student-designed restrictions. Application of these regulations to teachers is often predicated on the necessity of enforcing similar requirements for students. Three male teachers successfully challenged a Mississippi school board regulation restricting beards, moustaches, and long hair among students and teachers.[116] The court held that "a state sanctioned regulation which prescribes generally the grooming habits of adults as a condition of public employment, unrelated to one's ability to perform his work, can only be viewed with close judicial scrutiny." [117] The court found no legitimate state interest for the grooming regulation applied to teachers, and concluded that, absent proof of disruption, the board had no power to regulate employee appearance.

If the state impairs an individual's constitutionally protected rights, due process must be provided. It has been argued that the right to a particular mode of dress involves such a protected right or interest. However, the Seventh Circuit Court of Appeals emphasized that even if one accepts or assumes that an individual's personal appearance is a protected interest, this does not mean that every rule affecting appearance is unconstitutional.[118] The court found a restriction on employees' beards and sideburns to be a "relatively minor deprivation." Similarly, in 1978 the Fifth Circuit Court of Appeals held that the dismissal of a nontenured teacher for refusal to shave his beard did not impair any federal constitutional rights.[119] The court concluded that a protected interest would be involved only if the board's dismissal action attached a "badge of infamy." In the court's view, being discharged for refusal to shave could not be said to constitute infamy.

While the Supreme Court has not directly addressed grooming standards for teachers, it has upheld the right of other public employers to impose reasonable regulations on employee appearance. In *Kelley v. Johnson,* a case involving hair-grooming regulations for policemen, the Court established that the right to dress as one pleases is not a fundamental right involving a protected interest.[120] Applying the rational basis test, the Court held that a protected right would only be impaired if a regulation were "so irrational that it [could] be branded 'arbitrary.' " [121] The Court concluded that the question was not whether the state could establish a need for the regulation, but whether the police officer could "demonstrate that there was no rational connection between the regulation . . . and the promotion of safety of persons and property." [122] Thus the burden of proof was placed on the individual challenging the grooming regulation.

Shortly after the *Kelley* decision, a three-judge panel of the Second Circuit Court of Appeals invalidated a school board regulation requiring all males to wear ties. However, on rehearing before the full court, the appellate court relied on *Kelley* and upheld the school board regulation.[123] Although the teacher equated refusal to wear a tie with "symbolic speech," the court found that, "as conduct becomes less and less like 'pure speech' the showing of governmental interest required for its regulation is progressively lessened." [124] Recognizing that the role of teachers is uniquely influential, the court further stated, "as public servants in a special position of trust, teachers may properly be subjected to many restrictions in their professional lives which would be invalid if generally applied." [125]

Disparate treatment of men and women with regard to dress codes has been litigated under Title VII, which prohibits discrimination in employment based on race, color, national origin, religion, and sex. In a Seventh Circuit Court of Appeals case, a savings and loan association required its female employees to wear a uniform, while its male employees were required to wear regular business attire.[126] This policy was challenged and found to be discriminatory with respect to "compensation, terms, conditions, or privileges of employment." [127] The court found the differential treatment between two groups of employees performing the same functions to be impermissible under Title VII. Mandatory uniforms were not held to be discriminatory—only the unequal application of the requirement. Judicial scrutiny of this type of unequal treatment, of course, raises questions about the acceptability, under Title VII, of other personal appearance regulations that are applied to only one sex. The court noted that such variances are permissible if "reasonable," based on acceptable norms, and related to business needs.

Although courts generally acknowledge that the right to govern personal appearance is a protected interest, it has not been declared a fundamental right requiring close judicial scrutiny of regulations that might impair its exercise. School officials thus can restrict appearance as long as there is a rational basis for the regulation. Arbitrary rules, however, are vulnerable to challenge as a violation of personal liberty.

## REMEDIES UNDER CIVIL RIGHTS LEGISLATION

Increasingly, teachers are bringing legal actions against school boards, school administrators, and individual school board members to recover damages for actions that violate their constitutional rights. The legal basis for many of these constitutional tort suits has been grounded in the Civil Rights Act of 1871—a federal law rarely invoked until the 1960s. This law, which originally was enacted to prevent discrimination against black citizens, has been broadly interpreted as conferring liability upon school officials not only for racial discrimination but also for any actions that may result in the infringement of the constitutional rights of students and teachers. Specifically, these legal challenges usually are brought under Section 1983, which provides that any person who under color of state law deprives another individual of rights secured by the Federal Constitution or laws is subject to personal liability.[128]

Under Section 1983 school officials can be held personally liable for actions which impair a student's or teacher's constitutional rights; however, these officials may be protected by immunity under specific circumstances. Historically, certain governmental officials (for example, police officers) have been afforded qualified immunity under Section 1983 suits for their actions taken in good faith. More recently, this qualified immunity has been extended to a number of other governmental officials, including school board members.[129] The Supreme Court has concluded that individual school officials do not possess complete immunity, but a qualified immunity does exist when they have acted in good faith. In a student discipline case, the Court addressed qualified immunity, stating that

> A school board member is not immune from liability for damages under Section 1983 if he knew or reasonably should have known that the action he took within his sphere of official responsibility would violate the constitutional rights of the student affected, or if he took the action with the malicious intention to cause a deprivation of constitutional rights or other injury.[130]

The Court held that damages should be awarded only when a school board member has acted with "impermissible motivation" or such disregard of an individual's constitutional rights that a lack of good faith is demonstrated.[131] While recognizing motivation as a factor in determining violation of protected rights, the Court also emphasized that ignorance or disregard of established rights was not defensible.

Although school board members and administrators can be held personally liable for their actions under Section 1983, prior to 1978 school boards and school districts as entities were generally not viewed as "persons" subject to suit within the meaning of this Act. Precedent for this view was established in 1961 when the Supreme Court ruled that municipalities could not be held liable for damages in connection with civil rights abridgments.[132] Departing from this precedent in 1978, the Court in *Monell v. Department of Social Services of the City of New York* rejected its earlier interpretation and held that local governments are "persons" under Section 1983 of the Civil Rights Act of 1871.[133] In essence, school districts can now be assessed damages when actions taken pursuant to official policy violate federally protected rights. Thus, a teacher denied employment because of the exercise of first amendment rights can initiate a civil rights action directly against the school district.

In *Monell,* the court distinguished between acts performed on behalf of governmental agencies under official policy and acts committed by an individual employee. Following earlier precedent, the Court rejected the *respondeat superior* theory under Section 1983. That is, a governmental unit cannot be held liable for the wrongful acts committed solely by its employees. Liability against the agency can be imposed only when execution of official policy causes infringement of a constitutional right.

The Supreme Court in *Monell* firmly established that municipalities do not possess absolute immunity for official governmental actions; however, the Court did not address the issue of qualified immunity of governmental agencies. As a result, there has been disagreement among federal courts as to whether the qualified immunity of governmental officials in their individual capacities also extends to their official capacity (i.e., to the municipality itself). In essence, judgments rendered against officials in their individual capacities are paid from personal resources, whereas judgments against them in their official capacities are paid from public funds. The appellate courts in the Fourth and Eighth Circuits concluded that qualified good faith immunity applied to governmental officials acting in their individual as well as their official capacities.[134] In contrast, the Tenth Circuit Court of Appeals distinguished between personal and official liability.[135] The appellate court concluded that school board members possess qualified immunity in their individual capacities, but that the board members in their official capacities must be responsible to those they injure. According to the court, bad faith need not be established for liability to be assessed.

With conflicting appellate court decisions, the Supreme Court reviewed the Eighth Circuit Court's decision in *Owen v. City of Independence, Missouri.*[136] As noted above, the Eighth Circuit Court of Appeals did not distinguish between individual and official liability, but held that a municipality was entitled to qualified immunity when its officials acted in good faith. The Supreme Court reversed this decision, stating that

> By its terms, Section 1983 "creates a species of tort liability that on its face admits no immunities." . . . Its language is absolute and unqualified; no mention is made of any privileges, immunities, or defenses that may be asserted.[137] [citation omitted]

The Supreme Court's review of common law and congressional debate surrounding the Civil Rights Act of 1871 revealed that the Act was not intended to create qualified immunity for municipalities based on the good faith of their officials. The Court acknowledged that a form of sovereign immunity for tort liability has been provided for municipal corporations where "governmental" functions and "discretionary" activities have been involved. However, the Court concluded that governmental immunity had been abrogated in situations involving the impairment of federally protected rights by the enactment of Section 1983, which "abolished whatever vestige of the State's sovereign immunity the municipality possessed" in this regard.[138] Through the *Owen* decision and other prior precedents, the Court has clearly delineated that governmental bodies can be held liable for the impairment of rights under Section 1983.[139]

To avoid liability for the abridgment of constitutional rights, school districts have introduced claims of eleventh amendment immunity. The eleventh amendment has been interpreted as precluding legal challenges against a state by its citizens.[140] School districts have asserted similar eleventh amendment protection based on the fact that they perform a state function. Admittedly, education is a state function, but it does not necessarily follow that school districts gain eleventh amendment immunity against constitutional abridgments. For the eleventh amendment to be invoked in a suit against a school district, the state must be the "real party in interest." The Third Circuit Court of Appeals identified the following factors in determining if a governmental agency, such as a school district, is entitled to invoke eleventh amendment protection: whether payment of the judgment will be from the state treasury; whether a governmental or proprietary function is being performed; whether the agency has autonomy over its operation; whether it has the power to sue and be sued; whether it can enter into contracts; and whether the agency's property is immune from state taxation.[141] The most significant of these factors in determining if a district is shielded by eleventh amendment immunity has been whether or not the judgment will be recovered from state funds. If funds are to be paid from the state treasury, courts have declared the state to be the real party in interest, and thus school districts have been entitled to immunity.[142]

For many states, the eleventh amendment question with respect to school district immunity was resolved in *Mt. Healthy*.[143] In this case, the Supreme Court concluded that the issue turned on whether the Ohio school district was an arm of the state as opposed to that of a municipality or other political subdivision. This determination was dependent in part upon the "nature of the entity created by state law." [144] According to Ohio law, political subdivisions, including school districts, are not part of the "state." Considering also the taxing power and autonomy of district operations, the Supreme Court found school districts to be more like counties or cities than an extension of the state. Since the *Mt. Healthy* decision, other state/ local relationships have been similarly interpreted as excluding school districts from eleventh amendment immunity.

When a teacher prevails in a constitutional tort suit against a school district, the district may be subject to payment of damages. However, unless injury can be shown, the teacher will be entitled only to nominal damages. In a students' rights case, the Supreme Court held that, absent proof of injury, pupils who were denied procedural due process could not be awarded damages in excess of one dollar.[145] Although teachers can more easily substantiate entitlement to damages than can students, the burden remains with the teacher to show that actual injury, either monetary, emotional, or mental, has occurred.

In summary, school districts are "persons" under Section 1983 of the Civil Rights Act of 1871; thus, they can be held liable for actions that violate a teacher's constitutional rights. School districts cannot necessarily avoid legal challenges by claiming eleventh amendment immunity. Courts are reluctant to confer this immunity on districts as an arm of the state, generally holding that eleventh amendment coverage does not extend to such political subdivisions. Even though school districts can be sued, monetary damages awarded may be nominal unless injury can be shown. Unlike school districts, school officials may experience qualified immunity if action is characterized by "good faith." Ignorance of well-established law, however, is considered evidence of bad faith. With the interpretation of Section 1983 expanded to include school districts, teachers have a broader legal basis for seeking relief in connection with constitutional impairments.

## CONCLUSION

Although teachers' rights continue to be delineated by courts, the following generalizations reflect the present status in the substantive areas discussed in this chapter.

1. Teachers have a constitutional right to express their views on public issues related to the operation of the school system.
2. Speech that interferes with the management of the school or creates a disruptive situation can be restricted by school officials.
3. Dismissal or any other retaliatory personnel action, such as transfer or demotion, predicated solely on protected speech is unconstitutional.
4. Exercise of protected speech will not invalidate a dismissal action if the school board can show, by a preponderance of evidence, that it would have reached the same decision had the protected speech not occurred.
5. Private expression to a superior is protected under the first amendment.
6. Topics discussed in the classroom must be related to course objectives, and treatment of controversial issues must be objective.
7. Age and maturity of students are primary factors in evaluation of the appropriateness of teaching materials and methodology.
8. Teachers can be required to sign loyalty oaths pledging support of the Federal Constitution and their state constitution.
9. Membership in an organization with unlawful purposes is an unconstitutional basis for excluding an individual from public employment.
10. A teacher must answer questions posed by superiors if they are related to a determination of fitness to teach.
11. Political activities of teachers outside of the school cannot be the basis for employment decisions related to promotion, transfer, or dismissal.
12. Depending on individual state laws, restrictions may be placed on types of elected offices that may be held by a teacher (e.g., two incompatible positions cannot be held).
13. Employees can be required to take temporary leave from their positions to campaign for office if it is established that campaign demands would interfere with job responsibilities.

14. A teacher cannot promote the tenets of any religious belief in the classroom.
15. School officials must make reasonable accommodation for the exercise of a teacher's religious beliefs, unless such accommodation would result in undue hardship for the school district.
16. Private conduct of public employees can be restricted when it adversely affects students or the operation of the school.
17. Unwed pregnancy *per se* is not adequate evidence of immorality to justify dismissal, unless it can be related to fitness to teach.
18. Public knowledge of homosexuality may establish grounds for dismissal when teaching effectiveness is impaired.
19. Mere community disapproval of a teacher's personal activity is an impermissible basis for dismissal.
20. School officials can impose reasonable regulations on a teacher's personal appearance.
21. School officials and school districts can be held liable for damages in connection with actions that infringe on a teacher's constitutional rights.
22. An individual can recover only nominal damages for the impairment of constitutional rights unless monetary, emotional, or mental injury can be established.

## NOTES

1. 391 U.S. 563 (1968).
2. *Id.* at 567.
3. *Id.* at 570.
4. *Id.* at 572–73.
5. *Id.* at 573.
6. *Id.* at 574.
7. Birdwell v. Hazelwood School Dist., 491 F.2d 490 (8th Cir. 1974). *See also* Whitsel v. Southeast Local School Dist., 484 F.2d 1222 (6th Cir. 1973), in which the dismissal of a teacher was upheld because he addressed protesting students after the principal had ordered all students to return to class. The court reasoned that the teacher was speaking "in the capacity of a school teacher during school hours on school property." *Id.* at 1229.
8. James v. Board of Educ. of Central Dist. No. 1, 461 F.2d 566 (2d Cir. 1972), *cert. denied*, 409 U.S. 1042 (1972).
9. Adcock v. Board of Educ. of San Diego Unified School Dist., 513 P.2d 900 (Cal. 1973). *See also* Swilley v. Alexander, 448 F. Supp. 702 (S.D. Ala. 1978), in which a federal court held that a reprimand placed in a teacher's file did not abridge first amendment rights.

10. McGill v. Board of Educ. of Pekin Elementary School Dist. No. 108, 602 F.2d 774 (7th Cir. 1979).
11. Austin v. Mehlville R-9 School Dist., 564 S.W.2d 884 (Mo. 1978).
12. *Id.* at 887.
13. 429 U.S. 274 (1977).
14. *Id.* at 282.
15. *Id.* at 285–86.
16. Johnson v. Butler, 433 F. Supp. 531 (W.D. Va. 1977).
17. Zoll v. Eastern Allamakee Community School Dist., 588 F.2d 246 (8th Cir. 1978).
18. Bernasconi v. Tempe Elementary School Dist. No. 3, 548 F.2d 857 (9th Cir. 1977), *cert. denied,* 434 U.S. 825 (1977).
19. Hickman v. Valley Local School Dist., 619 F.2d 606 (6th Cir. 1980).
20. Johnson v. Cain, 430 F. Supp. 518 (N.D. Ala. 1977).
21. Williams v. Day, 553 F.2d 1160 (8th Cir. 1977).
22. Roseman v. Indiana University of Pennsylvania, 520 F.2d 1364 (3d Cir. 1975), *cert. denied,* 424 U.S. 921 (1976).
23. 439 U.S. 410 (1979).
24. Givhan v. Western Line Consolidated School Dist., 555 F.2d 1309, 1318 (5th Cir. 1977).
25. For a discussion and history of academic freedom, *see* Ralph F. Fuchs, "Academic Freedom—Its Basic Philosophy, Function, and History," *Law and Contemporary Problems,* Vol. 28, No. 3, 1968, pp. 431–46.
26. *Id.* at 436.
27. *Id.*
28. Mailloux v. Kiley, 448 F.2d 1242 (1st Cir. 1971).
29. *See* text with note 14, *supra,* and note 75, *infra.*
30. 393 U.S. 97 (1968).
31. 385 U.S. 589, 603 (1967).
32. Keefe v. Geanakos, 418 F.2d 359 (1st Cir. 1969).
33. *Id.* at 361.
34. *Id.* at 363.
35. Parducci v. Rutland, 316 F. Supp. 352 (M.D. Ala. 1970).
36. *Id.* at 353.
37. Brubacker v. Board of Educ. School Dist. 149, Cook County, Illinois, 502 F.2d 973 (7th Cir. 1974), *cert. denied,* 421 U.S. 965 (1975).
38. Simon v. Jefferson Davis Parish School Bd., 289 So. 2d 511 (La. App. 1974).
39. *Id.* at 517.
40. Mailloux v. Kiley, 323 F. Supp. 1387 (D. Mass. 1971).
41. *Id.* at 1392.
42. 448 F.2d 1242 (1st Cir. 1971).
43. Sterzing v. Fort Bend Independent School Dist., 376 F. Supp. 657 (S.D. Tex. 1972).
44. *Id.* at 662.
45. Wilson v. Chancellor, 418 F. Supp. 1358 (D. Ore. 1976).
46. *Id.* at 1364.
47. Kingsville Independent School Dist. v. Cooper, 611 F.2d 1109 (5th Cir. 1980).

48. *Id.* at 1111.
49. Adams v. Campbell County School Dist., Campbell County, Wyoming, 511 F.2d 1242 (10th Cir. 1975).
50. *Id.* at 1247.
51. Minarcini v. Strongsville City School Dist., 541 F.2d 577 (6th Cir. 1976).
52. *Id.* at 582. *See also* Right to Read Defense Committee of Chelsea v. School Committee of City of Chelsea, 454 F. Supp. 703 (D. Mass. 1978).
53. Presidents Council, Dist. 25 v. Community School Board No. 25, 457 F.2d 289 (2d Cir. 1972), *cert. denied*, 409 U.S. 998 (1972).
54. *Id.* at 291.
55. *See* text with note 31, Chapter 8, for an analysis of these cases.
56. Pico v. Board of Educ., Island Trees Union Free School Dist., 474 F. Supp. 387 (E.D.N.Y. 1979), *vacated and remanded,* No. 79-7690 (2d Cir., October 2, 1980); Salvail v. Nashua Bd. of Educ., 469 F. Supp. 1269 (D.N.H. 1979); Right to Read Defense Committee v. School Committee of the City of Chelsea, 454 F. Supp. 703 (D. Mass. 1978).
57. Bicknell v. Vergennes Union High School Bd. of Directors, 475 F. Supp. 615 (D. Vt. 1979), *aff'd* No. 79-7676 (2d Cir., October 2, 1980); Zykan v. Warsaw Community School Corp., No. 579-68 (N.D. Ind., December 3, 1979), *vacated and remanded,* 631 F.2d 1300 (7th Cir., 1980); Cary v. Board of Educ. of the Adams-Arapahoe School Dist., 598 F.2d 535 (10th Cir. 1979); Presidents Council, Dist. 25 v. Community School Bd. No. 25, 457 F.2d 289 (2d Cir. 1972), *cert. denied,* 409 U.S. 998 (1972).
58. Mailloux v. Kiley, 448 F.2d 1242 (1st Cir. 1971).
59. 342 U.S. 485 (1952).
60. *Id.* at 492.
61. Wieman v. Updegraff, 344 U.S. 183 (1952).
62. Cramp v. Board of Public Instruction of Orange County, 368 U.S. 278 (1961).
63. *Id.* at 287.
64. Baggett v. Bullitt, 377 U.S. 360 (1964).
65. Elfbrandt v. Russell, 384 U.S. 11 (1966).
66. Keyishian v. Board of Regents, 385 U.S. 589, 606 (1967).
67. Ohlson v. Phillips, 397 U.S. 317 (1970). *See also* Connell v. Higginbotham, 403 U.S. 207 (1971), where a required oath, affirming support for the constitutions of the United States and Florida, was upheld.
68. Familias Unidas v. Briscoe, 619 F.2d 391 (5th Cir. 1980).
69. 357 U.S. 399 (1958).
70. *See* Chapter 6 for a comprehensive discussion of teachers' collective bargaining rights.
71. Pickering v. Board of Educ., 391 U.S. 563 (1968).
72. Goldsmith v. Board of Educ., 225 P. 783 (Cal. App. 1924).
73. *Id.* at 783–84.
74. Los Angeles Teachers Union v. Los Angeles City Bd. of Educ., 455 P.2d 827 (Cal. 1969).
75. Ky. Rev. Stat. § 161.162.
76. Calhoun v. Cassady, 534 S.W.2d 806 (Ky. 1976).
77. 427 U.S. 347 (1976).

78. Miller v. Board of Educ. of the County of Lincoln, 450 F. Supp. 106 (S.D. W.Va. 1978).
79. *See* Visotcky v. City Council of the City of Garfield, 273 A.2d 597 (N.J. Super. 1971).
80. Haskins v. State *ex rel.* Harrington, 516 P.2d 1171, 1180 (Wyo. 1973).
81. Allen v. Board of Educ. of Jefferson County, Kentucky, 584 S.W.2d 408 (Ky. App. 1979).
82. Dougherty County, Georgia, Bd. of Educ. v. White, 439 U.S. 32 (1978).
83. *See* Chapter 10 for a discussion of these issues.
84. Knowlton v. Baumhover, 166 N.W. 202 (Iowa 1918).
85. LaRocca v. Board of Educ. of Rye City School Dist., 406 N.Y.S.2d 348 (App. Div. 1978).
86. Palmer v. Board of Educ. of City of Chicago, 603 F.2d 1271 (7th Cir. 1979), *cert. denied,* 444 U.S. 1026 (1980).
87. *Id.* at 1274.
88. West Virginia State Bd. of Educ. v. Barnette, 319 U.S. 624 (1943). *See* text with note 29, Chapter 10.
89. Russo v. Central School Dist. No. 1, 469 F.2d 623 (2d Cir. 1972).
90. *Id.* at 634.
91. Opinions of the Justices to the Governor, 363 N.E.2d 251 (Mass. 1977).
92. Hysong v. School Dist. of Gallitzin Borough, 30 A. 482 (Pa. 1894).
93. Commonwealth v. Herr, 78 A. 68 (Pa. 1910).
94. *Id.* at 71.
95. 42 U.S.C. § 2000e-2(a)(1) (1976). The Act provides that:
    (a) It shall be an unlawful employment practice for an employer—(1) to fail or refuse to hire or to discharge any individual, or otherwise to discriminate against any individual with respect to his compensation, terms, conditions, or privileges of employment, because of such individual's race, color, religion, sex, or national origin.
96. 42 U.S.C. § 2000e(j) (1976).
97. 432 U.S. 63 (1977).
98. *See* Rankin v. Commission on Professional Competence, 593 P.2d 852 (Cal. 1979), *cert. denied,* 444 U.S. 986 (1979); Wondzell v. Alaska Wood Products, Inc., 583 P.2d 860 (Alaska 1978).
99. Rankins, *supra,* at 853.
100. *Id.* at 856.
101. *Id.* at 859.
102. *See* text with note 91, Chapter 5, for a discussion of related cases involving dismissal for immorality.
103. Sullivan v. Meade Independent School Dist. No. 101, 530 F.2d 799 (8th Cir. 1976).
104. For an example of a case in which the school board did not establish a nexus between a teacher's living arrangements and classroom effectiveness, *see* Thompson v. Southwest School Dist., 483 F. Supp. 1170 (W.D. Mo. 1980).
105. Fisher v. Snyder, 476 F.2d 375 (8th Cir. 1973).
106. Drake v. Covington County Bd. of Educ., 371 F. Supp. 974 (M.D. Ala. 1974).

107. New Mexico State Bd. of Educ. v. Stoudt, 571 P.2d 1186 (N.M. 1977).
108. Stoddard v. School Dist. No. 1, Lincoln County, Wyoming, 590 F.2d 829 (10th Cir. 1979).
109. *Id.* at 833.
110. *See* text with note 107, Chapter 5, for a discussion of teacher dismissals related to homosexual conduct.
111. *See* Sarac v. State Bd. of Educ., 57 Cal. Rptr. 69 (Cal. App. 1967).
112. Morrison v. State Bd. of Educ., 461 P.2d 375 (Cal. 1969). For identification of criteria, *see* text with note 109, Chapter 5.
113. Gaylord v. Tacoma School Dist. No. 10, 559 P.2d 1340 (Wash. 1977), *cert. denied*, 434 U.S. 879 (1977).
114. Hollenbaugh and Philburn v. Carnegie Free Library, 578 F.2d 1374 (3d Cir. 1978), *cert. denied*, 439 U.S. 1052 (1979).
115. *Id.*
116. Conard v. Goolsby, 350 F. Supp. 713 (N.D. Miss. 1972).
117. *Id.* at 718.
118. Miller v. School Dist. No. 167, Cook County, Illinois, 495 F.2d 658 (7th Cir. 1974).
119. Ball v. Board of Trustees of the Kerrville Independent School Dist., 584 F.2d 684 (5th Cir. 1978), *cert. denied*, 440 U.S. 972 (1979).
120. 425 U.S. 238 (1976).
121. *Id.* at 247.
122. *Id.*
123. East Hartford Educ. Ass'n v. Board of Educ. of the Town of East Hartford, 562 F.2d 838 (2d Cir. 1977). *See also* Tardif v. Quinn, 545 F.2d 761 (1st Cir. 1976), in which the appellate court upheld the dismissal of a teacher for wearing short skirts.
124. *Id.* at 858.
125. *Id.* at 863.
126. Carroll v. Talman Federal Savings and Loan Ass'n of Chicago, 604 F.2d 1028 (7th Cir. 1979).
127. 42 U.S.C. § 2000e-2(a)(1) (1976).
128. 42 U.S.C. § 1980 (1976).
129. Wood v. Strickland, 420 U.S. 308 (1975). *See* text with note 45, Chapter 11.
130. *Id.* at 322.
131. *Id.* Recently, the Supreme Court held that a plaintiff asserting a cause of action under Section 1983 does not have to allege that a public official acted in bad faith to claim relief. To instigate action, the plaintiff must claim only (1) deprivation of a federal right and (2) that this right was deprived by a person acting under color of state law. A plaintiff is not required to anticipate that an official will employ a good faith defense and thus in the original action allege bad faith. Gomez v. Toledo, 100 S. Ct. 1920 (1980).
132. Monroe v. Pape, 365 U.S. 167 (1961).
133. 436 U.S. 658 (1978).
134. Paxman v. Campbell, 612 F.2d 848 (4th Cir. 1980); Owen v. City of

Independence, Missouri, 589 F.2d 335 (8th Cir. 1978), *rev'd,* 100 S. Ct. 1398 (1980).

135. Bertot v. School Dist. No. 1, Albany County, Wyoming, 613 F.2d 245 (10th Cir. 1979).

136. 100 S. Ct. 1398 (1980).

137. *Id.* at 1407.

138. *Id.* at 1414. This decision affects only liability for constitutional violations; it does not alter sovereign immunity which may exist under state laws for traditional tort liability.

139. This liability has become more onerous with the Supreme Court's decision in Maine v. Thiboutot, 100 S. Ct. 2502 (1980). The Court expanded the scope of the Civil Rights Act of 1871 to include impairment of rights guaranteed by any federal laws, not simply those related to civil rights legislation. According to the dissenting justices, this decision will "dramatically expand the liability of state and local officials." *Id.* at 2507–2508. For school districts, this means that civil rights actions can now be brought under such statutes as the Education Amendments of 1978 and the National School Lunch Act.

140. The eleventh amendment provides that a citizen of one state cannot bring suit against another state without its consent. This also has been interpreted as disallowing suits against a state of which one is a resident. *See* Floyd G. Delon, "Employees," *The Yearbook of School Law 1978,* edited by Philip K. Piele (Topeka, Kan.: National Organization on Legal Problems in Education, 1978), pp. 126–27.

141. Urbano v. Board of Managers, 415 F.2d 247, 250–51 (3d Cir. 1969). *See* Blake v. Kline, 612 F.2d 718 (3d Cir. 1979) for an application of *Urbano* criteria to the Public School Employees' Retirement Board of Pennsylvania.

142. The eleventh amendment immunity covers only suits that entail violations of constitutional rights; it does not have any bearing on immunity in negligence suits in tort actions under state law. *See* Chapter 7 for treatment of governmental immunity under tort law.

143. Mt. Healthy City School Dist. v. Doyle, 429 U.S. 274 (1977).

144. *Id.* at 280.

145. Carey v. Piphus, 435 U.S. 247 (1978). *See* text with note 45, Chapter 11.

# 4

# Discrimination in Employment

Beginning with *Brown v. Board of Education* in 1954, the judiciary has rendered a number of significant decisions restricting practices that discriminate against students and teachers in public education.[1] Many of these decisions have emanated from the fourteenth amendment which ensures in part that states must provide each person with equal protection of the laws. Additionally, decisions have been based on federal statutes that prohibit discrimination on the basis of race, color, national origin, religion, and sex in programs or activities receiving federal financial assistance. Litigation involving discriminatory employment practices has been extensive under both the Federal Constitution and statutory provisions. This chapter addresses legal protections that shield teachers from discrimination based on race, sex, age, and handicaps.[2]

## RACE DISCRIMINATION

Courts continue to interpret the legal protections afforded to minorities under the Federal Constitution and civil rights laws. These decisions have significant implications for teachers in the areas of employment, promotion, and discharge. To protect and ensure the minority employee's rights, courts have ordered remedies to restore individuals to their "rightful place" if they have been victims of past discrimination. As many of these affirmative remedies have impinged on the rights of the majority employees, charges of "reverse" discrimination have evolved. Issues relating to discriminatory employment practices in selection and hiring, staff reductions, and seniority are discussed in this section.

## SELECTION AND HIRING PRACTICES

Hiring practices often have been challenged as racially discriminatory because of the selection criteria upon which a final decision is based. Specifically, can an employer establish criteria for employee selection that disqualify a disproportionate number of minority applicants? In 1971, the Supreme Court addressed this question in *Griggs v. Duke Power Company* and identified principles for evaluating prerequisites to employment under Title VII of the Civil Rights Act of 1964.[3] The employer in *Griggs* required either a high school diploma or a specified score on a general intelligence test as a condition of employment. It was shown that the prerequisites effectively disqualified more black applicants than white applicants. In examining the intent and the impact of the requirements, the Court ruled that "consequences of employment practices, not simply motivation" must be the crucial test for assessment of the legality of such requirements.[4] The Court asserted that procedures, neutral on their face, could not be sanctioned if they continued to "freeze" prior discriminatory practices. The Court did not proscribe the use of tests or other selection criteria, but stated that a relationship must be demonstrated between the requirement and job performance in order to satisfy Title VII. Therefore, if a larger percentage of blacks than whites is excluded from employment by a test that cannot be shown to be job-related, use of the test would be prohibited under *Griggs*.

In 1975, the Supreme Court in *Albemarle Paper Company v. Moody* provided some clarification of the job-related requirement advanced in *Griggs*.[5] The Court addressed the issue of the burden placed on the employer to prove that pre-employment tests with a racially discriminatory impact are sufficiently job-related to satisfy Title VII. The Court concluded that the company's test validation study, which used experienced, white workers, could not be used to validate a test designed for job applicants who were primarily inexperienced and nonwhite. Also, the Court noted that a test cannot be used for jobs other than those for which it has been professionally validated unless there are "no significant differences" between the jobs.[6] The Court further held that if rankings made by supervisors are compared with employees' test scores in validating the test, there must be clear job performance criteria applied by all supervisors.

Through the mid-1970s, the standards formulated in *Griggs* and *Albemarle* constituted a legal framework for analyzing alleged discriminatory employment practices under Title VII. The primary focus was on the disproportionate impact of the practices. This Title VII standard of review also seemed to influence cases initiated on constitutional grounds.

However, in 1976 the Supreme Court in *Washington v. Davis* eroded the *Griggs* test for constitutional analysis by holding that discriminatory impact alone was insufficient to abridge the Federal Constitution.[7] This case involved a Washington, D.C., police training program that excluded a disproportionate number of black applicants on the basis of a written verbal skills test. In applying the *Griggs* principle, the appeals court found the test to be constitutionally impermissible. However, the Supreme Court reversed the decision, rejecting the assertion that the "constitutional standard for adjudicating claims of invidious racial discrimination is identical to the standards applicable under Title VII." [8] The Court noted that disproportionate impact is not irrelevant, but at the same time it is not the sole basis for determining prohibited discrimination under the Federal Constitution.[9] The disproportionate impact of the skills test did not conclusively support purposeful discrimination by the Washington police department. Absent a showing of discriminatory motive, the Court found the test to be an acceptable means for improving police effectiveness. The Court reasoned that the department's affirmative action program to recruit blacks and the increasing number of blacks on the force were sufficient to negate a discriminatory intent. While recognizing the job-relatedness requirement of *Griggs* for Title VII review, the Court concluded that a positive relationship between a test and success in a training program was sufficient to satisfy the Federal Constitution.

The rationale in *Washington v. Davis* subsequently was adopted by a federal district court in upholding the use of the National Teachers Examination for certification and salary purposes in South Carolina.[10] The required test score disqualified 83 percent of the black applicants for certification, as opposed to only 17.5 percent of the white applicants. Under the revised standards of this test, it was predicted that 96 percent of the new teachers certified to teach in South Carolina would be white. The district court ruled that plaintiffs did not prove a racially discriminatory purpose and that the state sufficiently justified its use of the test. The court relied on *Washington v. Davis* in holding that test validity could be established by showing a relationship with success in job training, which in this case was knowledge of course content of teacher education training programs. In spite of the disproportionate impact on blacks and the admonishment of the authors that the test was not designed for the purposes for which it was used, the Supreme Court affirmed the district court decision.

Hence, in order to establish a constitutional violation, the burden of proof is placed on the plaintiff to show that a disproportionate impact is, in fact, the result of purposeful discrimination. The employee's increased burden is further exemplified in more recent legal decisions involving issues of sex discrimination. The Supreme Court has noted that a neutral policy's predictable adverse impact on a protected class does not establish proof of unlawful intent.[11] To abridge the Federal Constitution, the decision makers must harbor a desire to discriminate rather than merely be aware that their actions will have discriminatory consequences. Thus, the issue has become more complex with the dichotomy between statutory analysis of disparate impact and constitutional assessment of discriminatory motive.[12]

Because of the difficulties involved in establishing unlawful intent to substantiate a constitutional impairment, most minority employees alleging discrimination in selection and hiring have relied on Title VII of the Civil Rights Act of 1964. Individuals seeking relief under Title VII bear the initial burden of establishing a prima facie case of discrimination. The Supreme Court in *McDonnell Douglas v. Green* concluded that, to establish this prima facie case, a plaintiff must show membership in a racial minority; show rejection for a position for which qualified; and show that the employer continued to seek similarly qualified applicants after rejecting the plaintiff.[13] Once the plaintiff establishes a prima facie case of discrimination, the burden shifts to the employer to "articulate some legitimate, nondiscriminatory reason for the employee's rejection."[14] This prima facie showing under *McDonnell Douglas* criteria does not mean that discrimination under Title VII ultimately will be established. It only raises an inference of discriminatory hiring practices which, if unexplained by the employer, can be used to substantiate discrimination. To rebut a claim, the Court has held that the employer must show that the decision was based on a legitimate business goal.[15] The plaintiff is then provided with an opportunity to refute the employer's evidence.

In *McDonnell Douglas,* the Supreme Court squarely placed on the plaintiff the burden of establishing a prima facie case of racial discrimination. In subsequent opinions, the Supreme Court has been compelled to deal with the exact nature of the proof needed by the employer to rebut such a prima facie showing of discrimination. Relying on *McDonnell Douglas,* in 1978 the Court concluded that "it is apparent that the burden which shifts to the employer is merely that of proving that he based his employment decision on a legitimate consideration, and not an illegitimate one such as race."[16]

Further clarification of the employer's burden in substantiating a nondiscriminatory motive was provided in a case related to sex discrimination, *Board of Trustees of Keene State College v. Sweeney.*[17] The case was brought by a faculty member at Keene State College, who claimed that she was twice denied promotion to full professor because of her sex. Sweeney met the *McDonnell Douglas* criteria for establishing an inference of discrimination, and since the employer did not sufficiently show a legitimate reason for its action, the appellate court ruled in favor of Sweeney. On appeal, the Supreme Court found that the employer was not required to "prove" a nondiscriminatory reason but merely to "articulate" such a reason. Noting that the words "prove," "articulate," and "show" are similar in meaning, the Supreme Court distinguished "articulate" as imposing a lesser burden than the appellate court had required. The dissenting justices admonished the majority for drawing a false distinction between "articulating some legitimate, nondiscriminatory reason and proving absence of discriminatory motive."[18] On remand, the appellate court again found evidence of sex discrimination, but emphasized that the employer's burden is "merely a burden of production," and "the burden of persuasion remains at all times with the plaintiff." [19] Thus, the ultimate burden to prove discrimination remains with the employee and may have been somewhat intensified, since the employer does not have to offer evidence of nondiscriminatory reasons but simply has to state reasons.

In determining discriminatory employment practices, statistical analyses pertaining to racial ratios have played a vital role for both plaintiffs and defendants. Title VII does not require that a work force mirror the racial composition of the local population; however, a substantial discrepancy may be a strong indicator of the existence of discrimination. The Supreme Court has acknowledged the important role of statistics in establishing either a pattern and practice of discrimination or a prima facie case, but also has noted that their usefulness depends on the circumstances of each case. [20] The Court also has recognized that the racial mix of the work force is a legitimate factor that an employer is entitled to proffer in rebutting charges of discrimination. [21]

It is commonly known that statistics can be used selectively to prove almost any point. This has been demonstrated in cases where the plaintiffs and defendants, by comparing different population groups and time periods, have used the same data to support claims of both discriminatory and nondiscriminatory practices. Through numerous federal court decisions, common points of comparison have evolved, such as comparison of the employer's work force with the composition of the surrounding labor market. For example, in establishing a pattern and practice of discriminatory hiring practices in the Hazelwood, Missouri, school district, the Supreme Court held that the proper comparison should be between the racial composition of the school district teaching staff and the composition of the teaching pool in the area. [22] The Court held that a comparison between the black teaching force and black pupils in the district was irrelevant. Depending on the geographic area of comparison, black teachers composed 5.7 percent or 15.4 percent of the labor market, whereas only 2 percent of the student population was black. The Court also noted that the proper time period for comparing hiring data was post-1972, since public employers were not subject to Title VII prior to that date.

STAFF REDUCTIONS

In addition to assessing selection and hiring criteria, judicial attention has focused on staff reductions in school systems under court-ordered desegregation. The dismantling of dual school systems to create unitary systems has resulted in teacher dismissals and demotions. Acceptable criteria to use in the identification of teachers for dismissal were articulated by the Fifth Circuit Court of Appeals in 1969. [23] In *Singleton v. Jackson Municipal Separate School District,* the appellate court held that professional staff members subject to dismissal "must be selected on the basis of objective and reasonable nondiscriminatory standards from among all the staff of the school district."[24] Although emanating from the Fifth Circuit, the *Singleton* criteria have been applied in other circuits confronting staffing reductions as a result of court-ordered desegregation.

Courts anticipated that movement from dual to unitary school systems might cause the displacement of a number of staff members due to duplicative positions as well as declines in enrollment resulting from the transfer of some students to private schools. To prevent black teachers from bearing a disproportionate burden, stringent criteria were formulated to regulate staff reductions. Criteria enunciated in *Singleton* provided that (1) race will not be a factor in hiring, assignment, promotion, demotion, salary, or dismissal; (2) a reduction in professional staff must be made on the basis of "objective and reasonable nondiscriminatory standards"; and (3) nonracial objective criteria must be developed by the school board prior to any reductions.[25] The court specifically defined demotion as a reassignment involving less pay, responsibility, or skill than the previous position, or a transfer to a teaching position for which one is not certified or does not have substantial experience.

To invoke the *Singleton* criteria, courts consistently have held that dismissals must be related to reductions occurring *as a result of court-ordered desegregation.*[26] This has been interpreted as an actual arithmetical reduction in the number of positions caused by the desegregation plan. Where the number of staff positions remains the same or increases, the *Singleton* criteria are inapplicable.[27] The *Singleton* requirements also do not apply if a district has entered into a voluntary desegregation effort,[28] or after a district has operated as a unitary system for several years.[29]

According to *Singleton* and earlier decisions, teachers released in consolidation efforts because of overstaffing must be given preference in reappointment. This has been strictly construed as entitling qualified displaced teachers preference when vacancies occur.[30] Preference must be afforded to displaced teachers as long as they possess minimum qualifications; such teachers cannot be rejected on the basis that other applicants have better qualifications.[31]

Upon establishing unitary school systems, a number of districts have tried to preserve the racial ratio in existence at the time of desegregation. That is, when vacancies occurred, whites were replaced with whites and blacks were replaced with blacks. The use of such quotas has been invalidated. The Fifth Circuit Court of Appeals has declared that "once a unitary system has been established the system-wide racial ratio may thereafter change from time to time as a result of nondiscriminatory application of objective merit standards in the selection and composition of faculty and staff."[32] The objective of *Singleton* and similar rulings was not to "freeze" the existing black/white ratio. Thus, a decrease in the number of black teachers alone does not substantiate discriminatory practices when objective merit standards are employed in the selection of teachers.[33]

During the transition from dual to unitary systems, transfers from one teaching position to another have often resulted in claims of demotion. As noted explicitly in *Singleton,* the factors that determine a demotion are level of responsibility, skills, salary, and certification.[34] In most cases, the level of responsibility has been the key factor or determinant in assessing demotion.[35] For example, when a black principal was transferred to a classroom teaching position, the court held that the significant difference in responsibilities constituted a demotion even though there was an increase in salary.[36] However, when a black high school counselor was reassigned as an elementary school counselor with the same title and salary, the court found that the old and new positions were essentially equivalent.[37] The court emphasized that there was no mandate of complete congruency of responsibilities between the two positions.

*Singleton* addressed staff reductions only as they related to court-ordered desegregation; however, another imperative issue confronting minorities is staff reductions necessitated by declining enrollments and financial exigency. Because of past discriminatory employment practices, minorities often have fewer years of experience. Thus, they have been the first released under a last hired, first fired seniority system. In effect, a seniority system, neutral on its face, may act to perpetuate the vestiges of past discrimination. To protect seniority rights and avoid reverse discrimination, Congress specifically exempted bona fide seniority systems from the operation of Title VII. Congress provided that

> . . . it shall not be an unlawful employment practice for an employer to apply different standards of compensation, or different terms, conditions, or privileges of employment pursuant to a bona fide seniority or merit system . . . provided that such differences are not the result of an intention to discriminate because of race.[38]

In light of Title VII, courts have been confronted with determining (1) what is a bona fide seniority system, and (2) how far an employer must go in remedying the effects of past discrimination.

The Fifth Circuit Court of Appeals was one of the first courts to address remedies to restore minority employees to their "rightful place" in a seniority system. In a case involving seniority rights and promotions in a paper mill, seniority had been granted to employees by job lines rather than time with the company.[39] Jobs were organized hierarchically in functional production lines segregated by race, with training and promotion occurring within the lines. Since black employees had been restricted to certain low-paying job lines prior to the implementation of Title VII, they were later unable to compete for vacancies on the white lines because of lack of job seniority on these particular lines. Applying the "rightful place" doctrine, the court of appeals held that the *future* awarding of vacant positions should not lock-in prior discrimination. The court did not advocate granting fictional seniority or bumping white employees, but stated that seniority must be based on total years in the company to ensure an employee's "rightful place" for future job vacancies.

The "rightful place" doctrine has been applied by other courts and has been extended by the United States Supreme Court to include the award of retroactive seniority.[40] The Supreme Court has held that one of the primary purposes of Title VII is to "make whole" individuals who have suffered employment discrimination.[41] Under Title VII, courts have wide discretion in ordering appropriate, affirmative relief. In addition to requiring victims of discrimination to be hired or reinstated, courts can order other relief. Courts may

> . . . order such affirmative action as may be appropriate, which may include, but is not limited to, reinstatement or hiring of employees, with or without back pay . . . or any other equitable relief as the court deems appropriate.[42]

In 1976, the Supreme Court held that adequate and equitable relief to achieve the "make whole" objective of Title VII may well require the awarding of retroactive seniority where racially discriminatory employment practices have existed.[43] The Court noted that retroactive seniority is not required in all circumstances, but it is relief that can be granted when considered appropriate. The Court's ruling did not alter the bona fide seniority system of the employer in this case, but rather required the hiring of individuals who had been unlawfully denied employment and the granting of seniority credit that presumably would have been earned if not for previous discrimination.

Last hired, first fired seniority systems have been sanctioned by the courts, but may be modified to reflect an employee's "rightful place" if prior discriminatory employment practices existed. The Second Circuit Court of Appeals upheld such a seniority system for the lay-off of supervisory personnel in a New York school district.[44] A disproportionate impact on minority supervisors did not invalidate the seniority system. However, the court acknowledged that certain minority supervisors might be entitled to "constructive or fictional" seniority because they had been deprived of their rightful place on the seniority list by a discriminatory examination.

Absent a showing of past discrimination, an employer cannot circumvent an established seniority system by using staff reductions to correct racial imbalance in the teaching force. For example, a Pennsylvania school district's suspension of white teachers with greater seniority than black teachers was held to constitute racial discrimination.[45] Although the district was attempting in good faith to achieve racial balance in its staff, the effort was impermissible because there had been no past discrimination in hiring practices.

As districts continue to face declining enrollments and financial problems, the necessity for staff reductions will be intensified. A bona fide seniority system is a legitimate mechanism for reduction in force, but prior discriminatory employment practices may require modifications for certain minority employees who are not in their "rightful place." However, this does not abrogate the seniority system itself. "Make whole" remedies, which include retroactive seniority for minorities, do not diminish the rights of other employees.

## REVERSE DISCRIMINATION

"Reverse discrimination" is a term that has surfaced in recent years as a reaction to affirmative efforts to eliminate patterns of racial segregation. It does not represent a new genre of employment discrimination, but is used to denote majority discrimination that occurs in the process of attempting to remedy minority discrimination. Employment discrimination, whether majority or minority, is impermissible. In safeguarding the rights of all individuals, courts have been faced with adjudication of what constitutes reverse discrimination or, more generally, employment discrimination.

The United States Supreme Court has held unconditionally that the terms of Title VII "are not limited to discrimination against members of any particular race." [46] In 1976, the Supreme Court reviewed a case where a charge of misappropriating cargo resulted in the termination of two white employees, but not a black employee who also had been accused.[47] The two white employees brought action against the company, claiming that the dismissals were determined on the basis of race. Noting that an employer can discharge an individual for a criminal offense, the Court emphasized that the same standard must be "applied alike to members of all races." [48] Failure to uniformly apply the same criterion violates Title VII.

The issue of "reverse" discrimination was directly addressed by the Supreme Court in the now famous case, *Regents of the University of California v. Bakke.*[49] Bakke, a white male, sought admission to the University of California Medical School at Davis. Upon denial of admission, he challenged the admissions practices under Title VI of the Civil Rights Act of 1964. Title VI provides that race cannot be the basis for excluding an individual from participation in any program or activity receiving federal financial assistance.[50] The university's admissions policies designated that sixteen of the one hundred openings available each year be reserved for minority students. As a result of the special admissions program, minority applicants with lower scores than Bakke's were admitted, thus resulting in his claim of discrimination. The university justified its differential treatment of applicants on the basis of correcting prior societal discrimination against minority applicants. However, the Supreme Court held that race could not be used to exclude an individual from a program receiving federal assistance. The use of a rigid quota system was declared impermissible where a history of discrimination had not been established.[51]

Although the Court disallowed the use of race as the basis for the Davis quota system, it did not hold that race could not be a consideration in screening applicants. In other words, to achieve diversity in the student body, an institution might include race along with academic credentials, overall potential, background, and numerous other factors in evaluating applicants. *Bakke* would indicate the need for a flexible admissions program rather than a rigidly defined program relying on numerical quotas. This is exemplified in a Washington Supreme Court decision involving the constitutionality of the University of Washington School of Medicine's admission criteria.[52] Candidates were considered on the basis of academic performance, admission test score, motivation, maturity, humanitarian qualities, and extenuating background. In upholding these criteria, the court distinguished this case from *Bakke* by noting that the Washington program did not establish a quota system or a separate admissions system for minority applicants.

With regard to employment discrimination, the *Bakke* decision resulted in more questions than answers. Doubts were raised as to the legal status of voluntary affirmative action plans, and employers questioned whether they could proceed with such plans in the absence of prior discriminatory practices. In June 1979, the Supreme Court confronted the issue of reverse discrimination and voluntary affirmative action programs in *Kaiser Aluminum and Chemical Corporation v. Weber.*[53] The Court did not address what Title VII requires or what a court might order, but "whether Title VII *forbids* private employers and unions from voluntarily agreeing upon bona fide affirmative action plans that accord racial preference." [54] In *Weber,* the employer and union had collectively bargained an on-the-job training program to fill skilled craft openings. The agreement specified that 50 percent of the training positions would be filled by black employees until the percentage of black employees in the skilled crafts reached the percentage of blacks in the local labor market. Since employees were selected on the basis of seniority and race, this arrangement resulted in the rejection of some white employees who had built up greater seniority than the black employees who were accepted for the program.

Kaiser adopted its in-plant craft training program in a good faith effort to mitigate historic discrimination against black employees. The company's training and experience requirements had resulted in an underrepresentation of blacks in the skilled crafts—2 percent in the crafts as opposed to 15 percent in the plant and 39 percent in the labor force. However, there was no indication that Kaiser's current employment practices were discriminatory. In fact, efforts had been made to recruit minorities, and the challenged training program was one of the affirmative measures that the company had initiated.

Earlier, the Supreme Court had announced that Title VII protects all employees from discrimination. The Court, however, did not alter this interpretation in *Weber,* but rather distinguished the *Weber* decision by noting that it involved an affirmative action plan adopted to remedy "traditional patterns of racial segregation." Relying on the legislative history of the Civil Rights Act of 1964, the Court concluded that Congress did not intend to prohibit voluntary private actions to eliminate discrimination. Title VII states that the Act shall not be interpreted "to require any employer . . . to grant preferential treatment to any individual or any group" to eliminate a racial imbalance.[55] However, the Court noted that Title VII did not state that an employer would not be *permitted* voluntarily to correct such an imbalance, only that an employer would not be required to do so. The Court reasoned that if Congress had intended to prohibit such plans, the law would have included explicit language to that effect. Accordingly, the Court held that Title VII *does permit* an affirmative action program where a job category has been "traditionally segregated." Justice Blackmun, in a concurring opinion in *Weber,* noted that it would be ironic indeed if Title VII, with its broad remedial purposes, were interpreted as locking-in the effects of prior segregation due to a lack of specified remedies.

In *Weber,* the Court did not attempt to delineate permissible and impermissible affirmative action programs. Rather, it merely found the Kaiser plan permissible—a plan which did not "unnecessarily trammel" the rights of white employees. The Kaiser plan was (1) a *temporary* plan to eliminate the effects of past discrimination; (2) a plan that did not exclude white employees from the program; and (3) a plan that was not designed to maintain an established racial balance.

The Supreme Court has not rendered an opinion on the constitutionality of preferential promotion and hiring programs, but rather has based its decisions on the Civil Rights Act of 1964. However, the Sixth Circuit Court of Appeals has outlined the criteria for acceptability of an affirmative action plan under the equal protection clause of the fourteenth amendment. In a case involving promotion practices of the Detroit police force, white police officers challenged the preferential promotion of black officers with lower numerical ratings than white officers who were not promoted.[56] The appellate court held that the police department's history of prior discrimination justified the plan under Title VI and Title VII. In addressing the constitutional question, the court advanced several criteria to determine the acceptance of an affirmative action plan under the fourteenth amendment. A plan would be constitutional in circumstances (1) where there is a sound basis for concluding that minorities are substantially underrepresented, (2) where past discrimination is impeding access to present positions, (3) where a plan does not stigmatize a particular group, and (4) where no other approach offers a practical means of overcoming racial imbalance in the foreseeable future.[57] The court noted that if the

Detroit affirmative action plan did not satisfy these criteria, the plan might still be constitutionally permissible on the basis of operational need. That is, the police department could possibly establish that the plan was needed in order to gain public support, respect, and confidence in effective law enforcement. The case was remanded for additional proceedings on the constitutional issue to ascertain if the affirmative action plan either satisfied the above criteria or was justified as an operational necessity.

The legal issues surrounding reverse discrimination are complex, and many questions still remain unresolved by the courts. Although the nature of the law in this area is somewhat ambiguous and sometimes appears contradictory, general principles have evolved which can guide school systems in designing affirmative programs for minority employees. All employees, regardless of race, are protected from employment discrimination. Where a district without a history of past discrimination is faced with reduction in force, white teachers with greater seniority cannot be suspended while black teachers with less seniority are re-employed to achieve a better racial balance.[58] In recruitment, promotion, and training, it is unlawful to use rigid racial quotas. A more defensible approach would be to establish a flexible plan with desirable ranges and to include race as a factor in screening, but not as the determinant of selection. If a job position has been historically segregated, a voluntary affirmative action program can be instituted without a judicial determination of prior discrimination. An acceptable plan might include one that is temporary, avoiding specific quotas or the maintenance of a specified racial balance.

## SEX DISCRIMINATION

Until the 1970s, unequal treatment in employment based on sex was legally sanctioned, reflecting itself in differences in working conditions, compensation, prerequisites for employment, and work-related benefits for women. A statement from an 1873 case is illustrative of the prevailing judicial attitude through much of the twentieth century toward differential treatment of men and women.

> Man is, or should be, woman's protector and defender. The natural and proper timidity and delicacy which belong to the female sex evidently unfits it for many of the occupations of civil life. The constitution of the family organization, which is founded in the divine ordinance, as well as in the nature of things, indicates the domestic sphere as that which properly belongs to the domain and functions of womanhood. The harmony, not to say identity, of interests and views which belong, or should belong, to the family institution is repugnant to the idea of a woman adopting a distinct and independent career from that of her husband. . . .[59]

Along with the equal rights gains of minorities, the status articulated above has given way to a recognition of greater equality in employment for women. Extensive litigation has challenged sex-based classifications that impose unequal employment burdens on female employees. These suits have been brought primarily under the equal protection clause of the fourteenth amendment, the Equal Pay Act, Title VII of the Civil Rights Act of 1964, and Title IX of the Education Amendments of 1972.

Although many discriminatory practices have been invalidated under the fourteenth amendment, sex has not been designated a "suspect class," as has race, which would necessitate strict judicial scrutiny under the equal protection clause. This distinction is critical in judicial review, for if sex were elevated to a "suspect class," a compelling justification would be required for any governmental classifications based on gender. At present, the government is required only to show a rational relationship between such classifications and a legitimate governmental purpose. However, from recent Supreme Court rulings, it is apparent that classifications based on sex must bear a "close and substantial relationship to important governmental objectives" [60] and require "an exceedingly persuasive justification to withstand a constitutional challenge." [61]

Since the Supreme Court has declined to apply the stringent equal protection standard to claims of sex discrimination, employees have been reluctant to bring sex-bias suits under constitutional guarantees and have turned to statutory protections instead. Most litigation has occurred under Title VII of the Civil Rights Act of 1964. Because of the comprehensive nature of the statute, Title VII is the most effective tool in combatting employment discrimination. Litigation also has resulted under Title IX of the Education Amendments of 1972, which proscribes discrimination based on sex in educational programs receiving federal assistance.[62] Although Title IX is significant for participants in and beneficiaries of educational programs (i.e., students), its application to employees has been severely curtailed.[63]

Several topics of particular import to educators are discussed in this section. Initially, policies related to maternity leave and pregnancy benefits are examined. Next, the legal issues pertaining to differential treatment of men and women in retirement programs are analyzed. Additionally, claims of sex bias in hiring and promotion are addressed. Finally, the current status of employees' standing to sue under Title IX is assessed.

## PREGNANCY-RELATED POLICIES

Employee disability programs often have excluded pregnancy-related disabilities. In *Geduldig v. Aiello,* a California disability program that excluded work loss occurring during pregnancy was challenged under the equal protection clause of the fourteenth amendment.[64] The Supreme Court upheld the program, finding that it did not discriminate against any definable group in terms of total protection. Neither group, men or women, was protected from a particular risk while the other group was denied protection. Rather than finding discrimination based on sex, the Court reasoned that employees were classified as either "pregnant women" or "nonpregnant persons." Since the latter group contained both men and women, the charge of sex discrimination was not supported.

Although the exclusion of maternity benefits was upheld under the Federal Constitution, it was assumed that such exclusion would not meet the more stringent criteria of Title VII. Enforcement regulations promulgated by the Equal Employment Opportunity Commission (EEOC) specifically provide that

> Disabilities caused or contributed to by pregnancy, miscarriage, abortion, childbirth, and recovery therefrom are, for all job-related purposes, temporary disabilities and should be treated as such under any health or temporary disability insurance or sick leave plan available in connection with employment.[65]

Following this reasoning, most lower courts relied on Title VII to invalidate disability programs that excluded pregnancy benefits or otherwise disadvantaged female employees.

However, two years after *Geduldig,* the Supreme Court rendered a decision regarding a disability benefits program challenged under Title VII and adhered to the rationale formulated in *Geduldig.* In *General Electric Company v. Gilbert,* the Court found no evidence of gender-based discrimination. It found only that one disability—pregnancy—had been excluded from the program.[66] Absent a showing that exclusion of pregnancy was a "pretext designed to effect an invidious discrimination against the members of one sex or the other," no violation could be established. The Court afforded little weight to the EEOC regulations cited above, reasoning that the EEOC lacked congressional authorization to issue such rules. Moreover, the Court noted the inconsistency in various pronouncements from the agency regarding disability benefits programs.

Judicial interpretations of statutory law rely heavily upon an interpretation of congressional "intent." In *Gilbert,* the Supreme Court concluded that Title VII was not intended to cover distinctions based on pregnancy. Congress, strongly disagreeing with the Supreme Court's interpretation, has since amended Title VII (1978 Pregnancy Disability Act, Public Law 95-555) specifically to prohibit employers from excluding pregnancy benefits in comprehensive medical and disability insurance plans.[67] According to the amendment, an employer must treat a pregnancy-related disability the same way as any other disability with respect to insurance and leaves of absences. It is predicted that the law will have the greatest effect on sick leave. If a school district permits sick leave for other disabilities, it must accord the same for pregnancy-related absences.[68]

As of April 29, 1979, all employers with disability programs were required to be in compliance with the amendment.

Like pregnancy benefits, school board mandatory leave policies have been the subject of litigation. The Supreme Court in *Cleveland Board of Education v. LaFleur* ruled that a compulsory maternity leave policy violated due process rights.[69] At issue in this case was a board rule requiring every pregnant teacher to take a leave of absence five months prior to the birth of her child and specifying a return date of the next semester after the child reached three months of age. In support of its mandatory leave policy, the board advanced the need for continuity of classroom instruction and noted the physical incapacity of teachers during latter months of pregnancy. The Supreme Court recognized the need for continuity of services but found the arbitrary five-month date to have no relationship to that purpose. The Court concluded that this need could be met by requiring teachers to give "substantial advance notice of their condition." [70] The second ground concerning physical incapacity was invalidated because there was an "irrebuttable presumption" that all pregnant teachers were physically incompetent as of a specified date.[71] The Court reasoned that the ability to continue teaching is an individual matter that was not considered in establishing the five-month rule. Similarly, the Court found the three-month return date following the birth of the child to suffer the same deficiencies.

*LaFleur* does not prohibit school boards from establishing maternity leave policies but prevents the establishment of arbitrary cut-off dates unrelated to a legitimate state interest. A reasonable leave policy was upheld by the Ninth Circuit Court of Appeals.[72] The challenged school board policy required all teachers to take maternity leave at the beginning of the ninth month of pregnancy. The board adequately demonstrated that this was a business necessity based on obtaining a replacement teacher, given the unpredictability of childbirth. In contrast, the Fourth Circuit Court of Appeals invalidated a school board practice of nonrenewal of teacher contracts where a foreseeable period of absence could be predicted for the ensuing year. Since female teachers were required to notify school administrators of their pregnancy and anticipated delivery date, this policy was found to impose a disproportionate burden on female teachers as opposed to male teachers.[73]

Employment policies that place a substantial burden on women and not on men have been closely scrutinized by courts. If policies cannot be justified as a business necessity, they have been found to constitute unlawful employment practices under Title VII. Denial of accumulated seniority upon return from maternity leave was found to be such a practice in *Nashville Gas Company v. Satty*.[74] In *Satty*, employees retained seniority rights when on leave for all disabilities except pregnancy. The Supreme Court concluded that the policy respecting pregnancy was not on its face discriminatory but that the impact on employment opportunities of women was discriminatory. The Court held that the employer failed to establish that the discriminatory seniority policy was justified by an overriding business need.

## RETIREMENT PROGRAMS

"As a class, women live longer than men." So begins the Supreme Court's opinion in its 1978 decision addressing a discriminatory retirement benefits program in *City of Los Angeles Department of Water v. Manhart*.[75] Recognition of women's longevity has traditionally resulted in differential treatment of women as a class with respect to retirement benefits. Employers have either required women to make a higher contribution as they pay into the system or paid lower benefits to women upon retirement. In *Manhart*, a program requiring women to pay approximately 15 percent more than men was challenged under Title VII.

Unlike stereotypic assumptions on which many personnel policies have been designed in the past, longevity is a true generalization of women as a class. Thus, the Court was faced with the task of determining whether it is acceptable to treat each individual woman, who may or may not fit the generalization, as a class member for retirement benefit purposes. In support of differential treatment, the City of Los Angeles argued that the distinction was based not on sex but on longevity. This argument was unacceptable to the Court, in that sex was the only factor considered in predicting life expectancy. The Court held that discrimination exists when individuals are treated as "simply components of a racial, religious, sexual, or national class."[76]

The Court was careful to narrowly define the issue in *Manhart* to unequal contributions in an employer-operated retirement program. However, since the ruling, the Department of Labor has proposed regulations that would require equal contributions as well as equal benefits.[77] This may impose a significant financial burden on school systems, as insurance companies are unaffected by the decision and can continue to use separate mortality tables for men and women. Rather than resolving the retirement issue, *Manhart* created uncertainties that continue to be the subject of legal debates.

For example, there have been several challenges to the use of sex-based mortality tables by the Teachers Insurance and Annuity Association and the College Retirement Equities Fund (TIAA-CREF). The company offers retirement plans in a large number of colleges and universities and a few private elementary and secondary schools. A New York district court held that TIAA was exempt from claims under Title VII because of the McCarran-Ferguson Act, a federal statute that reserves the regulation of insurance companies to the states.[78] But CREF was not considered an insurance company by the court; therefore, its use of the tables was held to be in violation of Title VII. A Michigan district court reached a different conclusion, holding that TIAA was not in the business of insurance and thus was subject to Title VII along with CREF.[79] The court reasoned that the service relationship between TIAA and educational institutions was not comparable to the relationship between an insurance company and its policyholders because of the lack of an "investment risk." Reacting to judicial pressure, TIAA-CREF announced in December 1979 that it plans to discontinue use of sex-based mortality tables.

## EMPLOYMENT OPPORTUNITIES

Issues relating to sex-biased employment practices in hiring, salary, promotion, and working conditions have been adjudicated primarily under Title VII. As in racial discrimination suits, the Supreme Court has held that the individual seeking recovery for sex discrimination has the initial burden of establishing a prima facie case of discrimination, with the burden then shifting to the employer to articulate a "legitimate, nondiscriminatory reason" for the practice.[80] If the employer shows a nondiscriminatory reason, then the plaintiff is given an opportunity to establish that the stated reason was only a pretext for discrimination.

In *Sweeney v. Board of Trustees of Keene State College,* the First Circuit Court of Appeals held, on remand from the Supreme Court, that the plaintiff proved by a preponderance of evidence that Keene State College's asserted reasons for not promoting her to full professor were a pretext for discrimination.[81] Sweeney had been denied promotion twice, but was promoted on her third attempt after filing charges of sex discrimination against the college. She subsequently sought backdating of her promotion to the date of her original promotion request, with appropriate salary adjustments. The court noted that the decision of the promotion committee, even if misguided, would not be overturned unless it was shown to be sex-biased. Among the reasons given by the college for denial of promotion were that Sweeney tended to be narrow-minded and rigid, to personalize professional matters, and in general to be a difficult individual with whom to work. She successfully rebutted these reasons by presenting evidence that she worked well with people, that she was as qualified as others who had been promoted in the past, and that a general atmosphere of sex discrimination pervaded the college. The court was careful to note that an institutional atmosphere of sex bias does not substantiate discrimination against an individual but may be considered along with other evidence in determination of an employer's motives. It is clear from this decision and others that an employer must apply similar standards of review to males and females; a female cannot be subjected to more stringent criteria.

In 1980, an appellate court ordered a university to award tenure to a female faculty member because of discriminatory counseling with regard to requirements for tenure.[82] Discrimination was established by the fact that male physical education teachers were advised that a master's degree was required for tenure, whereas the plaintiff teacher was not so informed. The Third Circuit Court of Appeals distinguished this case from other challenges to university tenure and promotion decisions by noting that, except for lack of a master's degree, the teacher would have been promoted because she had been considered highly qualified. The tenure review committees had unanimously approved her nomination, and the department chairman had consistently evaluated her favorably. Evidence substantiated the claim that if the teacher had obtained a master's degree she would have been promoted. In ordering the award of tenure, the court reasoned that the teacher should be placed in the position she would have occupied "but for" the disparate treatment.

Individuals are protected from sex-based discrimination in compensation under the Equal Pay Act as well as under Title VII. All employees are entitled to equal pay for equal work; jobs performed do not have to be identical but must be substantially equal with regard to skill, effort, and responsibility.[83] Differences in compensation of men and women can be defended by an employer on the basis of "a seniority system, a merit system, a system which measures earnings by quantity or quality of production, or a differential based on any other factor other than sex." [84] These affirmative defenses were incorporated into Title VII through amendment.[85] Although several courts have held that Title VII and the Equal Pay Act are coextensive, the Third and Ninth Circuit Courts of Appeals recently concluded that Title VII is broader in scope than he Equal Pay Act.[86] The Equal Pay Act was found to be determinative only where equal salary was an issue, whereas an individual was not precluded under Title VII from challenging other sex-related compensation differences. The Ninth Circuit Appellate Court reasoned that "if we were to limit Title VII's protection against sexually discriminatory compensation practices to those covered by the Equal Pay Act, we would in effect insulate other equally harmful discriminatory practices from review." [87] These interpretations could portend challenges to certain traditional salary differences among educational personnel, such as male and female athletic coaches.

Certain salary disparities have been held to be beyond the scope of Title VII and outside the protection of the fourteenth amendment. In a Tenth Circuit Court of Appeals case, a class action suit challenged the pay scale for municipal nurses in Denver.[88] The city uses a system whereby public employees' salaries are equalized with salaries for similar jobs in the private sector. Plaintiffs objected to the comparison with nurses in the community for salary purposes, because historically nurses have been underpaid. Instead, they asserted that a comparison should be made with other jobs of equal worth to an employer. However, the appeals court could find no basis for addressing this disparity under existing statutory or constitutional provisions. The crossing of job classification lines to achieve the parity sought in this case was held to be beyond judicial authority.

If an employer is found to have discriminated against an employee, Title VII provides broad remedies.[89] Such equitable relief, however, has not been interpreted as including the awarding of compensatory or punitive damages. The statute was designed to ensure equal opportunity in employment, not as a punitive measure against employers. Although not all courts are in agreement with this stance, the majority of federal courts have adopted such reasoning.[90] For example, the Sixth Circuit Court of Appeals held that proof of discrimination in working conditions did not entitle a teacher to compensatory damages.[91] Since she had retired from teaching in the school system, she also was ineligible for other equitable relief (i.e., improvement in teaching conditions). Further, the teacher was denied attorneys' fees, because she could not be called the "prevailing party" due to the fact that she was not awarded damages.

It should be noted that sex-bias suits, like allegations of racial discrimination, are subject to different standards of review depending on whether the basis for analysis is constitutional or statutory. Under constitutional review, a neutrally based classification that operates to the advantage of males is permissible unless accompanied by discriminatory motives. For example, the Massachusetts Veterans Preference Statute, which has a disparate impact on women, has been challenged and upheld under the Federal Constitution.[92] The statute gives veterans absolute lifetime preference for state employment, and in Massachusetts approximately 98 percent of the veterans are males. The Supreme Court examined the statute to determine whether it reflected gender-based discrimination. Because the law drew the distinction between veterans and nonveterans, it was found to be gender neutral; veteran status included both sexes. With respect to discriminatory intent, the Court concluded that the legislature did not intentionally attempt to exclude women from civil service positions, but merely gave preference to veterans even though the adverse impact of the law on women was foreseeable. The Court emphasized that evidence of unlawful *intent* rather than disparate *impact* was necessary to establish a constitutional impairment. According to the Court, a discriminatory purpose "implies that the decision maker, in this case a state legislature, selected or reaffirmed a particular course of action at least in part 'because of,' not merely 'in spite of,' its adverse effects upon an identifiable group." [93] Finding no unlawful intent, the Court upheld the Veterans Preference Statute.

## TITLE IX AND EMPLOYMENT DISCRIMINATION

Title IX of the Education Amendments of 1972 provides:

> No person in the United States shall, on the basis of sex, be excluded from participation in, be denied the benefits of, or be subjected to discrimination under any education program or activity receiving Federal financial assistance . . .[94]

The jurisdictional question before the courts has been whether this law covers employees in institutions with federally assisted programs as well as the students who are direct participants and beneficiaries.

The Department of Health, Education, and Welfare's (HEW) authority to terminate federal assistance to school districts for a discriminatory maternity leave policy was contested in *Islesboro School Committee v. Califano*.[95] The question before the First Circuit Court of Appeals was whether the issuance of employment-related regulations pursuant to Title IX exceeded HEW's authority. The court reviewed the language and legislative history of the statute and concluded that employees were not covered. In the appellate court's opinion, beneficiaries included students attending the institutions and teachers involved in special research projects funded by the federal government.

The Sixth, Eighth, and Ninth Circuit Courts of Appeal subsequently rendered similar decisions limiting the jurisdiction of Title IX to students.[96] These rulings have resulted in considerable doubt as to the validity of the HEW employment guidelines issued pursuant to Title IX. Over 50 percent of the Title IX cases pending before the Office of Civil Rights in the summer of 1979 involved employment practices.[97] The Supreme Court was petitioned to review the *Islesboro* case, as well as the Sixth and Eighth Circuit decisions, to resolve the uncertainty in the administration of Title IX. In December 1979, the Court declined to review these decisions, thus leaving the lower court rulings in effect.[98]

Subsequent conflicting appellate court decisions have further clouded the issue. In July 1980, the Second Circuit Court of Appeals became the first appellate court to rule that Title IX clearly applies to discriminatory employment practices. Within a week of this decision, the Fifth Circuit Court of Appeals concluded that employment practices are covered under Title IX, but only for employees in federally funded programs, not for all employees in the school district.[99] These decisions may provide an impetus for further consideration of the issue by the Supreme Court.

Despite court action, HEW has indicated that it will continue to investigate certain employment-biased practices against teachers under Title IX when there is a direct effect on students. Under a theory of "infection," HEW has maintained that discriminatory treatment of teachers in employment has an adverse effect on students and, therefore, comes within the purview of Title IX. A federal district court in New York has upheld this position, noting that the limited access of women to supervisory positions could have a "deleterious impact" on students.[100]

## AGE DISCRIMINATION

One of the greatest concerns of teachers with respect to age discrimination has been mandatory retirement ages. Compulsory retirement systems have been challenged as a violation of equal protection and due process guarantees of the fourteenth amendment. With few exceptions, these systems have been upheld as constitutional.

A 1978 decision by the Second Circuit Court of Appeals is reflective of the reasoning applied in assessing a state's right to prescribe retirement age. In *Palmer v. Ticcione,* a seventy-year-old kindergarten teacher claimed that compulsory retirement violated her rights under the equal protection clause and created an irrebuttable presumption of incompetency.[101] The court found the state statute to be rationally related to fulfilling a legitimate state objective and therefore not subject to due process attack. Emphasizing that rational bases must not be too narrowly defined, the court concluded that legitimate reasons for a mandatory system might include providing employment opportunities for young people and minorities, creating openings for individuals with new ideas and techniques, and assuring predictability in management of retirement systems. The court held that a system which is rationally based should not be invalidated simply because it might include a presumption of employee incompetency at a predetermined age.

In contrast to *Palmer,* an earlier decision by the Seventh Circuit Court of Appeals represented a departure from the prevailing precedent. In *Gault v. Garrison,* the appellate court upheld a teacher's right to a trial on an age discrimination claim involving mandatory retirement.[102] The court reasoned that fitness to teach should be determined on an individual basis—mandatory retirement *per se* violated an individual's rights whether the cut-off age was sixty or eighty. A distinction was drawn by the court between this case and an earlier Supreme Court decision in which a mandatory retirement age of fifty was upheld for uniformed policemen because of "physical preparedness." [103] Unlike the Supreme Court case, in *Gault* no evidence was introduced to show a rational relationship between age and fitness to teach. Thus, the appellate court concluded that in the absence of a valid justification, the mandatory retirement age deprived the affected teachers of their due process rights to an individual determination of teaching competency. Other courts have declined to view mandatory retirement as narrowly as the Seventh Circuit Court of Appeals did.

In *Palmer,* the Second Circuit Appellate Court noted that issues involving age classifications are surrounded by competing social goals, goals that must be resolved by legislative bodies rather than by courts. Congress, as well as state legislatures, has recognized this need by adopting legislation related to age discrimination. In 1967, Congress enacted the Age Discrimination in Employment Act (ADEA) to protect employees between the ages of forty and sixty-five.[104] This act was amended in 1978 to prohibit mandatory retirement for most employees before age seventy.[105] Approximately thirty-five states have implemented similar protections, with a number of state laws providing broader coverage with no upper age limits. Such legislation ensures that age, like sex and race, will not be the basis for unjustified employment practices.

Although federal and state statutes have extended mandatory retirement ages to seventy and upward, exceptions may be permissible for certain job categories. The Supreme Court has recognized such an exception for the Foreign Service Retirement System which mandates retirement at the age of sixty.[106] This decision was rendered even though civil service personnel face no mandatory retirement age. The Court held that the employer must have only a rational basis, not a compelling reason, to justify differential treatment of certain job categories. A similar rationale might be applicable to compulsory early retirement from certain positions in public education if the school board can justify such requirements.

The Age Discrimination in Employment Act coverage is not limited to retirement policies but prohibits any form of employment discrimination based on age. Under this federal statute, decisions related to such matters as promotions, transfers, and discharges cannot be premised on age. Allegations of age bias in employment have been evaluated under the *McDonnell Douglas* principles. Although these principles were enunciated in connection with racial discrimination in hiring, they have been applied to employment discrimination in general.

In adapting the *McDonnell Douglas* criteria to age discrimination, the First Circuit Court of Appeals held that in order for relief to be granted, an individual in a protected age group must establish that dismissal occurred even though job performance was satisfactory and that the employer sought another person to perform the same job.[107] Although accepting this format as a means of presenting an age discrimination case, the appellate court noted that a plaintiff could still establish discrimination under ADEA without meeting each element of the *McDonnell Douglas* criteria. However, the court recognized that to successfully challenge an employer's action under ADEA, a plaintiff must bear the burden of proving that age was the determining factor in an employer's decision, not merely a factor.

An Alabama federal district court decision is illustrative of the sufficiency and type of evidence necessary to support an age discrimination claim.[108] In this case, the Marshall Space Flight Center (MSFC) of the National Aeronautics and Space Administration (NASA) allegedly discriminated against certain employees on the basis of age during a centerwide reduction in force. The court held that discrimination was substantiated by statistics showing that older employees were disproportionately dismissed or downgraded as compared to younger employees, and by the fact that only 12.5 percent of the scientists and engineers at the MSFC were fifty-five years or older as compared to 39 percent of all such employees at the federal level. Additional considerations were evidence that the general management philosophy placed an emphasis, as well as preference, on retention of younger personnel and specific memoranda indicating that individuals identified for promotion should preferably be between the ages of twenty-eight and forty. Again, the *McDonnell Douglas* principles were followed in this case. However, the court noted that in order to establish age discrimination, a discharged employee does not have to be replaced by an individual outside the "protected group"—below forty years of age. That is, if age is the only factor in discharge, a sixty-two-year-old employee is entitled to reinstatement if displaced by a younger individual—whether forty-five or thirty.

## DISCRIMINATION BASED ON HANDICAPS

During the past decade increased attention has been focused on protecting the employment rights of handicapped individuals. Federal legislation, as well as some state statutory provisions, has sought to eliminate handicaps as a barrier to the employment of qualified individuals. The most significant legislation in this area has been Section 504 of the Rehabilitation Act of 1973.[109] Section 504 provides in part that "no otherwise qualified handicapped individual" shall be excluded from participation in a program receiving federal financial assistance "solely by reason of his handicap." [110] Because of the recency of the federal statute, only a limited number of cases have been litigated under its provisions; however, the number of cases can be expected to increase significantly as further efforts are made to protect the handicapped.

Discriminatory practices occurring prior to the implementation of the Rehabilitation Act of 1973 have been litigated on constitutional grounds. For example, a blind teacher challenged the Philadelphia School District's refusal to permit her to take the Philadelphia Teacher's Examination as a violation of her due process rights.[111] Applicants for teaching positions in Philadelphia who were found to have "chronic or acute physical defects" were not permitted to take the examination. In response to the plaintiff teacher's application in 1970, it was determined that she could not teach sighted students because of her blindness. Between 1970 and 1974 the plaintiff persistently petitioned to take the examination, and in 1974 she finally succeeded in being admitted to take the test. After passing the examination, she was placed on the eligibility list and eventually was offered several positions. However, she refused to accept the positions because they did not include retroactive seniority commencing from the date of her first attempt to obtain employment. In reviewing the case, the appellate court reasoned that the school district's original refusal to permit the teacher to take the exam constituted an irrebuttable presumption that blindness *per se* was evidence of incompetence. The court concluded that the school district violated the teacher's due process rights by refusing to give her an opportunity to demonstrate competence. An award of retroactive seniority dating from 1970 was found to be an appropriate remedy for the teacher, and in a subsequent appeal the appellate court also awarded back pay for the same time period.[112] However, the court refused to order the award of tenure, reasoning that tenure must be based on the school's evaluation of the teacher's performance.[113]

In 1977, a New York appeals court addressed the protections provided to handicapped employees under New York's Human Rights Law.[114] The statute prohibits employers from discriminating against any individual in employment because of a disability and specifically identifies disabilities as conditions unrelated to job performance. That is, handicaps related to an individual's ability to perform a job can be considered in an employment decision. In reviewing an order of the State Human Rights Appeal Board, the court concluded that a hearing impairment was related to a person's ability to drive a school bus. The appeal board had found the driver's hearing sufficient to allow him to adequately perform his duties. However, the court held that since hearing was an ability related to job performance, the Human Rights Appeal Board had improperly intervened. The court reasoned that the appeal board could provide relief only in situations where disabilities were unrelated to job performance.

While various state laws offer employment protection for the handicapped, Section 504 of the Rehabilitation Act of 1973 affords general protection for all handicapped individuals. In 1979, the first case involving an interpretation of Section 504 requirements reached the United States Supreme Court. *Southeastern Community College v. Davis* was initiated by a licensed practical nurse seeking admission to a college program to train registered nurses.[115] Mrs. Davis was denied admission to the program because of a serious hearing disability. During the interview process, it was discovered that even with the use of a hearing aid the applicant could communicate effectively only through lipreading. The college rejected her application based on her inability to participate in all aspects of the program and the danger she might pose to future patients. The Court, in addressing Section 504, concluded that the language of the statute does not compel an institution to ignore the disabilities of an individual or to substantially modify its program to enable a handicapped person to participate. Rather, it provides that a qualified individual cannot be excluded solely on the basis of a particular disability.[116] The Court interpreted an "otherwise qualified" person as "one who is able to meet all of a program's requirements in spite of his handicap." [117] This conclusion is reinforced by HEW's regulation pertaining to program admissions, which specifies that an individual must meet academic *and* technical standards, with technical standards defined as all nonacademic criteria. In this case, effective oral communication was considered critical to full participation in the program. The applicant's inability to communicate would have necessitated close supervision and substantial alteration in the curriculum to accommodate her disability. The Court determined that Section 504 does not require such modifications. Institutions do not have to lower or substantially modify their standards to accommodate handicapped individuals.

In 1980, the duty to accommodate the needs of handicapped persons also was addressed by the Fifth Circuit Court of Appeals.[118] In this case, a deaf graduate student at the University of Texas claimed that the university had violated Section 504 of the Rehabilitation Act by failing to provide him with a sign language interpreter. He relied on the Section 504 regulations which specifically require colleges to provide auxiliary aids, such as interpreters, for deaf students. The appellate court distinguished this case from the Supreme Court's decision in *Southeastern Community College,* noting that the Texas student *was* an "otherwise qualified handicapped" individual while Mrs. Davis was not. After acquiring a degree, he would be able to satisfactorily perform in his profession. It would appear from these decisions that courts will require institutions to make accommodations for handicapped individuals, but will not require them to provide special services when an individual is incapable of utilizing the training.

In employment decisions, courts have reiterated that Section 504 regulations require "reasonable accommodation" *only* for handicapped persons who are *otherwise* qualified. In an illustrative California case, a teacher challenged school officials for failure to appoint him to an administrative position because of his blindness.[119] To be placed on a list of those eligible for an administrative position, candidates were required to complete a written examination and an oral interview. During the course of this process, an administrative committee determined that the teacher did not possess the requisite administrative skills or leadership experience for an administrative position and further expressed reservations about the teacher's ability to cope with his blindness. The federal district court concluded that, aside from the teacher's disability, he was not qualified for an administrative position. Thus, it was unnecessary for the district to consider making accommodations for him. Furthermore, the court noted that it was permissible for the committee to inquire as to how the teacher would cope with his blindness in fulfilling job responsibilities.

A handicapped person cannot be eliminated arbitrarily from employment consideration solely on the basis of a disability. However, at the same time, an employer is not required to ignore a handicap or make substantial accommodations for the special needs of the individual. Under current legislation and judicial interpretations, an "otherwise qualified individual" is assured an equal opportunity for employment.

## CONCLUSION

Equal employment opportunity has been an elusive concept which has been continually refined through legislative enactments and judicial opinions. In general, it means that employers are prohibited from discriminating in employment against any individual on the basis of race, sex, age, or handicap. Courts have applied varying standards in assessing discriminatory employment practices. The standard of judicial review depends on the classification challenged (e.g., race or sex) and the basis for the litigation (i.e., constitutional or statutory grounds). Broad generalizations pertaining to discrimination in employment are enumerated below.

1. The Federal Constitution and various civil rights laws protect employees from discrimination in employment based on race, sex, age, and handicaps.
2. Under Title VII of the Civil Rights Act of 1964, the plaintiff bears the "burden of proof" in showing a prima facie case of discrimination; the burden then shifts to the employer to establish a legitimate, nondiscriminatory basis for the practice.[120]
3. The foreseeable adverse impact of an employment practice on a protected group does not establish discrimination under the Federal Constitution unless the practice is accompanied by unlawful intent; however, such disparate impact can violate Title VII if the employment practice is not justified as a business necessity.
4. A standardized test, such as the National Teachers Examination, can be used to screen teacher applicants, even though it has a disproportionate impact on minority applicants, as long as discriminatory motive does not accompany its use.
5. Staff reductions occurring under court-ordered desegregation must be based on objective and nondiscriminatory standards applied consistently to the total staff of the school district.
6. Where prior discriminatory employment practices have existed, retroactive seniority can be awarded to minority employees to ensure that individuals are in their "rightful place" for promotion and other employment benefits.
7. Absent a history of prior discriminatory employment practices, school officials cannot ignore a bona fide seniority system in making staff reductions in an effort to achieve racial balance in the teaching force.
8. Although Title VII protects *all* employees from discrimination in employment, it does permit an employer to implement an affirmative action plan to overcome "traditional patterns of segregation," even though the plan may restrict the rights of majority employees.
9. Pregnancy-related benefits cannot be excluded from an employer's medical and disability insurance plans.
10. Arbitrary cut-off dates cannot be used in compulsory maternity leave policies; however, school officials can establish dates for maternity leave if they show a business necessity for the policy.
11. Teacher retirement contributions and benefits cannot be gender-based.

12. In evaluating teachers, school officials must apply similar standards of review to males and females.
13. Equitable relief under Title VII is usually limited to employment-related opportunities (reinstatement, promotion, and back pay).
14. Mandatory retirement ages are constitutional.
15. An "otherwise qualified handicapped individual" cannot be excluded from employment solely on the basis of a disability, but employers are not obligated to make special accommodations for handicapped persons who are not qualified.

## NOTES

1. 347 U.S. 483 (1954).
2. *See* text with note 84, Chapter 3, for a discussion of protections against discrimination based on religion.
3. 401 U.S. 424 (1971). The question of constitutional infringement was not addressed in *Griggs*; rather, the decision was based solely on Title VII.
4. *Id.* at 432.
5. 422 U.S. 405 (1975).
6. *Id.* at 432.
7. 426 U.S. 229 (1976).
8. *Id.* at 239.
9. *Id.* at 242.
10. United States v. South Carolina, National Education Ass'n v. South Carolina, 445 F. Supp. 1094 (D. S.C. 1977), *aff'd*, 434 U.S. 1026 (1978).
11. Personnel Administrator of Massachusetts v. Feeney, 442 U.S. 256 (1979).
12. In 1979, the Supreme Court discussed constitutional versus statutory standards in assessing a school district's eligibility for federal funds under the Emergency School Aid Act (ESAA). ESAA was enacted to provide financial assistance in the voluntary elimination of minority group segregation and discrimination. The Act stipulates that an educational agency which has in effect any practice which discriminates in employment shall be ineligible for funds. In this case, the school board asserted that such ineligibility must be based on evidence of intentional discrimination in the constitutional sense. The Supreme Court, however, held that "disproportionate impact in assignment of employees is sufficient to occasion ineligibility. Specific intent to discriminate is not an imperative." The Court emphasized that Congress is empowered to establish standards more protective of minority rights than constitutional minimums require. Board of Educ. of the City of New York v. Harris, 444 U.S. 130, 149 (1979).
13. 411 U.S. 792, 802 (1973).
14. *Id.*
15. *See* Furnco Construction Corporation v. Waters, 438 U.S. 567 (1978).
16. *Id.* at 577.

17. 439 U.S. 24 (1978). *See* text with note 81, *infra.*
18. *Id.* at 27–28.
19. Sweeney v. Board of Trustees of Keene State College, 604 F.2d 106, 108 (1st Cir. 1979), *cert. denied,* 444 U.S. 1045 (1980). Although under the *McDonnell Douglas* criteria the burden of persuasion remains with the plaintiff, the Fifth Circuit Court of Appeals overturned a district court decision requiring a female faculty member to prove a "clear abuse of discretion" by the university. The court held this to be a heavier burden than that imposed by the Supreme Court in Title VII cases. Jepsen v. Florida Bd. of Regents, 610 F.2d 1379 (5th Cir. 1980).
20. International Brotherhood of Teamsters v. United States, 431 U.S. 324 (1977).
21. Furnco Construction Corporation v. Waters, 438 U.S. 567 (1978).
22. Hazelwood School Dist. v. United States, 433 U.S. 299 (1977).
23. Singleton v. Jackson Municipal Separate School Dist., 419 F.2d 1211 (5th Cir. 1970).
24. *Id.* at 1218.
25. *Id.*
26. *See* Lee v. Tuscaloosa County Bd. of Educ., 591 F.2d 324 (5th Cir. 1979); Wright v. Houston Independent School Dist., 569 F.2d 1383 (5th Cir. 1978); Barnes v. Jones County School Dist., 544 F.2d 804 (5th Cir. 1977); Pickens v. Okolona Municipal School Dist., 527 F.2d 358 (5th Cir. 1976).
27. This, however, does not negate the individual's right to initiate charges of racially discriminatory dismissal or demotion under the fourteenth amendment. *See* Barnes v. Jones County School Dist., 544 F.2d 804, 807 (5th Cir. 1977).
28. Harkless v. Sweeny Independent School Dist., 388 F. Supp. 738, 770 (S.D. Tex. 1975).
29. *See* Lee v. Walker County School System, 594 F.2d 156, 158 (5th Cir. 1979); Barnes v. Jones County School Dist., 544 F.2d 804, 806 (5th Cir. 1977).
30. Kelly v. West Baton Rouge Parish School Bd., 517 F.2d 194 (5th Cir. 1975).
31. United States v. Jefferson County Bd. of Educ., 380 F.2d 385, 394 (5th Cir. 1967).
32. Carter v. West Feliciana Parish School Bd., 432 F.2d 875, 878-79 (5th Cir. 1970).
33. Lee v. Walker, 594 F.2d 156, 159 (5th Cir. 1979).
34. 419 F.2d 1211, 1218 (5th Cir. 1970).
35. *See* Lee v. Macon County Bd. of Educ. (Thomasville), 470 F.2d 958 (5th Cir. 1972).
36. Lee v. Macon County Bd. of Educ. (Muscle Shoals), 453 F.2d 1104 (5th Cir. 1971).
37. Lee v. Russell County Bd. of Educ., 563 F.2d 1159 (5th Cir. 1977).
38. 42 U.S.C. § 2000e-2(h) (1976).
39. Local 189, United Papermakers and Paperworkers v. United States, 416 F.2d 980 (5th Cir. 1969).

40. *See* Franks v. Bowman Transportation Co. Inc., 424 U.S. 747 (1976).
41. *See* Albemarle Paper Co. v. Moody, 422 U.S. 405 (1975).
42. 42 U.S.C. § 2000e-5(g), § 706(g) (1976).
43. Franks v. Bowman Transportation Co. Inc., 424 U.S. 747 (1976).
44. Chance v. Board of Examiners and Bd. of Educ. of the City of New York, 534 F.2d 993 (2d Cir. 1976).
45. Bacica v. Board of Educ. of the School Dist. of the City of Erie, Pa., 451 F. Supp. 882 (W.D. Pa. 1978).
46. McDonald v. Santa Fe Trail Transportation Co., 427 U.S. 273, 278-79 (1976). This interpretation also has been consistently applied by the Equal Employment Opportunity Commission in proscribing discrimination against white employees.
47. *Id.*
48. *Id.* at 283.
49. 438 U.S. 265 (1978).
50. 42 U.S.C. § 2000d (1976).
51. In 1980, the Supreme Court addressed a congressional quota based on race. The Minority Business Enterprise (MBE) provision of the Public Works Employment Act of 1977 sets aside at least ten percent of federal funds granted for local public works projects to ensure minority contractor participation. This provision was challenged as a violation of the equal protection clause of the fourteenth amendment. The Court, recognizing the broad remedial powers of Congress, concluded that Congress could fashion a remedy with a racial factor in light of a history of prior discrimination. Fullilove v. Klutznick, 100 S. Ct. 2758 (1980).
52. McDonald v. Hogness, 598 P.2d 707 (Wash. 1979), *cert. denied*, 100 S. Ct. 1650 (1980).
53. 443 U.S. 153 (1979).
54. *Id.* at 200.
55. 42 U.S.C. § 2000e-2(j) (1976).
56. Detroit Police Officers' Ass'n v. Young, 608 F.2d 671 (6th Cir. 1979).
57. *Id.* at 694.
58. *See* Bacica v. Board of Educ. of School Dist. of the City of Erie, Pa., 451 F. Supp. 882 (W.D. Pa. 1978).
59. Bradwell v. Illinois, 16 Wall. 130, 141 (1873).
60. Craig v. Boren, 429 U.S. 190, 197 (1976).
61. Personnel Administrator of Massachusetts v. Feeney, 442 U.S. 256, 273 (1979). *See* text with note 1, Chapter 9, for a discussion of standards of review under the equal protection clause.
62. 20 U.S.C. § 1681 (1976).
63. *See* text with note 94, *infra.*
64. 417 U.S. 484 (1974).
65. 29 C.F.R. § 1604.10(b).
66. 429 U.S. 125 (1976).
67. 42 U.S.C.A. 2000e(k) (1978).
68. *Education U.S.A.*, Vol. 21, No. 9, October 30, 1978, p. 70.
69. 414 U.S. 632 (1974).
70. *Id.* at 643.

71. *Id.* at 644.
72. deLaurier v. San Diego Unified School Dist., 588 F.2d 674 (9th Cir. 1978).
73. Mitchell v. Board of Trustees of Pickens County School Dict., 599 F.2d 582 (4th Cir. 1979).
74. 434 U.S. 136 (1977).
75. 435 U.S. 702 (1978).
76. *Id.* at 708.
77. Thomas J. Flygare, "The Aftermath of *Manhart*: Are Teacher Pension Plans Illegal?" *Phi Delta Kappan*, Vol. 60, No. 4, 1978, p. 310.
78. Spirt v. TIAA-CREF, 475 F. Supp. 1298 (S.D. N.Y. 1979).
79. Peters v. Wayne State University, 476 F. Supp. 1343 (E.D. Mich. 1979).
80. *See* text with note 13, *supra*, for discussion of criteria established in McDonnell Douglas Corporation v. Green, 411 U.S. 792 (1973).
81. Sweeney v. Board of Trustees of Keene State College, 604 F.2d 106 (1st Cir. 1979), *cert. denied*, 444 U.S. 1045 (1980). *See* text with note 17, *supra*, for explanation of the Supreme Court's ruling.
82. Kunda v. Muhlenberg, 621 F.2d 532 (3d Cir. 1980).
83. 29 U.S.C. § 206(d) (1976).
84. 29 U.S.C. § 206(d) (1) (1976).
85. 42 U.S.C. § 2000e-2(h) (1976). This amendment is commonly referred to as the Bennett Amendment.
86. International Union of Electrical Radio and Machine Workers v. Westinghouse Electric Corp., 631 F.2d 1094 (3d Cir. 1980); Gunther v. County of Washington, 623 F.2d 1303 (9th Cir. 1979).
87. Gunther v. County of Washington, 623 F.2d 1303, 1312-13 (9th Cir. 1979).
88. Lemon v. City and County of Denver, 620 F.2d 228 (10th Cir. 1980), *cert. denied*, 101 S. Ct. 244 (1980).
89. 42 U.S.C. § 2000e-5(g) (1976).
90. *See* Curran v. Portland Superintending School Committee, 435 F. Supp. 1063 (D. Me. 1977).
91. Harrington v. Vandalia-Butler Bd. of Educ., 585 F.2d 192 (6th Cir. 1978), *cert. denied*, 441 U.S. 932 (1979).
92. Personnel Administrator of Massachusetts v. Feeney, 442 U.S. 256 (1979).
93. *Id.* at 279.
94. 20 U.S.C. § 1681(a) (1976).
95. Islesboro School Committee v. Califano, 593 F.2d 424 (1st Cir. 1979), *cert. denied*, 444 U.S. 972 (1979).
96. Seattle University v. HEW, 621 F.2d 992 (9th Cir. 1980); Junior College Dist. of St. Louis v. Califano, 597 F.2d 119 (8th Cir. 1979), *cert. denied*, 444 U.S. 972 (1979); Romeo Community Schools v. HEW, 600 F.2d 581 (6th Cir. 1979), *cert. denied*, 444 U.S. 972 (1979).
97. "Justice Department Asks Supreme Court to Hear Title IX Employment Cases," *Education Daily*, Vol. 12, No. 152, August 8, 1979, p. 1.
98. In Cannon v. University of Chicago, 441 U.S. 677 (1979), the Supreme Court held that an individual is permitted to sue under Title IX. This may be a moot victory for teachers if the appellate courts continue to rule that employment practices are not covered by Title IX.

99. North Haven Bd. of Educ. v. Hufstedler, 629 F.2d 773 (2d Cir. 1980); Dougherty County School System v. Harris, 622 F.2d 735 (5th Cir. 1980).
100. Caulfield v. New York City Bd. of Educ., 486 F. Supp. 862 (E.D. N.Y. 1979).
101. 576 F.2d 459 (2d Cir. 1978).
102. Gault v. Garrison, 569 F.2d 993 (7th Cir. 1977), *cert. denied*, 440 U.S. 945 (1979).
103. Massachusetts Bd. of Retirement v. Murgia, 427 U.S. 307 (1976).
104. 29 U.S.C. § 621 (1976).
105. Tenured college professors and certain executives are not covered by the law.
106. Vance v. Bradley, 440 U.S. 93 (1979).
107. Loeb v. Textron, Inc., 600 F.2d 1003, 1014 (1st Cir. 1979).
108. Polstorff v. Fletcher, 452 F. Supp. 17 (N.D. Ala. 1978).
109. 29 U.S.C. § 794 (1976).
110. *Id.*
111. Gurmankin v. Costanzo, 556 F.2d 184 (3d Cir. 1977).
112. Gurmankin v. Costanzo, 626 F.2d 1115 (3d Cir. 1980).
113. The court distinguished this case from Kunda v. Muhlenberg, 621 F.2d 532 (3d Cir. 1980), where it ordered the award of tenure to a professor who had been employed a sufficient length of time for performance to be assessed. *See* text with note 82, *supra*.
114. State Division of Human Rights v. Averill Park Central School Dist., 399 N.Y.S.2d 926 (App. Div. 1977).
115. 442 U.S. 397 (1979).
116. *Id.* at 405.
117. *Id.* at 406.
118. Camenisch v. University of Texas, 616 F.2d 127 (5th Cir. 1980).
119. Upshur v. Love, 474 F. Supp. 332 (N.D. Cal. 1979).
120. *See* text with note 13, *supra*, for discussion of *McDonnell Douglas* criteria for establishing a prima facie case of discrimination.

# 5

# Teacher Dismissal

State laws define the authority of school boards in teacher dismissal actions. Generally, these laws specify the causes for which a teacher may be terminated and the procedures that must be followed in dismissal. Legal requirements vary according to the employment status of the teacher, with more extensive safeguards afforded the tenured teacher. In permanent termination actions, a distinction is drawn between dismissals and nonrenewals. A *dismissal* is the termination of a tenured teacher at any point, or the termination of a probationary teacher within the contract period. A *nonrenewal,* on the other hand, is the termination of a probationary teacher's employment at the end of the contract period by board option not to renew. Implications of this distinction for due process of law are significant because dismissals require full procedural protections, whereas a nonrenewal may involve only notice that employment will not be continued.

The right of the school board to determine the fitness of teachers has been well established; in fact, courts have declared that school boards have a duty as well as a right to make such determinations. The United States Supreme Court has recognized that such authority is vested in school boards.

> A teacher works in a sensitive area in a schoolroom. There he shapes the attitude of young minds towards the society in which they live. In this, the state has a vital concern. It must preserve the integrity of the schools. That the school authorities have the right and the *duty to screen* the officials, teachers, and employees as to their fitness to maintain the integrity of the school as a part of ordered society, cannot be doubted.[1] [Emphasis added.]

A myriad of factors surround the screening process of the school board. This chapter, however, deals only with grounds for termination of a teacher's employment and procedures that must be followed. An overview of due process is presented, with a discussion of the critical elements as defined by the courts and state laws. Also, the special nature of due process guarantees as applied to the nontenured teacher is explicated. A survey of causes for dismissal is included in order to provide a broad perspective on statutory and judicial interpretations of the varied state laws. In conclusion, legal remedies for wrongful teacher dismissal are identified.

## DUE PROCESS

The fourteenth amendment guarantees that no state shall "deprive any person of life, liberty, or property without due process of law." Due process safeguards apply not only in judicial proceedings but also to acts of governmental agencies such as school boards. If school board action interferes with a constitutionally protected right of the teacher, certain due process procedures are required.

It has been established under the fourteenth amendment that teachers may possess certain "property" or "liberty" interests in their teaching positions.[2] A property interest is a "legitimate claim of entitlement" to continued employment that is created by state law.[3] The granting of tenure conveys such a right to a teacher. Also, a contract establishes a property right to employment within the terms of the contract. A liberty interest is involved when the action of an employer creates a stigma or damages an individual's reputation in a manner that forecloses future employment opportunities.[4] If either a property or liberty right is impaired, procedural due process must be afforded prior to termination of employment.

### WHAT IS DUE PROCESS OF LAW?

Legal authorities have noted that "it would be very difficult, if not impossible, to frame a definition of the term [due process] which would be accurate, complete, and appropriate under all circumstances. . . ."[5] Broadly, this means that an individual cannot be deprived of certain rights without notice and an opportunity for a hearing. Beyond these minimums, the actual procedural requirements will depend on the situation.

To determine a teacher's procedural rights in dismissal or nonrenewal actions, three sources must be consulted: (1) employment contract, (2) state laws, and (3) court decisions.[6] The contract may or may not specify the procedures for employment termination. If specified, such procedures must be followed when a teacher is dismissed during the term of the contract. Because of the nature of the probationary teacher's position, due process procedures usually are not required if the contract simply is not renewed; the school board is merely exercising its option each year either to rehire or not to rehire the teacher. However, once the teacher obtains tenure, the contract may stipulate that dismissal must be based on a reason specified in state law and that notice and a hearing must be provided prior to board action. Even if due process procedures are not addressed in the continuing contract, most state tenure laws delineate such requirements. These laws vary in specificity from detailed mandates including exact dates for notice, designated format and content of notice, and type of hearing, to general provisions, requiring only reasonable notice and an opportunity to be heard. In addition to contracts and state laws, court decisions have established guidelines for determining when a teacher is entitled to due process and what type of procedures must be followed.

Generally, due process of law must be provided in connection with any dismissal of a tenured teacher and dismissal of a nontenured teacher during the contract period. Additionally, the nontenured teacher may have a property or liberty interest that would necessitate procedural due process. The school board may have created an expectancy of reemployment, or its action may have damaged future employment opportunities. These rights of the nontenured teacher are discussed in a subsequent section of this chapter.

## PROCEDURAL REQUIREMENTS

Minimally, due process requires that dismissal proceedings be based on established rules or standards, and that the teacher be notified of the charges and provided an opportunity to be heard. Actual procedures will depend on state law, board regulations, and the status of the teacher (tenured or nontenured). It has been suggested that full procedural rights would include notice of charges, an impartial hearing, representation by counsel, cross-examination of witnesses, and an opportunity for appeal of an adverse decision.[7] The severity of the impact of the action on the teacher will influence the procedures required of the board. Nonrenewal of a probationary teacher may require only notice without specification of reasons, whereas dismissal of a tenured teacher may require a formal hearing with witnesses, extensive evidence, and counsel.

Many questions arise concerning the adequacy or sufficiency of the various elements of due process. Frequently asked questions include the following:

- What is adequate notice?
- Must specific charges be identified in notice of nonrenewal or dismissal?
- Is the school board an unbiased decision maker?
- Where is the burden of proof in a dismissal action?

- What type of evidence must be presented by the board to support dismissal?
- Is "substantial compliance" with state statutes by the board sufficient, or is "strict compliance" required?

In general, the authority to hire and to dismiss teachers is vested in the school board. Subject to statutory limitations, boards have broad discretion in this area. As long as a dismissal decision is not arbitrary, capricious, or unreasonable, courts will not interfere with this discretionary power of the board.[8] Courts do not attempt to second-guess boards, nor will they alter a decision because it is lacking in wisdom. In examining a challenged board decision, courts determine if statutory procedures have been followed. When such procedures are followed and there is no evidence of arbitrary action, board decisions are upheld. However, if statutory procedures are not followed, the dismissal action may be invalidated.

Courts have been asked to determine whether school authorities must act in "strict compliance" or merely "substantial compliance" with statutory provisions. Generally, courts have upheld school officials in controversies involving due process if a "standard of reasonability" has been followed.[9] Legal commentators have noted that when procedures are prescribed there must be substantial compliance with essential elements.[10] Most cases tend to support the notion that substantial compliance with statutory provisions is sufficient for a school board dismissal action to be upheld.[11] This means that a dismissal will not be overturned on a pure technical error when the board has attempted to meet the legal requirements. For example, if the tenure statute specifies that written notice must be given by registered mail and it is received through other means prior to the notification deadline, the notice will probably be declared adequate.[12] In contrast to the prevailing view, the Iowa Supreme Court required strict compliance with state law in a dismissal action and found substantial compliance to be inappropriate.[13]

**Notice.** Requirements for notice are specified in school board regulations and/or state statutes. Most statutes establish deadlines for notification, prescribe the form and content of notice, and designate the party to issue notice. Failure of the board to comply with these requirements can void a dismissal action.[14]

Notice of dismissal or nonrenewal must be reasonable and adequate. This has been interpreted as a notification that allows the teacher sufficient time to prepare for and appear before a hearing board. Additionally, an adequate notice is one in which charges are specific, not vague.[15]

Timeliness of notice is strictly construed by the courts. When a deadline is established by state statute, the school board *must* notify the teacher of dismissal or nonrenewal prior to the designated date. For example, Illinois law requires written notice sixty days before the end of the teaching period.[16] In Maine, a probationary teacher must receive notice six months in advance of nonrenewal in the third year of teaching.[17] Actual receipt of the notice is crucial. In a case where a state statute specified April 30 and notice was mailed on April 29 but not received until May 2, notice was deemed insufficient.[18]

Substance or form of notice is usually stipulated in statutes. In determining appropriateness of notice, courts have held that adequacy, rather than form, is the primary consideration.[19] However, oral notice does not satisfy the statutory requirement of written notice.[20] Additionally, citing only statutory cause as the grounds for dismissal is insufficient. That is, a charge of incompetence does not provide the teacher with specific grounds that can be contested. Furthermore, dismissal can be based only on charges identified in the notice. The Supreme Court of Montana reinstated a teacher who was dismissed for unexcused absences because the notice of charges specified only a single incident, while the hearing focused on absences during the previous nine years of employment.[21] Since the additional absences were not identified in the notice, the board could not consider them in dismissing the teacher. However, the Supreme Court of Kansas permitted a school board to amend a notice and provide supplemental reasons for nonrenewal after the statutory deadline.[22] The court concluded that additional reasons may be considered as long as the teacher is given an opportunity to refute the allegations. The court reasoned that this is especially proper where there is a close nexus between the supplemental reasons and the original notice.

Lack of proper notice can result in reinstatement of the probationary teacher for an additional year [23] or in the awarding of tenure.[24] For example, lack of proper notice in a Michigan case resulted in the reinstatement of and award of tenure to a probationary teacher.[25] The Michigan tenure statute provides that

> . . . at least 60 days before the close of each school year the controlling board shall provide the probationary teacher with a definite written statement as to whether or not his work has been satisfactory. Failure to submit a written statement shall be considered as conclusive evidence that the teacher's work is satisfactory.[26]

In this case a written notice was sent by certified mail prior to the deadline, but not actually received before the required sixty days. The Tenure Commission ordered reinstatement with tenure, and this decision was upheld by the Supreme Court of Michigan. In another case, a federal district court in Delaware held that if true reasons are not given in the notice for termination, reemployment is required for the following year.[27]

**Hearing.** All tenured teachers must be provided a hearing before dismissal. Similarly, probationary teachers terminated during the contract period must be given an opportunity to be heard.[28] Unlike judicial proceedings, hearings need not follow formal trial procedures. The Eighth Circuit Court of Appeals held that "an informal procedure which meets the minimal requirements of fair play and provides a dismissed teacher with a reasonable opportunity to be heard" satisfies state law.[29] Other courts have held that a school board hearing requires "orderly procedures" and "fundamental fairness," [30] and that as long as the board follows the mandates of due process, the hearing procedures are "entitled to great weight and will not be overruled." [31]

Although specific requirements for hearings have not been judicially mandated, courts have given broad guidelines. In 1970, the Fifth Circuit Court of Appeals stated that in general a teacher must be

1. advised of the cause or causes for termination in sufficient detail to fairly enable a defense to be prepared;
2. advised of the names and the nature of the testimony of adverse witnesses;
3. accorded a meaningful opportunity to be heard at a reasonable time after receiving notice; and
4. provided a hearing before a tribunal that both possesses some academic expertise and has an apparent impartiality toward the charges.[32]

The Supreme Court of Missouri identified the following elements of a valid hearing:

1. meaningful opportunity to be heard;
2. opportunity to state position;
3. opportunity to present witnesses;
4. right to counsel;
5. opportunity to cross-examine witnesses; and
6. access to written reports in advance of hearing.[33]

One persistent area of controversy has centered around the impartiality of the school board as the hearing tribunal in dismissals. Courts generally agree that the school board can serve as a neutral hearing board.[34] To challenge the school board, the teacher must clearly demonstrate that there is bias on the part of the board [35]; a "high probability of bias" is constitutionally unacceptable.[36]

The United States Supreme Court in *Joint School District No. 1 v. Hortonville Education Association* firmly established that the school board is the proper body under state law to conduct the hearing.[37] In *Hortonville,* the Wisconsin high court held that the school board was unable to provide striking teachers with an impartial hearing because of its involvement in the events. However, the Supreme Court reversed the state court decision, holding instead that

> A showing that the Board was "involved" in the events preceding this decision, in light of the important interest in leaving with the Board the power given by the state legislature, is not enough to overcome the presumption of honesty and integrity in policymakers with decision-making power.[38]

In a subsequent Iowa Supreme Court decision, it was concluded that extensive involvement of the board in initiating and investigating charges against a teacher rendered the board incapable of conducting a fair hearing.[39] The board, in this instance, determined that the teacher's performance was inadequate. A hearing was then conducted in which the only witnesses were board members calling upon their own knowledge of events.[40] Unless the bias of the board clearly can be demonstrated, as in this Iowa case, the school board will be considered the proper hearing body.

**Evidence.** Under tenure laws, the school board must show "cause" for dismissal. This places the burden of proof on the board to present substantial evidence to support a dismissal decision. If boards have produced adequate evidence in support of their decisions, courts have upheld dismissal actions.[41] However, when only minimum evidence has been presented, decisions have been overruled.[42] The Supreme Court of Nebraska reversed a teacher's dismissal for incompetency because the board did not have objective criteria for evaluating the teacher and, therefore, could not show substantial evidence to justify dismissal.[43] In a Connecticut case, an impartial hearing panel appointed pursuant to statute at a teacher's request found the evidence presented insufficient to warrant dismissal.[44] However, the school board rejected the impartial panel's decision and dismissed the teacher. The Supreme Court of Connecticut overruled the school board, noting that it did not produce a "preponderance of evidence" to support dismissal.[45]

A number of basic legal principles apply to type, form, content, and preparation of evidence required by school boards in dismissal proceedings. The following basic guidelines pertaining to the nature of evidence have emerged from judicial rulings.

1. It must be substantial.
2. It must be relevant to establish the alleged facts.
3. It must be developed in a constitutionally approved way.
4. It must be documented, which, in its simplest form, means recording the time, date, and place, with witnesses listed, if any.

5. Evidence presented at the hearing should be limited to charges made.

6. The rules of evidence applicable in court proceedings do not apply in a strict sense to dismissal hearings.[46]

## SUMMARY OF PROCEDURAL RIGHTS

In summary, the following general guidelines should be duly noted in assessing the teacher's procedural due process rights.

1. A teacher is entitled to due process of law prior to dismissal when a property or liberty interest exists.

2. A property interest is created through tenure, implied tenure, or contract.

3. A liberty interest may arise if the dismissal action imposes a stigma or damages the teacher's reputation.

4. At a minimum, due process requires that the teacher be provided with notice specifying reasons for dismissal and an opportunity for a hearing at which to present evidence and confront witnesses.

5. All procedures specified by statute or contract must be followed in the dismissal process.

## PROCEDURAL RIGHTS OF THE NONTENURED TEACHER

Prior to 1972, the due process rights of nontenured teachers were poorly defined. Clearly, a teacher was entitled to procedural safeguards if the exercise of a constitutionally protected right, such as freedom of speech, was involved. Beyond that basic right, however, a lack of unanimity existed among courts. The Supreme Court significantly clarified this area in two landmark decisions, *Board of Regents v. Roth* [47] and *Perry v. Sindermann.*[48] Although these cases involved faculty members at the post-secondary level, the rulings are equally applicable to public elementary and secondary school teachers, serving as precedent in teacher nonrenewal cases.

In *Roth,* a professor was hired on a fixed contract for one academic year. The university elected not to rehire him for a second year. Since Roth did not have tenure, there was no entitlement under Wisconsin law to an explanation of charges or a hearing; the university simply did not reemploy him for the succeeding year. Roth challenged the lack of notice and hearing as an infringement of his fourteenth amendment rights. Thus, the question presented to the Supreme Court was whether Roth had a constitutional right to procedural due process because of the university's decision not to reemploy him for a second year.

As noted previously, procedural due process is guaranteed by the fourteenth amendment if liberty or property interests are impaired. The Court found neither interest abridged in this case. To involve a liberty interest, nonretention must seriously damage the teacher's "standing and association in his community." [49] The Court declared: "Where a person's good name, reputation, honor, or integrity is at stake because of what the government is doing to him, notice and an opportunity to be heard are essential." [50] No evidence was presented indicating such damage to Roth. Additionally, the Court specified that the state had not created a "stigma" which might foreclose future employment opportunities. The Court concluded that "it stretches the concept too far to suggest that a person is deprived of 'liberty' when he simply is not rehired in one job but remains as free as before to seek another." [51]

The Court also rejected Roth's assertion that he had a protected property claim to continued employment. The Court held that in order to establish a valid property right an individual must have more than an "abstract need or desire" for a position; there must be a "legitimate claim of entitlement." [52] Property interests are not defined by the Federal Constitution, but by state laws. In this case, there was no statute or policy upon which Roth could base a "property" claim.

On the same day as the *Roth* decision, the Supreme Court handed down a second decision, *Perry v. Sindermann*,[53] which further explicated the conditions necessary to establish a property right to employment. Sindermann was employed in the Texas state college system for a period of ten years, the last four years of that period at Odessa Junior College. During Sindermann's fourth year at Odessa, the college elected, without explanation or a hearing, not to renew his annual contract. Sindermann contested the lack of procedural due process, maintaining that he was being dismissed because of public criticism of the college administration, and further that he had *de facto* tenure under the college's employment policy. Ruling in favor of Sindermann, the Supreme Court reiterated that if freedom of speech is implicated in a dismissal recommendation, a hearing must be provided. Furthermore, the Court concluded that Sindermann had a valid property right to due process. In addressing the property interest, the Court emphasized, as in *Roth,* that merely not being rehired for a position does not involve a property right. However, the Court differentiated between the "expectancy of reemployment" found in *Sindermann* and in *Roth.* As opposed to Roth's "abstract desire" for employment, Sindermann's expectancy was based on a *de facto* tenure policy that existed in the college. Although there was no formal tenure program, the college administration had promulgated an unofficial tenure program. In fact, the faculty guide stated: "The College wishes the faculty member to feel that he has permanent tenure as long as his teaching services are satisfactory. . . ." [54] A similar policy was also conveyed by the state college and university system for faculty members who had been in the system seven years or more. In finding that Sindermann did indeed have a legitimate property interest in continued employment, the Court noted that the lack of formal tenure did not foreclose the possibility of an institutionally created system. Such a property interest entitled Sindermann to an explanation and hearing prior to nonretention.

The *Roth* and *Sindermann* cases indicate that when a liberty or property interest is impaired, a nontenured teacher has the same constitutional right to due process as the tenured teacher. The question then arises as to what constitutes a violation of these interests. The courts have purposely avoided precisely defining the concepts of liberty and property, preferring to allow experience and time to shape their meanings.[55] Since 1972, the Supreme Court and federal appellate courts have rendered other decisions that provide some guidance in understanding these concepts.

In *Bishop v. Wood,* the Supreme Court recognized, as in *Sindermann,* that a property interest is created by state law rather than by the Federal Constitution; therefore, the scope of such property rights must be interpreted in light of a particular state's statutes or regulations.[56] Although the *Bishop* case involved a policeman rather than a teacher, it provided further guidance in defining property interests. Bishop, who was discharged without a hearing after approximately three years of employment, claimed that he was entitled to due process prior to dismissal. Bishop based his claim to continued employment on a city ordinance that stipulated that employees would have permanent employment status after six months of successful service. In North Carolina, where the *Bishop* case originated, the state supreme court earlier had ruled specifically that expectancy of reemployment can exist only if granted by statute or contract. The United States Supreme Court, in interpreting the city ordinance, concluded that Bishop "held his position at the will and pleasure of the city." [57] Based on this view, the plaintiff did not have a property claim under the fourteenth amendment.

In cases rendered since *Sindermann* and *Bishop,* courts generally have held that a nontenured or probationary teacher does not have a property entitlement to continued employment unless governmental action has clearly established such a right.[58] The Sixth Circuit Court of Appeals held that the basis for expectancy of reemployment must be grounded in state statute rather than in a school board regulation.[59] Similarly, a federal district court in Delaware ruled that a collective bargaining agreement, requiring an informal hearing to discuss the reasons for nonrenewal of nontenured teachers, did not constitute a property interest.[60] Thus, as long as the terms of the negotiated agreement were met, teachers facing nonrenewal were not entitled to more extensive due process procedures. A property interest can be created, however, if a school board fails to adhere to state statutory requirements regarding timely or proper notice of nonrenewal. As previously stated, once such a property right to continued employment is established, it cannot be deprived without due process.

Clarification also has been provided by the courts in defining an individual's liberty rights under the fourteenth amendment. The Supreme Court noted in *Roth* that liberty encompasses more than "freedom from bodily restraint" and includes

> . . . the right of the individual to contract, to engage in any of the common occupations of life, to acquire useful knowledge, to marry, establish a home and bring up children, to worship God according to the dictates of his own conscience, and generally to enjoy those privileges long recognized . . . as essential to the orderly pursuit of happiness by free men.[61]

Based on *Roth,* a liberty interest is impaired if through nonretention the person's reputation is damaged or a stigma is created of such magnitude that it forecloses future employment opportunities.

More recently, the Court recognized that unless employment is threatened, mere governmental stigmatization does not abridge a liberty interest which would require due process protections. This was demonstrated in a noneducation case involving an individual whose name was placed on an "active shoplifters" list by police.[62] The individual sued, claiming that his rights to enter business establishments and to obtain future employment were impaired. An attempt was made to establish defamation as a violation of his liberty interest. The Supreme Court noted that "the Court has never held that the mere defamation of an individual, whether by branding him disloyal or otherwise, was sufficient to invoke the guarantees of procedural due process absent an accompanying loss of government employment." [63] Vindication of reputation was clearly differentiated from a constitutional liberty interest under the fourteenth amendment. The Court indicated that defamation *unrelated to loss of employment* is a matter of tort law which should be settled in state courts.[64]

From the above case, a "stigma-plus" test has evolved: "To establish a liberty interest sufficient to implicate fourteenth amendment safeguards, the individual must be not only stigmatized but also stigmatized in connection with a denial of a right or status previously recognized under state law." [65] Under this test, courts have held that the transfer of teachers from one position to another (even one of lower rank) does not impair a liberty interest.[66] However, the Fifth Circuit Court of Appeals has held that defamation in the nonrenewal of a teacher's contract that damages future employment opportunities would meet the "stigma-plus" test. The appellate court concluded that the allegation of a drinking problem subjected the teacher to a "badge of infamy" which seriously damaged his reputation and standing in the community.[67] The court thus held that procedural due process was required to afford the teacher an opportunity to clear his name.

The purpose of a hearing is to provide an individual with an opportunity to refute allegations that the employer has made; there is an assumption of a factual dispute. If such is not the case, an individual may not be entitled to a hearing. The Supreme Court has noted "if [the plaintiff] does not challenge the substantial truth of the material in question, no hearing would afford a promise of achieving that result for him." [68]

During the past decade, courts have more clearly defined the liberty and property interests guaranteed under the fourteenth amendment. Although the concepts are still evolving, the nontenured teacher can rely on certain guarantees if threatened with job loss.

1. A hearing is required if the school board and its representatives create a stigma that might "foreclose future employment" opportunities.
2. The school board may create a *de facto* tenure policy, giving rise to an "expectancy of reemployment."
3. Expectancy of reemployment can be based on state statute or contract.

## DISMISSAL FOR CAUSE

Tenure laws are designed to provide competent teachers assurance of continued employment as long as their performance is satisfactory. With the protection of tenure, a teacher can be dismissed only for cause, and only in accordance with the procedures specified by law. Although acquiring tenure status gives a teacher a vested interest in continued employment that cannot be denied without due process of law, it does not guarantee permanent employment. The school district may discharge the teacher for cause, or because of conditions within the district, such as financial exigencies or declining enrollment, that necessitate reductions in the teaching force. Tenure rights accrue under individual state laws and therefore must be interpreted in light of each state's provisions.

Dismissal safeguards generally emanate from tenure statutes and are not applicable to the nontenured teacher. However, within the one-year contract period, certain procedural rights are constitutionally guaranteed. That is, a probationary teacher with an annual contract cannot be dismissed during the term of the contract without procedural due process. The contract itself establishes a property right to due process that extends throughout the contract period. In most states, school boards can decline to renew annual contracts without specification of cause, but in a few states reasons must be given for the termination or nonrenewal of all teachers.[69]

Dismissal of a permanent teacher must be based on causes identified in state laws. Where causes are identified by statute, the board cannot base the dismissal decision on reasons other than those contained in law.[70] To cover unexpected matters, statutes often include a catch-all phrase such as "other good and just cause." Causes included in statutes vary considerably among states, from an extensive listing of individual grounds to a simple statement that dismissal must be based on cause. Delon has compiled a breakdown of statutory grounds for dismissal of teachers by state that shows twenty-five causes (see Table 1).[71] The most frequently cited causes are incompetency, neglect of duty, insubordination, and immorality. As can be seen from the table, these categories are not discrete areas. Many of the individual causes noted could be subsumed under a broader cause; for example, failure to provide instruction might be covered by incompetency or neglect of duty.

Statutory provisions from three selected states illustrate the range in specificity of causes stipulated for dismissal. California law includes an extensive listing.

No permanent employee shall be dismissed except for one or more of the following causes:

(a) Immoral or unprofessional conduct.
(b) Commission, aiding, or advocating the commission of criminal syndicalism.
(c) Dishonesty.
(d) Incompetency.
(e) Evident unfitness for service.
(f) Physical or mental condition unfitting him to instruct or associate with children.
(g) Persistent violation of or refusal to obey the school laws of the state or reasonable regulations prescribed for the government of the public schools by the State Board of Education or by the governing board of the school district employing him.
(h) Conviction of a felony or of any crime involving moral turpitude . . . .[72]

Illinois law provides an example of a typical provision.

One of the duties of the school board is to dismiss a teacher for incompetency, cruelty, negligence, immorality, or other sufficient cause and to dismiss any teacher, whenever, in its opinion, he is not qualified to teach, or whenever, in its opinion, the interest of the schools requires it . . . .[73]

The Maine statute exemplifies a very general provision.

After investigation, due notice of hearing and hearing thereon, [the School Committee] shall dismiss any teacher, although having the requisite certificate, who proves unfit to teach or whose services they deem unprofitable to the school, and give to said teacher a certificate of dismissal and of the reasons therefore . . . .[74]

## STATUTORY GROUNDS FOR THE DISMISSAL OR SUSPENSION OF TEACHERS

| State | Incompetency | Unfitness for Service | Negligence, Neglect of Duty | Failure to Provide Designated Instruction | Failure to Attend Required Institutes | Inefficiency | Incapacity | Insubordination | Refusal to Obey School Board Regulations | Noncompliance with School Laws | Disloyalty, Subversive Activity | Contract Violation, Cancellation, Annulment, Breach | Conviction of Specified Crime | Immorality | Untruthfulness, Dishonesty, Falsification of Application, Records | Drunkenness, Intemperance | Addiction to Drugs and/or Selling Drugs | Cruelty | Conduct Unbecoming a Teacher, Misconduct in Office | Unprofessional Conduct | Violation of Code of Ethics | Revocation of Certificate | Cause (Good, Just, Sufficient) | Failure to Obey State Laws | Other |
|---|---|---|---|---|---|---|---|---|---|---|---|---|---|---|---|---|---|---|---|---|---|---|---|---|---|
| Alabama | X |  | X | X |  |  |  | X |  |  |  |  |  | X |  |  |  |  |  |  |  |  | X |  |  |
| Alaska | X |  |  |  |  |  |  |  |  |  | X |  | X | X |  |  |  |  |  | X |  |  |  |  |  |
| Arizona |  |  |  |  |  |  |  |  |  |  |  |  |  |  |  |  |  |  |  |  |  |  |  |  | X |
| Arkansas |  |  |  |  |  |  |  |  |  |  |  |  |  | X |  |  |  |  |  |  |  |  |  |  |  |
| California | X | X |  |  |  |  |  |  |  |  | X | X | X | X | X | X |  |  |  | X |  | X |  | X | X |
| Colorado | X |  | X | X |  |  |  |  | X |  |  |  | X | X | X |  |  |  |  |  |  |  | X |  |  |
| Connecticut | X |  |  | X | X |  |  |  | X |  |  |  |  | X |  |  |  |  |  |  |  |  | X |  |  |
| Delaware | X | X |  |  |  |  |  |  | X |  |  | X |  | X |  |  |  |  | X |  |  |  |  |  |  |
| Florida | X | X |  |  |  |  |  |  | X |  |  |  | X | X |  | X | X |  | X |  |  |  |  |  |  |
| Georgia | X |  |  |  |  |  |  |  | X |  |  |  |  | X |  |  |  |  |  |  |  |  |  | X | X |
| Hawaii |  |  |  |  |  |  |  | X | X | X |  |  |  | X |  |  |  |  |  |  |  |  |  | X |  |
| Idaho |  |  |  |  |  |  |  |  |  | X |  |  | X |  |  |  |  |  | X |  |  |  |  |  | X |
| Illinois | X | X |  |  |  |  |  |  |  |  |  |  |  | X |  |  |  |  | X |  |  |  |  | X |  |
| Indiana | X | X |  |  |  |  |  | X | X | X |  |  |  | X |  |  |  |  |  |  |  |  |  | X |  |
| Iowa | X | X |  |  |  |  |  |  |  |  |  |  |  | X |  |  |  |  |  |  |  |  |  | X |  |
| Kansas |  |  |  |  |  |  |  |  |  |  |  |  |  |  |  |  |  |  |  |  |  |  |  | X |  |
| Kentucky | X | X |  |  |  |  |  | X | X |  |  |  |  | X |  |  |  |  | X |  |  |  |  | X |  |
| Louisiana | X | X |  |  |  |  |  |  |  |  |  |  |  | X | X |  |  |  |  |  |  |  |  |  | X |
| Maine |  |  |  |  |  |  |  |  |  |  |  |  |  |  |  |  |  |  |  |  |  |  | X |  |  |
| Maryland | X | X |  |  |  |  |  |  | X |  |  |  |  | X |  |  |  |  | X |  |  |  |  | X |  |
| Massachusetts |  |  |  |  |  | X | X | X | X | X |  |  | X | X |  |  |  |  | X |  |  |  |  | X |  |
| Michigan |  | X |  |  |  |  |  |  |  | X |  |  |  |  |  | X |  |  |  |  |  |  |  | X |  |
| Minnesota |  | X |  |  |  | X | X |  | X |  | X |  | X | X | X |  |  |  | X |  |  |  |  | X |  |
| Mississippi | X | X |  |  |  |  |  |  |  |  |  |  | X | X |  | X |  | X |  |  |  |  |  | X |  |
| Missouri | X | X |  |  |  | X | X | X | X |  |  |  | X | X |  |  |  |  |  |  |  |  |  |  | X |
| Montana | X | X |  |  |  | X |  |  | X | X |  |  | X | X |  |  |  |  |  |  |  |  |  |  |  |
| Nebraska | X | X |  |  |  |  | X |  | X | X |  |  |  | X |  |  |  |  |  |  |  |  |  | X | X |
| Nevada |  | X | X |  |  | X | X |  | X |  |  | X | X | X | X | X |  |  |  | X | X |  | X |  |  |
| New Hampshire | X |  |  |  |  |  |  |  |  |  |  |  |  | X |  |  |  |  | X |  |  |  |  |  |  |
| New Jersey |  |  |  |  |  | X | X |  |  |  |  |  |  |  |  |  |  |  | X |  |  |  | X |  | X |
| New Mexico |  |  |  |  |  |  |  |  |  |  |  |  |  |  |  |  |  |  |  |  |  |  |  | X |  |
| New York | X | X |  |  |  | X | X |  |  |  |  |  |  |  |  |  |  |  | X |  | X |  |  | X |  |
| North Carolina | X | X |  |  |  | X | X | X | X |  | X |  | X | X |  |  | X |  |  |  |  |  |  | X |  |
| North Dakota |  |  |  |  |  | X | X | X |  |  |  | X | X | X |  |  |  |  | X |  |  |  |  | X |  |
| Ohio |  |  |  |  |  | X |  |  | X |  |  |  |  | X |  |  |  |  |  |  |  |  |  | X |  |
| Oklahoma | X | X |  |  |  |  |  |  |  |  | X |  |  | X |  |  |  |  |  | X |  |  |  |  |  |
| Oregon |  | X |  |  |  | X | X | X | X |  |  |  | X | X |  |  |  |  |  |  |  |  | X |  | X |
| Pennsylvania | X | X |  |  |  |  |  |  |  |  | X |  |  | X |  |  | X | X |  |  |  |  | X |  | X |
| Rhode Island |  |  |  |  |  |  |  |  | X |  |  |  |  |  |  |  |  |  |  |  |  |  | X |  |  |
| South Carolina | X | X |  |  |  |  |  |  | X |  |  |  | X | X | X | X | X |  |  |  |  |  | X |  |  |
| South Dakota | X | X |  |  |  |  |  |  | X |  | X |  | X | X | X | X |  |  |  |  |  | X |  |  |  |
| Tennessee | X | X |  | X | X |  | X | X | X |  | X |  | X | X |  | X | X | X | X | X |  | X |  |  |  |
| Texas |  | X |  |  |  |  |  |  | X |  | X |  | X | X |  |  |  | X |  |  |  |  |  |  |  |
| Utah |  |  |  |  |  |  |  |  |  |  |  |  |  |  |  |  |  |  |  |  |  |  |  |  |  |
| Vermont | X | X |  |  |  |  |  |  | X |  |  | X |  |  |  |  |  |  | X |  |  |  |  | X |  |
| Virginia | X | X |  |  |  | X | X |  | X |  |  |  |  | X |  |  |  |  |  |  |  |  |  | X |  |
| Washington |  |  |  |  |  |  |  |  |  |  |  |  |  |  |  |  |  |  |  |  |  |  |  |  |  |
| West Virginia | X | X |  |  |  |  | X |  |  |  |  |  | X | X |  |  |  |  | X | X | X |  |  | X |  |
| Wisconsin |  |  |  |  |  | X |  |  | X |  | X |  |  | X |  |  |  |  |  |  |  |  |  | X |  |
| Wyoming | X | X | X |  |  |  | X |  |  |  |  |  |  | X |  |  |  |  |  |  |  |  |  | X |  |

TABLE 1. Reprinted from NOLPE Monograph, F. Delon, *Legal Controls on Teacher Conduct: Teacher Discipline* 12 (rev. ERIC/CEM—NOLPE Monograph, 1977).

Since dismissal is statutorily determined, it is difficult to provide generalizations for all teachers. The causes are broad in scope and application; in fact, individual causes often have been attacked for impermissible vagueness. It is not unusual to find dismissal cases with similar factual situations based on different grounds. Additionally, a number of grounds often are introduced and supported in a single case. Illustrative case law is examined in this section in relation to several of the more frequently cited grounds for dismissal.

## INCOMPETENCY

Incompetency has been broadly defined by the courts. Although it usually refers to classroom performance, it has been extended in a few cases to a teacher's private life. The term is legally defined as "lack of ability, legal qualifications, or fitness to discharge the required duty." [75] Incompetency cases often involve issues of classroom management, teaching methods, grading procedures, and professional relationships.

An early Pennsylvania case, *Horosko v. School District of Mt. Pleasant,*[76] dealt with a teacher's working in her husband's "beer garden," where she occasionally had a drink of beer, served beer, and played a pinball machine with customers. The Pennsylvania Supreme Court held that the loss of respect and good will of the community that resulted from her outside activities was evidence of incompetency. In a later Pennsylvania case, the United States Supreme Court reiterated that classroom performance alone was not the only basis for determining a teacher's fitness.[77] The superintendent in this case was seeking information concerning a teacher's loyalty as related to alleged prior activities in the Communist Party. Since the teacher refused to answer the superintendent's questions, he was dismissed on the ground of incompetency. The Supreme Court, in upholding the dismissal, agreed with the Pennsylvania high court that incompetency included the teacher's "deliberate and insubordinate refusal to answer the questions of his administrative superior in a vitally important matter pertaining to his fitness." [78]

Lack of proper classroom management and control is frequently cited by boards in dismissals based on incompetency. Such dismissals often have been contested on the grounds that discharge is too severe a penalty for the offense. Courts generally have held that school boards have latitude in determining penalties [79] and their decisions will be vacated only if "disproportionate to offense." [80] As long as evidence is presented to substantiate the board's charge, poor classroom management can result in termination.[81]

Boards often cite a number of factors related to classroom performance in attempting to establish incompetency as a basis for dismissal. A Louisiana school board noted that repeated violations of rules in the administrative handbook, lack of control of students, and neglect of instructions of the principal as to grading procedures, lesson plans, and lunch counts constituted incompetence.[82] Similarly, in a New Mexico case, indicators of incompetency included deficiencies in grading and teaching methods, lack of pupil discipline, and failure to exhibit initiative.[83]

Courts examine dismissals based on incompetency to determine if the teacher received adequate prior notice of the need to improve performance. In Illinois, by law, the teacher must be given notice of deficiencies and provided an opportunity to correct them. To substantiate dismissal, the factors cited against a teacher must be irremediable. In one Illinois case, a school board advanced fourteen causes for dismissal, but the appellate court concluded that none was uncorrectable.[84] Causes in this case included irregular work assignments, leaving classes unattended, poor disciplinary procedures, and lack of pupil/teacher rapport. Although the teacher was informed that her performance was unacceptable, she was never told that it could result in dismissal. In another case, the Supreme Court of Illinois invalidated a teacher dismissal because of lack of warning of deficiencies.[85] The teacher had failed to submit lesson plans and attendance reports and to perform football duties adequately. In finding these causes remediable, the court held that the teacher should have been notified and given an opportunity to correct the problems. In contrast, where a school board provided notice and an opportunity for remediation, the dismissal of a teacher for incompetency was upheld by a Missouri appeals court.[86]

A wide range of issues has been litigated under incompetency. For example, in an Iowa case, a teacher was dismissed for incompetency because her students scored poorly on standardized basic skills tests.[87] In this case, the court noted that the board has responsibility for evaluation of teachers and that such evaluations are not subject to judicial review. A Louisiana appellate court upheld a teacher's dismissal for incompetency because the teacher required two eleven-year-old girls to write a vulgar, four-letter word one thousand times.[88] Inadequate supervision of the school newspaper and general improper appearance and dress justified a dismissal based on incompetency in a Wyoming case.[89] In a Pennsylvania case, physical confrontations with students on several occasions, along with inadequate handling of discipline problems and an unsatisfactory rating by the principal, resulted in dismissal for incompetency.[90]

## IMMORALITY

Immorality, the cause for dismissal most frequently cited in state statutes,[91] is subject to wide interpretation. In recent years, courts have become more restrictive in construing its meaning in dismissal cases and have required that a relationship be shown between the immoral conduct and fitness to teach. For a determination of the adverse impact of the conduct on the teacher's role in the classroom, the opinion of school personnel alone does not suffice. The judiciary frequently calls upon the expert testimony of psychiatrists and other specialists to assess potential harmful consequences.

Although ideas have been tempered somewhat since the early 1900s when female teachers were prohibited even from marrying, the teacher is still viewed as an exemplar whose conduct is influential in shaping the lives of young students. This high standard of expectation was noted by the Supreme Court of Pennsylvania.

It has always been the recognized duty of the teacher to conduct himself in such a way as to command the respect and good will of the community, though one result of the choice of a teacher's vocation may be to deprive him of the same freedom of action enjoyed by persons in other vocations. Educators have always regarded the example set by the teacher as of great importance . . . .[92]

Teachers have claimed that school policies regulating certain behavior and activities have impaired their constitutionally protected rights to privacy and free association. However, in balancing the interests of the teacher and the board, courts uniformly have held that classroom effectiveness is not measured solely on classroom performance.

Sexually related conduct between a teacher and student consistently has been held to constitute sufficient cause for dismissal. The Supreme Court of Colorado stated that "whenever a male teacher engages in sexually provocative or exploitative conduct with his minor female students a strong presumption of unfitness arises against the teacher."[93] Similarly, a Washington appeals court found that a male teacher's sexual relationship with a minor student justified dismissal.[94] The court declined to hold that an adverse effect on fitness to teach must be shown. Rather, the court concluded that when a teacher and a minor student are involved, the board may reasonably decide that such conduct is harmful to the school district. An Alabama teacher challenged his dismissal for sexual advances toward female students on the vagueness of the statutory causes of "immorality" and "other good and just cause."[95] He asserted that the law did not adequately warn a teacher as to what behavior would constitute an offense. The court acknowledged the lack of clarity in defining immorality but rejected the teacher's contention, reasoning that his behavior fell "squarely within the hard core of the statute's proscription."[96] The court noted that the teacher should have been aware that his conduct was improper, and the claim of vagueness or overbreadth could not invalidate his dismissal.

The teacher does not have the freedom to select any desired lifestyle if there is a potential for adverse impact on pupils. An Eighth Circuit Court of Appeals decision exemplifies the judiciary's reasoning in circumscribing the teacher's freedom outside the classroom.[97] In this case, an unmarried teacher was living with a boyfriend in a mobile home in close proximity to the school. School officials gave her several opportunities to alter her living arrangements, but she declined, claiming that this demand violated her rights to privacy and free association. The board, reluctant to use the statutory cause of "gross immorality," dismissed the teacher on the grounds of incompetency and immorality. In upholding the dismissal, the appellate court found that the conduct offended community mores and had an adverse effect on pupils. A strong connection was established between the teacher's actions and her effectiveness as a teacher.[98]

Community disapproval alone, however, is not sufficient to justify termination of a teacher's employment. In a Nebraska case, a middle-aged divorced teacher occasionally was visited by friends of her son.[99] Because of the lack of motel accommodations, these guests stayed in her apartment. One young man, who was a frequent visitor, spent one week with her while he attended classes in the district to complete certain college course requirements. Following his visit, the teacher was notified that her contract would not be renewed based on "conduct unbecoming a teacher." The Eighth Circuit Court of Appeals affirmed that the dismissal was arbitrary and capricious. The court rejected the board's assertion that the teacher's behavior exhibited a "strong potential for sexual misconduct." [100]

Some school boards have used immorality as the basis for dismissing unwed pregnant employees. Policies promulgated by boards regarding unwed pregnancies often conflict with the constitutional rights of teachers. In a Mississippi school district, a rule was adopted prohibiting employment of anyone who was an unwed parent.[101] The constitutionality of the policy was challenged by a teacher aide who was dismissed pursuant to the rule. Finding the rule unconstitutional, the Fifth Circuit Court of Appeals refused to equate giving birth to an illegitimate child with immorality. With such a presumption of immorality, the policy did not allow for consideration of the qualifications or character of each individual applicant. Additionally, the court in this case did not accept the board's supposition that unmarried parents contribute to increased pregnancies among students.

In an Alabama case, the immorality cause was applied to an unmarried, pregnant teacher in such a way that it violated her constitutional right to privacy.[102] Upon hearing rumors of the teacher's pregnancy, the superintendent contacted her doctor for verification and then instigated dismissal procedures. Throughout the proceedings, the board did not attempt to show that the plaintiff's condition affected fitness to teach, but relied solely on her pregnancy and unwed status as grounds for dismissal. The court, in overturning the board's decision, held the action to be an invasion of privacy.

An Arkansas teacher was successful in obtaining damages and reinstatement because the board had not informed employees that unwed pregnancy constituted grounds for dismissal.[103] The school board concluded in this situation that the teacher's pregnancy violated community standards and thus justified dismissal. However, the federal district court reasoned that without an explicit school board policy the plaintiff had no means of knowing that pregnancy out of wedlock would result in termination. A New Mexico school board cited immoral conduct as good and just cause for dismissal and identified unwed pregnancy as evidence of immoral conduct.[104] While the New Mexico Supreme Court did not address whether unwed pregnancy constituted "immoral conduct," the court nonetheless found the board's decision arbitrary and unreasonable based on the evidence presented. Facts considered by the court were that (1) at the time of dismissal five other unwed mothers were teaching in the school system, and (2) the teacher had been rated above average in performance, recommended for reemployment by the principal, and supported by the community for continued employment.

Whether an unwed pregnancy is sufficient to justify termination will depend on harm to the pupils, other teachers, and the school itself.[105] If such adverse impact can be demonstrated, then a basis for dismissal can be established. A Nebraska federal district court concluded that there was "a rational connection between the plaintiff's pregnancy out of wedlock and the school board's interest in conserving marital values when acts probably destructive of those values are revealed . . . in the classroom. . . ."[106] Thus, the court upheld the discharge of the pregnant, unwed teacher.

With increased attention being focused on individual rights, the issue of teacher homosexuality has been the focal point in several controversial dismissal cases. Courts have confronted the question of whether homosexuality *per se* is evidence of unfitness to teach, or whether it must be shown that teaching effectiveness has been impaired. Diversity is found in judicial opinion among the courts that have addressed this issue. According to the Supreme Court of California, immoral or unprofessional conduct or moral turpitude must be related to unfitness to teach.[107] Consequently, the school board does not possess the right to dismiss an employee simply because it does not approve of a particular private lifestyle.[108] In *Morrison v. State Board of Education,* where a male teacher was involved in a limited one-week relationship with another male, the California court enumerated criteria for evaluating the fitness of a teacher.[109] The court stated:

> The board may consider such matters as the likelihood that the conduct may have adversely affected students or fellow teachers, the degree of such adversity anticipated, the proximity or remoteness of time of the conduct, the type of teaching certificate held by the party involved, the extenuating or aggravating circumstances, if any, surrounding the conduct, the likelihood of the recurrence of the questioned conduct, and the

extent to which disciplinary action may inflict an adverse impact or chilling effect upon the constitutional rights of the teacher involved or other teachers.[110]

The Supreme Court of California subsequently relied on the *Morrison* criteria in a case in which a teacher's homosexual solicitation of a police officer in a public restroom resulted in charges of immoral conduct and unfitness to teach.[111] Evidence of unfitness was not found in that (1) the act did not come to the attention of the public, students, or other teachers, (2) it was an isolated incident, and (3) there was no threat to students.[112]

Publicity and notoriety are often critical factors in determining the legality of an employer's action in dealing with homosexual conduct of employees. In a case where an offer to a male librarian of the position of division head was rescinded after he applied for a marriage license with another male, the Eighth Circuit Court of Appeals differentiated between pursuing a particular lifestyle clandestinely and "pursuing an activist role in implementing . . . unconventional ideas." [113] No duty is imposed on an employer when the employee seeks employment "on his own terms." Approaching the issue of notoriety from the teacher's right to freedom of speech, the Fourth Circuit Court of Appeals found the right to make public statements regarding homosexuality to newspapers and television to be a protected right that could not be used as a basis for reassignment from a classroom to an administrative position.[114] However, because the teacher falsified his job application, relief was barred.

The Supreme Court of Washington held that public knowledge of a teacher's homosexuality could impair teaching effectiveness. In *Gaylord v. Tacoma School District Number 10,* the vice principal was informed by a former high school student of a male teacher's homosexual conduct.[115] Upon being confronted by the vice principal, the teacher admitted his homosexuality. He was discharged shortly thereafter on the ground of being a known homosexual. The lower court found the discharge to be proper on immorality grounds. The state supreme court accepted the lower court's conclusion that "the knowledge thereof would and did impair his efficiency as a teacher with resulting injury to the school had he not been discharged." [116] Refusal of the United States Supreme Court to grant *certiorari* in *Gaylord* has left widely varying standards for judging teacher conduct in this area.

## INSUBORDINATION

Insubordination, another frequently cited cause for dismissal,[117] is the willful disregard for or refusal to obey school regulations and official orders. The *Kentucky Revised Statute* defines insubordination as

. . . including but not limited to (1) violation of lawful rules and regulations established by the local board of education for the operation of schools, and (2) refusal to recognize or obey the authority of the superintendent, principal or any other supervisory personnel of the board in the performance of their duties.[118]

With the plethora of regulations promulgated by school districts, wide diversity is found in types of behavior adjudicated as insubordination. Dismissals based on insubordination have been upheld in cases involving refusal to shave a beard, use of excessive physical punishment, failure to obtain a master's degree, unwillingness to cooperate with superiors, and numerous other actions. Since conduct is measured against the existence of a rule or policy, insubordination is more readily documented by a school board, and thus is more supportable, than most other legal causes.

Numerous dismissal cases involving insubordination have resulted from the inappropriate use of corporal punishment. If the school board has adopted policies prohibiting corporal punishment or prescribing procedures for its administration, teachers must strictly adhere to board requirements. Dismissal of an Illinois teacher was upheld because he failed to follow prescribed procedures which specified that a teacher must explain the reasons for the punishment to the child and must have another adult present while administering corporal punishment.[119] Shaking students and shoving them into chairs and the wall, along with general physical attacks on students, exceeded an Oregon board policy which limited physical discipline to the use of a paddle.[120] Administering physical punishment on five occasions over a two-year period in opposition to an established policy was held to constitute "willful and persistent violation" of regulations in a Missouri school district.[121] In contrast to the preceding cases, the Colorado Supreme Court invalidated a teacher's dismissal for insubordination in connection with excessive use of corporal punishment because the school board had not adopted any regulations pertaining to this disciplinary technique.[122]

Although corporal punishment may be allowable under state law, violation of a local board policy forbidding its use still constitutes grounds for dismissal as insubordination. A Philadelphia teacher who administered corporal punishment on several different occasions was warned that continued use could result in dismissal.[123] Challenging the board policy, the teacher contended that corporal punishment was legally permissible under state law. The court affirmed the board's prerogative to determine whether corporal punishment would be allowed, and concluded from the evidence that the teacher's action showed intentional disregard for school regulations.[124]

As in many other dismissal cases, courts have examined corporal punishment offenses for prior admonishment that actions might result in dismissal. A New York teacher's discharge was upheld because he continued to use corporal punishment after repeated warnings to cease.[125] On the other hand, insubordination could not be established in a North Carolina case where the teacher discontinued inappropriate punishment after being warned of the potential consequences.[126]

Dismissals for insubordination also have resulted from the failure of teachers to abide by grooming regulations.[127] Generally, in the area of personal appearance, boards can adopt rules and regulations that are necessary for the smooth operation of the school as long as there is a rational basis for the action.[128] To support dismissal for insubordination, there must be a policy or rule prohibiting the practice.[129] An unwritten rule of a particular administrator was found to be arbitrary and insufficient as a basis for dismissing a teacher for wearing a moustache.[130] No justification was provided for the rule; that is, no evidence was introduced to show that moustaches had caused or would cause disruption.

Insubordination charges often have arisen from conflicts within the administrator/teacher relationship. For example, a teacher cannot refuse to meet with a principal to discuss classroom matters. A Florida teacher's discharge was upheld for refusal to meet with her principal to discuss leaving her class unattended.[131] In another case, insubordination was established because a teacher allowed boycotting students to attend classes in violation of a school policy and refused to attend two football games, as all male teachers were required to do.[132] Where a teacher's remarks to an unauthorized assembly of students encouraged disobedience of the principal's orders, the Sixth Circuit Court of Appeals upheld the teacher's dismissal based on insubordination.[133] In a Minnesota case, a teacher's continuous refusal to complete program evaluation forms resulted in insubordination charges.[134] The Minnesota Supreme Court, upholding the dismissal, defined insubordination as "constant or continuing intentional refusal to obey a direct or implied order, reasonable in nature, and given by and with proper authority."[135] The Wyoming Supreme Court presented an opposing view on whether repeated refusals to obey orders were necessary to justify dismissal.[136] The court concluded that the dismissal of a teacher who refused a split assignment between two schools was proper. In the court's opinion, repeated refusals were unnecessary if other elements of insubordination were present, such as reasonableness of the order and direct refusal to obey. Similarly, a Kansas teacher's dismissal was sustained for a one-time refusal to obey the superintendent's direct order to supervise recess.[137]

Failure to abide by residency requirements established by the school board can also result in dismissal for insubordination. The Cincinnati, Ohio school district's policy requiring school employees to reside within the district boundaries was upheld by the Sixth Circuit Court of Appeals as constitutional, and hence the refusal to abide by the requirement could be the basis for dismissal.[138] However, a federal district court in Kansas found no reasonable basis for such a regulation and thus concluded that the school board's residency requirement violated the teacher's right to equal protection of the laws.[139]

## OTHER CAUSES

Among other causes that have been adjudicated in dismissal actions are neglect of duty, unprofessional conduct, unfitness to teach, and other good and just cause. Each cause is briefly discussed below in relation to conduct that may justify termination under various state laws.

**Neglect of Duty.** Neglect of duty arises when a teacher fails to carry out assigned duties. This may involve an intentional omission or may result from ineffectual performance. In a Colorado case, neglect of duty was found when a teacher was absent from class for observance of certain holy days after having been denied permission for leave.[140] A North Carolina appellate court concluded that a teacher's lack of control of pupils constituted neglect of duty.[141] However, the West Virginia Supreme Court held that missing one parent-teacher conference was not sufficient to justify dismissal based on neglect of duty.[142]

As noted earlier, a tenured teacher can be dismissed only for "just cause." The Supreme Court of Nebraska recently dealt with the issue of what constitutes "just cause" in connection with neglect of duty.[143] Under Nebraska law, just cause is defined as incompetency, neglect of duty, unprofessional conduct, insubordination, immorality, physical or mental incapacity, or other conduct which interferes substantially with performance. The Nebraska high court examined charges of neglect of duty and incompetency where a teacher had failed on several occasions to perform certain duties, and at other times had not performed duties competently. Evidence revealed that the teacher had not violated any administrative orders or school laws, had received good evaluations (only three of twenty categories had been noted as needing improvement), and had been recommended for retention by administrators. In the opinion of the court, the facts did not support just cause for dismissal. The court cautioned that in evaluating a teacher's performance "incompetency or neglect of duty [is] not measured in a vacuum nor against a standard of perfection, but, instead, must be measured against the standard required of others performing the same or similar duties." [144] It was not demonstrated that the teacher's performance was below that expected of other teachers in similar positions.

The United States Supreme Court recently upheld the dismissal of an Oklahoma teacher for "willful neglect of duty" in failing to comply with the school board's continuing education requirement.[145] For a period of time, lack of compliance was dealt with through denial of salary increases. Upon enactment of a law requiring salary increases for all teachers, the board notified teachers that noncompliance with the requirement would result in termination. Affirming the board's action, the Supreme Court found the sanction of dismissal to be "rationally related" to the board's objective of improving its teaching force through continuing education requirements.

**Unprofessional Conduct.** Approximately fourteen states identify either unprofessional conduct or conduct unbecoming a teacher as a cause for dismissal.[146] A teacher's activities both inside and outside of school can be used to establish grounds for discharge. Similarity of facts is often found among dismissals for unprofessional conduct, neglect of duty, and unfitness to teach. For instance, a New York teacher was dismissed for unprofessional conduct for being absent after having been denied permission for a leave, whereas the Colorado teacher noted above was charged with neglect of duty.[147] In a case similar to the New York case, a Missouri teacher's absences also resulted in dismissal for unprofessional conduct,[148] whereas a Maine school board classified a teacher's unauthorized absences as unfitness to teach.[149] It must be remembered that causes for dismissal are usually identified in statute, but are defined through case law and various administrative rulings in individual states. Consequently, there are wide variances in the meaning of the same legal cause.

Courts have upheld dismissals for unprofessional conduct based on a number of grounds, such as arrest for alleged shoplifting,[150] failure of a teacher's children to attend school in violation of the compulsory attendance law,[151] refusal to attend faculty in-service meetings and to supervise children during recess duty,[152] participation in a demonstration,[153] and inappropriate discipline.[154] As in incompetency cases, courts often require prior warning that the behavior may result in dismissal.[155]

**Unfitness to Teach.** Unfitness to teach covers a wide array of teacher behavior. An Illinois appellate court defined unfitness as "conduct detrimental to the operation of the school." [156] Under this definition, the court held that improper sexual conduct toward students constituted unfitness. The question of incapacity as unfitness was addressed by a New Jersey court.[157] In this case, a male teacher who underwent a sex change operation was dismissed on the ground that retention would result in psychological harm to students. The court concluded that the teacher's presence could potentially result in emotional harm to students, and therefore dismissal was appropriate. The judiciary has recognized that a determination of fitness or capacity must extend beyond actual classroom performance.

Two recent decisions from the Supreme Court of Maine dealt with dismissals for one-time incidents that allegedly affected fitness to teach. In the first case, a teacher who was a licensed gunsmith inadvertently brought a gun and ammunition to school in his jacket.[158] The gun was stolen from his room but later returned. The school board initiated dismissal proceedings for "grave lack of judgment." Overturning the board action, the court held that one isolated incident does not represent such "moral impropriety, professional incompetence, or unsuitability" as to warrant unfitness to teach.[159] The second case involved a teacher striking a student across the face with his hand during a voluntary basketball game.[160] The blow was severe, causing the loss of one tooth, damage to another, and extensive bruises. In this case, as opposed to the first case, the court concluded that the single incident was sufficient to justify dismissal because of its direct impact on the teacher's effectiveness as a coach. Dismissals for one-time incidents, regardless of the grounds, are always scrutinized closely by the courts.

A California appeals court addressed the question of whether a teacher's false bomb threat, *per se,* justified dismissal for unfitness to teach.[161] During a teacher's strike, the plaintiff teacher had falsely reported that a bomb had been planted in the intermediate school. The teacher's motive was to challenge what he believed to be inflated attendance reports by bringing public attention to the actual number of students in school. The appellate court assessed the teacher's fitness in light of such factors as the effect of the unlawful action on students and the likelihood of its recurrence.[162] Noting that the crime itself was only one factor to be considered in determining fitness, the court concluded that the teacher should be retained in his position.

Rather than being dismissed for unfitness to teach, under some state laws a teacher may be placed on an involuntary leave of absence when found to be medically unfit to teach. New York law provides that the superintendent of schools, upon recommendation of a building principal, may require a tenured teacher to submit to a medical examination to determine mental fitness to teach.[163] According to the New York courts, this law also empowers a school board to place a teacher on involuntary leave of absence without a hearing. However, the Second Circuit Court of Appeals has recognized that such action by the school board must be followed by a fair postsuspension hearing, as suspended teachers do not relinquish their procedural due process rights.[164]

**Other Good and Just Cause.** Not unexpectedly, "other good and just cause" often has been challenged as vague and overbroad. Courts have been faced with the task of determining whether the phrase's meaning is limited to the enumerated grounds or whether it is a separate, expanded cause. An Indiana appellate court interpreted it as permitting termination for reasons other than those specified in the tenure law, if evidence indicated that the board's decision was based on "good cause."[165] As such, dismissal of a teacher convicted of a misdemeanor was upheld even though the teacher had no prior indication that such conduct was sufficient cause.

The Second Circuit Court of Appeals found "other due and sufficient cause" to be

> . . . appropriate in an area such as discipline of teachers, where a myriad of uncontemplated situations may arise and it is not reasonable to require a legislature to elucidate in advance every act that requires sanction. Some general "catch-all" phrase may be incorporated to ensure that the legislature's inability to detail all matters meant to be proscribed does not permit clearly improper conduct to go uncorrected.[166]

The appellate court declined to rule on the vagueness of "other due and sufficient cause," but rather noted that courts generally assess the teacher's conduct in relation to the statutory grounds for dismissal.[167] That is, if the specific behavior is sufficiently related to the causes specified in state law, it is assumed that the teacher should have reasonably known that the conduct was improper. In this case, where a teacher repeatedly humiliated and harassed students (and school administrators had discussed the problem with him), the court concluded that the teacher was aware of the impropriety of his conduct.

## REDUCTION IN FORCE

A teacher must be provided with a hearing when released because of budget cuts or declining enrollment if a property interest in employment can be established.[168] The Pennsylvania Commonwealth Court has held that a hearing must be provided to assure the teacher (1) that termination is for reasons specified by law, and (2) that the board followed the correct statutory procedures in selecting the teacher for discharge.[169] Adopting an opposing stance, the Michigan Court of Appeals found no need for a hearing over staff reductions, because there were no charges to refute.[170] The court emphasized that the law protected the released teacher, who, subject to qualifications, was entitled to be hired for the next vacancy.

If a statute exists for teacher layoffs, it must be followed.[171] One of the protections most frequently found is the requirement that release be based on seniority.[172] In general, a tenured teacher must be retained rather than a nontenured teacher if both are qualified to fill the same position.[173] Oregon statutes require that both legal qualifications and seniority be considered; a teacher lacking legal qualifications and seniority would not be permitted to teach while a permanent, legally qualified teacher with more seniority was dismissed.[174] Along with seniority, merit rating systems are often included in the determination of reductions.[175] Pennsylvania uses a combination of ratings and seniority; ratings are the primary determinant unless no substantial difference exists in ratings, and then seniority becomes the basis for layoffs.[176]

Preference in reemployment is often given to the teacher who is dismissed because of unavoidable staff reductions.[177] However, a teacher must be certified for the available position. A French teacher whose tenure was in the secondary academic area was found to be unqualified to teach English or science because of lack of certification in those subjects.[178] Although statutes often require that a teacher be appointed to the first vacancy for which certified and qualified, courts have held that reappointment still is at the board's discretion. The terms certified and qualified are not synonymous. A Michigan appeals court recognized that a teacher could be certified in an area but not necessarily qualified in the opinion of the board.[179]

SUMMARY OF DISMISSAL GROUNDS

Since legal causes for dismissal vary from state to state, it is incumbent on the teacher to become familiar with an individual state's statutory provisions. Many statutes are published in annotated editions that provide summary statements of legal decisions interpreting the law. This enables the reader to more fully define the meaning of identified state causes, such as incompetency or neglect of duty. As noted, specific grounds are not discrete among states, and identical causes may encompass disparate behavior.

## REMEDIES FOR WRONGFUL DISMISSALS

A teacher who has been improperly dismissed may be entitled to reinstatement, damages, and/or attorneys' fees. Specific remedies vary according to statutory provisions and the discretionary power of the courts. For example, whereas the failure to provide timely notice in a teacher nonrenewal may result in reinstatement and tenure in one state, another state may provide only reinstatement and a one-year extension of the probationary period.

DAMAGES

As noted in Chapter 3, court decisions over the past several years have increased the potential for teachers to recover monetary damages when their civil rights have been violated. This is partly because school districts are now viewed as "persons" under Section 1983 of the Civil Rights Act of 1871, and thus can be sued directly for official actions that deprive an individual of a constitutional right. Other factors that have enhanced the possibility for recovery of damages have been determinations that school districts cannot plead good faith immunity and, in most states, are not an extension or arm of the state subject to eleventh amendment immunity.[180]

Additionally, school board members and administrators can be sued in their individual capacities. Such individuals, however, are protected by immunity if they have acted in good faith.

Damages may include back pay, interest on back pay, and compensatory or punitive amounts. The Tenth Circuit Court of Appeals awarded $33,000 in compensatory damages to a teacher who had not been renewed for constitutionally impermissible reasons.[181] The Ninth Circuit Court of Appeals found payment of the balance due under a contract and an additional one-half year's salary adequate compensation when a teacher was wrongfully dismissed for admitted homosexuality.[182] The court, however, declined to order reinstatement. In another Ninth Circuit case, a teacher who was dismissed on the basis of protected speech was awarded $50,000 in damages.[183]

REINSTATEMENT

Whether or not reinstatement is ordered by a court as a remedy for school board action will depend on the protected interest involved and the discretion of the court, unless specific provisions are included in state law. If a tenured teacher is unjustly dismissed, the property interest gives rise to an expectation of reemployment. Reinstatement in such instances is usually the appropriate remedy. A nontenured teacher, wrongfully dismissed during the contract period, is normally only entitled to damages, not reinstatement. Again, the court remedy will depend on the protected interest.

A Delaware district court held that if a liberty interest is involved in dismissal, the proper remedy is an opportunity to clear one's name, not reinstatement.[184] In this case, a nontenured teacher was dismissed after her third year of employment without being provided procedural due process. Because of unsupported statements made by the superintendent, it was established that a liberty interest was impaired, and the court ordered a hearing to allow the teacher to clear her name.

The failure to comply with statutory procedures in nonrenewals and dismissals may result in reinstatement. When statutory dates are specified for notice of nonrenewal, failure to strictly comply with the deadline provides grounds for reinstatement of the teacher. Courts may interpret this as continued employment for an additional year,[185] or reinstatement with tenure if nonrenewal occurs at the end of the probationary period.[186] In contrast to the remedy for lack of proper notice, the remedy for failure to provide a required hearing is generally remand for a hearing, not reinstatement.[187]

ATTORNEYS' FEES

Unless provided by state or federal laws, attorneys' fees are not assured the teacher who prevails in challenging improper board action. Courts in some states without statutory provisions have ruled that an equitable remedy includes fees, but usually courts rely on statutory authorization for such awards.

In 1975, the Supreme Court specifically held that "the prevailing litigant is ordinarily not entitled to collect a reasonable attorney's fee from the loser." [188] Congress responded to the Court's statement on attorneys' fees by enacting the Civil Rights Attorneys' Fees Awards Act in 1976.[189] This law gives the federal courts discretion to award attorneys' fees to prevailing parties in civil rights suits. Previously Congress had provided for attorneys' fees only under Title VII of the Civil Rights Act of 1964, but the attorneys' fees act extends similar rights to Section 1983 suits in order to encourage private actions under civil rights laws.[190] Congress viewed the disallowance of attorneys' fees as a significant bar to individuals who might seek judicial relief. In congressional debate concerning attorneys' fees, it was stated that "private citizens must be given not only the rights to go to court, but also the legal resources. If the citizen does not have the resources, his day in court is denied him." [191]

To be awarded attorneys' fees, the teacher must be the prevailing party; that is, damages or some form of equitable relief must be granted to the teacher. Without an award of damages, the teacher is not considered the prevailing party, and attorneys' fees are denied.[192] Courts base the amount of attorneys' fees to be awarded on time involved, current hourly rates, skill required, uniqueness of the issue, statutory provisions, and other appropriate considerations.

Although it has been established that the plaintiff who prevails in a civil rights suit may, at the court's discretion, be entitled to attorneys' fees, the same standard is not applied to defendants. When a plaintiff teacher is awarded attorneys' fees, the assessment is against a party who has violated a federal law. Different criteria must be applied when a prevailing defendant seeks attorneys' fees. The Supreme Court has held that such fees cannot be imposed on a plaintiff unless the claim was "frivolous, unreasonable, or groundless." [193]

## CONCLUSION

An area of general concern among all teachers is employment security. Through state laws and the Federal Constitution, extensive safeguards exist to prevent arbitrary or capricious actions of school officials. Most states have adopted teacher tenure laws that precisely delineate teachers' employment rights in termination proceedings. Additionally, in the abscence of specific state guarantees, the fourteenth amendment ensures that a teacher will be afforded procedural due process when a property or liberty interest exists in employment. Legal decisions, interpreting both state and federal rights in dismissal actions, have established broad guidelines as to when due process is required and the types of procedures that must be provided. Generalizations applicable to teacher employment termination are enumerated below.

1. A teacher is entitled to procedural due process if dismissal action impairs a property or liberty interest.
2. Due process requires, at a minimum, that a teacher be notified of charges and provided with an opportunity for a hearing.
3. Full procedural rights in a dismissal hearing include representation by counsel, examination and cross-examination of witnesses, and a record of the proceedings; however, formal trial procedures are not required.
4. An adequate notice of dismissal must adhere to statutory deadlines, follow designated form, allow the teacher time to prepare for a hearing, and specify charges.
5. Lack of proper notice can result in reinstatement of the teacher.
6. The school board is considered an impartial hearing tribunal unless bias of its members can be clearly established.
7. The burden of proof is placed on the school board to introduce sufficient evidence to support a teacher's dismissal.
8. Courts generally have held that probationary employment does not involve a property interest, except within the contract period.
9. A probationary teacher may establish a liberty interest, and thus entitlement to a hearing, if nonrenewal imposes a stigma or forecloses opportunities for future employment.
10. Tenure status, defined by state law, confers upon teachers a property interest in continued employment, and tenured teachers can be dismissed only for cause.
11. Cause for dismissal varies extensively among the states, but may include such grounds as incompetency, neglect of duty, immorality, insubordination, unprofessional conduct, and other good and just cause.
12. Incompetency is generally defined in relation to classroom performance—classroom management, teaching methods, grading, pupil/teacher relationships, and general attitude.
13. Immoral conduct can result in dismissal when a relationship is established between the conduct and the teacher's effectiveness in the school system.
14. Dismissal for insubordination is based on the refusal to follow school regulations and policies.
15. Declining enrollment and financial exigencies constitute adequate cause for dismissal of tenured teachers.
16. An improper dismissal can result in an award of damages, reinstatement, and/or attorneys' fees.

# NOTES

1. Adler v. Board of Educ., 342 U.S. 485, 493 (1952).
2. Board of Regents v. Roth, 408 U.S. 564 (1972).
3. *Id.* at 577.
4. *Id.* at 573.
5. 16 Am. Jr. 2d § 545.
6. Thomas J. Flygare, *The Legal Rights of Teachers* (Bloomington, Ind.: Phi Delta Kappa, 1976), pp. 20–21.
7. William Van Alystyne, "The Constitutional Rights of Teachers and Professors," *Duke Law Journal*, No. 5, 1970, pp. 864–65.
8. Lombardo v. Board of Educ. of School Dist. No. 27 Cook County, 241 N.E.2d 495 (Ill. App. 1968).
9. Virginia D. Nordin, "Employees," *The Yearbook of School Law 1977*, ed. Philip K. Piele (Topeka, Kan.: National Organization on Legal Problems in Education, 1977), p. 189.
10. Leroy J. Peterson, Richard A. Rossmiller, and Marlin M. Volz, *The Law and Public School Operation* (New York: Harper & Row, 1978), p. 447.
11. Alexander v. School Dist. No. 17 of Thurston City, 248 N.W.2d 335 (Neb. 1976); Williams v. School Dist. No. 40 of Gila County, 417 P.2d 376 (Ariz. App. 1966).
12. Glover v. Board of Educ. of Macon Community Unit Dist. No. 5, 340 N.E.2d 4 (Ill. 1975).
13. Kruse v. Board of Directors of Lamoni Community School Dist., 231 N.W.2d 626 (Iowa 1975).
14. Neal v. Board of Educ., School Dist. No. 189, 371 N.E.2d 869 (Ill. App. 1977); Perry v. Independent School Dist. No. 696, 210 N.W.2d 283 (Minn. 1973).
15. Powell v. Board of Trustees of Crook County School Dist. No. 1, 550 P.2d 1112 (Wyo. 1976).
16. Illinois Educ. Ass'n Local Community High School Dist. 218 v. Board of Educ. of School Dist. 218, 340 N.E.2d 7 (Ill. 1975).
17. Beattie v. Roberts, 436 F.2d 747 (1st Cir. 1971).
18. State *ex rel.* Peake v. Board of Educ. of South Point Local School Dist., 339 N.E.2d 249 (Ohio 1975).
19. School Dist. No. 4, Lincoln County v. Colburg, 547 P.2d 84 (Mont. 1976).
20. McDonald v. East Jasper County Dist., 351 So. 2d 531 (Miss. 1977).
21. Board of Trustees v. Superintendent of Public Instruction, 557 P.2d 1048 (Mont. 1976).
22. Gillett v. Unified School Dist. No. 276 Jewell County, 605 P.2d 105 (Kan. 1980).
23. Boyce v. Alexis I. duPont School Dist., 341 F. Supp. 678 (D. Del. 1972); Board of Trustees of Nogales Elementary School Dist. v. Cartier, 559 P.2d 216 (Ariz. App. 1977).
24. Weckerly v. Mona Shores Bd. of Educ., 202 N.W.2d 777 (Mich. 1972). *See also* Lipka v. Brown City Community Schools, 271 N.W.2d 771 (Mich. 1978).

25. *Id.*, 202 N.W.2d 777.
26. *Id.* at 780.
27. Boyce v. Alexis I. duPont School Dist., 341 F. Supp. 678 (D. Del. 1972).
28. Valter v. Orchard Farm Dist., 541 S.W.2d 550 (Mo. 1976); Ahern v. Board of Educ. of School Dist. of Grand Island, 456 F.2d 399 (8th Cir. 1972); Cooley v. Board of Educ. of Forrest City School Dist., 453 F.2d 282 (8th Cir. 1972).
29. Brouillette v. Board of Directors of Merged Area IX, 519 F.2d 126, 128 (8th Cir. 1975).
30. Knox County Bd. of Educ. v. Willis, 405 S.W.2d 952 (Ky. 1966).
31. Callahan v. Price, 505 F.2d 83, 87 (5th Cir. 1974).
32. Ferguson v. Thomas, 430 F.2d 852, 856 (5th Cir. 1970).
33. Valter v. Orchard Farm School Dist., 541 S.W.2d 550 (Mo. 1976).
34. Hoffman v. Jannarone, 401 F. Supp. 1095 (D. N.J. 1975).
35. Swab v. Cedar Rapids Community School Dist., 494 F.2d 353 (8th Cir. 1974).
36. Naus v. Joint School Dist. No. 1 of the City of Sheboygan Falls, 250 N.W.2d 725 (Wis. 1977).
37. 426 U.S. 482 (1976).
38. *Id.* at 497.
39. Keith v. Community School Dist. of Wilton, 262 N.W.2d 249 (Iowa 1978).
40. *Id.* at 260.
41. Toups v. Authement, 496 F.2d 700 (5th Cir. 1974).
42. Sanders v. Board of Educ., 263 N.W.2d 461 (Neb. 1978).
43. *Id.*
44. Catino v. Board of Educ. of the Town of Hamden, 389 A.2d 754 (Conn. 1978). According to statutory provisions, an impartial hearing panel can be requested by either the teacher or the board. The panel in this case consisted of three persons—one selected by the teacher, one selected by the board, and one selected by the other two panel members.
45. *Id.* at 755.
46. Shirley B. Neill and Jerry Curtis, *Staff Dismissal: Problems and Solutions* (Sacramento, Cal.: American Association of School Administrators, 1978), p. 37.
47. 408 U.S. 564 (1972).
48. 408 U.S. 593 (1972).
49. Board of Regents v. Roth, 408 U.S. 564, 573 (1972).
50. *Id.*
51. *Id.* at 575.
52. *Id.* at 577.
53. 408 U.S. 593 (1972).
54. *Id.* at 600.
55. Board of Regents v. Roth, 408 U.S. 564, 572 (1972).
56. 426 U.S. 341 (1976).
57. *Id.* at 345.
58. Longarzo v. Anker, 578 F.2d 469 (2d Cir. 1978); Gentile v. Wallen, 562 F.2d 193 (2d Cir. 1977); Buhr v. Buffalo Public School Dist., No.

38, 509 F.2d 1196 (8th Cir. 1974); Turner v. Board of Trustees, Calexico Unified School Dist., 548 P.2d 1115 (Cal. 1976); Abbott v. Board of Educ. of Nebo School Dist., 558 P.2d 1307 (Utah 1976).
59. Ryan v. Aurora County Bd. of Educ., 540 F.2d 222 (6th Cir. 1976).
60. New Castle–Gunning Bedford Educ. Ass'n v. Board of Educ. of New Castle–Gunning Bedford, 421 F. Supp. 960 (D. Del. 1976).
61. Board of Regents v. Roth, 408 U.S. 564, 572 (1972).
62. Paul v. Davis, 424 U.S. 693 (1976).
63. *Id.* at 706.
64. *See* text with note 75, Chapter 7, for a discussion of defamation.
65. Moore v. Otero, 557 F.2d 435, 437 (5th Cir. 1977).
66. *Id. See also* Sullivan v. Brown, 544 F.2d 279, 283 (6th Cir. 1976); Danno v. Peterson, 421 F. Supp. 950, 954 (N.D. Ill. 1976).
67. Dennis v. S&S Consolidated Rural High School Dist., 577 F.2d 338 (5th Cir. 1978). *See also* Colaizzi v. Walker, 542 F.2d 969 (7th Cir. 1976), where a discharge accompanied by publication of defamatory remarks about the teacher resulted in a liberty deprivation necessitating due process.
68. Codd v. Velger, 429 U.S. 624, 627–28 (1977).
69. Peterson, Rossmiller, and Volz, *The Law and Public School Operation,* p. 446.
70. 78 CJS § 202.
71. Floyd G. Delon, *Legal Controls on Teacher Conduct: Teacher Discipline* (Topeka, Kan.: National Organization on Legal Problems in Education, 1977), p. 12.
72. Cal. [Education Reorganized] Code § 44932.
73. Ill. Ann. Stat. 122 § 10-22.4.
74. Me. Rev. Stat. 20 § 477.
75. Henry Black, *Black's Law Dictionary,* 4th ed. (St. Paul, Minn.: West Publishing Company, 1968), p. 906.
76. 6 A.2d 866 (Pa. 1939).
77. Beilan v. Board of Public Educ. of Philadelphia, 357 U.S. 399 (1958).
78. *Id.* at 408.
79. Hatta v. Board of Educ., Union Endicott Central School Dist., Broome County, 394 N.Y.S.2d 301 (App. Div. 1977).
80. Kinsella v. Board of Educ. of Central School Dist. No. 7, 407 N.Y.S.2d 78 (App. Div. 1978).
81. *See* Phillips v. Board of Educ. of Smyrna School Dist., 330 A.2d 151 (Del. Sup. 1974); Wickersham v. New Mexico State Bd. of Educ. 464 P.2d 918 (N.M. App. 1970).
82. Mims v. West Baton Rouge Parish School Bd., 315 So. 2d 349 (La. App. 1975).
83. Wickersham v. New Mexico State Bd. of Educ., 464 P.2d 918 (N.M. App. 1970).
84. Gilliland v. Board of Educ. of Pleasant View Consolidated School Dist., 343 N.E.2d 704 (Ill. App. 1976).
85. Aulwurm v. Board of Educ. of Murphysboro Community Unit School Dist. No. 186, 367 N.E.2d 1337 (Ill. 1977).

86. Condor v. Board of Directors of Windsor School, Community School Dist. No. 1, 567 S.W.2d 377 (Mo. App. 1978).
87. Scheelhaase v. Woodbury Central Community School Dist., 488 F.2d 237 (8th Cir. 1973), *cert. denied*, 417 U.S. 969 (1974).
88. Celestine v. Lafayette Parish School Bd., 284 So. 2d 650 (La. App. 1973).
89. Jergeson v. Board of Trustees of School Dist. No. 7, 476 P.2d 481 (Wyo. 1970).
90. Board of Public Education of the School Dist. of Pittsburgh v. Pyle, 390 A.2d 904 (Pa. Commw. 1978).
91. *See* Table 1.
92. Horosko v. School Dist. of Mt. Pleasant, 6 A.2d 866, 868 (Pa. 1939).
93. Weissman v. Board of Educ. of Jefferson County School Dist., 547 P.2d 1267 (Colo. 1976).
94. Denton v. South Kitsap School Dist. No. 402, 516 P.2d 1080 (Wash. App. 1973).
95. Kilpatrick v. Wright, 437 F. Supp. 397 (M.D. Ala. 1977).
96. *Id.* at 399.
97. Sullivan v. Meade Independent School Dist. No. 101, 530 F.2d 799 (8th Cir. 1976). *See also* Dominy v. Mays, 257 S.E.2d 317 (Ga. App. 1979). A tenured teacher's arrest and plea of guilty to possession of marijuana and cocaine were sufficient for the school board to dismiss the teacher for "immorality" under the Georgia statutory code.
98. It should be noted that a Missouri federal district court reached an opposite conclusion and enjoined a school board from dismissing a teacher for living with her boyfriend. Evidence was not presented in this case to document that the teacher's living arrangement impaired her teaching effectiveness. Thompson v. Southwest School Dist., 483 F. Supp. 1170 (W.D. Mo. 1980).
99. Fisher v. Snyder, 476 F.2d 375 (8th Cir. 1973).
100. *Id.* at 377.
101. Andrews v. Drew Municipal Separate School Dist., 507 F.2d 611 (5th Cir. 1975).
102. Drake v. Covington County Bd. of Educ., 371 F. Supp. 974 (M.D. Ala. 1974).
103. Cochran v. Chidester School Dist. of Ouachita County, Arkansas, 456 F. Supp. 390 (W.D. Ark. 1978).
104. New Mexico State Bd. of Educ. v. Stoudt, 571 P.2d 1186 (N.M. 1977).
105. Reinhardt v. Board of Educ. of Alton Community Unit School Dist. No. 11, 311 N.E.2d 710 (Ill. App. 1974).
106. Brown v. Bathke, 416 F. Supp. 1194, 1198 (D. Neb. 1976). Upon appeal to the Eighth Circuit Court of Appeals, damages were awarded in this case because of the lack of a predetermination hearing, 566 F.2d 588 (8th Cir. 1977).
107. Morrison v. State Bd. of Educ., 461 P.2d 375 (Cal. 1969).
108. *Id.* at 382.
109. *Id.* at 386. It should be noted that this case dealt with the revocation of a male teacher's certificate because of homosexual conduct. Although it

was not a dismissal case, the criteria listed have been relied on in dismissals for immorality.

110. *Id.*

111. Board of Educ. of Long Beach v. Jack M., 566 P.2d 602 (Cal. 1977).

112. *Id.* at 605.

113. McConnell v. Anderson, 451 F.2d 193, 196 (8th Cir. 1971).

114. Acanfora v. Board of Educ. of Montgomery County, 491 F.2d 498 (4th Cir. 1974).

115. 559 P.2d 1340 (Wash. 1977), *cert. denied*, 434 U.S. 879 (1977).

116. *Id.* at 1346.

117. Delon, *Legal Controls on Teacher Conduct*, p. 36.

118. Ky. Rev. Stat. § 161.790.

119. Welch v. Board of Educ. of Bement Community Unit School Dist. No. 5, 358 N.E.2d 1364 (Ill. App. 1977).

120. Barnes v. Fair Dismissal Appeals Bd., 548 P.2d 988 (Ore. App. 1976).

121. Board of Educ., Mt. Vernon Schools v. Shank, 542 S.W.2d 779 (Mo. 1976).

122. Nordstrom v. Hansford, 435 P.2d 397 (Colo. 1967).

123. Harris v. Commonwealth of Pennsylvania Secretary of Educ., 372 A.2d 953 (Pa. Commw. 1977).

124. *Id.* at 957.

125. Jerry v. Board of Educ. of the City School Dist. of the City of Syracuse, 376 N.Y.S.2d 737 (App. Div. 1975).

126. Thompson v. Wake City Bd. of Educ., 230 S.E.2d 164 (N.C. App. 1976).

127. *See* text with note 115, Chapter 3, for discussion of personal appearance as a constitutional right.

128. Kelley v. Johnson, 425 U.S. 238 (1976); Morrison v. Hamilton County Bd. of Educ., 494 S.W.2d 770 (Tenn. 1973).

129. Lucia v. Duggan, 303 F. Supp. 112 (D. Mass. 1969).

130. Ramsey v. Hopkins, 320 F. Supp. 477 (N.D. Ala. 1970).

131. Seitz v. Duval County School Bd., 346 So. 2d 644 (Fla. App. 1977).

132. Blair v. Robstown Independent School Dist., 556 F.2d 1331 (5th Cir. 1977).

133. Whitsel v. Southeast Local School Dist., 484 F.2d 1222 (6th Cir. 1973).

134. Ray v. Minneapolis Bd. of Educ., Special School Dist. No. 1, 202 N.W.2d 375 (Minn. 1972).

135. *Id.* at 378.

136. Board of Trustees of School Dist. No. 4 v. Colwell, 611 P.2d 427 (Wyo. 1980).

137. Warner v. Board of Educ., 604 P.2d 295 (Kan. App. 1979).

138. Wardwell v. Board of Educ. of the City School Dist. of the City of Cincinnati, 529 F.2d 625 (6th Cir. 1976). *See* text with note 73, Chapter 2.

139. Hanson v. Unified School Dist. No. 500, Wyandotte County, Kansas, 364 F. Supp. 330 (D. Kan. 1973).

140. School Dist. #11, Joint Counties of Archuleta and La Plata v. Umberfield, 512 P.2d 1166 (Colo. App. 1973). It should be noted that the

California Supreme Court recently held that "reasonable accommodation" must be made for teacher absences for holy days. The court applied Article I, Section 8 of the California constitution, which forbids religious discrimination. *See* text with note 95, Chapter 3, for further discussion of absences for religious reasons.

141. Thompson v. Wake County Bd. of Educ., 230 S.E.2d 164 (N.C. App. 1976).

142. Fox v. Board of Educ. of Doddridge County, 236 S.E.2d 243 (W.Va. 1977).

143. Sanders v. Board of Educ. of the South Sioux City Community Dist. No. 11, 263 N.W.2d 461 (Neb. 1978).

144. *Id.* at 465.

145. Harrah Independent School Dist. v. Martin, 440 U.S. 194 (1979).

146. *See* Table 1.

147. Pell v. Board of Educ. of Union Free School Dist. No. 1, 313 N.E.2d 321 (N.Y. 1974).

148. Aubuchon v. Gasconade County R-1 School Dist., 541 S.W.2d 322 (Mo. App. 1976).

149. Fernald v. City of Ellsworth Superintending School Committee, 342 A.2d 704 (Me. 1975).

150. Caravello v. Board of Educ., Norwich City School Dist., 369 N.Y.S.2d 829 (App. Div. 1975).

151. Meinhold v. Clark County School Dist. Bd. of School Trustees, 506 P.2d 420 (Nev. 1973).

152. DiCaprio v. Redmond, 350 N.E.2d 119 (Ill. App. 1976).

153. DeCanio v. School Committee of Boston, 260 N.E.2d 676 (Mass. 1970).

154. Celestine v. Lafayette Parish School Bd., 284 So. 2d 650 (La. App. 1973).

155. Board of Trustees of the Clark County School Dist. v. Rathbun, 556 P.2d 548 (Nev. 1976).

156. Lombardo v. Board of Educ. of School Dist. No. 27, 241 N.E.2d 495 (Ill. App. 1968).

157. *In re* Grossman, 316 A.2d 39 (N.J. App. 1974).

158. Wright v. Superintending Committee, City of Portland, 331 A.2d 640 (Me. 1975).

159. *Id.* at 647.

160. McLaughlin v. Machias School Committee, 385 A.2d 53 (Me. 1978).

161. Board of Educ. of the Sunnyvale Elementary School v. Commission on Professional Competence, 162 Cal. Rptr. 590 (Cal. App. 1980).

162. In assessing the teacher's fitness, the court applied the criteria announced in Morrison v. State Bd. of Educ., 461 P.2d 375 (Cal. 1969). *See* text with note 109, *supra.*

163. Newman v. Board of Educ. of the City School Dist. of New York, 594 F.2d 299 (2d Cir. 1979).

164. *Id.*

165. Gary Teachers Union, Local No. 4, AFT v. School City of Gary, 332 N.E.2d 256, 263 (Ind. App. 1975).

166. diLeo v. Greenfield, 541 F.2d 949, 954 (2d Cir. 1976).

167. *Id.* at 953.

168. Kodish v. Spring-Ford Area School Dist., 373 A.2d 124 (Pa Commw. 1977); DiCello v. Board of Directors of Riverside School Dist., 380 A.2d 944 (Pa. Commw. 1977).
169. Fatscher v. Board of School Directors, Springfield School Dist., 367 A.2d 1130 (Pa. Commw. 1977).
170. Steeby v. School Dist. of the City of Highland Park, 224 N.W.2d 97 (Mich. App. 1974).
171. Gassman v. Governing Bd. of Rincon Valley Union School Dist. of Sonoma County, 133 Cal. Rptr. 1 (Cal. 1976).
172. Thayer v. Anacortes School Dist., 504 P.2d 1130 (Wash. 1972). *See also* Ohio Rev. Code. § 6.34.
173. Fedele v. Board of Educ. of the Town of Branford, 394 A.2d 737 (Conn. C. P. 1977).
174. Cooper v. Fair Dismissal Appeals Bd., 570 P.2d 1005 (Ore. App. 1977).
175. Stets v. McKeesport Area School Dist., 350 A.2d 185 (Pa. Commw. 1975); Gabriel v. Trinity Area School Dist., 350 A.2d 203 (Pa. Commw. 1976).
176. Pa. Stat. Ann. 24 § 11-1124.
177. Bilek v. Board of Educ. of Berkeley School Dist., 377 N.E.2d 1259 (Ill. App. 1978); Relph v. Board of Educ. of DePue Unit School Dist. No. 103, 366 N.E.2d 1125 (Ill. App. 1977).
178. Chauvel v. Nyquist, 389 N.Y.S.2d 636 (App. Div. 1976).
179. Chester v. Harper Woods School Dist., 273 N.W.2d 916 (Mich. App. 1979).
180. *See* text with note 136, Chapter 3, for discussion of school district immunity under Section 1983 of the Civil Rights Act of 1871, and text with note 140, Chapter 3, for an explanation of eleventh amendment immunity.
181. Stoddard v. School Dist. No. 1, 590 F.2d 829 (10th Cir. 1979).
182. Burton v. Cascade School Dist. Union High School No. 5, 512 F.2d 850 (9th Cir. 1975).
183. Wagle v. Murray, 560 F.2d 401 (9th Cir. 1977).
184. Morris v. Board of Educ. of Laurel School Dist., 401 F. Supp. 188 (D. Del. 1975).
185. State v. Grant Valley Local School Bd., 375 N.E.2d 48 (Ohio 1978); Board of Trustees of Nogales Elementary School Dist. v. Cartier, 559 P.2d 216 (Ariz. App. 1977); Jackson v. Board of Educ. of Oktibbeha City, 349 So. 2d 550 (Miss. 1977); Neal v. Board of Educ., School Dist. No. 189, 371 N.E.2d 869 (Ill. App. 1977); Boyce v. Alexis I. duPont School Dist., 341 F. Supp. 678 (D. Del. 1972).
186. Weckerly v. Mona Shores Bd. of Educ., 202 N.W.2d 777 (Mich. 1972).
187. DiCello v. Board of Directors of Riverside School Dist., 380 A.2d 944 (Pa. Commw. 1977).
188. Alyeska Pipeline Service Co. v. Wilderness Society, 421 U.S. 240, 247 (1975).
189. 42 U.S.C. § 1988 (1976).
190. The Supreme Court has extended the Civil Rights Attorneys' Fees Award Act to all types of Section 1983 suits, not just civil rights violations.

Maine v. Thiboutot, 100 S.Ct. 2502 (1980). *See*, specifically, Maher v. Gagne, 100 S.Ct. 2570 (1980), where attorneys' fees were awarded in a consent decree for a violation of the Social Security Act.

191. 122 Cong. Rec. S. 17051 (Sept. 29, 1976).

192. *See* Harrington v. Vandalia-Butler Bd. of Educ., 585 F.2d 192 (6th Cir. 1978), *cert. denied*, 441 U.S. 932 (1979).

193. Christiansburg Garment Co. v. Equal Employment Opportunity Commission, 434 U.S. 412, 422 (1978).

# 6

# Collective Bargaining

The 1960s brought about dramatic changes in the teacher/school board relationship. Traditionally, boards of education have had unilateral managerial control over the operation of public schools. As employees of the school board, teachers were minimally involved in the decision-making process. Teachers, seeking greater participation and voice in school affairs, turned to collective group action to achieve a balance of power. Since the early 1960s when the United Federation of Teachers in New York City attained bargaining rights, most teachers throughout the nation have become involved in collective bargaining.

This chapter presents an overview of the legal structure in which collective bargaining occurs. The private versus public sector dichotomy is highlighted in order to place public school negotiations in a historical perspective. Teachers' rights in the bargaining process are delineated through an analysis of judicial decisions and statutory law. Additionally, two issues with special significance for teachers are discussed: scope of negotiations and strikes.

## PRIVATE AND PUBLIC SECTOR BARGAINING

Collective bargaining is a rather recent phenomenon in the public sector and has been influenced significantly by the bargaining process in the private sector. Although there are a number of similarities in public and private sector bargaining, several basic differences distinguish the two areas. First, the removal of decision-making authority from public officials through bargaining is viewed as an infringement on the sovereign power of government. This position is widely quoted by individuals and groups who support anti–collective bargaining policies in the public sector. Second, whereas the strike is considered essential to the effective operation of collective decision making in the private sector, this view has been rejected in the public sector because of the nature and structure of governmental services.

In spite of the basic differences between the public and private sectors, collective bargaining legislation in the private sector has been significant in shaping statutory and judicial regulation of public negotiations. Similarities between the two sectors can be noted in a number of areas, such as unfair labor practices, union representation, and impasse procedures. Because of the influence of private sector legislation on the public sector, a brief overview of major legislative acts is presented in this section. This presentation is followed by a discussion of the development of organizational rights in public employment.

### HISTORICAL DEVELOPMENT OF BARGAINING RIGHTS IN THE PRIVATE SECTOR

Prior to the 1930s, private labor relations were dominated by the judiciary, which strongly favored management. The extensive use of judicial injunctions against strikes and boycotts effectively countered employee efforts to obtain recognition for purposes of bargaining.[1] Consequently, courts reinforced the powers of management and substantially curtailed the development and influence of unions. To bolster the position of the worker, Congress enacted the Norris-LaGuardia Act in 1932. The purpose of this federal legislation was to circumscribe the role of courts in labor disputes. The Act achieved this by preventing the use of the injunction except where union activities would jeopardize public safety and health or would violate the law. In essence, the legislation did not confer any new rights on employees or unions but simply removed judicial control that had impeded the development of unions.

Following the Norris-LaGuardia Act, in 1935 Congress passed the National Labor Relations Act, commonly known as the Wagner Act. While this Act created substantial rights for the private employee, one of the most important outcomes was that it granted legitimacy to the collective bargaining process.[2] In addition to defining employees' rights to organize and collectively bargain, the Act established a mechanism to safeguard these rights.[3] The National Labor Relations Board (NLRB) was created specifically to monitor claims of unfair labor practices such as interference with employees' rights to organize, discrimination against employees in hiring or discharge because of union membership, and failure to bargain in good faith.

The National Labor Relations Act was amended in 1947 by the Labor Management Relations Act (known as the Taft-Hartley Act).

While the Wagner Act regulated the activities of employers, the Taft-Hartley Act was an attempt to balance the scales in collective bargaining by regulating abusive union practices. Since 1947 other amendments to the Taft-Hartley Act have further limited union abuses. Federal legislation has restricted interference from both the employer and the union, thereby ensuring the individual employee greater freedom of choice in collective bargaining.

## ORGANIZATIONAL RIGHTS OF PUBLIC EMPLOYEES

President Kennedy's Executive Order 10988 in 1962 gave federal employees "the right, freely and without fear of penalty or reprisal, to form, join, and assist any employee organization. . . ." [4] This was a significant milestone for public employees, who historically had been deprived of the right to organize and collectively bargain. The granting of organizational rights to federal employees provided the impetus for similar gains at the state and local levels.

Until the late 1960s, the constitutional right of public employees to join a union had not been fully established. A large number of public employees actively participated in collective bargaining, but statutes and regulations existed in some states prohibiting union membership. Restrictions against union membership were challenged as impairing freedom of association protected by the first amendment. Although not addressing union membership, the Supreme Court held in *Keyishian v. Board of Education* that public employment could not be conditioned on the relinquishment of free association rights.[5] In a later decision, the Seventh Circuit Court of Appeals clearly announced that "an individual's right to form and join a union is protected by the first amendment." [6] Other courts followed this precedent by invalidating state statutory provisions that blocked union membership.[7]

## EMPLOYEES' RIGHTS IN THE BARGAINING PROCESS

While the United States Constitution has been interpreted as protecting public employees' rights to organize, the right to form and join a union does not ensure the right to bargain collectively with a public employer. Individual state statutes and constitutions govern such bargaining rights. Whether identified as professional negotiations, collective negotiations, or collective bargaining, the bargaining process entails bilateral decision making in which the teachers' representative and the school board attempt to reach mutual agreement on subjects that relate to or affect the teachers' employment. This process is governed in thirty-two states by legislation granting specific bargaining rights to teachers and their professional associations. Because of the variety of the existing legislation, as well as the absence of legislation in some states, collective bargaining rights of teachers vary substantially.

States with laws permitting public sector bargaining differ as to the rights conferred on employees. Provisions range from limited mandates for public employers to "meet and confer" with employees to comprehensive requirements defining the scope of the bargaining process. Courts, viewing collective bargaining as within the ambit of legislative authority, have restricted their involvement to interpretation of state statutes and federal and state constitutions. Courts have been reluctant to interfere with the legislature's authority to define the collective bargaining relationship between public employer and employees unless protected rights have been compromised.

## DIVERSITY IN BARGAINING PRACTICES

There is no uniformity among the states in bargaining practices. Some states, such as New York, have a very detailed, comprehensive collective bargaining statute that delineates specific bargaining rights. In contrast, laws in Virginia and North Carolina strictly prohibit negotiated contracts between teachers' organizations and school boards. Between these two polar positions, a range of practices exists among states.

This diversity in protected bargaining rights has led many individuals and groups to advocate a federal bargaining law for all state and local employees. Supporting such a proposal are a number of national organizations, including the National Education Association, the American Federation of Teachers, and the American Federation of State, County, and Municipal Employees. Several laws were considered by Congress in 1975 but were abruptly abandoned with the Supreme Court's 1976 decision in *National League of Cities v. Usery*.[8] This decision involved a challenge to the 1974 congressional amendments to the Fair Labor Standards Act that extended the federal minimum wage and maximum hour provisions to employees of state and local governments. The Court concluded that the amendments unconstitutionally interfered with the states' rights to structure the public employer-employee relationship. Affirming the states' sovereignty, the Court concluded that "Congress may not exercise [its] power so as to force directly upon the states its choices as to how essential decisions regarding the conduct of integral governmental functions are to be made."[9] This decision has effectively foreclosed federal efforts to initiate uniform collective bargaining legislation for the present; however, options continue to be investigated that might meet the balancing test between the national interest and states' rights imposed in *Usery*. For the immediate future, bargaining rights seem destined to be controlled by individual state legislation or, in the absence of legislation, court rulings.

As noted, teachers in the states of North Carolina and Virginia are not allowed to enter into negotiated agreements. Under North Carolina law, all contracts entered into by public employers and employee associations are invalid. A federal district court has upheld the constitutionality of this legislation.[10] Similarly, in 1977 the Virginia Supreme Court declared that a negotiated contract between a teachers' organization and the school board was null and void.[11] The board maintained that its power to enter into contracts enabled it also to bargain collectively with employee organizations. However, the court concluded that such implied power was contrary to legislative intent.

In the absence of enabling legislation, other states have permitted negotiated agreements. Most recently, the Kentucky Supreme Court ruled that a public employer *may* recognize an employee organization for the purpose of collective bargaining, even though state law is silent regarding public employee bargaining rights.[12] The ruling does not impose a duty on local school boards but merely allows a board the discretion to negotiate. This ruling is consistent with a number of other decisions permitting negotiated contracts in the absence of legislation. The power and authority of the board to enter into contracts for the operation and maintenance of the school system have been construed to include the ability to enter into negotiated agreements with employee organizations.[13]

Unless negotiation is mandated by statute, courts have not compelled school boards to negotiate. Whether or not to negotiate is thus at the school board's discretion. However, once a school board extends recognition to a bargaining agent and commences bargaining, the board's actions in the negotiation process are governed by established judicial principles. The employer maintains certain prerogatives, such as recognition of the bargaining unit, determination of bargainable items, and establishment of impasse procedures, but designated rights also are conferred on the employee organization. For example, there is a legal duty for the board to bargain in good faith. Furthermore, if negotiations reach an impasse, the board may not unilaterally terminate the bargaining process. Also, after signing a contract, the board is bound by the provisions and cannot abrogate the contract on the basis that no duty existed to bargain. Hence, the school board is subject to a number of legal constraints once it enters into the negotiation process.

BARGAINING STATUTES

The majority of the states have enacted statutes governing bargaining rights, and school boards must negotiate with teachers in accordance with the statutorily prescribed process. Generally, public employee bargaining laws address employer and employee rights, bargaining units, scope of bargaining, impasse resolution, grievance procedures, unfair labor practices, and penalties for prohibited practices. Many states have established labor relations boards to monitor bargaining under the statute.

Although the specific functions of these boards vary widely, their general purpose is to resolve questions arising from the implementation of state law. Functions assigned to such boards include determination of membership in bargaining units, resolution of union recognition claims, investigation of unfair labor practices, and interpretation of the general intent of statutory bargaining clauses.

Like the National Labor Relations Act (NLRA), state statutes require bargaining "in good faith." A number of states have followed the federal law in stipulating that this "does not compel either party to agree to a proposal or to require the making of a concession." [14] Since good faith bargaining has been open to a range of interpretations, judicial decisions in the public sector have relied extensively on private sector rulings that have clarified the phrase.[15] Good faith bargaining has been interpreted as requiring parties to meet at reasonable times and attempt to reach mutual agreement without compulsion on either side to agree. Failure of the board or teachers' organization to bargain in good faith can result in the imposition of a penalty for an unfair labor practice.

Statutes impose certain restrictions or obligations on the school board and the employee organization. Violation of the law, by either party, can result in an unfair labor practice claim. Allegations of unfair labor practices are brought before the state public employee relations board for a hearing and judgment. Specific unfair labor practices, modeled after those in the National Labor Relations Act, are included in state statutes.[16] The unfair labor practices listed below from the Florida public employee bargaining law are illustrative.

Public employers or their agents or representatives are prohibited from:

(a) Interfering with, restraining, or coercing public employees in the exercise of any rights guaranteed them . . .

(b) Encouraging or discouraging membership in any employee organization by discrimination in regard to hiring, tenure, or other conditions of employment.

(c) Refusing to bargain collectively, failing to bargain collectively in good faith, or refusing to sign a final agreement agreed upon with the certified bargaining agent for the public employees in the bargaining unit.

(d) Discharging or discriminating against a public employee because he has filed charges or given testimony . . .

(e) Dominating, interfering with, or assisting in the formation, existence, or administration of any employee organization or contributing financial support to such an organization.

(f) Refusing to discuss grievances in good faith pursuant to the terms of the collective bargaining agreement with either the certified bargaining agent for the public employee or the employee involved.

A public employee organization is prohibited from:

(a) Interfering with, restraining, or coercing public employees in the exercise of any rights guaranteed them . . .

(b) Causing or attempting to cause a public employer to discriminate against an employee because of the employee's membership or non-membership in an employee organization or attempting to cause the public employer to violate any of the provisions of [law].

(c) Refusing to bargain collectively or failing to bargain collectively in good faith with a public employer.

(d) Participating in a strike against the public employer by instigating or supporting, in any positive manner, a strike.[17]

Another topic often addressed in a comprehensive bargaining statute is impasse resolution. An impasse occurs in bargaining when an agreement cannot be reached and neither party will compromise. When negotiations reach such an impasse, several options are available for resolution—mediation, fact finding, and arbitration. Most state statutes address impasse procedures; statutory provisions range from allowing impasse procedures to be negotiated (e.g., Hawaii) to mandating detailed steps that must be followed (e.g., Kansas). Alternatives that are most frequently employed to resolve impasse are identified below.

Mediation is often the first step to reopening negotiations. A neutral third party assists both sides in finding a basis for agreement. The mediator serves as a facilitator rather than a decision maker, thus enabling the board and teachers' association jointly to reach an agreement. Mediation may be optional or required by law; the mediator is selected by the negotiation teams or, upon request, appointed by a public employee relations board.

Failure to reach agreement through mediation frequently results in fact finding (often called advisory arbitration). The process may be mandated by law, or may be entered into by mutual agreement of both parties. Fact finding involves the efforts of a third party to investigate the causes for the dispute, collect facts and testimony to clarify the dispute, and formulate a judgment accordingly. Because of the advisory nature of the process, proposed solutions are not binding on either party.

One of the most controversial issues in bargaining involves what should be the final step in impasse procedures. In a number of states, the final step is fact finding, which may leave both parties without a satisfactory solution. A few states permit a third alternative—binding arbitration. This process is similar to fact finding, except that the decision of the arbitrator is binding on both parties. States that permit binding arbitration vary as to how it can be used. For example, Maine permits binding arbitration on matters of mutual consent,[18] Rhode Island allows binding arbitration only on nonmonetary items,[19] and Oregon merely provides that impasse procedures with final and binding arbitration may be negotiated.[20]

It is generally agreed that mediation and fact finding, because of their advisory nature, do not provide the most effective means for resolving negotiation disputes. Since the strike is prohibited among public employees in most states, conditional binding arbitration has been considered a viable alternative in resolving deadlocks. Although a greater balance of power is achieved between the school board and the teachers' association with binding arbitration, it has not been met with enthusiasm by public sector employers, who often view it as an illegal delegation of power. As a result, statutory provisions for arbitration have been implemented only on a voluntary or conditional basis.

## NONUNION TEACHERS' RIGHTS

In a short period of time, teachers have achieved significant gains in negotiation rights; most of these rights apply to teachers as members of a collective body. The question then arises as to how these gains for the increasing number of union members have impinged on the nonunion teachers' rights. Two important issues have been litigated: (1) payment of agency shop fees, and (2) freedom of speech at public meetings.

An "agency shop" provision in a collective bargaining contract is an arrangement whereby a nonunion employee in a bargaining unit must pay a service charge that may be equal to union dues. Such a requirement is predicated on the rationale that a union represents all members of the bargaining unit, and payment of this "fair share" from all employees is necessary because of the high costs of bargaining and handling grievances under the contract. Approximately fifteen states have legislation permitting the negotiation of an agency fee.[21] Until recently, the constitutionality of payment of these fees by the nonunion teacher had not been clarified by the courts. The Supreme Court, as well as a number of state courts, now have addressed the question of whether the nonunion teacher can be compelled to pay union dues.

In 1969, the Detroit Board of Education entered into a negotiated contract containing an agency fee provision. This fee was contested by nonunion teachers and was eventually invalidated by the Michigan Supreme Court because of the lack of legislative authorization.[22] In response to this decision, legislation was passed to permit the negotiation of an agency fee. Nonunion teachers in Detroit again protested the fee, this time claiming violation of first and fourteenth amendment rights because of forced support of the political activities of unions. A Michigan appellate court,[23] and later the United States Supreme Court, upheld the constitutionality of the agency shop clause in *Abood v. Detroit Board of Education*.[24] However, the Supreme Court stated that under the protections of the first amendment an employee could not be compelled "to contribute to the support of an ideological cause he may oppose as a condition of holding a job as a public school teacher." [25] Therefore, the nonunion teacher's payment can reflect only union costs of bargaining and administration of the contract, not costs for other causes such as political activities.

According to the Supreme Court, an agency shop statute is permissible under the Federal Constitution; however, a number of courts have declared such provisions illegal in states without specific statutory authority. The Maine Supreme Court held that forced payment of dues was "tantamount to coercion toward membership." [26] The Maine statute ensures employees the right to join a union *voluntarily*. This was interpreted by the court as including the right to *refrain* from joining. Similarly, a Florida appeals court rejected a fair share checkoff requirement, finding that such an agency shop provision violated the state constitution.[27] In 1979, an Indiana superior court reinforced this view, holding that absent statutory authority, agency shop was illegal in Indiana.[28]

Substantial clarity has been provided as to the constitutionality of agency shop clauses; but ambiguity exists as to whether teachers can be dismissed for refusing to pay union dues in states allowing agency shop provisions. In Pennsylvania, an appellate court overturned the dismissal of two teachers, stating that refusal to pay dues did not constitute "persistent and willful violation of the school laws" to justify dismissal.[29] The Michigan State Tenure Commission also ruled that failure to pay agency shop fees was not a valid basis for dismissal of a tenured teacher.[30] Further litigation will be necessary to clarify the nature of the sanctions that can be imposed if teachers fail to adhere to agency shop provisions.

A second topic of interest to the nonunion teacher is whether or not the teacher's freedom of speech is subordinate to the union's bargaining rights. While a teacher's right to free expression is well established,[31] the nonunion teacher's right to address a school board on a subject of negotiation has been the source of recent litigation. The Wisconsin Supreme Court concluded that allowing a nonunion teacher to comment on a bargaining issue at a public school board meeting violated the exclusive recognition of the union.[32] In this case, negotiations had reached a deadlock on the issue of an agency shop provision. A nonunion teacher, representing a minority group of teachers, addressed the board at a regular public meeting and requested postponement of a decision on the issue until further study could be made. Although the Wisconsin high court upheld the union's position, the United States Supreme Court reversed the decision, concluding that the nonunion teacher did possess the right to express concerns to the board.[33] The teacher was not attempting to negotiate, but merely to speak on an important issue before the board—a right any citizen possesses. The Court noted that teachers have never been "compelled to relinquish the first amendment rights they would otherwise enjoy as citizens to comment on matters of public interest in connection with the operation of the public school in which they work." [34] Further, the Court stated that the board "may not be required to discriminate between speakers on the basis of their employment, or the content of their speech." [35] This decision firmly established the individual teacher's right to present views on an issue to the school board. However, it must be noted that the Court did differentiate between stating a position and negotiating; the latter must be performed only by representative bargaining units.

## SCOPE OF NEGOTIATIONS

Should the teachers' organization have input into class size? Who will determine the length of the school day? How will extra duty assignments be determined? Will reductions in force, necessitated by declining enrollment, be based on seniority or merit? These questions and others are raised in connection with determining the scope of negotiations. "Scope" refers to the range of issues or subjects that are negotiable. Parameters establishing scope of bargaining vary considerably among the states. Thus, to determine negotiable items in a particular state, the state's statutes and regulations as well as resulting litigation must be examined.

The specification of negotiable items in statutes varies from broad general guidelines to detailed enumerations. Many of the states with bargaining laws have modeled their statutes after the National Labor Relations Act (NLRA), which stipulates that the employer's and employees' representatives must meet and confer "with respect to wages, hours, and other terms and conditions of employment." [36] Pennsylvania [37] and Hawaii [38] have adopted identical language, while Florida [39] specifies only "terms and conditions of employment." Other states have elected to deal directly with the issue by identifying each item that must be negotiated; Tennessee [40] lists ten items, while Nevada [41] lists approximately twenty.

All proposed subjects for teacher negotiations can be classified as either mandatory, permissive, or prohibited. Mandatory items must be negotiated. Failure of the school board to meet and confer on such items is evidence of lack of good faith bargaining. Permissive items can be negotiated if both parties agree; however, there is no legal duty to consider the items. Prohibited items are beyond the power of the board to negotiate; an illegal delegation of power is involved if the board subjects these items to the bargaining process. Since most statutory scope provisions are general in nature, a number of court decisions have been rendered that differentiate negotiable items from nonnegotiable items.

Although collective bargaining for public school teachers has a short history, two generations of negotiated agreements can be identified. The first generation of teacher contracts dealt primarily with salaries, hours, insurance, and other fringe benefits. These contracts focused essentially on economic gains for the teacher. As teacher associations have become more experienced in bargaining, negotiations have moved into a second generation of contracts, which can be classified more aptly as "conditions of employment." Such contracts have dealt with the school curriculum, class size, transfers and promotions, and general policy areas. This has led to conflicts between school boards exercising their legal duties and teachers asserting a claim to bilateral decision making in areas that affect their teaching.

## GOVERNMENTAL POLICY

Defining managerial rights is one of the key elements in establishing parameters of negotiable items at the bargaining table. State laws and court decisions indicate that public employers cannot be required to negotiate regarding governmental policy. It has been held impermissible for a school board to bargain away certain rights and responsibilities in the public policy area. Established boundaries distinguishing such policy issues from other items that can be negotiated vary widely among the states.

Educational policy matters are defined through provisions in collective bargaining statutes, such as "management rights" and "scope of bargaining" clauses, as well as through court interpretations of policy rights. The policy matters are totally excluded as negotiable items in some states; however, most states generally stipulate only that employers will not be required to bargain such policy rights. The excerpt below from the Pennsylvania Public Employees Act illustrates a typical provision.

> Public employers *shall not be required* to bargain over matters of inherent managerial policy, which shall not be limited to such areas of discretion or policy as the functions and programs of the public employer, standards of services, its overall budget, utilization of technology, the organizational structure and selection and direction of personnel.[42] [Emphasis added.]

Thus, employers cannot be compelled to bargain governmental policy. However, bargaining agreements may be permitted on policy subjects as long as there is no conflict with state constitutions, statutes, or court rulings.[43] Therefore, to interpret policy rights in a particular state, judicial rulings must be examined.

In a significant 1978 New Jersey decision, the state supreme court limited negotiated contracts strictly to terms and conditions of employment.[44] This decision resulted from a 1974 amendment to the state's collective bargaining law which appeared to make most items permissive in negotiations. By interpreting this amendment narrowly, the court removed governmental policy items that previously had been negotiated, such as teacher transfers, course offerings, and evaluations. In effect, the decision limited negotiations primarily to wages, benefits, and work schedules. The court emphasized that a collective bargaining contract could not supplant state laws. Further restricting employee rights, the court concluded that nonnegotiable items could not be submitted to arbitration.

The phrase "conditions of employment," as it was used in the New Jersey case, can include a myriad of items—unless policy matters that cannot be negotiated are clearly delineated. Conditions of employment can affect almost every aspect of the school system, since most decisions made by the school board either directly or indirectly influence the teacher at the classroom level. Although the New Jersey court's ruling was quite restrictive with regard to scope,[45] a number of courts have construed conditions of employment in broader terms. The South Dakota Supreme Court held that subjects that *materially* affect teachers' employment are negotiable.[46] In an even broader interpretation, the Nevada Supreme Court ruled that items *significantly* related to wages, hours, and working conditions are negotiable.[47] The Pennsylvania Supreme Court, depicting a more moderate position, concluded that an issue's *impact* on conditions of employment should be weighed in determining whether it should be considered outside the educational policy area.[48]

Courts are in agreement that school boards cannot be required to negotiate inherent managerial rights pertaining to policy matters. While there is no requirement to bargain management rights, these rights are viewed as permissive subjects in some states. That is, the board may agree to negotiate a particular "right" in the absence of statutory or judicial prohibitions. If the board does negotiate the policy item, it is bound by the agreement in the same manner as if the issue were a mandatory item.[49]

## MANDATORY, PERMISSIVE, OR PROHIBITED ITEMS

Beyond wages, hours, and fringe benefits, there is a lack of agreement among states as to what is negotiable. Similar enabling legislation has been interpreted quite differently among states, as illustrated by the subjects discussed below.

**Class Size.** Class size has been one of the most controversial policy subjects, and one that courts and state legislatures have been reluctant to designate as negotiable. With the exception of California, it is not specifically identified as a negotiable item in the statutes of any state. However, the Nevada Supreme Court interpreted the state collective bargaining statute as including class size among mandatory subjects by implication.[50]

In response to this decision, the state law was revised to exclude class size from a detailed list of bargainable items, thus placing it in the category of permissive subjects.[51] An Oregon appeals court held that class size is a policy right that is not mandatorily negotiable, but can be a permissive item.[52] New York courts have ruled, in a similar manner, that the subject is permissive only.[53] In a recent decision by the Alaska Supreme Court, class size was declared a nonnegotiable item because of its effect on educational policy.[54]

**Work Day/School Calendar.** Determination of the school calendar generally is held to be a managerial prerogative. The Supreme Court of Alaska held it to be nonnegotiable under state law.[55] Courts in Nevada [56] and Oregon [57] have concluded that it is a policy issue that can be permissively negotiated. On the other hand, the Wisconsin Supreme Court upheld a ruling of the Wisconsin Employment Relations Commission declaring the school calendar mandatorily bargainable.[58] The court reasoned that the school board is "required to meet, confer and bargain as to any calendaring proposal that is *primarily* related to 'wages, hours, and conditions of employment.' " [59] Thus, the court interpreted calendar issues as more closely related to terms of employment than to policy matters. Unlike the school calendar, the length of the work day and related issues such as hours, work load, and planning and lunch periods are usually defined as "conditions of employment" and therefore mandatory subjects of negotiation.[60]

**Teacher Evaluation.** Significant gains have been made by teacher unions in securing teacher performance evaluations. A number of states, including California, Iowa, Massachusetts, and Kansas, have specified teacher evaluation as a mandatory item in negotiations. The Wisconsin Supreme Court considered evaluation to be primarily related to wages, hours, and conditions of employment.[61] Even though "who will evaluate" was held nonnegotiable, the Wisconsin court stated that evaluation procedures to be used must be negotiated. Courts in Oregon [62] and Nevada [63] have ruled that teacher evaluation is a permissive item, but it has been declared nonnegotiable in Alaska and New Jersey.[64]

**Reduction in Force.** With declining enrollments and the economic crisis faced by many school districts, reduction in force (RIF) has become a very real threat to tenured as well as nontenured teachers. The threat has nurtured teachers' union demands for input into criteria or guidelines for selecting teachers for nonretention. Generally, if reduction in force is necessitated by economic reasons, the subject is nonnegotiable.[65] A New Jersey appellate court ruled that criteria for nonretention and re-employment rights pertaining to RIF did not have to be negotiated.[66] Even though a number of courts have viewed reduction in force as a managerial prerogative, the impact of such a reduction on employee rights may necessitate the negotiation of RIF procedures.[67]

**Probationary Teachers.** Granting of tenure to teachers is a discretionary decision of the school board. It is not considered a mandatory subject for negotiation. The awarding of tenure has been declared a prohibited subject for negotiations in New Jersey [68] and New York.[69] The New York Supreme Court considered a negotiated agreement regarding tenure rights as *ultra vires* (beyond the power of the board).[70] In another New York case, an education association had obtained a collective bargaining contract which provided that nontenured teachers could be dismissed only for cause.[71] This limited the board's discretion in conferring tenure at the end of the probationary period, since nonrenewal had to be based on cause. The court emphasized that only a school board can grant tenure, and concluded that the negotiated agreement applied exclusively to employment within the probationary period, not to the granting of tenure.

**Grievance Procedures.** Negotiated grievance procedures for teachers are far less extensive than procedures for employees in the private sector. Public employers, adhering to the doctrine of the sovereign power of government, have been reluctant to provide procedures that might result in a loss of public authority. Allowing grievance procedures to include final decision making by a neutral third party lessens a school board's power, effectively equating the positions of the teachers' organization and the school board.

Nonetheless, one of the greatest gains in public collective bargaining in recent years has been in the area of grievance procedures.[72] Over twenty-five states have made some provision for the negotiation of such procedures in their public employee bargaining laws.[73] The majority of these states *permit* school boards to negotiate grievance procedures with binding arbitration.[74] Four states (Alaska, Florida, Minnesota, and Pennsylvania) *compel* the negotiation of a grievance mechanism with binding arbitration. In Iowa, school boards may negotiate a grievance procedure, but final and binding arbitration is not permitted. The Iowa Supreme Court has invalidated the use of binding arbitration as a surrender of the statutory duty of the school board.[75]

Central to the establishment of grievance procedures is the definition of a grievance. In the private sector, a grievance is usually defined as any dispute between employer and employee. Teachers' grievances, on the other hand, are most often limited to controversies arising from the interpretation or application of the negotiated contract. The Ohio Supreme Court upheld the right of school boards to enter into contracts containing binding grievance arbitration, as long as grievances were related to the terms of the contract.[76] Many state statutes providing binding arbitration specifically restrict the arbitrator to grievances related to interpretation of the contract.[77]

## STRIKES

Although numerous rights have been obtained in the area of public sector bargaining, the right to strike has not been gained by teachers. It is argued that there can be no true collective bargaining without the right to withhold services, which characterizes the bargaining process in the private sector. Opponents of public employee strikes assert that the essential nature of public services, the loss of governmental discretionary decision-making power, and the general disfavor of the public toward work stoppages prevent the legalization of strikes. Except in a few limited cases, legislation and judicial rulings consistently prohibit strikes by teachers.

In those states that have legislation granting public employees a limited right to strike, certain mandatory conditions, specified in statute, must be met prior to the initiation of a work stoppage. Designated conditions vary, but usually include: (1) the exhaustion of statutory mediation and fact finding steps; (2) elapse of a certain time period prior to commencing the strike; (3) written notice by the union of intent to strike; and (4) evidence that the strike will not constitute a danger to public health or safety. Among the states permitting the limited right to work stoppages for certain public employees are Alaska, Hawaii, Minnesota, Montana, Oregon, Pennsylvania, Vermont, and Wisconsin. In contrast to the few states noted above, most states with statutes pertaining to collective bargaining for public employees have specific "no strike" provisions. The provision in the Florida public employee bargaining law is representative of those found in other states.

> No public employee or employee organization may participate in a strike against a public employer by instigating or supporting, in any manner, a strike. Any violation . . . shall subject the violator to the penalties provided.[78]

Through a number of court decisions, the judicial framework for viewing public school strikes has evolved. In one of the first notable decisions, the Supreme Court of Connecticut stated that permitting teachers to strike could be equated with asserting that "they can deny the authority of government." [79] The court in this case denied teachers the right to strike, emphasizing that a teacher is an agent of the government, possessing a portion of the sovereignty of the state. In a later case, the Supreme Court of Indiana issued a restraining order against striking teachers, affirming the same public welfare issue. The court stated that "public employees occupy a status entirely different from private employees because they are agents of the government serving a public purpose and a strike by them contravenes the public welfare and results in paralysis of the society." [80] Addressing the legality of strikes, a Michigan appeals court declared that "it is well settled that there is neither a common law nor a constitutional right of public employees to strike." [81]

In addition to prohibiting work stoppages, state laws usually identify penalties for involvement in strikes. Such penalties can include withholding compensation for strike days and prohibiting salary increases for designated periods of time (e.g., one year). Despite the statutory prohibitions against strikes, an increasing number of teachers, as well as other public employees, participate in work stoppages each year. Public employers can request a court injunction against teachers who threaten to strike or initiate a strike. Failure of teachers to comply with such a restraining order can result in charges of contempt of court, with resulting fines and/or imprisonment. For example, teachers in Maryland who refused to obey an injunction were found guilty of criminal contempt.[82] In Newark, New Jersey, refusal to comply with an injunction resulted in a contempt of court charge, with fines and imprisonment for teachers and an additional fine for the union.[83] An order imposing a fine of ten dollars per day on striking teachers was upheld by the Wisconsin Supreme Court.[84] The court interpreted the statutory penalty as remaining in force from date of issuance of the injunction until the teachers returned to the classroom.

Even though the injunction has been the accepted legal response to strikes, recently there has been some reluctance on the part of courts to impose this sanction automatically. Other factors are being considered, such as whether the board bargained in "good faith," whether the strike constitutes a clear and present danger to public safety, and whether irreparable harm may result from the strike.[85] Demonstration by school boards of sufficient cause for an injunction will vary according to the jurisdictions and interpretation of applicable state statutes.

In addition to penalties for violation of court injunctions, teachers are subject to penalties provided in state statutes. Under the Taylor law, New York teachers are assessed two days' pay for each strike day.[86] Massachusetts law does not allow for compensation of strike days, even if teachers are required to work additional days to complete the required school term.[87] Several states disallow any salary increases for striking teachers. For example, Florida law prohibits any increase in compensation for a period of one year after a strike.[88] Minnesota has a similar antistrike statute that prevents a salary increase for one year and imposes a loss of pay for strike days.[89] Until the Pennsylvania strike statute was amended, salary increases were prevented for a three-year period following a strike.

A recent United States Tax Court ruling augments the impact of strike penalties by stipulating that employees must pay taxes on income lost during an illegal strike.[90] A New York teacher on strike for twenty-one days and assessed a penalty of loss of pay for an additional twenty-one days was held liable for taxes on forty-two days' salary.

The procedures required in the dismissal of striking teachers have received increasing judicial attention. In 1975, the Michigan Supreme Court held that a hearing was not required prior to the dismissal of striking teachers.[91] The Michigan Public Employees Relations Act (PERA) stipulates that if dismissal is based on participation in a strike, a hearing is not required until after dismissal, and then only upon request of the teacher. However, the Michigan Teachers' Tenure Act specifies that teachers can be dismissed only after all procedural steps have been followed. Thus, the court in this instance had to determine which act would govern. Since the dismissals were related to a labor dispute, the court ruled that PERA would govern the school board action. Generally, in strike-related dismissals, the fourteenth amendment ensures that teachers must be afforded procedural due process protections; however, in some situations, as in Michigan, the requirement can be legally met after the actual dismissal.

Since due process procedures are required for teachers, the question arises as to the nature and type of hearing that must be provided by the school system. The leading case on this issue involved Hortonville, Wisconsin, teachers who entered the 1973–74 school year without a negotiated contract and continued to work until March 1974, when they went on strike. After issuing two notices for the teachers to return to work, the board conducted a hearing and terminated the striking teachers. The Wisconsin Supreme Court ruled that striking teachers must be provided with an impartial and fair hearing, and that the board of education was not sufficiently impartial to serve as the hearing panel.[92] On appeal, the United States Supreme Court reversed the decision.[93] The Court maintained that the involvement on the part of the board did not overcome "the presumption of honesty and integrity in policy makers with decision making power." [94] The Court further held that "permitting the board to make the decision at issue here preserves its control over school district affairs, leaves the balance of power in labor relations where the state legislature struck it, and assures that the decision whether to dismiss the teacher will be made by the body responsible for that decision under state law." [95] Thus, the Supreme Court concluded that the fourteenth amendment guarantees each teacher a hearing, but only before the school board.

State legislatures and courts consistently have refused to grant public school teachers the right to strike. Even in the few states where a limited right to strike has been gained, extensive restrictions have been placed on its use. Teachers participating in an illegal strike are subject to court-imposed penalties, and also in most states to statutory penalties. Refusal of teachers to return to the classroom can result in dismissal.


## CONCLUSION

Because of the diversity in collective bargaining laws among states, legal principles with universal application are necessarily broad. Generalizations concerning collective bargaining rights that are applicable to most teachers are set forth below.

1. Teachers have a constitutionally protected right to form and join a union.
2. Specific bargaining rights are conferred through state statutes or judicial interpretations of state constitutions, thus creating wide divergence in bargaining rights among teachers.
3. School boards are not required to bargain with employee organizations unless so mandated by state law.
4. Collective bargaining must be conducted "in good faith," which means that the school board and teachers' organization attempt to reach agreement without compulsion on either side to agree.
5. Impasse procedures for public sector bargaining generally are limited to mediation and fact finding, with the public employer retaining final decision-making authority.
6. State legislation permitting the negotiation of an agency shop provision is constitutional.
7. Nonunion teachers have the right to express a viewpoint before the school board on an issue under negotiation between the board and union.
8. Scope of negotiation generally is defined to include wages, hours, and other terms and conditions of employment, such as teaching load, planning time, and lunch periods.
9. Subjects related to managerial policy making, such as class size, evaluations, and school calendar, are not mandatorily bargainable but may be permissive subjects unless prohibited by law.
10. Teacher strikes, except in limited situations in a few states, are illegal and punishable by dismissal, fines, and/or imprisonment.

## NOTES

1. *See* Benjamin Taylor and Fred Witney, *Labor Relations Law* (Englewood Cliffs, N.J.: Prentice-Hall, Inc., 1975), pp. 69–99, for a discussion of use and control of the labor injunction.
2. *Id.* at 154.
3. The Wagner Act states that "employees shall have the right to self-organization, to form, join or assist labor organizations, to bargain collectively through representatives of their own choosing, and to engage in concerted activities, for the purpose of collective bargaining or other mutual aid or protection." 29 U.S.C. § 157 (1976).
4. 3 C.F.R. 521 (Supp. 1962).
5. 385 U.S. 589 (1967).

6. McLaughlin v. Tilendis, 398 F.2d 287 (7th Cir. 1968).

7. Atkins v. City of Charlotte, 296 F. Supp. 1068 (W.D.N.C. 1969); Dade County Classroom Teachers' Ass'n v. Ryan, 225 So. 2d 903 (Fla. 1969). *See also* AFSCME v. Woodward, 406 F.2d 137 (8th Cir. 1969).

8. 426 U.S. 833 (1976).

9. *Id.* at 855.

10. Winston-Salem/Forsyth County Unit of the North Carolina Ass'n of Educators v. Phillips, 381 F. Supp. 644 (M.D.N.C. 1974).

11. Commonwealth of Virginia v. County Bd. of Arlington County, 232 S.E.2d 30 (Va. 1977).

12. Board of Trustees of University of Kentucky v. Public Employees Council No. 51, AFSCME, 571 S.W.2d 616 (Ky. 1978).

13. *See* Gary Teachers Union, Local No. 4, AFT v. School City of Gary, 284 N.E.2d 108 (Ind. App. 1972); Chicago Division of Ill. Educ. Ass'n v. Board of Educ., 222 N.E.2d 243 (Ill. App. 1966).

14. 29 U.S.C. § 158(d) (1976).

15. Perry A. Zirkel, "An Analysis of Selected Aspects of State Teacher-Board Negotiations Statutes," *NOLPE School Law Journal*, Vol. 6, No. 1, 1976, pp. 9–22.

16. *Id.* at 20. *See* Table IV for a summary, by state, of prohibited practices.

17. Fla. Stat. 447 § 501.

18. Me. Rev. Stat. 26 § 979.D(4).

19. R.I. Gen. Laws 28 § 9.3-9.

20. Ore. Rev. Stat. 243 § 706.

21. Education Commission of the States, *State Education Collective Bargaining Laws* (Denver, Colo.: Education Commission of the States, 1978).

22. Smigel v. Southgate Community School Dist., 202 N.W.2d 305 (Mich. 1972).

23. Abood v. Detroit Bd. of Educ., 230 N.W.2d 322 (Mich. App. 1975).

24. 431 U.S. 209 (1977).

25. *Id.* at 235.

26. Churchill v. School Adm'r Dist. No. 49 Teachers Ass'n, 380 A.2d 186 (Me. 1977).

27. Florida Educ. Ass'n/United v. PERC, 346 So. 2d 551 (Fla. App. 1977).

28. Alexander v. Anderson Fed'n, No. 25-77-861 (Super. Ct., Madison County, Ind., May 10, 1979).

29. Langley v. Uniontown Area School Dist., 367 A.2d 736 (Pa. Commw. 1977).

30. *NOLPE Notes*, Vol. 13, No. 5, May 1978, p. 1.

31. *See* Tinker v. Des Moines Independent Community School Dist., 393 U.S. 503 (1969); Pickering v. Board of Educ., 391 U.S. 563 (1968); Keyishian v. Board of Regents, 385 U.S. 589 (1967).

32. City of Madison v. Wisconsin Employment Relations Comm'n, 231 N.W.2d 206 (Wis. 1975).

33. City of Madison Joint School Dist. No. 8 v. Wisconsin Employment Relations Comm'n, 429 U.S. 167 (1976).

34. *Id.* at 175.

35. *Id.* at 176.

36. 29 U.S.C. § 158(d) (1976).

37. Pa. Stat. Ann. 43 § 1101.701.
38. Haw. Rev. Stat. 89 § 9(a). The statute goes beyond the NLRA provision and in § 9(d) specifies those items which cannot be negotiated, i.e., retirement benefits, public employees' health fund, classification and reclassification, and so forth.
39. Fla. Stat. 447 § 301(2).
40. Tenn. Code Ann. 49 § 11.
41. Nev. Rev. Stat. 228 § 150.
42. Pa. Stat. Ann. 43 § 1702.
43. Pa. Stat. Ann. 43 § 1101.703.
44. Ridgefield Park Educ. Ass'n v. Ridgefield Park Bd. of Educ., 393 A.2d 278 (N.J. 1978).
45. Id.
46. Aberdeen Educ. Ass'n v. Aberdeen Bd. of Educ., 215 N.W.2d 837 (S.D. 1974).
47. Clarke County School Dist. v. Local Gov't Employee Management Relations Bd., 530 P.2d 114 (Nev. 1974).
48. Pennsylvania Labor Relations Bd. v. State College Area School Dist., 337 A.2d 262 (Pa. 1975).
49. Scranton School Bd. v. Scranton Fed'n of Teachers, 365 A.2d 1339 (Pa. Commw. 1976).
50. Clarke County School Dist. v. Local Gov't Employee Management Relations Bd., 530 P.2d 114 (Nev. 1974).
51. Nev. Rev. Stat. 288 § 150.
52. Springfield Educ. Ass'n v. Springfield School Dist. No. 19, 547 P.2d 647 (Ore. App. 1976).
53. See West Irondequoit Teachers Ass'n v. Helsby, 315 N.E.2d 775 (N.Y. 1974); Susquehanna Valley Central School Dist. v. Susquehanna Valley Teachers Ass'n, 358 N.Y.S.2d 235 (App. Div. 1974).
54. Kenai Peninsula Borough v. Kenai Peninsula Educ. Ass'n, 572 P.2d 416 (Alaska 1977).
55. Id.
56. Clarke County School Dist. v. Local Gov't Employee Management Relations, 530 P.2d 114 (Nev. 1974).
57. Springfield Educ. Ass'n v. Springfield School Dist. No. 19, 547 P.2d 647 (Ore. App. 1976).
58. Beloit Educ. Ass'n v. Wisconsin Employment Relations Comm'n, 242 N.W.2d 231 (Wis. 1976).
59. Id.
60. See Galloway Township Bd. of Educ. v. Galloway Township Educ. Ass'n, 384 A.2d 547 (N.J. App. 1978); Byram Township Bd. of Educ. v. Byram Township Educ. Ass'n, 377 A.2d 745 (N.J. App. 1977); Clarke County School Dist. v. Local Gov't Employee Management Relations, 530 P.2d 114 (Nev. 1974).
61. Beloit Educ. Ass'n v. Wisconsin Employment Relations Comm'n, 242 N.W.2d 231 (Wis. 1976).
62. Springfield Educ. Ass'n v. Springfield School Dist. No. 19, 547 P.2d 647 (Ore. App. 1976).

63. Clarke County School Dist. v. Local Gov't Employee Management Relations, 530 P.2d 114 (Nev. 1974).
64. Teaneck Bd. of Educ. v. Teaneck Teachers Ass'n, 390 A.2d 1198 (N.J. Super. 1978); Kenai Peninsula Borough v. Kenai Peninsula Educ. Ass'n, 572 P.2d 416 (Alaska 1977).
65. PLRB v. Mars Area School Dist., 344 A.2d 284 (Pa. Commw. 1975); Hill v. Dayton School Dist. No. 2, 532 P.2d 1154 (Wash. 1975).
66. Union County Regional High School Bd. of Educ. v. Union County Regional High School Teachers Ass'n, Inc., 368 A.2d 364 (N.J. App. 1976).
67. See Minnesota Fed'n of Teachers Local 59 v. Minnesota School Dist. No. 1, 258 N.W.2d 802 (Minn. 1977).
68. Board of Educ. of the City of Englewood v. Englewood Teachers' Ass'n, 375 A.2d 669 (N.J. App. 1977).
69. Cohoes City School Dist. v. Cohoes Teachers Ass'n, 358 N.E.2d 878 (N.Y. 1976).
70. Id.
71. Morris Central School Dist. v. Morris Educ. Ass'n, 388 N.Y.S.2d 371 (App. Div. 1976). See also Lake County Educ. Ass'n v. School Bd. of Lake County, 360 So. 2d 1280 (Fla. App. 1978).
72. In a Bureau of Labor Statistics Study of 318 public sector collective bargaining agreements, approximately 90 percent contained grievance procedures. Bureau of Labor Statistics, Collective Bargaining Agreements for State and County Government Employees (Washington, D.C.: Government Printing Office, 1976).
73. See Education Commission of the States, State Education Collective Bargaining Laws.
74. Binding arbitration is a procedure whereby both parties (employee organization and school board) are bound by the decision of a third party.
75. Moravek v. Davenport Community School Dist., 262 N.W.2d 797 (Iowa 1978).
76. Dayton Classroom Teachers Ass'n v. Dayton Bd. of Educ., 323 N.E.2d 714 (Ohio 1975).
77. See Education Commission of the States, State Education Collective Bargaining Laws.
78. Fla. Stat. 447 § 505.
79. Norwalk Teachers Ass'n v. Board of Educ. of City of Norwalk, 83 A.2d 482, 485 (Conn. 1951).
80. Anderson Fed'n of Teachers v. School City of Anderson, 251 N.E.2d 15 (Ind. 1969).
81. Rockwell v. Board of Educ. of Crestwood, 226 N.W.2d 596 (Mich. App. 1975).
82. Harford County Educ. Ass'n v. Board of Educ. of Harford County, 380 A.2d 1041 (Md. 1977).
83. Board of Educ. of Newark v. Newark Teachers Union, 276 A.2d 175 (N.J. Super. 1971).
84. Joint School Dist. No. 1, City of Wisconsin Rapids v. Wisconsin Rapids Educ. Ass'n, 234 N.W.2d 289 (Wis. 1975).
85. Joint School Dist. No. 1, City of Wisconsin Rapids v. Wisconsin Rapids

Educ. Ass'n, 234 N.W.2d 289 (Wis. 1975); Bristol Township Educ. Ass'n v. School Dist. of Bristol Township, 322 A.2d 767 (Pa. Commw. 1974); Timberlane Regional School Dist. v. Timberlane Regional Educ. Ass'n, 317 A.2d 555 (N.H. 1974); School Dist. for City of Holland v. Holland Educ. Ass'n, 157 N.W.2d 206 (Mich. 1968).

86. Lawson v. Board of Educ. of Vestal Central School Dist. No. 1, 315 N.Y.S.2d 877 (App. Div. 1970).

87. Mass. Gen. Laws 150E § 15.

88. Fla. Stat. 447 § 507.(5)(6).

89. Head v. Special School Dist. No. 1, 182 N.W.2d 887 (Minn. 1970).

90. Tucker v. Commissioner of Internal Revenue, 69 T.C. No. 54 (1978).

91. Rockwell v. Board of Educ. of School Dist. of Crestwood, 227 N.W.2d 736 (Mich. 1975).

92. Hortonville Educ. Ass'n v. Hortonville Joint School Dist., 225 N.W.2d 658 (Wis. 1975).

93. Hortonville Joint School Dist. v. Hortonville Educ. Ass'n, 426 U.S. 482 (1976).

94. *Id.* at 497.

95. *Id.* at 496.

# 7

# Tort Liability

Other chapters in this book focus primarily on the legal resolution of conflicts between governmental interests in maintaining public schools and individual interests in exercising constitutional and statutory rights. In contrast, this chapter examines principles of tort law which offer remedies to individuals for harm caused by the unreasonable conduct of others. This branch of law involves civil suits, which pertain to the private rights of citizens, as opposed to criminal suits, which are initiated by the state to redress public offenses. Generally, a tort is defined as a civil wrong, independent of breach of contract, for which a court will provide relief in the form of damages. Tort cases are mainly handled on the basis of state laws[1] and are grounded in the fundamental premise that all individuals are liable for the consequences of their conduct.

Tort actions can be grouped into three major categories: negligence, intentional torts, and strict liability. Negligence involves conduct that falls below an acceptable standard of care and results in injury.[2] Intentional torts are committed with the desire to inflict harm, and include assault, battery, false imprisonment, trespass, and defamation. Strict liability occurs when an injury results from the creation of an unusual hazard (e.g., the storage of explosives), and the injured party need not establish that the injury was knowingly or negligently caused. Seldom have allegations of strict liability appeared in education cases. Some school-related injuries have generated intentional tort actions, but the vast majority of tort cases involving school districts and educational employees have entailed allegations of negligence. Accordingly, this chapter primarily deals with the conditions necessary to establish negligence and the legal defenses employed by school personnel to rebut negligence charges.

## ELEMENTS OF NEGLIGENCE

Negligence is a breach of one's legal duty to protect others from unreasonable risks of harm. A charge of negligence can result when the failure to act or an improper act causes injury to another person.[3] In order for negligence to exist, the person causing the injury must fail to exercise a standard of care commensurate with the duty owed to the injured party and the risks involved. Also, there must be a causal relationship between the alleged negligent conduct and the injury sustained. The ability to foresee harm is an important factor in determining whether or not an individual's conduct is negligent. Courts assess whether a reasonably prudent person under the same or similar circumstances would have anticipated the harmful consequences. A teacher's conduct is gauged by how a reasonable teacher, who has had special training to assume that role, would have acted in a similar situation.

Negligence cases include questions of law, which are determined by judges, and questions of fact, which are decided by juries. In some instances, a judge may conclude that there are no material factual issues to submit to a jury and thus return a directed verdict. Where a trial does take place, a judge can reverse the jury's decision if clearly erroneous. Judges, however, will not exercise this authority unless supported by overwhelming evidence.

### BREACH OF DUTY TO PROTECT OTHERS FROM HARM

Various courts have noted that teachers owe students a duty to provide adequate supervision and instruction, to maintain equipment in good repair, and to provide warnings regarding any known dangers.[4] The nature of the duty owed is determined by factors such as the age of the pupils, the environment, and the type of instructional activities taking place. The duty to protect students from harm is increased in laboratory classes, gymnasiums, and other environments where risk of harm is great.

A teacher, however, does not have a duty to keep each student under constant surveillance or to anticipate every possible accident that might occur; teachers cannot be held liable for unforeseeable injuries. Even if supervision is inadequate, a teacher will not be held negligent if it is established that the injury could have occurred as easily in the presence of proper supervision.[5] In an illustrative Missouri case, an appeals court concluded that a kindergarten teacher did not breach her duty of supervision simply because she was attending to other students when a child fell during recess while attempting to swing down from a jungle gym.[6] The court concluded that the teacher was not required to have each pupil in sight at all times. Similarly, a Louisiana appeals court held that a teacher was not negligent with respect to an injury sustained by a child who fell on a tree stump at recess.[7] The court reasoned that the stump was not so hazardous as to place a special duty on the teacher to anticipate harm.

Courts, however, have awarded damages in suits involving pupil injuries if school employees were aware of, or should have been aware of, hazardous conditions and breached their duty to protect students from the special risks of harm. In a Washington, D.C., case, school personnel were found negligent for breaching their duty to provide safety precautions or additional supervisors on a playground with a fence in disrepair.[8] Other courts have recognized that school personnel have a duty to maintain play areas in proper condition and to warn students of any known dangers.[9]

Courts also have ruled that school districts have a duty to maintain school facilities, as well as playgrounds, in good repair.[10] If school officials are aware of a defective condition and do not act to rectify it, they can be held liable for resulting injuries. On the other hand, the duty to provide reasonable maintenance of facilities does not place an obligation on school personnel to be aware of and correct every minor defect as soon as the condition occurs. For example, in a Louisiana case a student was unsuccessful in establishing a breach of duty in connection with an injury sustained on a defective door latch.[11] The appeals court concluded that there was no evidence that any school employee had knowledge of, or should have had knowledge of, the broken latch. Therefore, a duty to protect the student from the resulting injury could not be imposed.

Allegations that school personnel have breached their duty to maintain equipment in proper condition have often arisen in connection with student injuries sustained during athletic events. In 1978, an Illinois appeals court concluded that football coaches had a duty to inspect equipment provided to team members and were liable for student injuries resulting from the failure to conduct such inspections.[12] In the same year, the Illinois Supreme Court held that a school district breached its duty to protect athletes from harm by providing an ill-fitting and inadequate football helmet to a student.[13] The Massachusetts high court also concluded that a school district was liable for supplying a defective helmet to a student hockey player. The court noted that the student had every reason to expect the hockey coach to supply team members with proper equipment.[14]

In 1967, the New Jersey Supreme Court discussed the liability of school personnel in situations where they have *assumed a duty* to provide supervision and have not acted appropriately.[15] The case involved a student who was seriously injured by a paper clip shot by another child on school grounds before school opened. Children regularly gathered on the premises before the start of classes to connect with buses for other schools. The court concluded that the principal was aware of the need for supervision before school and had assumed the duty of providing this service between 8:00 A.M. and 8:15 A.M., at which time he had instructed teachers to arrive. However, the principal had not established conduct rules for the students, nor had he attempted to secure additional adult supervisors to assist him. Concluding that the provision of proper supervision might have prevented the injury sustained, the court held that the principal was liable for damages.

Some cases have dealt with the responsibility of school personnel to supervise students on school grounds after regular school hours. In Louisiana, a teacher was relieved of liability in connection with an after-school injury. In this case, a third-grade pupil was cut on the eye by a knife wielded by another pupil.[16] The teacher had gone home after school, leaving three boys in her classroom unsupervised. She had forbidden the students to go near her desk, where a knife was kept in a drawer. The court concluded that the teacher did not have a duty to supervise the students after school, even though one of the students had been asked to stay and do chores in the classroom.

Courts have rendered conflicting decisions on the school's duty to protect students from harm on school playgrounds after school. Damages have been awarded to students injured after school hours if the injuries have resulted from unsafe playground conditions.[17] A student in Michigan was successful in obtaining damages for the loss of sight in his right eye.[18] He sustained this injury while playing among piles of dirt and sand on the playground after school. The area was not fenced, and prior to the incident parents had complained to the school district concerning the dirt piles and "dirt fights" among children playing there. The Michigan appeals court concluded that the school district breached its duty to maintain the school grounds in a safe condition. In contrast, a California appeals court concluded that the school district was not liable for the death of a student on school grounds after school.[19] Although the playground was accessible to the public, unsupervised, and in disrepair, the court concluded that the student's death resulted from his own conduct in performing a hazardous skateboard activity, not from the defective condition of the playground. The court further stated that school employees were not responsible for students after school hours (except for school-related activities), even if school officials were aware that children used the playground.

The school's duty to protect truant students from injury was addressed by the California Supreme Court in 1978. The case involved a pupil who left school without permission and was struck by a motorcycle several blocks from school.[20] The trial court concluded that the duty of school personnel to protect the student from harm terminated when he became truant. The California Supreme Court, however, reversed the trial court's decision, reasoning that the provision of proper supervision at school might have prevented the student's truancy and subsequent injury.

While school personnel have a duty to provide appropriate supervision and instruction and to protect students from unreasonable hazards, educators are not the absolute insurers of pupil safety. Students themselves also are expected to act reasonably and to take appropriate precautions against known dangers. Courts will assess the facts of each situation when determining the extent of the school's duty to shield pupils from injury.

## FAILURE TO EXERCISE REASONABLE CARE

All school personnel are expected to exercise a reasonable standard of care commensurate with their duty to protect others from risks of harm. As noted previously, the appropriate standard of care will fluctuate according to each set of circumstances. If a situation entails special dangers, the provision of additional safety precautions and supervision is expected.

Many cases challenging the adequacy of a teacher's standard of care have involved injuries sustained in gymnasiums, where appropriate supervision and instruction are essential.[21] An Illinois appeals court concluded that a physical education teacher did not exercise a reasonable standard of care in forcing an overweight student to perform a backwards somersault which resulted in injury.[22] The court noted that the teacher was aware of the child's fear of completing the exercise and of the special risks associated with the student's obesity. Similarly, a New York teacher was found to have exercised an improper standard of care in connection with an injury sustained by a student who was instructed to participate in physical education activities in his bare feet because he had forgotten his gym shoes.[23] In another New York case, a student who was injured while attempting a high jump during physical education class was awarded damages. The court ruled that the teacher was negligent in encouraging the student to try the jump when he had unsuccessfully attempted jumps with the bar at a lower level.[24] A teacher also was found negligent for permitting two male students to engage in boxing without proper training, while the teacher sat in the bleachers.[25] One of the students was fatally injured, and the teacher was held liable for providing inadequate instruction and supervision.

Although a teacher's mere absence from the classroom is not sufficient to establish negligence, the length of the absence may be a controlling factor in determining whether the teacher exercised reasonable care. The Supreme Court of Wisconsin held that there were legitimate issues of negligence in a situation where a fourteen-year-old pupil was injured in a rowdy game in the school gymnasium. The game took place while the teacher was gone for twenty-five minutes, leaving fifty adolescent males unsupervised.[26]

Foreseeability of harm is a crucial consideration in assessing the adequacy of a teacher's standard of care. In a California case, a teacher was held negligent because he was careless in failing to observe and stop dangerous activity that resulted in an injury.[27] The teacher took his class outside on the school lawn for instruction, and one of the students picked up a homemade knife on the way out of the classroom. The student, who was seated with other pupils around the teacher, began throwing the knife into the ground. This activity continued for some time. Eventually, the knife hit a drawing board, was deflected, and struck another pupil in the eye. The court concluded that the teacher should have been aware of the dangerous activity, which could have been curbed prior to the injury.

Courts, however, have not assessed damages against school personnel unless the injury might have been prevented by the exercise of proper supervision typically required by the circumstances. Two pupil injury cases involving rock throwing incidents illuminate the importance of "foreseeability of harm" in determining the outcome of negligence cases. In one instance, where student rock throwing had continued for almost ten minutes before the injury occurred, the court found the supervising teacher liable for negligence.[28] In contrast, in a situation where a teacher aide had walked past a group of students moments before one child threw a rock that was deflected and hit another pupil, no liability was assessed against the aide.[29] The court concluded that the teacher aide had provided adequate supervision and had no reason to have anticipated the event that caused the injury.

In a Louisiana case, negligence charges against a teacher also were dismissed due to evidence that the pupil injury was unforeseeable.[30] The child was injured by an explosion in a trash burner while emptying a classroom wastebasket. The Louisiana appeals court noted that there had been no accidents associated with the burner for forty years, and that the burner could not be considered so dangerous as to warrant special safety precautions. Thus, the teacher had no reason to predict that an explosion would occur. In contrast, a Michigan appeals court concluded that a student who was injured when an alcohol wick lamp exploded during science class was entitled to seek damages for negligence. The court reasoned that the principal and teacher should have anticipated the special risks associated with conducting science experiments in a room that was neither designed nor equipped for laboratory work.[31]

In some situations, teachers have successfully rebutted charges of negligence by establishing that proper instructions were given to the students, but were disregarded. In a case involving a shop class injury resulting from a nail thrown by a student, the South Carolina Supreme Court concluded that the teacher provided adequate supervision and was not negligent, since he had forbidden students to throw objects.[32] The court emphasized that the teacher could not be held responsible for an injury caused by a student who disobeyed orders.

Pupil injuries during field trips often have evoked tort actions challenging the adequacy of adult supervision. It is a widely held misconception that permission slips signed by parents relieve school personnel of liability for injuries that occur during such school-related activities. Permission slips serve a useful purpose in documenting that parents are aware of their child's whereabouts and participation in the special activities, but parents cannot waive their child's entitlement to proper supervision. In an illustrative case, the Supreme Court of Oregon assessed liability against a teacher for an injury sustained by a student at a beach during a school outing.[33] The court concluded that the unusual wave action on the Oregon coast was a known hazard, and that the teacher failed to take reasonable safety precautions.

While a high standard of care is required during field trips to unfamiliar places, school personnel are not held liable for every injury that occurs, as long as students are adequately supervised. For example, no liability was assessed in connection with the death of a student on a band trip who drowned when he dove into the deep end of the swimming pool at the hotel.[34] The Louisiana appeals court reasoned that appropriate supervision was provided by school personnel, who had not been informed that the student could not swim. In fact, the child's parents had given permission for him to use the pool. The court concluded that he voluntarily dove into the deep end, and thus drowned through no fault of the supervisors.

Some lawsuits have challenged the standard of care exercised by school personnel in the treatment of students after accidents have occurred. Courts have upheld the right of teachers and administrators to provide emergency first aid treatment to pupils if the treatment has been reasonable. However, courts have recognized that students should not be moved or treated unless such emergency aid is absolutely necessary prior to the arrival of appropriate medical personnel. Liability has been assessed in instances where injured students have been negligently moved from playing fields during athletic events.[35] Improperly administered first aid also has resulted in liability. In 1979, an Illinois appeals court recognized that public policy considerations dictate an obligation to ensure that medical treatment undertaken by a school or its agent is competently rendered.[36] In a Pennsylvania case, two teachers were held personally liable for administering medical treatment to a student by holding his infected finger under boiling water.[37] The superior court held that the action was not reasonable, and noted that the situation did not necessitate emergency first aid.

Teachers and administrators, because of their special training to assume such roles, are expected to make sound judgments as to the appropriate standard of care required in any given school situation. The adequacy of care is measured against the risks of harm involved. Reasonable actions in one instance may be considered unreasonable under other conditions. Courts assess the facts of each case in determining whether the standard of care is proper in light of the attendant circumstances.

## DEFENSES AGAINST NEGLIGENCE

There are several defenses that school districts and school employees may use in rebutting charges of negligence.[38] Traditionally, the most frequently used defense has been governmental immunity which is based on the common law notion that governmental agencies cannot be held liable for torts committed by their employees. The defense of contributory negligence, which relies on evidence that the action of the injured party was a substantial factor in causing the injury, also has appeared in educational litigation. In some instances, liability has been awarded in relation to the fault of each party involved (comparative negligence). Procedural defects in the suits, such as failure to adhere to statutory requirements regarding notice of claim, also have been used to relieve defendants of liability for damages. Other defenses proffered in educational negligence cases have included assertions that an intervening event caused the injury, that the injured party assumed the risk of a known danger, or that the injury was caused by uncontrollable events of nature. Given the frequency with which they have appeared in school litigation, several of these defenses warrant additional explication.

## GOVERNMENTAL IMMUNITY

The doctrine of governmental or sovereign immunity originated in the middle ages from the notion that "the king can do no wrong." Subsequently, this idea was translated into the common law principle that government agencies cannot be held liable for the negligent acts of their officers, agents, or employees.[39] Various rationales have been offered for applying sovereign immunity to school districts, such as the involuntary status of government agencies and their legal inability to pay tort claims since public funds are to be used only for statutorily prescribed purposes.[40]

While governmental immunity for torts still exists under common law, several legislative and judicial inroads have partially eroded the vitality of this doctrine.[41] In many states, immunity has been abrogated by legislative action, and in others, the use of immunity has been curtailed by judicial decree.[42] In states where governmental immunity has not been totally dissolved, certain restrictions have been placed on its use as a defense in negligence cases.

For example, most states have enacted "safe place" statutes that protect frequenters of public buildings from danger to life, health, safety, or welfare. Such statutes have been used successfully by individuals to obtain damages from school districts for injuries resulting from defective conditions of school buildings and grounds.[43] However, such "safe place" statutes do not cover the *use* of facilities or the equipment contained in the buildings. A Michigan appeals court noted that the absence of a safety net between tennis courts did not come within the "public building exception" to immunity. Therefore, a school district could not be held liable for an injury sustained by a student who was struck by a tennis ball during physical education class.[44]

In addition to being restricted by safe place statutes from using sovereign immunity as a defense, government agencies also cannot plead immunity if they maintain a public nuisance that results in harm to an individual.[45] A nuisance is defined as an annoyance that interferes with common public rights.[46] Swimming pools or ponds on school property are classified as attractive nuisances, and therefore school districts are not shielded by immunity if proper precautions are not taken to prevent public access to such areas.

In some jurisdictions, a distinction has been made between governmental functions and proprietary functions in limiting the immunity of school districts. Governmental functions, which are performed in discharging the agency's official duties, have been considered immune from liability. On the other hand, proprietary functions, which could be provided as easily by a private corporation, have been legitimate targets for tort actions. Courts have not agreed, however, as to which school functions should be considered proprietary in nature. Some courts have held that profit-making extracurricular activities are proprietary functions, while other courts have ruled that all extracurricular activities are part of the educational mission of the school district and thus protected by immunity.[47]

Several courts have rejected the governmental/proprietary distinction and have instead distinguished between ministerial and discretionary functions in determining a school district's potential liability. For example, in 1977 the Massachusetts Supreme Judicial Court concluded that school districts were liable for negligence involving ministerial duties in the administration of policies, but were immune from liability for negligence associated with discretionary, policy-making activities.[48]

Despite judicial and legislative action limiting governmental immunity, this defense continues to be used in some jurisdictions to protect school districts against liability for negligence. In two 1979 Missouri cases, school districts successfully relied on governmental immunity to bar recovery for pupil injuries sustained at school.[49] The Missouri Supreme Court concluded that school districts were not considered municipal corporations for purposes of the state law abrogating immunity of municipalities under certain circumstances. Furthermore, the court held that their purchase of liability insurance did not waive the immunity of school districts.[50] In Illinois, the procurement of such insurance has been interpreted as waiving immunity within the limits of the policy, but school districts declining to obtain insurance can rely on governmental immunity to shield them from liability for negligence.[51]

While school employees are not protected by the common law notion of governmental immunity, some states have enacted statutes that provide partial immunity for the negligent acts of teachers. Illinois law, for example, confers in loco parentis (in place of parent) status on educational employees and stipulates that willful and wanton misconduct must be established in order for liability to be assessed in connection with strictly educational activities. A state appeals court noted, however, that this protection applies only to negligence arising in the direct student-teacher relationship. Consequently, negligence associated with duties such as providing equipment to student athletes need not be accompanied by willful or wanton misconduct in order for liability to be assessed.[52]

## CONTRIBUTORY NEGLIGENCE

The assertion that an injured student's own acts contributed to the injury often has been used by school personnel as a defense against negligence charges. If contributory negligence were not considered by courts, an impossible burden would be placed on teachers to ensure the safety of students regardless of the students' own actions in disobeying instructions properly given.[53] In determining the validity of contributory negligence as a defense, courts have evaluated whether or not the teacher exercised a reasonable standard of care in anticipating dangers and in warning students about any special risks of harm.

School personnel have been successful in using contributory negligence if they have been able to prove that the child was aware of, or should have been aware of, the consequences of the actions and nonetheless engaged in dangerous conduct.[54] However, school personnel have been unsuccessful in using this defense if the child did not know of the hazards involved in the activity.[55] For example, a student who was waiting for a teacher outside an area marked "danger" in an industrial arts class was injured when a cylinder exploded.[56] The Louisiana appeals court concluded that the student was acting appropriately in waiting outside the danger area and had no reason to expect the injury to occur. Therefore, the defense of contributory negligence could not be used.

## INTERVENING ACT

Even in situations in which a teacher breaches the duty to supervise students and exercises an improper standard of care, liability will not be assessed if the teacher's actions were not the proximate cause of the injury sustained. In some instances an intervening event, such as the negligence of a third party, has relieved school personnel of liability. In an illustrative case, school officials had excused students to ride with the mother of one of the pupils to a wrestling tournament that was not sponsored by the school.[57] During the trip, two of the boys spilled gasoline on their pants at a service station. Subsequently, one child ignited the clothing, causing second and third degree burns to the plaintiff. The Supreme Court of Alaska ruled that the intervening acts of the parent relieved the school district of any liability for the resulting injuries. The court noted that it would be unreasonable to force the school to supervise continuously students or to prohibit parents from transporting students to athletic events. The court concluded that even if the school's failure to supervise the students was a factor in producing the injury, the mother's intervening negligence was the superseding cause.

In determining liability for negligence, courts have evaluated whether or not school personnel should have anticipated and prevented the intervening act. A Maryland appeals court concluded that a teacher had no reason to predict an intervening event that caused injury to a fourth-grade pupil who was engaged in a program of calisthenics while the teacher was absent briefly from the room.[58] The injury occurred when another child moved from his position, contrary to instructions, and struck the plaintiff with his feet while performing the exercises. The court reasoned that the incident could have occurred with the teacher in the classroom, and therefore her absence was not the proximate cause of the injury sustained. Similarly, a New York appeals court held that a teacher who was absent from the room was not liable for a pupil injury occasioned when a child sat down on the point of a pencil placed on his chair by another student.[59] The court concluded that the teacher could not have anticipated the intervening act of the student, and therefore was not negligent.

The existence of intervening events, however, has not always relieved teachers of liability for their negligent conduct. In a California case involving a student who was killed while engaging in an unsupervised "slap boxing" match on school grounds, the state supreme court held that the negligent supervision provided by school personnel was the proximate cause of the student's fatal injury.[60] While noting that another student's misconduct was the precipitating cause of the injury, the court concluded that with proper supervision the dangerous "slap boxing" activity would have been curtailed. Even when an intervening event actually causes a given injury, if school personnel place students in a dangerous situation, or if they reasonably should anticipate special risks of harm, they will not be relieved of liability for their negligent conduct.

## NOTICE OF CLAIM

Procedural defects in the process of filing a tort action can preclude recovery by the injured party. Most states specify the form to be used when initiating a suit and the time period within which a claim must be filed. Such requirements are designed to afford defendants an opportunity to investigate the claim while the facts surrounding it are still relatively recent.

When minors have been involved in the suits, some courts have allowed late petitions to be filed as long as they have been filed within a reasonable period of time, such as one year, from the date of the injury.[61] For example, the Supreme Court of Utah held that a minor's period of disability resulting from a shop class injury should not be considered part of the elapsed time for purposes of limiting the filing of a suit for damages.[62] In ruling that special consideration should be given to minors, the court noted that children are incapable of bringing suit and are left unprotected unless parents file the claim. A California appeals court also concluded that a minor should not be penalized because his parents neglected to initiate a timely action.[63] In contrast, a New York appeals court interpreted state law as not allowing time extensions for the filing of claims involving minors.[64]

## ASSAULT AND BATTERY

Although negligence cases have dominated educational tort litigation, a few intentional tort actions have been initiated. An intentional tort need not be maliciously planned, but may be committed if a person intentionally proceeds to act in a manner that impairs the rights of others. Intentional tort actions in school settings mainly have involved charges of assault and battery.

Assault consists of an overt attempt to place another in fear of bodily harm; no actual physical contact need take place. When an assault is consummated and physical injury occurs, battery is committed. A person wielding a knife and threatening harm is guilty of assault; the actual stabbing constitutes battery.

Assault and battery cases in the school context generally have focused on the administration of corporal punishment by school personnel. Courts have been reluctant to interfere with a teacher's authority to discipline students, and have sanctioned the use of reasonable force to control pupil behavior. For example, an Oregon appeals court ruled that a teacher was not guilty of assault and battery for using force to remove a student from the classroom.[65] After the pupil defiantly refused to leave the room, the teacher held his arms and led him toward the door. The student extricated himself, swung at the teacher, and broke a window, thereby cutting his arm. Concluding that the teacher used reasonable force with the student, the court dismissed the assault and battery charges.

A Louisiana appeals court also dismissed battery charges against a teacher who gently kicked a student.[66] Testimony revealed that the student had repeatedly disobeyed the teacher and had turned around in his chair to talk to classmates when the incident occurred. The teacher, who was holding chalk and an eraser in his hands, pushed the student with his foot in the right buttock to gain the pupil's attention. The court rejected the battery charge, reasoning that the blow was of little force and resulted in embarrassment more than pain. The court considered this situation to be one of the few circumstances in which a kick would meet the test of reasonableness.

In another Louisiana case, however, a student was successful in obtaining damages for assault and battery.[67] The pupil sustained a broken arm when a teacher shook him against bleachers in the gymnasium and then let him fall to the floor. The court reasoned that the teacher's action was unnecessary to discipline the student or to protect himself. Recognizing that the use of excessive or brutal force with pupils can result in liability for assault and battery, the court assessed damages against the teacher.

## WORKERS' COMPENSATION

Personal injury suits on behalf of school employees usually have been initiated under workers' compensation laws. Under such statutes, negligence on the part of the employer need not be established; employees can recover damages for accidental injuries as long as they are work-related. Although the application of workers' compensation statutes to school employees has been challenged, courts have ruled that such provisions waive the immunity of school districts for employee injuries, and that the purchase of workers' compensation insurance is a legitimate expenditure of public funds.[68]

Generally, workers' compensation statutes exclude coverage for injuries sustained enroute to or from work. In a South Carolina case, an assistant principal was unsuccessful in obtaining workers' compensation benefits for an automobile accident that occurred while he was driving to his out-of-town residence after supervising an evening football game.[69] He claimed that his permanent disabilities were employment related, because his journey home was part of the special evening duties he was performing for the school. The Supreme Court of South Carolina disagreed. It held that the assistant principal was not performing a service for his employer during his normal trip home, nor was the trip required by his school duties. Other courts also have disallowed damages in situations where employees have been injured in transit to or from work and such travel has not been a specific job requirement.[70]

However, if employees must drive as part of their regular employment activities (e.g., a librarian who serves two schools) and an accident occurs during such work-related travel, valid grounds for recovery under workers' compensation laws can be established. A Pennsylvania appeals court concluded that a principal who was injured while on his way to transact business with the state department of education was covered by workers' compensation.[71]

The mere fact that an injury occurs at school does not entitle an employee to workers' compensation benefits unless it is established that the injury is job-related. For example, a teacher's widow was unsuccessful in securing benefits after her husband was murdered at school.[72] The deceased was murdered by another teacher's jealous husband, and the New Mexico appeals court ruled that the action, taken for personal reasons, was not a risk associated with employment. In contrast, a New York appeals court held that the death of an elementary school principal who had a heart attack at school was work-related.[73] The court noted that during the school year preceding the fatal attack, the deceased had been involved in preparing an extensive report in addition to his regular duties, and that he had been instructed by his physician to lessen his work activities. Based on the physician's testimony, the court concluded that the principal's death was sufficiently related to employment to entitle his estate to workers' compensation benefits.

Questions have arisen concerning the status of student teachers under workers' compensation provisions. In 1978, the Michigan Supreme Court interpreted the state law as covering university students who were injured while student teaching in local school districts.[74] The court reasoned that such individuals were considered employees, since they performed a service in the school and were compensated in the form of training experience.

## DEFAMATION

While most tort actions have involved claims for damages due to physical injuries, some plaintiffs have sought recovery for injuries to their reputations. Generally, *defamation* is defined as false and intentional communication that places another person in a position of disgrace, ridicule, or contempt.[75] *Slander* is spoken defamation, and *libel* is written defamation.

Under certain circumstances, communication is considered privileged and cannot be the grounds for a defamation suit. Statements made by justices and state officials in carrying out governmental services are usually considered absolutely privileged. Qualified privilege is often applied to statements made by educational personnel, and such communication is immune from liability as long as it is made "upon a proper occasion, from a proper motive, in a proper manner, and based upon reasonable or probable cause." [76] Qualified privilege will not shield educators if statements are made with malicious intent. The mere transmittal of erroneous information, however, does not constitute evidence of malice, as long as the communication is believed to be accurate and is conveyed in good faith. In some states, truth can be used as a defamation defense, but usually, even if the communication is true, it must be made with good intentions in order to thwart defamation charges.

Despite the recent interest in the privacy rights of students, there has been a dearth of defamation cases involving students. Most defamation cases pertaining to schools have been initiated by teachers challenging evaluations placed in their personnel files or statements made by parents to school officials. In one such case, an Arizona appeals court held that parents were not liable for defamation of character simply because they submitted to the school board a list of grievances against a teacher.[77] Similarly, in a California case, a vice-principal was unsuccessful in a defamation suit brought against a group of parents who made several allegations about him to the school board.[78] The court concluded that communication between citizens and public officials who are charged with investigating activities of employees is privileged. In another California case, an appeals court also rejected charges of libel against parents for writing a letter to a school principal in which they made derogatory statements about a teacher. The court stated:

> One of the crosses a public school teacher must bear is intemperate complaint addressed to school administrators by overly-solicitous parents concerned about the teacher's conduct in the classroom. Since the law compels parents to send their children to school, appropriate channels for the airing of supposed grievances against the operation of the school system must remain open.[79]

## LIABILITY INSURANCE

Many states have enacted statutes that require or permit school boards to purchase insurance to cover damages for negligence assessed against the school district. If the purchase of such insurance is mandated by law and a school board fails to procure adequate coverage, the board may be held liable for the difference between the district's effective coverage and the statutory limits placed on awards against school districts for negligence.[80]

In a few states in which the application of sovereign immunity has not been limited, courts have ruled that the purchase of insurance to indemnify school districts is unnecessary because it protects a government agency against a threat that cannot exist. Under such circumstances, courts have concluded that the use of public funds to purchase liability insurance is illegal.[81] In states authorizing the purchase of liability insurance to protect government agencies, conflicting rulings have been rendered as to whether the acquisition of such insurance waives the sovereign immunity of the school district. In 1978, the Illinois Supreme Court held that a school board's purchase of insurance suggested a waiver of immunity up to the amount covered by the policy.[82] The same year, however, the Michigan Supreme Court concluded that a school district did not waive its immunity by providing a policy of general liability insurance.[83] In 1979, the Supreme Court of Missouri also ruled that the purchase of insurance did not alter the immune status of a school district.[84]

Some states that have abrogated immunity for government agencies have enacted statutes requiring or allowing school districts to purchase insurance to "save harmless" and protect employees from financial loss in connection with charges of negligence. Mandatory "save harmless" legislation places an obligation on school boards to defend employees in negligence suits arising out of employment duties as long as the employees' actions were taken in good faith.[85] In states with such laws, school employees can still be found negligent, but they are relieved of responsibility for any monetary damages assessed by the courts.

## CONCLUSION

Tort actions, primarily involving pupil injuries resulting from alleged negligence on the part of school personnel, undoubtedly will continue to generate extensive litigation. To guard against liability, teachers and administrators should be cognizant of the following basic principles of tort law:

1. All individuals are responsible for any harmful consequences of their conduct.
2. The propriety of a teacher's conduct in a given situation is gauged by whether a reasonably prudent teacher (with the special skills and training associated with that role) would have acted in a similar fashion under like conditions.
3. Teachers owe students a duty to provide proper instruction and adequate supervision, to maintain equipment in proper repair, and to provide warnings regarding any known hazards.
4. Teachers are expected to exercise a standard of care commensurate with the duty owed; with more dangerous activities, a higher standard of care is required.
5. Foreseeability of harm is a crucial element in determining whether a teacher's actions are negligent in a given situation.
6. An intervening act can relieve a teacher of liability for negligence if the intervening event caused the injury and the teacher had no reason to anticipate that the event would occur.
7. The common law doctrine that government agencies cannot be held liable in tort actions (sovereign immunity) has been abrogated by legislative or judicial action in some states; in states still adhering to this doctrine, certain restrictions have been placed on its use to defend school districts against negligence claims (e.g., "safe place" statutes, exceptions to immunity for proprietary functions or ministerial duties).
8. While sovereign immunity does not protect school employees from liability in tort actions, some states by law require evidence of willful or wanton misconduct in order for school personnel to be liable for negligent acts in connection with educational activities.
9. Contributory negligence can be used to relieve school personnel of liability if it is established that the injured party's own actions were a significant factor in producing the injury.

10. Procedural defects in filing a claim can preclude recovery on the part of the injured party.
11. School personnel can be held liable for assault and battery if they use excessive or brutal force with students.
12. Under workers' compensation laws, employers are strictly liable for employee injuries that are work-related; employees need not establish that such injuries were negligently or knowingly caused in order to be eligible for workers' compensation benefits.
13. Employees cannot recover under workers' compensation for injuries sustained outside the scope of employment (e.g., in transit to or from work).
14. Educators are protected from defamation charges by "qualified privilege," whereby written or spoken communication cannot be the subject of tort actions as long as statements are made to appropriate persons and with proper intentions.

While all individuals, including school personnel, have a responsibility to act reasonably and to respect the rights of others, some negligent conduct is likely to occur and to generate claims for damages. Consequently, educators should be knowledgeable about their potential liability under applicable state laws, and should ensure that they have adequate insurance protection to cover any awards that might be assessed against them.

## NOTES

1. The only exceptions involve cases brought in the District of Columbia and actions initiated under 42 U.S.C. § 1983, which entitles individuals to sue other persons for damages in connection with the impairment of constitutional rights. Constitutional tort cases involving civil rights abridgments are discussed in Chapters 3, 4, 5, and 11.
2. *See generally*, William Prosser, *Law of Torts*, 4th ed. (St. Paul, Minn.: West Publishing Co., 1971).
3. *See* text with note 49, Chapter 8, for a discussion of educational negligence/malpractice litigation in which plaintiffs have alleged that school districts breached their duty to assure student literacy upon high school graduation.
4. *See* Bottorf v. Waltz, 369 A.2d 332 (Pa. Super. 1976).
5. *See* Segerman v. Jones, 259 A.2d 794 (Md. App. 1969).
6. Clark v. Furch, 567 S.W.2d 457 (Mo. App. 1978).
7. Partin v. Vernon Parish School Bd., 343 So. 2d 417 (La. App. 1977).
8. Ballard v. Polly, 387 F. Supp. 895 (D.D.C. 1975).
9. *See* Ardoin v. Evangeline Parish School Bd., 376 So. 2d 372 (La. App. 1979); Zaepfel v. City of Yonkers, 392 N.Y.S.2d 336 (App. Div. 1977); text with note 17, *infra*.

10. *See* Kingsley v. Independent School Dist. No. 2, 251 N.W.2d 634 (Minn. 1977).
11. Lewis v. Saint Bernard Parish School Bd., 350 So. 2d 1256 (La. App. 1977).
12. Thomas v. Chicago Bd. of Educ., 377 N.E.2d 55 (Ill. App. 1978).
13. Gerrity v. Beatty, 373 N.E.2d 1323 (Ill. 1978).
14. Everett v. Bucky Warren, Inc., 380 N.E.2d 653 (Mass. 1978).
15. Titus v. Lindberg, 228 A.2d 65 (N.J. 1967).
16. Richard v. Saint Landry Parish School Bd., 344 So. 2d 1116 (La. App. 1977).
17. *See* Pichette v. Manistique Public Schools, 269 N.W.2d 143 (Mich. 1978); Zaepfel v. City of Yonkers, 392 N.Y.S.2d 336 (App. Div. 1977).
18. Monfils v. City of Sterling Heights, 269 N.W.2d 588 (Mich. App. 1978).
19. Bartell v. Palos Verdes Peninsula School Dist., 83 Cal. App. 3d 492, 147 Cal. Rptr. 898 (Cal. App. 1978).
20. Hoyem v. Manhattan Beach School Dist., 150 Cal. Rptr. 1, 585 P.2d 851 (Cal. 1978).
21. *See* Baird v. Hosmer, 347 N.E.2d 533 (Ohio 1976); Talmadge v. District School Bd. of Lake County, 355 So. 2d 502 (Fla. Dist. Ct. App. 1978).
22. Landers v. School Dist. No. 203, O'Fallon, Illinois, 383 N.E.2d 645 (Ill. App. 1978).
23. Brod v. School Dist. No. 1, 386 N.Y.S.2d 125 (App. Div. 1976).
24. Hauser v. South Orangetown Central School Dist. No. 1, 376 N.Y.S.2d 608 (App. Div. 1976).
25. LaValley v. Stanford, 70 N.Y.S.2d 460 (App. Div. 1947). *See also* Brahatcek v. Millard School Dist. No. 17, 273 N.W.2d 680 (Neb. 1979).
26. Cirillo v. City of Milwaukee, 150 N.W.2d 460 (Wis. 1967).
27. Lilienthal v. San Leandro Unified School Dist., 139 Cal. App. 2d 453, 293 P.2d 889 (Cal. App. 1956).
28. Sheehan v. Saint Peter's Catholic School, 188 N.W.2d 868 (Minn. 1971).
29. Fagan v. Summers, 498 P.2d 1227 (Wyo. 1972).
30. Prier v. Horace Mann Insurance Co., 351 So. 2d 265 (La. App. 1977).
31. Bush v. Oscoda Area Schools, 250 N.W.2d 759 (Mich. App. 1977).
32. Hammond v. Scott, 232 S.E.2d 336 (S.C. 1977).
33. Morris v. Douglas County School Dist. No. 9, 403 P.2d 775 (Ore. 1965).
34. Powell v. Orleans Parish School Bd., 354 So. 2d 229 (La. App. 1978).
35. *See* Welch v. Dunsmuir Joint Union High School Dist., 326 P.2d 633 (Cal. App. 1958).
36. O'Brien v. Township High School Dist., 392 N.E.2d 615 (Ill. App. 1979).
37. Guerrieri v. Tyson, 147 Pa. Super. 239, 24 A.2d 468 (1942).
38. *See generally,* Martha McCarthy, "Torts," *The Yearbook of School Law 1979,* edited by Philip Piele (Topeka, Kan.: National Organization on Legal Problems of Education, 1979).
39. *See* text with note 140, Chapter 3, for a discussion of immunity of school districts under the eleventh amendment. This amendment pertains to suits initiated against government agencies for alleged constitutional abridgments rather than for negligent acts.
40. *See* Kern Alexander, Ray Corns, and Walter McCann, *Public School Law: Cases and Materials* (St. Paul, Minn.: West Publishing Co., 1969), p. 336.

41. For a discussion of the abrogation of school district immunity in connection with abridgments of federal rights under Section 1983 of the Civil Rights Act of 1871 (42 U.S.C. § 1983), *see* text with note 136, Chapter 3.

42. *See* Whitney v. City of Worcester, 366 N.E.2d 1210 (Mass. 1977); Molitor v. Kaneland Community School Dist., 163 N.E.2d 89 (Ill. 1959).

43. *See* Monfils v. City of Sterling Heights, 269 N.W.2d 588 (Mich. App. 1978); Hudson v. Union Free School Dist. No. 2, 391 N.Y.S.2d 487 (App. Div. 1977).

44. Zawadzki v. Taylor, 246 N.W.2d 161 (Mich. App. 1976).

45. *See* Wilson v. United States, 425 F. Supp. 143 (E.D. Va. 1977).

46. Prosser, *Law of Torts*, p. 583.

47. *See* Richards v. School Dist. of City of Birmingham, 83 N.W.2d 643 (Mich. 1957); Sawaya v. Tucson High School Dist., 281 P.2d 105 (Ariz. 1955); Robert Schaerer and Marion McGhehey, *Tort Liability of School Districts* (Bloomington, Ind.: Beanblossom Publishers, 1960), pp. 13–14.

48. Whitney v. City of Worcester, 366 N.E.2d 1210 (Mass. 1977).

49. Beiser v. Parkway School Dist., 589 S.W.2d 277 (Mo. 1979); Kuhn v. LaDue School Dist., 589 S.W.2d 281 (Mo. 1979).

50. Beiser v. Parkway School Dist., *id. See* text with note 84, *infra*.

51. Beckus v. Chicago Bd. of Educ., 397 N.E.2d 175 (Ill. App. 1979). *See* text with note 82, *infra*.

52. Thomas v. Chicago Bd. of Educ., 377 N.E.2d 55 (Ill. App. 1978).

53. *See* Scott v. Independent School Dist. No. 709, Duluth, 256 N.W.2d 485 (Minn. 1977).

54. *See* Bartell v. Palos Verdes Peninsula School Dist., 83 Cal. App. 3d 492, 147 Cal. Rptr. 898 (Cal. App. 1978); Powell v. Orleans Parish School Bd., 354 So. 2d 229 (La. App. 1978).

55. *See* Potter v. North Carolina School of Arts, 245 S.E.2d 188 (N.C. App. 1978); Sansonni v. Jefferson Parish School Bd., 344 So. 2d 42 (La. App. 1977).

56. Danos v. Foret, 354 So. 2d 667 (La. App. 1977).

57. Sharp v. Fairbanks N. Star Borough, 569 P.2d 178 (Alaska 1977).

58. Segerman v. Jones, 259 A.2d 794 (Md. App. 1969).

59. Swaitkowski v. Board of Educ. of City of Buffalo 319 N.Y.S.2d 783 (App. Div. 1971).

60. Dailey v. Los Angeles Unified School Dist., 470 P.2d 360 (Cal. 1970).

61. *See* Rocha v. Lodi Unified School Dist., 152 Cal. Rptr. 307 (Cal. App. 1979).

62. Scott v. School Bd. of Granite School Dist., 568 P.2d 746 (Utah 1977).

63. Williams v. Mariposa County Unified School Dist., 147 Cal. Rptr. 452 (Cal. App. 1978).

64. Cohen v. Pearl River Union Free School Dist., 419 N.Y.S.2d 998 (App. Div. 1979). *See also* McGrath v. Board of Educ., South Colonie Central School Dist., 405 N.Y.S.2d 798 (App. Div. 1978).

65. Simms v. School Dist. No. 1, 508 P.2d 236 (Ore. App. 1973). *See* Chapter 11 for a more detailed discussion of the legal issues involved in the administration of corporal punishment.

66. Thompson v. Iberville Parish School Bd., 372 So. 2d 642 (La. App. 1979).

67. Frank v. Orleans Parish School Bd., 195 So. 2d 451 (La. App. 1967).

68. *See* Hickey v. Board of Educ. of City of St. Louis, 256 S.W.2d 775 (Mo. 1953); Kroncke v. Caddo Parish School Bd., 183 So. 86 (La. App. 1938).
69. Gregg v. Dorchester County School System, 241 S.E.2d 554 (S.C. 1978).
70. *See* Freebern and Workers' Compensation Bd. v. North Rockland CDA, 410 N.Y.S.2d 371 (App. Div. 1978).
71. Howell v. Kingston Township School Dist., 161 A. 559 (Pa. Super. 1932). *See also* City and County of Denver School Dist. No. 1 v. Industrial Comm'n, 581 P.2d 1162 (Colo. 1978).
72. Gutierrez v. Artesia Public Schools, 583 P.2d 476 (N.M. App. 1978).
73. Faso v. Pioneer Central School System, 406 N.Y.S.2d 901 (App. Div. 1978).
74. Betts v. Ann Arbor Public Schools, 271 N.W.2d 498 (Mich. 1978).
75. *See* Alexander, Corns, and McCann, *Public School Law*, pp. 324–25.
76. Baskett v. Crossfield, 228 S.W. 673, 675 (Ky. 1921).
77. Sewell v. Brookbank, 581 P.2d 267 (Ariz. App. 1978).
78. Brody v. Montalbano, 151 Cal. Rptr. 206 (Cal. App. 1978).
79. Martin v. Kearney, 124 Cal. Rptr. 281, 283 (Cal. App. 1975).
80. *See* Scott v. Independent School Dist. No. 709, Duluth, 256 N.W.2d 485 (Minn. 1977).
81. *See* Board of Educ. of County of Raleigh v. Commercial Casualty Insurance Co., 116 W. Va. 503, 182 S.E. 87 (1935).
82. Edmonson v. Chicago Board of Educ., 379 N.E.2d 27 (Ill. App. 1978). *See also* Beckus v. Chicago Bd. of Educ., 397 N.E.2d 175 (Ill. App. 1979).
83. Pichette v. Manistique Public Schools, 269 N.W.2d 143 (Mich. 1978). *See also* Smith v. Board of Educ. of Caney School Dist. No. 34, 464 P.2d 571 (Kan. 1970).
84. Beiser v. Parkway School Dist., 589 S.W.2d 277 (Mo. 1979).
85. *See* Schaerer and McGhehey, *Tort Liability of School Districts*, pp. 21–23.

# PART II

# Students and the Law

The law pertaining to students' rights and responsibilities has changed
dramatically since 1950. This change has focused primarily on the
application of federal constitutional guarantees to children in school
settings. Numerous facets of the state's sovereign power to control
education have been challenged as interfering with the free exercise of
protected rights. Traditionally, state agencies had almost complete
discretion in attaching conditions to school attendance and regulating
student behavior, but recently courts have delved more deeply into the
justification for school policies and practices that restrict personal
freedoms. The current status of the law governing students in public
schools is described in this section.

Chapters 8 and 9 focus on students and the law in relation to the
school's curricular and extracurricular offerings. Chapter 8 covers rather
diverse topics that pertain to requirements and rights associated with
public school attendance. Governmental controls and individual freedoms
are analyzed in connection with compulsory attendance, instructional
program requirements, pupil achievement and academic standards,
extracurricular activities, and student records. Chapter 9 elaborates on
students' rights to equal educational opportunities. Pupil classification
practices and constitutional and statutory protections against governmental
discrimination are explored. Classifications based on race, sex, age, ability,
handicaps, and native language are analyzed in relation to the legality of
various criteria for distinguishing among students and the rights of certain
children to receive special services because of their unique needs.

The next two chapters focus on the rights of students to exercise protected freedoms in school and the authority of school personnel to restrict such freedoms in the interest of maintaining a proper school environment. Chapter 10 deals with students' first amendment rights, including religious guarantees and freedoms of speech, press, and association. In Chapter 11, school policies and practices pertaining to student discipline are addressed. This chapter covers the types of student behavior that can be curtailed, legitimate forms of punishment, and procedures that must be followed in administering student discipline.

Taken together, the following four chapters portray the legal parameters within which educators must operate in relation to students. An attempt is also made to depict for parents and students the extent of the individual's rights to equal and appropriate educational opportunities.

# 8

# School Attendance: Requirements and Rights

Although there is no inherent right to a public education under the United States Constitution,[1] once a state establishes an educational system, such opportunities must be made available to all children on equal terms.[2] Not only can children within the state assert a right to attend school, but also the state can mandate school attendance and specify curricular offerings to ensure an educated citizenry. Much litigation has resulted from the collision of state interests in providing schools for the general welfare and individual interests in exercising rights protected by constitutional and statutory law. In these instances, the judiciary must weigh the public and private interests involved. This chapter focuses on legal mandates pertaining to various general requirements and rights associated with school attendance. Selected aspects of students' rights and responsibilities are explored in more detail in subsequent chapters.

## COMPULSORY ATTENDANCE

Presently, all fifty states have some type of compulsory school attendance statute that includes penalties for noncompliance. The legal basis for compulsory education is grounded in the common law doctrine of *parens patriae* which means that the state, in its guardian role, has the authority to enact reasonable laws for the well-being of its citizens. Kentucky's compulsory attendance law is typical in requiring "each parent, guardian or other person residing in the state and having in custody or charge any child between the ages of seven and sixteen" to send the child to school for the full school term.[3] Courts consistently have recognized that mandated school attendance does not compromise parents' rights to govern the upbringing of their children. In an early case, the Supreme Court of Indiana held that compulsory attendance statutes were necessary to carry out the purposes of the state constitution.[4]

While states can require schooling, it was settled in 1925 that private school attendance can satisfy such compulsory attendance mandates. In *Pierce v. Society of Sisters,* the United States Supreme Court invalidated an Oregon statute requiring children between eight and sixteen years of age to attend public schools. The Court concluded that by restricting attendance to public institutions, the state interfered with private schools' rights to exist and with parents' rights to govern the upbringing of their children. The Court recognized that "the fundamental theory of liberty upon which all governments in this union repose excludes any general power of the state to standardize its children by forcing them to accept instruction from public teachers only." [5] In essence, parents do not have the right to determine *whether* their children are educated, but they do have some control over *where* such education takes place.

In many states, compulsory attendance laws permit pupil instruction outside of formal school settings as well as in public and private schools. Such equivalent instruction, however, must in fact be comparable to that available in the public educational system; home instruction by unqualified teachers will not fulfill compulsory education requirements.[6] Courts generally have ruled that state agencies have the authority to monitor and regulate private schools and all recognized equivalent instructional programs within the state to ensure that appropriate educational programs are being provided.[7]

In 1980, however, the United States Supreme Court declined to review a case in which the Kentucky Supreme Court held that the state could not require private schools to meet state accreditation standards, employ certified teachers, or use prescribed textbooks.[8] The Kentucky high court reasoned that applying such stipulations to private schools violated the state constitutional prohibition against requiring children to attend a school to which their parents might be conscientiously opposed. The court recognized that the state could compel school attendance, but held that specified branches of study could not be required in church-related schools as long as the schools provided instruction sufficient to enable children to exercise their right of suffrage and to participate in a democratic system of government.

EXCEPTIONS TO COMPULSORY ATTENDANCE

State laws generally recognize certain exceptions to compulsory attendance mandates. The most common exemption pertains to married students. It is reasoned that students assume adult responsibilities when they marry, and thus should be emancipated from compulsory school attendance.

Statutes often include other exceptions. In Indiana, for example, students who are serving as pages for the state legislature for a limited period of time and children who have reached age fourteen and have obtained lawful employment certificates are exempted from compulsory attendance requirements.[9]

In addition to statutory exceptions, an exemption from compulsory attendance mandates has been granted on first amendment grounds to Amish children who have successfully completed the eighth grade. In *State of Wisconsin v. Yoder,* the Court emphasized that the Amish religion is unique in that for centuries Amish youth have been prepared to enter a cloistered agrarian community in contrast to mainstream American society.[10] Furthermore, the Court recognized that the Amish community provides instructional programs in the form of vocational education for children after grammar school. The Court reasoned that under first amendment religious guarantees Amish adolescents have the right to devote their full attention to preparing for the responsibilities they will assume as adults in the Amish community.

Justice Douglas, however, issued a strong dissent in this case, arguing that the children rather than their parents should have testified regarding their religious views. He contended that the future of some children who may wish to break with the Amish tradition is "imperiled" by their not attending high school. He further asserted that if a student "is harnessed to the Amish way of life by those in authority over him or if his education is truncated, his entire life may be stunted and deformed." [11] Nonetheless, the Court majority concluded that an exception to compulsory attendance mandates was justified by the unique characteristics of the Amish religion and lifestyle.

## ATTEMPTS TO EVADE COMPULSORY ATTENDANCE LAWS

In contrast to the special consideration given the Amish, most other attempts to keep children out of school based on religious convictions have not met with receptive judicial forums. Parents have been subjected to civil or criminal penalties for failing to send their children to school. In some instances, truant children have been made wards of juvenile courts, with school attendance supervised by probation officers.

In an illustrative case, the Virginia Supreme Court ruled that parents violated compulsory attendance laws by keeping their children out of school because of their belief that the Bible commanded them to teach their children at home. In ruling against the parents, who were not licensed teachers, the court stated that "no amount of religious fervor . . . in opposition to adequate instruction should be allowed to work a lifelong injury" to their children. Furthermore, the court concluded that the parents should not be allowed "to inflict another illiterate citizen" on their community or state.[12]

In 1978, a Wisconsin appeals court also ruled that parents who withdrew their eight children from public school for religious reasons were acting in violation of compulsory attendance laws. Noting that there was no evidence that the children were being taught in a private school, the court declared:

> A way of life, however virtuous and admirable, may not be interposed as a barrier to reasonable state regulation of education if it is based on purely secular considerations.[13]

Reasons other than religious convictions also have been unsuccessfully proffered as justification for noncompliance with compulsory attendance laws. For example, a North Carolina appeals court ruled that a "deep-rooted conviction for Indian heritage was an insufficient basis for keeping children out of school." [14] The father, who was an Indian, testified that he would not send his children to school because they were not taught about Indian history and culture. The court concluded that the children were "neglected" within the meaning of state law, because they were not permitted to attend public school or provided with any alternative education.

### REQUIRED IMMUNIZATION

State agencies have the power not only to mandate school attendance, but also to require students attending school to be in good health so as not to endanger the well-being of others. Parents have been convicted for indirectly violating compulsory attendance laws because they have refused to have their children vaccinated as a prerequisite to school admission.[15] In a typical case, a New Jersey school board adopted a policy requiring immunization against diphtheria as a condition of school attendance.[16] A group of Christian Scientists challenged the policy, and a state superior court upheld the school board, noting that the board had the authority to mandate immunization without waiting for an epidemic to occur.

In some states, statutes provide for religiously based exemptions from required immunization as long as the welfare of others is not endangered by the exemption. For example, Kentucky law makes an exception for "members of a nationally recognized and established church or religious denomination, the teachings of which are opposed to medical immunization against disease." [17] In 1976, however, a federal district court ruled that a parent could not rely on this statute merely because he was "philosophically opposed" to having his children immunized.[18] The court was not persuaded by the argument that the law was discriminatory because it granted an exemption to members of religious groups while denying the same privilege to those opposed to immunization on nonreligious grounds.

In 1979, the Supreme Court of Mississippi invalidated a similar state statutory provision allowing an exemption from mandatory vaccination based on religious convictions.[19] In contrast to the Kentucky Supreme Court, the Mississippi high court concluded that such a provision discriminated against parents who opposed immunization for nonreligious reasons. Furthermore, the court held that such an exemption defeated the purpose of an immunization requirement, which is to protect all students from exposure to communicable diseases. Accordingly, the court ruled that the state law requiring immunization as a prerequisite to school attendance must be applied to all students, regardless of the religious beliefs of parents.

In general, states are granted broad discretion in governing school attendance,[20] and courts will not interfere with this discretionary authority unless it is exercised in a manner that violates constitutional rights of students or parents. Courts have reasoned that state interests must prevail over parental interests if the welfare of the child or society is at stake.

## REQUIREMENTS PERTAINING TO THE INSTRUCTIONAL PROGRAM

Can the state and its agents prescribe instructional offerings and books? Can student access to certain materials be restricted? Can pupils be charged fees for books, courses, or supplies? These and related questions have generated litigation in which various school instructional policies have been challenged as violating protected rights.

### CURRICULAR REQUIREMENTS AND PROHIBITIONS

Courts repeatedly have recognized that the state retains the power to determine the public school curriculum as long as federal constitutional guarantees are respected. Although a few state constitutions include specific curricular mandates,[21] more typically a duty is imposed on the legislature to make such curricular determinations. States vary as to the specificity of legislative directives, but all states require instruction pertaining to the Federal Constitution. Most legislatures also mandate the teaching of American history. Other subjects commonly required are English, mathematics, drug education, health, safety, and physical education. Some state statutes specify what subjects will be taught in which grades, and many states provide detailed legislation for the provision of vocational education, bilingual education, and special services for handicapped children. State laws usually stipulate that local school boards must offer the state-mandated minimum curriculum and may supplement this curriculum unless there is a statutory prohibition.[22]

Parents often have challenged specific curricular offerings or prohibitions and have asserted a right to control their children's course of study in public schools. While it is clear that the state and its agents can determine the public school curriculum, courts have invalidated curricular requirements or prohibitions that impair constitutional rights. In particular, courts have scrutinized legislative attempts to ban certain topics from the curriculum.

The first curriculum case to reach the United States Supreme Court involved a 1923 challenge to a Nebraska law that prohibited the teaching of a foreign language in any private or public school to children who had not successfully completed the eighth grade.[23] The state high court had upheld the dismissal of a private school teacher for teaching reading in German to elementary school students. In striking down the statute, the Supreme Court reasoned that the teacher's right to teach, the parents' right to engage him to instruct their children, and the children's right to acquire useful knowledge were protected liberties under the due process clause of the fourteenth amendment.

More recently, the Supreme Court invalidated an Arkansas law prohibiting the teaching of Darwin's theory of evolution in public schools as abridging first amendment rights. The Court held that a state could not prohibit the teaching of a particular segment of knowledge simply because it conflicted with religious views. The Court declared that "the First Amendment does not permit the State to require that teaching and learning must be tailored to the principles or prohibitions of any religious sect or dogma." [24] A state law requiring instruction in the biblical theory of creation also has been invalidated as impairing first amendment guarantees.[25]

If constitutional rights have not been implicated, however, curricular decisions made by state and local education agencies have been upheld by the judiciary. Courts have shown great reverence for the authority of state and local educational personnel to make curricular determinations. They have been reluctant to intervene in the resolution of conflicts that arise in the daily operation of school systems, unless constitutional rights are compromised. As early as 1859, the Vermont Supreme Court upheld disciplinary action against a student for refusing to write a composition, even though the parent had requested that the child be excused from the assignment.[26] Also, in an early Indiana case, the state high court upheld the expulsion of a student who refused, on his father's orders, to study music.[27] More recently, a federal district court in Georgia upheld the school board's power to require male students to take an officers' training course.[28] The court did recognize, however, that students could be excused from this requirement on religious grounds.

Parental challenges to the school board's authority to include certain subjects in the public school curriculum, such as sex education, also have been unsuccessful.[29] As long as school boards have been able to justify curricular decisions in terms of expanding the spectrum of knowledge or providing instruction necessary for the general welfare of students, such decisions have been endorsed by the courts. Also, school authorities have been upheld in establishing academic prerequisites for specific courses.

Accordingly, students cannot assert a right to be admitted to any class that is offered in the public school.[30] Such course admission criteria, however, cannot be arbitrary or serve to disadvantage certain groups of students.

## PRESCRIBED BOOKS

In addition to authority over the public school curriculum, the state also has the power to specify school textbooks and to regulate the method by which such books are obtained and distributed. In most states, textbooks are prescribed by the state board of education or by a textbook commission. A list of acceptable books usually is developed at the state level, and local school boards then select from the list the specific books to adopt for various course offerings within the district. However, in some states, such as Colorado, the local board is given almost complete authority to make textbook selections.

Several cases have involved controversies over books selected by local school boards for courses and school libraries. Unless a board has abused its discretionary authority or violated protected rights by including or excluding certain books from either the school library or course curricula, courts have upheld the board's power to make textbook decisions pursuant to state law.

One of the most dramatic incidents regarding the selection of textbooks occurred in Kanawha County, West Virginia. In 1974, parents protested the school board's adoption of a series of English materials which they considered to be godless, communistic, profane, and otherwise inappropriate for use in the schools. National attention was focused on Kanawha County as the parental protests evolved into school boycotts, a strike by coal miners, shootings, bombing of the courthouse, and even public prayer for the death of school board members. Although the federal district court upheld the board's action and rejected the parents' contention that these books represented an infringement of constitutionally protected rights, book burnings and other public demonstrations continued.[31]

In contrast to the West Virginia case, most challenges to the school board's authority to select textbooks and library books have focused on a board's attempt to remove controversial books from the school or to restrict student access, rather than a board's attempt to add such materials to the curriculum. In an illustrative New York case, the Second Circuit Court of Appeals upheld a school board's right to remove a particular book from a junior high school library, reasoning that the state legislature had clearly delegated the responsibility for selecting library materials to local school boards.[32] The court noted that a book does not acquire tenure, and therefore can be removed by the same authority that made the initial selection.

In a more recent Vermont case, the Second Circuit Court of Appeals affirmed the federal district court's holding that a school board has authority to remove or restrict access to certain "obscene" and "vulgar" books in the high school library, and to screen future library acquisitions.[33] The district court recognized that the selection of library books is a curricular matter within the discretionary authority of school boards. While the court noted that it did not entirely agree with the board's actions, it concluded that the policies did not impair any constitutional rights. Accordingly, the court held that it was not appropriate for the judiciary to review either the wisdom or the efficacy of the board's determinations.

Similarly, in 1980 the Seventh Circuit Court of Appeals endorsed an Indiana federal district court's conclusion that school boards have the authority to remove books from classroom use and from the school library based on board members' "social, political, and moral" beliefs.[34] Students had challenged the censorship of instructional materials and the elimination of certain courses from the high school curriculum as violating their "right to know" and imposing a chilling effect on the free exchange of ideas. Rejecting these assertions, the federal district court concluded that "it is legitimate for school officials to develop an opinion about what type of citizens are good citizens, to determine what curriculum and material will best develop good citizens, and to prohibit the use of texts, remove library books, and delete courses from the curriculum as a part of the effort to shape students into good citizens." [35] Although the appellate court vacated the district court's ruling to allow the students to initiate an amended complaint, it seems unlikely that the students will be able to satisfy the court's standard for establishing a constitutional violation. The appeals court emphasized that there are "limited constitutional constraints on the form and content of decisions of local school boards acting within the bounds of their statutory powers." [36] Recognizing that challenges by secondary school students to educational decisions made by local authorities can sometimes be legitimate, the court emphasized that such complaints must "cross a relatively high threshold" before implicating constitutional rights to justify federal court intervention. According to the Seventh Circuit Court of Appeals, the judiciary should not interfere with a school board's broad discretion in making curricular determinations unless there is a "flagrant abuse" of such discretion.

Some courts, however, have reached a different conclusion regarding the authority of school boards to censor classroom and library materials. In 1976, the Sixth Circuit Court of Appeals ruled that a school board acted beyond its scope of authority in removing books from the school library.[37] In this case, the board refused to accept the recommendation of the teaching staff to purchase several novels for the English curriculum and ordered the controversial books removed from the school library shelves. Students challenged the board's action, claiming that it created an unconstitutional censorship of classroom materials and impaired their protected freedom to learn. The court upheld the board's right to disregard faculty recommendations as to the initial purchase of books but rejected the board's contention that it could remove books that had already been placed in the library. Since there was no claim that the books were obscene or that they lacked literary value, the court concluded that the board failed to demonstrate any compelling reason for removing the books. The court stated that the board was not forced to establish a library, but having done so, it could not place conditions on the use of the library simply to conform to the social or political attitudes of board members. Nonetheless, the appellate court did uphold the board's authority to override faculty judgments on the selection of books for academic courses.

In 1979, the federal district court in New Hampshire held that the removal of *Ms.* magazine from the school library violated first amendment rights of students.[38] Echoing the Sixth Circuit Court of Appeals, the district court held that once a library is established, arbitrary conditions cannot be placed on its use. The court concluded that board members' disapproval of the political orientation of *Ms.* was not a sufficient justification for removing the magazine from the high school library.

In 1980, the Second Circuit Court of Appeals ruled that a New York school board may have impaired the constitutional rights of students by banning books from the junior high school and high school libraries.[39] The federal district court had dismissed the suit, reasoning that although the book ban might have been based on misguided educational philosophy, it did not implicate any first amendment rights. The appellate court disagreed and questioned the board's motivation and procedures for removing objectionable books. The case was returned to the district court for a trial to determine whether the school board's actions created a sufficient risk of suppressing the exchange of ideas to abridge the first amendment.

Presumably, as long as public schools exist, there will be controversy surrounding the selection of materials for the curriculum. The debated issues will change to reflect shifts in public sentiments, but parental assaults on the public school curriculum undoubtedly will continue. Although there are some conflicting opinions, most courts seem inclined to uphold the school board's authority to prescribe curricular materials. The burden is on the party challenging such decisions to establish that the state agency has acted beyond its scope of authority, has violated its own policies, or has impaired constitutionally protected rights.

## REQUIRED FEES FOR TEXTBOOKS AND COURSES

The legality of charging students for the use of public school textbooks has been contested with some regularity. In 1972, the United States Supreme Court was asked to determine whether the Federal Constitution prohibits the imposition of such fees. This case involved a New York law that allowed local school districts to decide by election whether to charge elementary school students a book rental fee.[40] The law was challenged in connection with a school district that had elected to impose a rental system. The Second Circuit Court of Appeals concluded that the law was constitutional, even though it served to disadvantage children from poor families. The United States Supreme Court agreed to review the case, but before it had the opportunity to address the constitutional issue, voters in the district under litigation decided to assess a tax to purchase all textbooks in grades one through six. The Supreme Court, therefore, vacated the court of appeals judgment.[41]

Since the Supreme Court has not ruled on the validity of textbook fees under the Federal Constitution, resolution of this issue has been handled on the basis of each individual state's constitutional and statutory mandates. In several states, such as Virginia, Colorado, Arizona, and Indiana, constitutional provisions have been interpreted as allowing fees to be charged for public school textbooks.[42] In contrast, the Supreme Court of North Dakota has ruled that the legislature is prohibited from authorizing school districts to charge students for textbooks.[43] The Illinois Supreme Court likewise has interpreted state law as requiring school boards to furnish textbooks without charge, and the West Virginia high court has ruled that textbooks, workbooks, or other materials necessary for use in the state-required curriculum must be provided free for students who cannot afford to purchase such materials.[44]

In addition to fees for textbooks, fees for courses and supplies also have been challenged in the courts. The Illinois Supreme Court has sanctioned the imposition of supply fees for courses, but not tuition fees.[45] The Supreme Court of Missouri also has ruled that the practice of charging course fees as a prerequisite to enrollment in academic classes impairs students' rights to free public schooling.[46] The court, however, did not address the issue of whether students could be required to furnish certain materials and equipment for use in classes. In New Mexico, the high court has interpreted its state constitution as prohibiting fees for courses required of every student, but allowing reasonable fees for elective courses.[47]

In 1978, a New York appeals court prohibited a school district from charging students an annual supply fee for classroom materials.[48] While recognizing that the school district was not required to furnish consumable supplies to students free of charge, the court concluded that the contested supply fee schedule was not based on the quantity of supplies actually used or on the voluntary purchase of such supplies by the parents. Accordingly, the court reasoned that state law was violated by the imposition of a charge on parents who were unwilling to purchase the supplies through the school district.

Currently, school districts in many states solicit fees from students for various consumable materials. The permissibility of such practices will remain in question until the Supreme Court or individual state courts either sanction or invalidate the collection of these fees in public schools.

## STUDENT ACHIEVEMENT: RIGHT OR RESPONSIBILITY?

It is well established that state education agencies have the authority to determine the public school instructional program (as long as constitutional rights are not abridged) and to establish academic standards for courses. But do they also have the obligation to guarantee that student learning actually takes place and to certify that high school graduates have minimum skills? In other words, should the individual student or the school be held responsible for academic achievement? There has been a growing public demand for schools to assume greater accountability for pupil performance. This accountability movement has nurtured two distinct, but related, thrusts: educational malpractice suits and minimum competency testing programs.

### EDUCATIONAL MALPRACTICE

A question that has received recent judicial attention is whether or not students have a right to attain a predetermined level of achievement in return for state-mandated school attendance. This question has resulted in educational malpractice/negligence suits, in which parents have claimed that they have a right to expect their children to be functionally literate upon high school graduation.

In the most widely publicized case of this type, *Peter W. v. San Francisco Unified School District,* a student asserted that the school district was negligent in teaching, promoting, and graduating him from high school with the ability to read only at the fifth-grade level.[49] He also claimed that his performance and progress had been misrepresented to his parents, who testified that they were unaware of his deficiencies until he was tested by a private agency after high school graduation. Both the trial court and the appeals court dismissed the charges against the school district. The appellate court reasoned that the complexities of the teaching/learning process made it impossible to place the entire burden on the school to assure student literacy. Noting "public policy considerations," the court concluded that the school district did not have a duty to guarantee that the student mastered basic academic skills.

> The "injury" claimed here is plaintiff's inability to read and write. Substantial professional authority attests that the achievement of literacy in the schools, or its failure, are influenced by a host of factors which affect the pupil subjectively, from outside the formal teaching process, and

beyond the control of its ministers. They may be physical, neurological, emotional, cultural, environmental; they may be present but not perceived, recognized but not identified.[50]

Finding no legitimate connection between the school district's conduct and the injury suffered, the court reasoned that to hold the school district liable would expose all educational agencies to countless "real or imagined" tort claims of "disaffected students and parents." [51]

More recently, the New York Court of Appeals dismissed a similar five-million-dollar educational malpractice suit brought by a learning disabled high school graduate who claimed that he was unable to complete job applications and cope with the problems of everyday life.[52] As in the California case, the court concluded that the school could not be held accountable for ensuring that all students, with their varying abilities to learn, attained a specified reading level before high school graduation. Also, a Maryland court ruled that a public high school student, who alleged that misdiagnosis of his mental abilities caused him to be almost illiterate, could not sue a county school board for educational malpractice.[53] The court found no breach of statutory or common law duty owed to the student.

In December 1979, the New York Court of Appeals dismissed what had appeared to be the only successful educational malpractice suit. In *Hoffman v. Board of Education,* a state appellate court had awarded a former public school student $500,000 in damages after concluding that the New York City Board of Education had negligently diagnosed his needs and erroneously instructed him in a program for the mentally retarded.[54] At age five, Hoffman's I.Q. was assessed by the school psychologist using a test that required verbal responses, despite the fact that he had a severe speech defect. He scored one point below the score required for placement in a regular class. Hoffman's I.Q. was never reevaluated through twelve years of public school, during which time he was instructed in classes for the retarded. The thrust of the negligence claim was that the school psychologist's report, recommending reassessment of the child's intelligence within two years of the original evaluation, was ignored for the next eleven years—even though Hoffman scored in the ninetieth percentile on reading readiness tests at ages eight and nine. Upon high school graduation, he was required by Social Security to have his intelligence tested in order to continue receiving payments after his eighteenth birthday. At that time he scored over 100, and thus became ineligible to remain in the occupational training program for the retarded.. According to a psychologist and psychiatrist who testified at the trial, Hoffman suffered a lengthy depression caused by his awareness that he was in essence uneducated and could not earn a living.

In distinguishing *Hoffman* from previous educational malpractice suits, the lower court noted that school personnel committed affirmative acts of negligence (i.e., ignoring the psychologist's report) that placed crippling burdens on the student. Nonetheless, the New York Court of Appeals, in a four-to-three decision, reversed the lower court ruling and held that it was not the role of the judiciary to make such educational determinations. The New York high court emphasized that instructional negligence claims, as a matter of public policy, should not be entertained by the judiciary. Instead, the court reasoned that such allegations should be handled within the administrative appeals network of the state educational system.

Even though it appears unlikely that public schools in the near future will be held accountable for a specified quantum of student achievement, it is quite probable that schools will be held accountable for accurately diagnosing pupils' needs, reporting their progress to parents, and providing special services if warranted. In litigation involving handicapped students, courts already have articulated that schools have an obligation to keep parents accurately informed regarding the needs as well as the achievement of their children.[55] Furthermore, schools must be able to substantiate that they have provided appropriate remedial services for students with identified academic deficiencies.

## COMPETENCY TESTING

In reaction to allegations that students are not acquiring basic academic skills, some school districts have instituted minimum competency tests as prerequisites to graduation. Although teachers' organizations have voiced opposition to the use of proficiency tests in public schools, over two-thirds of the states have enacted some type of competency examination legislation.[56] Some states administer a uniform test to all students at specified grade levels, while in others local school boards design competency standards based on local norms. States also differ in the use of the examinations. In seventeen states, students must pass the tests in order to graduate. In the other states with competency legislation, either local school boards have the option of using the tests as graduation requirements or proficiency examinations are used solely to determine remediation needs.

The rationale for enacting such competency legislation is grounded in evidence that some students have graduated from high school without minimum skills thought to be necessary for one to function successfully as an adult. Proficiency exams have been instituted to ensure that students have at least the basic verbal and quantitative skills needed to perform such tasks as writing checks and completing job applications. Advocates of competency testing programs have asserted that statewide standards make local schools more accountable for teaching such fundamental skills.[57]

The establishment of competency testing programs has been widely criticized by various national education associations. Criticisms have included allegations that such tests are racially discriminatory and impair protected rights by attaching arbitrary conditions to the receipt of a high school diploma. Critics also have alleged that there is no sound foundation for determining what is "minimal," and that teachers will teach only those skills required for the test, neglecting other important subjects in the curriculum.[58] In 1979, the Association for Supervision and Curriculum Development issued a statement endorsing competency-based education, but opposing the use of statewide minimum competency tests as prerequisites to graduation or promotion.[59]

It is somewhat ironic that threats of malpractice suits have encouraged the establishment of proficiency testing programs, yet the tests employed have been attacked as impairing protected rights. In the first federal suit involving the use of minimum competency tests, ten black Florida high school students challenged the state law authorizing the Florida Department of Education to withhold regular high school diplomas from graduating seniors who had not passed a functional literacy test.[60] The ten students, all of whom failed the test, asserted that the test was discriminatory in that a disproportionate number of the black students did not pass. Evidence indicated that 77 percent of the black students, compared to 24 percent of the white students, failed the math portion of the test; and 26 percent of the black students, compared to 3 percent of the white students, failed the communications section. Moreover, plaintiffs claimed that the students were not given proper notice to prepare for the 1977–78 tests (since the enabling legislation was not passed until 1976) and that the test items were not validated for reliability. The students sought a permanent injunction to ban the use of such test scores as a prerequisite to graduation and as a basis for assigning pupils to remedial classes.

The federal district court in Florida sanctioned the use of competency tests for remediation purposes, but prohibited their use as a graduation requirement until the 1982–83 school year. This phase-in period was considered necessary to "purge the taint" of past racial discrimination in the state and to provide students adequate notice of the skills required to pass the tests. The court recognized that students are constitutionally protected against arbitrary governmental stigmatization. Furthermore, students have a state-created property right to attend school, including the right to receive a diploma, which cannot be impaired without appropriate procedural safeguards. Accordingly, the court held that the premature application of the test requirement impaired protected rights of the students who satisfied other graduation criteria but failed the tests. While deferring the use of proficiency tests as a prerequisite to graduation, the court recognized the state's authority to establish such academic standards.[61]

If state laws continue to become more specific as to the student competencies required for high school graduation, the next step may be greater uniformity in statewide curricular offerings.[62] It seems logical for states to exhibit increasing interest in monitoring the instructional practices of local school districts if students are expected to pass proficiency tests developed at the state level.

## EXTRACURRICULAR ACTIVITIES

Legal controversies have not been confined to academic programs; there also has been substantial litigation pertaining to requirements and rights associated with extracurricular activities. Extracurricular activities usually are defined as those that are school-sponsored, but are not part of regular class activities or the basis for academic credit.[63] It is clear that once a state provides public education, students cannot be denied attendance without due process of law,[64] but there is less agreement regarding students' rights to participate in school-related activities.

Historically, school officials successfully asserted that extracurricular activities were additional benefits bestowed at the will of the school board, and courts endorsed the notion that the right to attend school did not include the right to participate in such activities.[65] More recently, conflicting decisions have been rendered as to whether involvement in extracurricular activities is a privilege or a right. In 1976, the Tenth Circuit Court of Appeals recognized that school attendance could not be denied without procedural safeguards, but concluded that similar constitutional protections did not extend to each component of the educational process.[66] In 1979, a North Carolina federal court held that total exclusion from extracurricular participation would abridge students' rights, while exclusion from one or several activities would not.[67] In contrast, other courts have held that extracurricular activities are an integral part of the total school program, and that the right to attend school includes the right to participate in extracurricular activities.[68] Regardless of whether they have considered such participation a privilege or a right, courts generally have allowed governing bodies great flexibility in formulating rules that pertain to extracurricular activities. Regulations have not been invalidated unless clearly arbitrary.[69]

### TRAINING REGULATIONS

Indicative of the judicial posture toward extracurricular activities is the fact that reasonable training rules have been endorsed as conditions of participation on athletic teams. A New York trial court upheld the denial of a high school football letter to a student who violated a training regulation after the football season was over.[70] In other cases, courts have held that school officials should be given latitude in establishing training standards for high school athletes in order to foster discipline on competitive teams.[71]

In 1978, the Nebraska Supreme Court upheld the suspension of students from interscholastic athletic competition for violating a training regulation prohibiting smoking and drinking among athletes.[72] The court concluded that the rule involved in this case clearly served "a legitimate rational interest" and directly affected the discipline of student athletes.

> It cannot be said that the prescribed penalty was an arbitrary and unreasonable means to attain the legitimate end of deterrence of the use of alcoholic liquor by student athletes.[73]

Furthermore, the Nebraska Supreme Court held that the trial court erred in granting an injunction, because the students had failed to exhaust the "prompt and reasonable" administrative procedures available for appealing the order of the school board. The United States Supreme Court declined to review this case, and thus left the Nebraska high court ruling intact.[74]

In another Nebraska case the following year, a student was suspended from interscholastic wrestling competition after being arrested and charged with intoxication in violation of training regulations.[75] The student challenged the suspension as violating his due process rights. The Nebraska Supreme Court ruled that the school's procedures were quite adequate, and that a six-week suspension from wrestling competition did not violate any protected rights of the student. The court reasoned that state law governing long-term suspensions from school did not apply to a suspension from an extracurricular athletic team.

In Iowa, a controversy over a training rule violation raised issues regarding the relationship between local school boards and state athletic associations. The Iowa High School Athletic Association enacted a rule forbidding the use of alcoholic beverages by athletes of schools belonging to the association.[76] A student athlete was arrested with a case of beer in his car. Subsequently, he was suspended from interscholastic competition under the association rule. The Iowa Supreme Court held that the school board had unlawfully delegated its policy-making powers to the athletic association. The court was not persuaded by the argument that the school had independently adopted the rule, noting that schools electing not to enforce such a rule would have to withdraw from the association. Hence, the court granted the student relief because of the school board's unlawful delegation of its rule-making authority, and did not address the validity of the rule prohibiting the use of alcoholic beverages among student athletes.

TRANSFER POLICIES

In addition to upholding training regulations, courts usually have approved residency requirements as conditions of participation on extracurricular athletic teams. Stipulations that prohibit involvement in extracurricular activities for one year after a change in a student's school without a change in the parents' address are intended to prevent high schools from recruiting student athletes. In 1978, an Illinois federal district court upheld a state high school athletic association regulation prohibiting eighteen-year-old transfer students from playing on interscholastic teams for one year if the transfer was not accompanied by a change in their parents' residence.[77] The court reasoned that the regulation was justified in order to deter eighteen-year-old students from deciding to attend school in a certain district because of athletic considerations. Similarly, the Indiana Supreme Court upheld a trial court's denial of an injunction to a student who was declared ineligible to play varsity basketball when he moved from his mother's residence to another town to reside with friends who later became his guardians.[78] The court concluded that the guardianship had been created primarily for the purpose of making him eligible to participate in interscholastic sports, and that the move was a result of "undue influence" based on athletic reasons. Accordingly, the court held that the student was obligated to comply with the state high school association rule barring him from team play for one year. Eligibility restrictions have been upheld as reasonable even in situations of interstate transfers.[79]

Exceptions to transfer policies have been made in some situations if a student's physical or mental welfare has necessitated the move. In an illustrative Texas case, a student with severe psychiatric difficulties was taken out of his family home and placed with his maternal grandparents on his therapist's recommendation.[80] He was told that he could not play varsity football in the new school because of the interscholastic league's transfer policy. The therapist believed that the student's participation on the football team was therapeutically beneficial, and therefore an injunction was sought. The federal court held that the student was a handicapped individual under 29 U.S.C., Section 794, which prohibits discrimination against the handicapped in programs or activities receiving federal financial assistance. The court granted the injunction, reasoning that it must balance the harm that would be inflicted on the student if relief were denied against the harm that would result to the defendants if the injunction were granted. Concluding that there was no evidence that athletic considerations accompanied the student's move, the court ruled that there were compelling medical and psychiatric reasons necessitating the change of residence and supporting the need for the student to play on the football team.

OTHER CONDITIONS

It is well established that schools can use academic criteria to determine student eligibility for extracurricular activities.[81] Similarly, age restrictions can be placed on such participation in order to equalize competitive conditions.[82] In addition, courts have endorsed time limitations on a student's eligibility for interscholastic teams. The Supreme Court of Georgia, for example, upheld a rule specifying that eligibility for interscholastic competition would be for eight consecutive semesters, or four consecutive years, from the date of initial entrance into the ninth grade.[83] While noting that the rule appeared "harsh," the court concluded that the regulation was justified in order to equalize competition among teams.

Some courts have endorsed the use of special grooming regulations as conditions of participation in athletic activities, if such regulations can be justified for health or safety reasons.[84] Other courts, however, have ruled that students have a right to govern their appearance in all school activities, not merely academic programs.[85] In 1970, the Vermont Federal District Court struck down a hair regulation for high school athletes that was designed to "enhance esprit de corps, prevent adverse public reaction, prevent dissension on teams," and foster the general welfare of the teams and participants.[86] The court concluded that the regulation had no legitimate relationship to team performance, discipline, or conformity and could not be justified in terms of the school's educational mission. In contrast, a federal court in California upheld the legality of a hair regulation for student athletes that had been devised by a committee of students, coaches, community members, and administrators.[87]

A recent controversy pertaining to extracurricular activities has involved the school's authority to exclude handicapped students from participation on certain athletic teams. A New York case is illustrative of the lack of judicial agreement in this area. In 1977, the Second Circuit Court of Appeals sanctioned a contested school board policy barring students with defective vision from participating in contact sports.[88] The appellate court concluded that federal civil rights laws were not abridged, and that the school board had a sufficient medical basis for making such a decision in the interest of the students' health. Subsequently, one of the partially sighted students brought suit under state law and was granted relief.[89] The New York appeals court enjoined the school district from barring the student from contact teams, noting that she was athletically inclined and had protective eyewear to minimize the risk of injury. The court concluded that it was in the best interest of the student to participate in the athletic program, and that such an opportunity could not be denied simply because of a physical impairment.

While extracurricular activities remain a heavily contested aspect of public school offerings, courts generally have allowed school personnel latitude in attaching conditions to student participation in school-related activities. Academic standards, skill criteria, residency rules, and training regulations can be used as prerequisites to such participation as long as the conditions are reasonable and related to legitimate school purposes. Educators should ensure, however, that all policies pertaining to extracurricular activities are clearly stated, publicized to parents and students, and applied without discrimination.[90]

## STUDENT RECORDS

The Supreme Court has recognized that the constitutional meaning of "liberty" includes the right to privacy.[91] One dimension of this guarantee is the right to have personal information about oneself kept confidential. As a result of this recognized right, questions about who has access to a student's permanent file and what can go into a student's file have been the source of much controversy. It appears that the information contained in pupil records has become more personal as demands for such information have increased.

Legal challenges to school record-keeping procedures have resulted in school officials being ordered to expunge irrelevant and/or damaging information from students' permanent folders. In an early case, the Supreme Court of Oklahoma ordered removal from the school register of a notation that a pupil had been "ruined by tobacco and whiskey."[92] Finding no evidence to support the veracity of the statement, the court concluded that the student was unjustly defamed. Courts also have required school officials to allow parents and eighteen-year-old students to have access to their school files. In upholding a father's right to inspect his son's records, a New York court declared that "it needs no further citation of authority to recognize the obvious interest which a parent has in the school records of his child."[93]

Because of widespread dissatisfaction with educators' efforts to ameliorate abuses associated with student record–keeping practices, the Family Educational Rights and Privacy Act (FERPA), commonly known as the Buckley Amendment, was passed in 1974.[94] Proposed regulations for FERPA were issued the following year, and after extensive comment by school personnel, final regulations became effective in 1976.[95] This law stipulates that federal funds may be withdrawn from any educational agency or institution that (1) fails to provide parents access to their child's educational records, or (2) disseminates such information (with some exceptions) to third parties without parental permission. Also, parents must be given a hearing if they wish to challenge the contents of their child's records. Upon reaching age eighteen, students may exercise the rights guaranteed to parents under this law.

A teacher's daily records pertaining to pupil progress are exempted from coverage under the law, as long as the records are kept in the sole possession of the faculty member. Also, parental consent is not required prior to the release of certain public directory information, such as the student's name, address, telephone number, date and place of birth, major field of study, and degrees and awards received. In addition, federal and state education authorities are entitled to have access to data needed to audit and evaluate federally supported education programs. These data, however, are to be collected in a way that prevents the disclosure of personally identifiable information.

After reviewing a student's permanent file, the parent or eligible student can request that the information be amended if it is believed to be inaccurate, misleading, or in violation of the student's protected rights. If school authorities decide that an amendment is not warranted, the parent or eligible student must be advised of the right to a hearing. The hearing officer may be an employee of the school district, but may not be an individual with a direct interest in the outcome of the hearing. Either party may be represented by counsel at the hearing, and the hearing officer must issue a written decision summarizing the evidence presented and the rationale for the ruling. If the hearing officer concludes that the records should not be amended, the parent or eligible student has the right to place in the file a personal statement specifying objections.

Other federal laws include further protections pertaining to the confidentiality and accessibility of student records. For example, the Education for All Handicapped Children Act of 1975 (Public Law 94-142) stipulates that records of handicapped children must be accessible to their parents or guardians.[96] Furthermore, interpreters must be hired if necessary to interpret the contents of students' files for parents, and parental consent is required before such records can be disclosed to third parties.

Many states also have enacted legislation pertaining to the privacy of student records. Indiana law is typical in stipulating that school boards must maintain a list of all persons or agencies having access to personal files, furnish prior notice before such information is disclosed to a third party, and inform individuals of their right to access to their records and their right to contest the accuracy or appropriateness of the material in such files.[97]

Since Congress, state legislatures, and the judiciary have indicated a continuing interest in safeguarding the privacy rights of students, school boards would be wise to reassess their policies and ensure that they are adhering to the protections included in federal and state laws. If student records are improperly managed or disseminated, school officials may be held liable in a civil rights action for violating students' protected rights to privacy. School personnel, however, should use some restraint before purging information from student files. Pertinent material that is necessary to provide continuity in the instructional program for a student *should* be included in a permanent record and should be available for use by authorized personnel. It is unfortunate that fear of federal sanctions under the Family Educational Rights and Privacy Act has resulted in deletion of useful information (along with irrelevant material) from student records.

The mere fact that information in a student's file is negative does not imply that the material is inappropriate. Courts have held that school authorities have an obligation to record relevant data pertaining to students' activities as long as such information is accurate. In an illustrative Pennsylvania case, students sought to enjoin school officials from noting in their permanent records and communicating to institutions of higher education that they had participated in a demonstration at graduation ceremonies.[98] The federal district court denied the injunction, reasoning that the objective account of what occurred at the graduation exercises, with no reference as to the propriety of the demonstration, did not result in any "immediate, irreparable harm" to the students. Furthermore, the court held that school officials have a *duty* to record and communicate true factual information about students to institutions of higher learning in order to present an accurate picture of applicants for admission.

## CONCLUSION

Our nation was founded on the basic premise of liberty and justice for all. Until recently, however, this concept often was not applied to students in public schools. Given that children are deprived of a certain amount of their liberty by the mere fact that schooling is required for the general welfare of society, students are further denied justice in instances where arbitrary conditions are attached to school attendance. While school personnel are granted latitude in regulating various aspects of public education, any requirements that restrict students' activities must be reasonable and necessary to carry out the mission of the school. Whenever students' or parents' constitutional rights are impaired, school authorities must be able to substantiate that there is an overriding public interest to be served.

From an analysis of court cases and legislation pertaining to general requirements and rights associated with school attendance, the following generalizations seem warranted:

1. Once a state provides public education, such opportunities must be made available to all on equal terms.
2. The state can compel children between specified ages to attend school even if such attendance conflicts with religious convictions of the parents or children.[99]
3. Students can satisfy compulsory attendance mandates by attending private schools and, in most states, by receiving equivalent instruction (e.g., tutoring) that is comparable to the public school program.
4. School officials can require good health, including necessary immunization against diseases, as a condition of school attendance.
5. The state and its agencies have the authority to determine public school course offerings and instructional materials, and such curricular determinations will be upheld by courts unless clearly arbitrary or in violation of constitutional or statutory rights.
6. Fees can be charged for the use of public school textbooks unless prohibited by state constitutional or statutory provisions.

7. Students do not have an inherent right to attain a specified level of achievement upon high school graduation.

8. Proficiency examinations can be used to determine pupil remediation needs, and also as prerequisites to high school graduation if students are given sufficient preparation time prior to implementation of the examination requirements.

9. Student participation in extracurricular activities can be regulated by reasonable conditions (e.g., academic and skill criteria, age and residency requirements, training regulations).

10. Rules pertaining to extracurricular activities must be well publicized, uniformly applied, and based on legitimate educational objectives.

11. Parents and eighteen-year-old students must be granted access to the student's school records and an opportunity to contest the contents.

12. School personnel must ensure the accuracy of information contained in student records and maintain the confidentiality of such records.

# NOTES

1. *See* San Antonio Independent School Dist. v. Rodriguez, 411 U.S. 1 (1973); text with note 4, Chapter 9.
2. *See* Brown v. Board of Educ. of Topeka, 347 U.S. 483 (1954); text with note 11, Chapter 9.
3. Ky. Rev. Stat. § 159.010.
4. State v. Bailey, 157 Ind. 324, 61 N.E. 730, 731 (1901).
5. Pierce v. Society of Sisters, 268 U.S. 510, 535 (1925).
6. *See* Scoma v. Chicago Bd. of Educ., 391 F. Supp. 452 (N.D. Ill. 1974); State v. Garber, 197 Kan. 567, 419 P.2d 896 (1966); State *ex rel.* Shoreline School Dist. No. 412 v. Superior Court for King County, 55 Wash. 2d 177, 346 P.2d 999 (1960). According to a survey conducted by the New Hampshire State Department of Education, at least thirty-nine states have some type of statutory provision for home education, and twenty-three of these states require home education to be substantially equivalent to education in the public schools. *See Education U.S.A.*, Vol. 22, No. 50, August 11, 1980, p. 366. In 1980, New Hampshire became the first state to trial-test guidelines allowing parents to educate their child at home if it was demonstrated that a hardship (which might be based on philosophical beliefs) would result from sending the child to school. Under the home education rules, the course work must be reasonably equivalent to public school courses and must be approved by the local school board. *See Education Daily*, Vol. 13, No. 119, June 18, 1980, p. 6.

7. *See* State v. Vietto, 247 S.E.2d 298 (N.C. App. 1978); State v. Hershberger, 103 Ohio App. 188, 144 N.E.2d 693 (1955). In 1980, a Missouri appeals court ruled that parents could not be convicted of violating the compulsory attendance law in the absence of proof that they failed to provide the child proper instruction at home, State v. Davis, 598 S.W.2d 189 (Mo. App. 1980).

8. Kentucky State Bd. for Elementary and Secondary Educ. v. Rudasill, 589 S.W.2d 877 (Ky. 1979), *cert. denied*, 100 S. Ct. 2158 (1980).

9. Ind. Code Ann. §§ 20-8.1-3-18; 20-8.1-4-3.

10. 406 U.S. 205 (1972).

11. *Id.* at 245–46 (Douglas, J., dissenting).

12. Rice v. Commonwealth, 188 Va. 224, 49 S.E.2d 342, 348 (1948). *See also* Matter of Franz, 390 N.Y.S.2d 940 (App. Div. 1977); F. and F. v. Duval County, 273 So. 2d 15 (Fla. 1973).

13. State v. Kasuboski, 275 N.W.2d 101, 105 (Wis. App. 1978).

14. Matter of McMillan, 226 S.E.2d 693 (N.C. App. 1976). *See also* Matter of Baum, 61 A.2d 123, 401 N.Y.S.2d 514 (App. Div. 1978).

15. *See* State v. Drew, 89 N.H. 54, 192 A. 629 (1937).

16. Board of Educ. of Mountain Lakes v. Maas, 56 N.J. Super. 245, 152 A.2d 394 (1959).

17. Ky. Rev. Stat. § 214.036.

18. Kleid v. Board of Educ. of Fulton, Kentucky Independent School Dist., 406 F. Supp. 902 (W.D. Ky. 1976).

19. Brown v. Stone, 378 So. 2d 218 (Miss. 1979).

20. School officials also have the authority to assign pupils to attendance zones and to require legal residence within a school district as a condition of public school attendance. While students can elect to attend a nonpublic school, if they remain in the public educational system they do not have the right to attend the specific school of their choosing.

21. For example, the Utah Constitution, art. X, § 11, requires teaching of the metric system, and the Oklahoma Constitution, art. XIII, § 7, stipulates that agriculture, horticulture, stock raising, and domestic science must be taught.

22. *See* Woodson v. School Dist. No. 28, Kingsman County, 127 Kansas 651, 274 P. 728 (1929).

23. Meyer v. Nebraska, 262 U.S. 390 (1923).

24. Epperson v. Arkansas, 393 U.S. 97, 106 (1968).

25. Daniel v. Walters, 515 F.2d 485 (6th Cir. 1975).

26. Lander v. Seaver, 32 Vt. 114 (Vt. 1859).

27. State v. Webber, 108 Ind. 31 (1886).

28. Sapp v. Renfroe, 372 F. Supp. 1193 (N.D. Ga. 1974). In an earlier decision, Spence v. Bailey, 465 F.2d 797 (6th Cir. 1972), the Sixth Circuit Court of Appeals held that a mandatory officers' training course for male students violated first amendment rights.

29. *See* text with note 40, Chapter 10.

30. *See* Arundar v. Dekalb County School Dist., 620 F.2d 493 (5th Cir.1980).

31. Williams v. Board of Educ. of County of Kanawha, 388 F. Supp. 93 (S.D. W.Va. 1975). For a discussion of the Kanawha situation, *see* Ralph N.

Fuller, "Textbook Selection: Burning Issue?" *Compact*, Vol. 9, No. 3, June 1975, pp. 6–8; *Censoring Textbooks: Is West Virginia the Tip of the Iceberg?* (Washington, D.C.: Institute for Educational Leadership, 1974).

32. Presidents Council, Dist. 25 v. Community School Bd. No. 25, 457 F.2d 289 (2d Cir. 1972), *cert. denied*, 409 U.S. 998 (1972). *See* Chapter 3 for a discussion of teachers' rights to academic freedom.

33. Bicknell v. Vergennes Union High School Bd. of Directors, 475 F. Supp. 615 (D. Vt. 1979), *aff'd* No. 79-7676 (2d Cir., October 2, 1980). For a discussion of the most-censored items in educational institutions, *see* L. B. Woods, "Is Academic Freedom Dead in Public Schools?" *Phi Delta Kappan*, Vol. 61, No. 2, October 1979, p. 104.

34. Zykan v. Warsaw Community School Corp., No. S79-68 (N.D. Ind., December 3, 1979), *vacated and remanded*, 631 F.2d 1300 (7th Cir. 1980). The students also alleged that the contracts of two teachers were not renewed for improper motives. Finding such allegations "creative," the appellate court concluded that such claims are properly initiated by employees who have allegedly suffered the harm and not by students. *See also* Cary v. Board of Educ. of Adams-Arapahoe School Dist., 598 F.2d 535 (10th Cir. 1979).

35. *Id.*, No. S79-68, slip opinion, p. 4.

36. *Id.*, 631 F.2d 1305.

37. Minarcini v. Strongsville City School Dist., 541 F.2d 577 (6th Cir. 1976). *See also* Right to Read Defense Committee v. School Committee of the City of Chelsea, 454 F. Supp. 703 (D. Mass. 1978), in which the federal district court held that the removal of an anthology from the high school library violated first amendment rights of students and faculty.

38. Salvail v. Nashua Bd. of Educ., 469 F. Supp. 1269 (D.N.H. 1979).

39. Pico v. Board of Educ., Island Trees Union Free School Dist., 474 F. Supp. 387 (E.D.N.Y. 1979), *vacated and remanded*, No. 79-7690 (2d Cir., October 2, 1980).

40. Johnson v. New York State Educ. Depart., 449 F.2d 871 (2d Cir. 1971), *vacated and remanded*, 409 U.S. 75 (1972) (per curiam).

41. *Id.*, 409 U.S. 75.

42. *See* Foster v. County School Bd. of Prince William County, 48 U.S.L.W. 3128 (Va., Aug. 28, 1979), *cert. denied*, 100 S.Ct. 23 (1979); Marshall v. School Dist. Re No. 3 Morgan County, 553 P.2d 784 (Colo. 1976); Carpio v. Tucson High School Dist. No. 1 of Pima County, 524 P.2d 948 (Ariz. 1974); Chandler v. South Bend Community School Corp., 312 N.E.2d 915 (Ind. 1974).

43. Cardiff v. Bismarck Public School Dist., 263 N.W.2d 105 (N.D. 1978).

44. Beck v. Board of Educ. of Harlem Consolidated School Dist., 344 N.E.2d 440 (Ill. 1976); Vandevender v. Cassell, 208 S.E.2d 436 (W. Va. 1974).

45. Beck v. Board of Educ., *id. See also* Sneed v. Greensboro City Bd. of Educ., 264 S.E.2d 106 (N.C. 1980).

46. Concerned Parents v. Caruthersville School Dist., 548 S.W.2d 554 (Mo. 1977).

47. Norton v. Board of Educ. of School Dist. No. 16, Hobbs Municipal Schools, 553 P.2d 1277 (N.M. 1976).

48. Sodus Central School v. Rhine, 406 N.Y.S.2d 175 (App. Div. 1978).
49. 131 Cal. Rptr. 854 (Cal. App. 1976). *See* Chapter 7 for a general discussion of tort law pertaining to negligence suits.
50. *Id.* at 861.
51. *Id.*
52. Donohue v. Copiague Union Free Schools, 407 N.Y.S.2d 874 (App. Div. 1978), *aff'd* 418 N.Y.S.2d 375, 391 N.E.2d 1352 (N.Y. 1979).
53. Doe v. Board of Educ. of Montgomery County, 48 U.S.L.W. 2077 (Md. Cir. Ct., Montgomery County, July 6, 1979).
54. Hoffman v. Board of Educ. of the City of New York, 410 N.Y.S.2d 99 (App. Div. 1978), *rev'd* 424 N.Y.S.2d 376 (Ct. App. 1979).
55. *See* Mills v. Board of Educ., 348 F. Supp. 866 (D.D.C. 1972), text with note 96, Chapter 9.
56. *See* Chris Pipho, *Update VIII: Minimum Competency Testing* (Denver, Colo.: Education Commission of the States, July, 1979); *The Competency Movement*, AASA Critical Issues Report (Arlington, Va.: American Ass'n of School Administrators, 1978).
57. *See* Warren Newman, "Competency Testing: A Response to Arthur Wise," *Educational Leadership*, Vol. 36, No. 8, May 1979, pp. 549–50; *The Competency Challenge: What Schools Are Doing* (Arlington, Va.: National School Public Relations Ass'n, 1978).
58. *See* "Tyler—NEA Panel Criticizes Florida's Basic Skills Standards," *News Exchange* (Ass'n for Supervision and Curriculum Development), Vol. 20, No. 3, Summer 1978, p. 3; Merle McClung, "Competency Testing Programs: Legal and Educational Issues," *Fordham Law Review*, Vol. 47, No. 5, April 1979, pp. 668–672.
59. "ASCD Board Opposes Statewide Tests for Graduation, Favors Competency-Based Education," *Educational Leadership*, Vol. 36, No. 8, May 1979, p. 554.
60. Debra P. v. Turlington, 474 F. Supp. 244 (M.D. Fla. 1979). *See also* Florida State Bd. of Educ. v. Brady, 368 So. 2d 661 (Fla. App. 1979), in which a state appeals court rejected a parental challenge to the scoring criterion by which functional literacy was measured; Brady v. Turlington, 372 So. 2d 1164 (Fla. App. 1979), in which a state appeals court upheld a rule of the state board of education requiring students to qualify for a high school diploma by attaining a minimum performance standard as measured by a test taken before or after the effective date of the rule.
61. A North Carolina federal district court dismissed a class action suit on behalf of eleventh- and twelfth-grade black, poor white, and American Indian students who claimed that the state-mandated proficiency test violated their due process and equal protection rights due to its cultural and racial bias, Green v. Hunt, No. 78-539-CIV-5 (E.D.N.C., April 4, 1979). *See also* Wells v. Banks, 266 S.E.2d 270 (Ga. App. 1980), in which a Georgia appeals court held that local school boards have the authority to require passage of a competency test as a prerequisite for a high school diploma and that such requirements do not violate due process or equal protection rights of students.
62. *See* Arthur Wise, "Why Minimum Competency Testing Will Not Improve Education," *Educational Leadership*, Vol. 36, No. 8, May 1979, p. 549.

63. Edward L. Winn, "Legal Control of Student Extracurricular Activities," *School Law Bulletin*, Vol. VII, No. 3, July 1976, p. 2.
64. See Goss v. Lopez, 419 U.S. 565 (1975); text with note 33, Chapter 11.
65. See State *ex rel*. Indiana High School Athletic Ass'n v. Lawrence Circuit Court, 162 N.E.2d 250 (Ind. 1959).
66. Albach v. Odle, 531 F.2d 983 (10th Cir. 1976).
67. Pegram v. Nelson, 469 F. Supp. 1134 (M.D.N.C. 1979).
68. See Davis v. Meek, 344 F. Supp. 298 (N.D. Ohio 1972); Moran v. School Dist. No. 7, 350 F. Supp. 1180 (D. Mont. 1972); Kelley v. Metropolitan County Bd. of Educ. of Nashville, 293 F. Supp. 485 (M.D. Tenn. 1968).
69. See Chapter 9 for a discussion of regulations dealing with special treatment of married and female students in connection with extracurricular activities.
70. O'Connor v. Board of Educ., 316 N.Y.S.2d 799 (Sup. Ct., Herkimer County, 1970).
71. See Hasson v. Boothby, 318 F. Supp. 1183 (D. Mass. 1970); Stevenson v. Wheeler County Bd. of Educ., 306 F. Supp. 97 (D. Ga. 1969).
72. Braesch v. DePasquale, 200 Neb. 726, 265 N.W.2d 842 (1978), *cert. denied*, 439 U.S. 1068 (1979).
73. *Id.*, 265 N.W.2d 846.
74. *Id.*, 439 U.S. 1068.
75. French v. Cornwall, 202 Neb. 569, 276 N.W.2d 216 (1979).
76. Bunger v. Iowa High School Athletic Ass'n, 197 N.W.2d 555, 561–62 (Iowa 1972).
77. Kulovitz v. Illinois High School Ass'n, 462 F. Supp. 875 (N.D. Ill. 1978). *See also* Walsh v. Louisiana High School Athletic Ass'n, 616 F.2d 152 (5th Cir. 1980); Albach v. Odle, 531 F.2d 983 (10th Cir. 1976).
78. Kriss v. Brown, 390 N.E.2d 193 (Ind. App. 1979). *See also* Florida High School Activities Ass'n, Inc. v. Bradshaw, 369 So. 2d 398 (Fla. App. 1979); Mozingo v. Oklahoma Secondary School Activities Ass'n, 575 P.2d 1379 (Okla. App. 1978).
79. See Crandall v. North Dakota High School Activities Ass'n, 261 N.W.2d 921 (N.D. 1978); Sanders v. Louisiana High School Athletic Ass'n, 242 So. 2d 19 (La. App. 1970); Scott v. Kilpatrick, 237 So. 2d 652 (Ala. 1970).
80. Doe v. Marshall, 459 F. Supp. 1190 (S.D. Tex. 1978).
81. See Parish v. NCAA, 361 F. Supp. 1220 (W.D. La. 1973), *aff'd* 506 F.2d 1028 (5th Cir. 1975).
82. See Missouri State High School Activities Ass'n v. Schoenlaub, 507 S.W.2d 354 (Mo. 1974).
83. Smith v. Crim, 240 S.E.2d 884 (Ga. 1977). *See also* DeKalb County School System v. White, 260 S.E.2d 853 (Ga. 1979).
84. See Neuhaus v. Torrey, 310 F. Supp. 192 (N.D. Cal. 1970).
85. See Long v. Zopp, 476 F.2d 180 (4th Cir. 1973).
86. Dunham v. Pulsifer, 312 F. Supp. 411, 413 (D. Vt. 1970).
87. Neuhaus v. Torrey, 310 F. Supp. 192 (N.D. Cal. 1970).
88. Kampmeier v. Nyquist, 553 F.2d 296 (2d Cir. 1977).
89. Kampmeier v. Harris, 411 N.Y.S.2d 744 (App. Div. 1978). *See also*

Swiderski v. Board of Educ.–City School Dist. of Albany, 408 N.Y.S.2d 744 (Sup. Ct., Albany County, 1978).

90. *See* Elwood Clayton and Gene Jacobsen, "An Analysis of Court Cases Concerned with Student Rights, 1960–1971," *NASSP Bulletin*, Vol. 58, No. 379, February 1974, p. 53.

91. *See* Griswold v. Connecticut, 381 U.S. 479 (1965).

92. Dawkins v. Billingsley, 172 P. 69 (Okla. 1918).

93. Van Allen v. McCleary, 211 N.Y.S.2d 501 (Sup. Ct., Nassau County, 1961). *See also* Valentine v. Independent School Dist., 174 N.W. 334 (Iowa 1919).

94. 20 U.S.C. § 1232g (1976).

95. *See* 45 C.F.R. 99 *et seq.* (1978).

96. *See* text with note 111, Chapter 9, for a more detailed discussion of this law.

97. Ind. Code Ann. §§ 4-1-6-2 to 4-1-6-5.

98. Einhorn v. Maus, 300 F. Supp. 1169 (E.D. Pa. 1969). *See also* Elder v. Anderson, 23 Cal. Rptr. 48 (Cal. App. 1962).

99. The one notable exception to compulsory attendance pertains to Amish children who have successfully completed the eighth grade. *See* State of Wisconsin v. Yoder, 406 U.S. 205 (1972); text with note 10, *supra*.

# 9

# Equal Educational Opportunity: Pupil Classification Practices

The preceding chapter dealt with general requirements and rights attached to public school attendance. Because of its importance, the right to equal educational opportunities warrants closer examination. The theoretical concept of equal opportunity is rooted firmly in democratic philosophy and shares an exalted position with brotherhood and peace. However, the applauded principle has not been easily translated into concrete school policies and practices. Although during much of the twentieth century noted educators have asserted that all children should have an equal chance to develop their capabilities, only recently have judicial and legislative bodies addressed the nature of the equal treatment that is constitutionally required in public schools. Various classification practices have been scrutinized to determine if they have impeded students' rights to equal access to appropriate instructional programs. After a brief discussion of equal protection mandates in general, this chapter focuses on student classifications based on race, sex, marriage and pregnancy, age, ability or achievement, and ethnic background/native language.

## EQUAL PROTECTION GUARANTEES

The fourteenth amendment to the United States Constitution provides in part that "no State shall . . . deny to any person within its jurisdiction, the equal protection of the laws." [1] Historically, courts allowed differential treatment of individuals, as long as the bases for the distinctions were reasonably related to legitimate governmental goals. Since challenged state

action usually has prevailed under this *rational basis* test, the Warren
Supreme Court developed a second equal protection standard to afford
greater protection to individuals. If the classification of individuals for
differential treatment is considered "suspect" or affects a fundamental interest, evidence of a compelling governmental objective is required to
justify the state action. As legislation rarely has withstood analysis under
this *strict scrutiny* standard of review, the decision as to which test to
apply often has determined the outcome in equal protection cases. In
essence, the identification of either a suspect classification or fundamental
interest has been the critical factor in shifting the burden of proof to the
state to justify its policies.

The Supreme Court has defined fundamental interests as those specifically mentioned in the Constitution, such as freedom of speech, as well
as rights that are closely related to constitutional guarantees (i.e., "fundamental" by implication), such as the rights to vote, procreate, and travel.[2]
While many lower courts had assumed that education was a fundamental
interest,[3] in 1973 the Supreme Court announced that education was not
among the implied fundamental rights under the Federal Constitution.[4]
Therefore, the Court majority reasoned that challenged state action involving education would trigger only the rational basis equal protection
test, unless a suspect classification (e.g., race, alienage, or national origin[5])
was implicated. In identifying suspect classifications, the Supreme Court
has assessed whether the classification is based on an immutable characteristic, whether members of the class are stigmatized, whether there has
been a history of discrimination against the class, and whether the class is
politically powerless. To date, the judiciary has not declared that classifications based on gender, handicaps, or wealth are "suspect," and thus
state action based on such distinctions has not been subject to the strict
scrutiny standard of review.[6]

Because of dissatisfaction with having to choose between the lenient
rational basis and the stringent strict scrutiny standards, an in-between
test for evaluating equal protection claims seems to have emerged during
the Burger Supreme Court era. While declining to expand the category of
suspect classes and fundamental interests, the Court has invalidated state
action that traditionally would have withstood analysis under the rational
basis test. During the past decade the Court has noted that it should evaluate three items in equal protection disputes: "the character of the classification in question; the individual interests affected by the classification;
and the governmental interests asserted in support of the classification."[7]
Using this in-between standard, the Court has required state-imposed
classifications to be necessary, not merely convenient, to achieve legitimate
governmental goals, and has invalidated classification schemes if there
have been reasonable less restrictive means of reaching the same goal.[8]

How are these equal protection guarantees applied to public education? While it might appear from a literal translation of the equal protection clause that once a state establishes an educational system all stu-

dents must be treated in the same manner, courts have recognized that individuals are different and that equal treatment of unequals can have negative consequences. Accordingly, valid classification practices, designed to enhance the educational experiences of children by recognizing their unique needs, generally have been accepted as a legitimate prerogative of educators. Indeed, all schools classify students in some fashion, and state laws often specifically authorize school boards to set criteria for pupil classification schemes. Children are grouped by academic levels, social maturity, athletic ability, sex, age, and many other distinguishing traits. It has been asserted that without these various classifications, the business of public education could not proceed.[9]

While the authority of educators to classify pupils has not been contested, the bases for certain classifications and the procedures used to make distinctions among students recently have been the focus of substantial litigation. To the extent that school classifications determine a pupil's access to various types of educational resources, courts and legislatures have looked closely at the practices, particularly if they have an adverse impact on vulnerable minority groups. In some instances, courts have interpreted "equal educational opportunity" as requiring more than neutral treatment of students and have ordered school officials to take affirmative steps to overcome the deficiencies of certain groups of pupils.[10]

## RACIAL CLASSIFICATIONS

Greater public attention has focused on the courts' involvement in desegregating public schools than on any other aspect of judicial intervention in the public education arena. The controversy created in legislative and judicial forums over busing to achieve desegregation is unparalleled in the history of American education. While this chapter focuses primarily on within-school classifications, it seems appropriate to begin a discussion of pupil classification practices with a brief overview of desegregation developments. These race discrimination cases have provided the impetus for courts and legislatures to evaluate the legality of other bases used to make distinctions among students. Suits involving sex discrimination, age discrimination, and the rights of handicapped, married, pregnant, and English-deficient students have relied on precedents established in desegregation cases.

In the landmark decision *Brown v. Board of Education of Topeka,* the Supreme Court announced that state-imposed segregation in public schools violates the Federal Constitution. Justice Warren's often-quoted passage set the stage for subsequent litigation pertaining to students' rights to equal educational opportunities.

Today, education is perhaps the most important function of state and local governments. Compulsory school attendance laws and the great expenditures for education both demonstrate our recognition of the importance of education to our democratic society. It is required in the performance of our most basic public responsibilities, even service in the armed forces. It is the very foundation of good citizenship. Today it is a prinicipal instrument in awakening the child to cultural values, in preparing him for later professional training, and in helping him to adjust normally to his environment. In these days, it is doubtful that any child may reasonably be expected to succeed in life if he is denied the opportunity of an education. Such an opportunity, where the state has undertaken to provide it, is a right which must be made available to all on equal terms.[11]

Since this *Brown* proclamation was delivered in 1954, courts have grappled with two main tasks: (1) determining whether a constitutional violation has occurred, and (2) if so, fashioning an appropriate remedy. The judiciary has placed an affirmative duty on school officials to eliminate *de jure* segregation resulting from state laws or other governmental actions (e.g., gerrymandering school attendance zones) that serve to perpetuate school segregation. The failure to act as well as discriminatory acts can provide evidence that this affirmative duty has not been satisfied.[12]

In contrast to *de jure* segregation, the judiciary has not considered segregation resulting from residential patterns or other racially neutral conditions (*de facto* segregation) to be unconstitutional and subject to remedial action. The touchstone in determining whether segregation should be considered *de jure* or *de facto* is evidence or lack of evidence of discriminatory governmental intent. This assessment of intent has been crucial in school systems that were not segregated by law in 1954. In the Supreme Court's first desegregation opinion pertaining to a district outside the south, the Court concluded that a finding of discriminatory intent in a meaningful part of the school system created a presumption of *de jure* segregation in the remainder of the system.[13] The Court placed the burden on school authorities to substantiate that other segregated schools within the system were not the result of intentional discrimination.

Several federal courts have taken the position that such a discriminatory motive can be inferred if the foreseeable consequences of official actions have maintained school segregation.[14] In 1976, however, the Supreme Court declared that mere evidence of a policy's disproportionate impact on a minority group does not justify a presumption that neutral practices are automatically unconstitutional.[15] Thus, evidence of racial imbalance is not sufficient to violate the Constitution; there must be proof of deliberate acts of discrimination on the part of school decision makers. The nature of proof required to establish this discriminatory intent continues to generate substantial judicial debate.

Delineation of the appropriate criteria to apply in assessing the existence of a constitutional violation has not been the only troublesome task facing federal courts. Once a constitutional abridgment has been established, courts have had to fashion suitable remedies. The Supreme Court has instructed lower courts to tailor "the scope of the remedy to fit the nature and extent of the constitutional violation" and at the same time to ensure that the remedy restores the victims of discriminatory conduct to the position they would have occupied in the absence of the violation.[16]

During the past decade the Supreme Court has voiced displeasure with court-ordered remedies that are more extensive than warranted by evidence of constitutional abridgments and has noted that in devising remedies, courts must consider the interests of state and local authorities in managing their own affairs.[17] The Court also has declared that metropolitan desegregation remedies are inappropriate, unless there is proof of intentional segregation on the part of all school districts involved in the remedial plan.[18] Furthermore, the Court has ruled that only with evidence of a system-wide impact of segregation may lower courts impose a system-wide remedy,[19] and that school districts do not have an obligation to make annual adjustments in the racial compositions of schools as long as the implementation of a desegregation plan has achieved its original objective.[20]

Despite the Supreme Court's cautionary statements, lower federal courts have remained aggressive in finding constitutional violations and in ordering and monitoring remedial measures. Many courts have mandated compensatory educational programs and in-service staff training in desegregation plans as necessary in order to eliminate the lingering effects of past discrimination.[21] Courts also have assessed schemes intended to curb "white flight," such as the use of magnet alternative schools.[22] Regardless of other features, however, most remedial plans continue to include the transfer of pupils between paired or clustered schools to integrate student bodies.[23] Until the judiciary becomes convinced of the effectiveness of alternative plans to achieve desegregation, it seems likely that some degree of student busing will appear in most remedial orders.

Numerous school districts remain involved in desegregation controversies, and three decades of litigation have not clarified the obligations placed on school districts to achieve desegregated schools. Moreover, various practices within schools are being attacked as racially discriminatory. For example, the disproportionate representation of minority children in special education classes and lower instructional tracks is being challenged, as is the use of racially biased testing instruments. Such allegations of racial discrimination in connection with student classifications by aptitude and achievement are explored later in this chapter.

## CLASSIFICATIONS BASED ON SEX

The judiciary has been called upon to review a growing number of claims of sex discrimination in public schools, but the applicable principles of law in this area are less settled than those pertaining to racial discrimination. Sex, like race, is "an immutable characteristic determined solely by the accident of birth,"[24] but the Supreme Court has been reluctant to apply strict judicial scrutiny to sex-based distinctions. In 1973, four justices on the high court argued that sex should be elevated to the category of suspect classes.

> . . . the imposition of special disabilities upon the members of a particular sex because of their sex would seem to violate "the basic concept of our system that legal burdens should bear some relationship to individual responsibility . . . ."[25]

To date, however, a Supreme Court majority has not been persuaded to apply the rigorous equal protection test to sex-based classifications. Hence, the arguments that have been so persuasive in desegregation litigation have been less effective when applied to claims of sex discrimination. Courts, nonetheless, have invalidated gender-based classifications if they have not been sufficiently related to the achievement of a valid governmental objective.[26]

## HIGH SCHOOL ATHLETICS

In the school context, the most publicized cases dealing with sex discrimination have involved high school athletics and have focused on the denial of equal opportunities to female students. Such sex-bias suits have been based primarily on the equal protection clause of the fourteenth amendment and on equal rights amendments of individual states. Recently, suits also have relied on Title IX of the Education Amendments of 1972, which prohibits discrimination against the beneficiaries of or participants in any educational programs receiving federal financial assistance.[27]

Courts generally have ordered school districts to allow female athletes to compete with males in noncontact sports if no comparable programs have been available for female students. In the first case to receive notable attention, the Eighth Circuit Court of Appeals invalidated a policy restricting participation on the interscholastic tennis, track, and cross-country skiing teams to male students.[28] The court concluded that the lack of alternative competitive programs for females raised a valid equal protection claim. The court rejected the high school athletic league's contention that relief was inappropriate because participation in interscholastic sports was a privilege and not a right. The court reasoned that whether or not there was an absolute right to engage in interscholastic athletics, female students were denied equal protection of the laws because benefits provided by the state to male students were denied to them. While there have been isolated cases to the contrary,[29] most courts have echoed the rationale espoused by the Eighth Circuit Appellate Court in mandating that qualified female students be allowed to participate on interscholastic tennis, track, and other noncontact teams that traditionally have been reserved for male students.[30]

Courts generally have held that the establishment of comparable women's athletic programs removes the necessity for providing "mixed" teams because of the psychological and physiological differences between men and women. For example, an Indiana appeals court upheld the state high school athletic association rule prohibiting mixed gender competition in sports where separate, comparable teams were provided for both sexes.[31] In opposition to this view, the Sixth Circuit Court of Appeals ruled in 1973 that female students had the right to participate with males in all noncontact interscholastic athletic activities, even if teams for females were provided.[32] The appeals court, however, did recognize the permissibility of selecting members for competitive teams on the basis of athletic skills.

Without question, the most controversial issue involving high school athletics is the participation of males and females together in *contact* sports. Several courts have ruled that female students must be allowed to compete for positions on all school-sponsored teams, including those in contact sports. For example, the Washington Supreme Court held that two fully qualified female high school students were entitled to try out for the interscholastic football team.[33] Similarly, the Supreme Court of Pennsylvania relied on the state's equal rights amendment in ruling that females must be allowed to compete with males in all contact sports, including football and wrestling.[34] The court noted that even if women's teams are available, female athletes are denied the opportunity to reach their full potential when they are limited to playing on such teams, which usually offer a lower level of competition.

In 1978, a federal district court in Ohio rendered a sweeping decision in which a high school athletic association rule and a portion of the regulations for Title IX of the Education Amendments of 1972 were declared invalid.[35] In this case, a school district brought suit against the state athletic association, challenging the constitutionality of its regulation forbidding coeducational contact teams. The federal court struck down the association rule under the fourteenth amendment. The court held that qualified females were deprived of their liberty rights without due process of law by being prohibited from participating on contact teams traditionally reserved for males. The court reasoned that the exclusionary rule created a conclusive presumption that females were physically weaker than males, and an equally conclusive presumption that females were less proficient athletes. Furthermore, the court held that the Title IX regulation stipulating that female students be provided comparable programs or be allowed to participate on teams with male students "unless the sport involved is a contact sport" violated the due process clause of the fifth amendment.[36] The court concluded that the last phrase of this regulation could be interpreted as giving school districts the option of maintaining contact teams limited to male athletes (without providing comparable competitive activities for females), which was not the intent of the framers of Title IX.

A federal district court in Wisconsin also ruled that female students have the right to compete for positions on traditionally male contact teams.[37] Although the Wisconsin court did not offer an opinion as to the constitutionality of Title IX regulations, it did declare that once a state undertakes to provide interscholastic competition, such opportunities must be provided to all students on equal terms. The court reasoned that the objective of preventing injury to female athletes was not sufficient to justify the prohibition of coeducational teams in contact sports. In enjoining the school district from absolutely denying female students the opportunity to participate in varsity interscholastic competition in contact sports, the court noted that school officials had options available other than establishing coeducational teams: Interscholastic competition in these sports could be eliminated for all students, or separate teams for females could be established. The court also recognized that if comparable sex-segregated programs were provided, female athletes could not assert the right to try out for the male team simply because of its higher level of competition arising from the abilities of team members themselves.

In addition to challenging their exclusion from varsity contact teams, female athletes have contested the use of different rules for women's basketball (split court rules) and men's basketball. In Tennessee, a federal district court held that the use of different rules was not rationally related to any legitimate objective, and thus deprived female students of their constitutional rights.[38] The court reasoned that the objective of protecting weaker athletes from the more strenuous form of basketball could be applied to both sexes, in that many female athletes could easily play full court basketball, while some male students could benefit from using the modified rules. However, the Sixth Circuit Court of Appeals overturned the district court ruling and concluded that sex-based classifications in athletics were legitimate because of the differences in physical characteristics and capabilities between the sexes. The court held that there was no equal protection violation simply because basketball rules were tailored to accommodate differences between male and female athletes. A federal court in Oklahoma followed the Sixth Circuit Appellate Court's reasoning,[39] but in 1979 a federal district court in Arkansas invalidated the use of separate rules for males and females as lacking a rational basis.[40] Noting that tradition was the only justification offered for the differential treatment, the Arkansas court concluded that the practice violated equal protection rights.

It appears that female athletes cannot rely on Title IX in challenging such sex-based modifications in sports. In January 1979, the Department of Health, Education, and Welfare issued a policy statement interpreting Title IX as allowing split court rules for women's basketball. According to the statement, Title IX requires schools to offer *comparable* athletic opportunities, but *not identical versions* of a single sport.[41] It follows that the provision of a softball team for females and a baseball team for males also would be legally permissible under this law.

While the majority of the suits alleging sex discrimination in high school athletics have been initiated by women, a few male students have asserted their right to compete for positions on all-female teams. In Rhode Island, for example, a federal district court granted a male high school student the right to compete for a position on the women's volleyball team because there was no separate team provided for males.[42] The student asserted that the interscholastic league's policy of limiting competitive volleyball competition to females violated Title IX as well as the equal protection clause of the Federal Constitution. Defendants contended that since overall athletic opportunities had not been limited for male students, Title IX was not violated by restricting volleyball competition to female athletes. Although recognizing that males occupied the vast majority of the positions on teams open to mixed-gender competition, the district court concluded that males had been excluded from this particular sport and therefore were entitled to participate on coeducational teams. The First Circuit Court of Appeals, however, stayed implementation of the order pending appellate review. Subsequently, the appeals court dismissed the case as moot, because the league's volleyball season had ended and the plaintiff was about to graduate from high school.[43] Thus, the appellate court did not offer an opinion as to whether Title IX regulations were intended to provide relief for the previously disadvantaged sex in *each sport* or in *overall* athletic opportunities.

Other courts have rendered conflicting opinions on this issue. The Massachusetts high court invalidated an interscholastic athletic association rule that barred male students from teams established for females while allowing female athletes to participate on previously all-male teams in sports without comparable teams for both sexes.[44] The court held that such sex-based discrimination could not be justified by health or safety considerations or by the assertion that the rule was necessary to shield the emergent women's sports program from inundation by male athletes. In contrast, an Illinois appeals court concluded that the state high school athletic conference rule excluding males from all-female volleyball teams did not abridge state or federal constitutional provisions.[45] The court reasoned that the objective of providing general equality in athletic opportunities would be impeded by allowing male students to compete on the teams reserved for females. Since the United States Supreme Court has not addressed this issue, the intent of Title IX remains subject to differing interpretations among lower courts.

## ACADEMIC PROGRAMS

Allegations of sex bias in public schools have not been confined to athletic programs. Differential treatment of males and females in academic courses and schools also has generated litigation. Again, the "separate but equal" doctrine seems to be the prevailing legal principle applied by courts. In suits challenging the maintenance of sex-segregated schools or programs, the excluded sex must be able to substantiate that specific disadvantages result from the exclusion in order to receive relief.[46]

In a significant case, *Vorchheimer v. School District of Philadelphia,* the Third Circuit Court of Appeals sanctioned the operation of sex-segregated public high schools in 1976. Subsequently, the United States Supreme Court, equally divided, affirmed the decision without delivering an opinion. Essentially, the appellate court concluded that the maintenance of single-sex public high schools, in which enrollment is voluntary and educational offerings are essentially equal, is permissible under the equal protection clause of the fourteenth amendment and the Equal Educational Opportunities Act of 1974.[47]

The Third Circuit Court of Appeals distinguished *Vorchheimer* from prior decisions in which sex-based classifications had been invalidated because of the absence of a rational basis for differential treatment disadvantaging one sex. Noting that Philadelphia's sex-segregated college preparatory schools offered functionally equivalent programs, the court concluded that the separation of the sexes was justified because adolescents may study more effectively in single-sex high schools. The appellate court reiterated that "gender has never been rejected as an impermissible classification in all instances." [48] The court also emphasized that the female plaintiff was not compelled to attend the sex-segregated academic school; she had the option of enrolling in a coeducational school within her attendance zone. Furthermore, the court stated that her petition to attend the male academic high school was based on personal preference rather than on an objective evaluation of the offerings available in the two schools.[49]

Although the Supreme Court endorsed the operation of separate but equal academic schools for males and females in *Vorchheimer,* this decision should not be interpreted as sanctioning *unequal* educational opportunities for the two sexes. Female students have been successful in gaining admission to specific courses that traditionally have been offered only for males. For example, the exclusion of female students from auto mechanics classes, wood shop, and metal shop has been invalidated as a denial of equal protection guarantees.[50] Also, courts have required industrial arts and home economics classes to be made available to male and female students on equal terms.[51]

Most cases challenging the exclusion of one sex from specific curricular offerings have been settled on constitutional grounds, but future challenges to sex-segregated classes probably will rely on Title IX regulations. These regulations prohibit sex-segregated health, industrial arts, business, vocational-technical, home economics, and music classes. They also ban sex discrimination in counseling and sex-based differential course requirements for graduation (e.g., home economics for females and industrial arts for males). Separate physical education classes also are prohibited under Title IX, although students may be grouped by skill levels.[52]

Like sex-segregated programs and schools, sex-based admission criteria have been challenged, and courts have used constitutional grounds in voiding standards that blatantly disadvantage either sex.[53] For example, the admission practices of the Boston Latin Schools were invalidated because they discriminated against female applicants.[54] Because of the different seating capacities of the two schools, the Latin School for males required a lower score on the entrance examination than did the school for females. While sanctioning the operation of sex-segregated schools, the federal district court was unsympathetic to the physical plant problems and ruled that the same entrance requirements had to be applied to both sexes. Similarly, the Ninth Circuit Court of Appeals concluded that a school district's plan to admit an equal number of male and female students to the high school with an advanced college preparatory curriculum violated equal protection guarantees, because it resulted in stricter admission criteria for female applicants.[55] The appellate court rejected the assertion that the school district's admission policy was a legitimate means of reaching its admittedly desirable goal of balancing the number of male and female students enrolled in the school.

UNRESOLVED QUESTIONS

Many diverse issues have been raised in these sex-bias suits, and it appears that claims of sex discrimination in academic as well as athletic programs will continue to be a popular source of litigation. The doctrine of "separate but equal" remains viable in these cases, but courts have not agreed as to the *type* of equality required under constitutional or statutory provisions. Questions such as the following persist: Are sex-segregated varsity teams in noncontact and contact sports comparable if they have different levels of competition? What criteria should be used to gauge the equality between sex-segregated academic programs and/or schools? Under what circumstances is sex segregation unjustified, even if comparable opportunities are provided for both sexes? In the absence of a federal equal rights amendment,[56] it appears that the Supreme Court eventually will have to address these questions and take a stand on the nature of sex equality required in public education.

## CLASSIFICATIONS BASED ON MARRIAGE
## AND PREGNANCY

Legal principles governing the rights of married and pregnant students have changed dramatically since 1960. The evolution of the law in this area is indicative of the increasing judicial commitment to protect students from unjustified classifications that limit educational opportunities.

## MARRIED STUDENTS

Courts historically sanctioned differential treatment of married students in public education. In 1957, the Supreme Court of Tennessee upheld a school regulation requiring students to withdraw from school for the remainder of the term following their marriage.[57] More recently, an Ohio regulation barring married students from participation in extracurricular activities was upheld by a common pleas court, because school officials demonstrated that married athletes were often in a position to be idolized and copied by other students.[58] The court concluded that the school's purpose of attempting to curtail underage marriages justified the policy.

During the past decade, however, most courts have rejected the traditional view that students can be denied school attendance or participation in extracurricular activities because of their marital status. A Kentucky appeals court declared that a policy excluding married students from school was arbitrary, unrelated to the school's asserted purpose, and a denial of the students' right to obtain an education.[59] In 1972, an Ohio federal court held that married students were entitled to equal treatment in all aspects of public education, including school-related activities. The court recognized extracurricular functions as "an integral part" of the total school program and declared that the Federal Constitution prohibited discrimination against married students in any school offerings.[60] Similarly, a Tennessee federal district court held that school regulations preventing married students from participating in extracurricular activities unconstitutionally infringed upon the students' right to marry and right to attend school.[61] Other courts have invalidated the exclusion of married students from extracurricular activities on the rationale that once a state establishes such programs, it cannot exclude a certain class of students without showing a compelling state interest.[62]

## PREGNANT STUDENTS

School regulations that deny pregnant students an education or discriminate against pregnant students also have been questioned through litigation. Since the latter part of the 1960s, courts generally have placed the burden on school officials to demonstrate that any differential treatment of pregnant students is absolutely necessary for health reasons. In an illustrative Texas case, a school rule was challenged which prohibited married mothers from attending regular public school classes. The only alternative available to the excluded students was to attend adult education classes, for which one had to be at least twenty-one years of age. A Texas civil appeals court invalidated the school board policy, ruling that it violated pregnant students' entitlement to free public schooling.[63]

In a Massachusetts case, the federal district court similarly held that school authorities could not exclude a pregnant, unmarried student from regular high school classes.[64] School officials had proposed that the pregnant student be allowed to use all school facilities, attend school functions, participate in senior activities, and receive assistance from teachers in continuing her studies. However, she was not to attend school during regular school hours. Since there was no evidence of any educational or medical reason for this special treatment, the court held that the pregnant student had a constitutional right to attend classes with other pupils.

Although most litigation has been settled on constitutional grounds, Title IX regulations also bar discrimination based on marital or parental status in educational programs receiving federal financial assistance.[65] Thus, it would appear that any denial of equal opportunities to married and pregnant students must be justified by an overriding educational objective. While school districts may offer special courses designed to address pregnant students' unique needs (e.g., instruction in child care), such students should not be forced to enroll in special classes that segregate them from other pupils. Courts have held that pregnant students cannot be relegated to evening programs that offer limited instruction or require fees for academic courses.[66] Restrictions placed on pregnant, unwed students because of their alleged lack of moral character, or other such reasons not grounded in valid health or safety considerations, no longer will be tolerated by the courts.

## CLASSIFICATIONS BASED ON AGE

Age is one of the factors most commonly used to classify individuals, not only in schools but also in general society. A specified age is used as a prerequisite to obtaining a driver's license, buying alcoholic beverages, and voting in state and national elections. Also, age is used to classify individuals for employment eligibility (e.g., child labor laws) and for mandatory retirement. While discrimination based on age has generated more litigation in connection with teachers and college students[67] than with public elementary and secondary pupils, there are a few public school situations that have evoked legal challenges.

It is generally accepted that a specified age can be used as a school entrance requirement, as a criterion for compulsory education, and as a condition of participation in certain extracurricular activities. In an illustrative Pennsylvania case, a school district refused to admit a potential kindergarten student who did not meet the minimum age requirement.[68] The student's birthday was in October, and the school district policy stipulated that all students had to be five years old by September 1 in order to enroll in kindergarten. The commonwealth court upheld the board policy as rationally related to a legitimate educational purpose.

In a Maine case, the controversy focused on a state law rather than a school board policy. Parents contested a statute that required all children entering first grade to be six years old by October 15.[69] It was asserted that the student, whose birthday fell short of the deadline by over two months, was academically ready for first grade and that he would lose interest in school if denied admission. Nonetheless, the federal court upheld the school board in enforcing the state's minimum age law. The court relied on evidence that substantiated a correlation between chronological age and school readiness in concluding that the law had a reasonable educational basis and, therefore, was constitutionally sound. Furthermore, the court noted the prohibitive costs that would be involved in making such a determination of readiness for each individual child.

A different type of age discrimination suit was initiated against school officials in New York City. Parents challenged the refusal of school authorities to admit their son to a two-year special progress class conducted at his junior high school.[70] The student had completed elementary school and was academically qualified for the program, but was denied admission because he was six months younger than the required age. The special progress classes were accelerated to cover the regular three-year junior high school curriculum in two years. The board asserted that the age requirement for admission to the special class was justified because younger students needed an additional year at the junior high school level in order to develop emotionally, socially, and physiologically. The New York court upheld the requirement, concluding that "to thrust a youngster into an environment where all his classmates are older may well result in the consequent impairment of the necessary social integration of the child with his classmates." [71] Also, the court emphasized that actions of school officials, taken in the best interests of students, should not be disturbed by the judiciary as long as such administrative determinations are reasonable.

Although parents undoubtedly will continue to use constitutional and statutory grounds to challenge various age restrictions placed on public school students, it appears that the Age Discrimination Act passed by Congress in 1975 and amended in 1978 will have little impact on such suits. The Department of Health, Education, and Welfare carefully designed the regulations for this Act so as to permit the use of age as a factor necessary to the "normal operation of the achievement of any statutory objective." [72] While all federally funded programs must review age distinctions and eliminate those that cannot be justified, the Act does not prohibit youth organizations from imposing a maximum age limit on membership or bar school districts from focusing funds, such as those from Title I of the Elementary and Secondary Education Act, on particular grades or age groups of students. Also, age limits for compulsory attendance as well as for free public education are permissible.

To date, courts have not concluded that the Federal Constitution requires governmental action to reflect an "age blind" society. The judiciary has recognized the unique characteristics of childhood in sanctioning reasonable age restrictions on students' activities, as long as age-based classifications are related to valid educational objectives.

## CLASSIFICATIONS BASED ON ABILITY OR ACHIEVEMENT

Schools use a variety of evaluative techniques to divide students into instructional groups and to determine grade placements. It is claimed that ability grouping permits more effective and efficient teaching by allowing teachers to concentrate their efforts on students with similar needs. While ability grouping is clearly permissible, several legal challenges have focused on the use of standardized intelligence and achievement tests for determining pupil placements. These suits have alleged that such tests are racially and culturally biased, and that their use to classify pupils often results in erroneous placements that stigmatize the children involved.

### TRACKING SCHEMES

In a widely publicized case, *Hobson v. Hansen,* the use of standardized intelligence test scores to place students in various ability tracks in Washington, D.C., was attacked as unconstitutional. Plaintiffs contended that some children were erroneously assigned to the lower tracks and had very little chance of advancing to higher tracks because of the limited curriculum and the absence of remedial instruction. They also charged that the track system placed "a dear price on teacher misjudgments." [73] The federal district court closely examined the test scores used to assign students to the various tracks, analyzed the accuracy of the test measurements, and concluded that mistakes often resulted from assigning pupils to instructional programs on this basis. For the first time, a federal court evaluated testing methods and concluded that they discriminated against minority children. In prohibiting the continuation of ability grouping schemes that resulted in *de jure* segregation, the court emphasized that it was *not* abolishing the use of track systems *per se:* "What is at issue here is not whether defendants are entitled to provide different kinds of students with different kinds of education." [74] The court noted that classifications reasonably related to educational purposes are constitutionally permissible unless they result in discrimination against identifiable groups of children.

Other ability grouping plans with racial overtones also have been invalidated. Two years after *Hobson,* the Fifth Circuit Court of Appeals reviewed the legality of a tracking scheme used in Jackson, Mississippi. The court struck down the plan and held that students could not be placed in classes on the basis of standardized test scores until a desegregated school district had been established to the court's satisfaction.[75] A similar Louisiana case involved ability grouping that resulted in classes segregated by race. The federal district court held that the classification of students on a nondiscriminatory basis would be permissible, but that tracking could not be used to perpetuate racial discrimination.[76] In a 1978 Alabama case, the Fifth Circuit Court of Appeals also concluded that an ability grouping scheme violated protected rights.[77] The scheme had been initiated shortly after a court order to desegregate schools, and it resulted in the continuation of racially segregated classes.

In contrast to the preceding situations, an ability grouping plan was considered permissible in a 1979 case.[78] An Alabama federal district court ruled that a school district's use of test scores to place students in various levels of a nongraded elementary school did not impair any protected rights of pupils. The court concluded that the tests were not administered on the basis of racial criteria. Instead, they were used for the legitimate purpose of ensuring that all students were placed in appropriate instructional groups. The court emphasized that grouping schemes designed to enhance educational opportunities for pupils are not only permissible, but indeed desirable.

## SPECIAL EDUCATION PLACEMENTS

Courts have paid particular attention to the use of test scores to assign students to special education classes because of the adverse effects that an incorrect placement can have on a child's entire future. In several situations, children labeled as "retarded" have been found to be of normal intelligence when retested with valid instruments.[79] In Louisiana, a federal district court imposed specific requirements regarding the use of test scores for pupil placement purposes.[80] The court declared that a child could not be assigned to a class for the mentally retarded unless the pupil's adaptive behavior was subnormal and allowances were made for the effects of sociocultural background in making the placement decision. In short, program assignment could not be based solely on a low intelligence test score, even though the child's intelligence was measured by an individually administered test.

In a significant California case, *Larry P. v. Riles,* plaintiffs alleged that standardized intelligence tests used for placement purposes were culturally biased against black children. Noting that a disproportionate ratio of black students were assigned to classes for the educable mentally retarded (EMR), the federal district court issued an injunction prohibiting school authorities from using the results of intelligence tests as the primary criterion for placing minority students in such classes.[81] Subsequently, the temporary injunction was made a permanent prohibition against using intelligence tests to place students in classes for the mentally retarded.[82]

The court concluded that the testimony overwhelmingly demonstrated that I.Q. tests were racially discriminatory. While this decision is binding only in the northern federal district of California, it may serve as a catalyst for other challenges to the use of I.Q. tests for pupil placement purposes.

In another California case, Mexican-American students claimed that they had been erroneously placed in an EMR class on the basis of standardized achievement tests administered in English.[83] When the children were retested in Spanish, they gained an average of fifteen points. This case resulted in state regulations prohibiting the placement of non-English-speaking children in special education classes on the basis of tests measuring English language skills.

While courts are continuing to scrutinize the use of tests in "mislabeling" students, the Supreme Court decision in *Washington v. Davis* may affect the extent to which the equal protection clause can be relied upon to invalidate the use of standardized tests that allegedly are biased against minority children.[84] In *Davis,* the use of a standardized aptitude test resulted in the rejection of a disproportionate number of minority applicants to the police training program in Washington, D.C. Nonetheless, the Supreme Court held that evidence of a disproportionate impact alone did not violate constitutional guarantees, as long as there was no intent to discriminate against black applicants. Applying the *Davis* rationale in the public school context, plaintiffs challenging the use of intelligence tests or other standardized instruments on constitutional grounds may be required to substantiate that the tests result in deliberate, purposeful discrimination, or that they are totally inappropriate criteria for classifying students.

The Constitution, however, is not the only legal basis for challenging the use of standardized tests to determine pupil placements. Federal legislation has been enacted that restricts the use of standardized test scores in making instructional assignments. For example, in legislation designed to protect the rights of handicapped children, Congress has stipulated that before such pupils can be placed in special instructional programs, a full and individual evaluation of each child's educational needs must be conducted.[85] Tests used for placement purposes must be administered in the child's native language, validated for the specific purpose for which they are used, and administered by trained personnel. Furthermore, the federal regulations specify that no single criterion can be used to determine a handicapped child's placement; pupil assignments must be based on a composite analysis of such data as test scores, teacher recommendations, and the child's cultural background and adaptive behavior.[86] Parents also have the right to contest any placement recommendation that does not comply with these mandates. Legislative action, in concert with court decisions, eventually may effect changes in public school testing procedures used to determine *all* instructional assignments—not only those involving special education placements.[87]

## GIFTED AND TALENTED STUDENTS

A discussion of classifications based on ability would be incomplete without brief mention of children labeled as gifted or talented. Congress has defined such children as those "who have outstanding intellectual ability or creative talent, the development of which requires special activities not ordinarily provided by local educational agencies." [88] While lobbyists on behalf of gifted students have not been as well organized or vocal as advocates of handicapped children have been, recently, courts and legislatures have started to address gifted students' rights to appropriate instructional programs.

Most of the legal activity thus far has taken place in legislative forums and has focused on the services provided for gifted students rather than on the criteria used to identify such pupils. Congress has enacted legislation providing financial assistance to state and local education agencies, institutions of higher education, and other public and private organizations for the implementation of programs designed to meet the special needs of gifted and talented students.[89] The legislation also has provided funds on a competitive basis for research and evaluation in the field of education for the gifted.

Many states also have enacted laws regarding the rights of gifted and talented students. In Pennsylvania, for example, the statutory definition of exceptional children includes gifted and talented pupils who require special education facilities or services. A Pennsylvania commonwealth court interpreted this law as placing a mandatory obligation on school districts to establish appropriate educational programs for gifted children.[90] Furthermore, the court recognized that this duty was not contingent upon state reimbursement for such programs. In Connecticut, gifted students also are covered by statutory protections pertaining to other categories of exceptional children, and are entitled to private school placements if appropriate programs are not available for them in the public education system.[91]

Despite the recent legislative efforts on behalf of gifted students, it was estimated in February 1980 that only 10 percent of the nation's gifted and talented children were receiving some type of special instruction.[92] To date, there have been few lawsuits asserting the rights of gifted pupils, but such litigation seems destined to escalate in light of the legal activity pertaining to other types of exceptional children. In an unsuccessful Illinois suit, plaintiff parents asked for injunctive relief and one million dollars in damages because of the school district's alleged failure to meet the needs of their son, with a measured intelligence of 170.[93] Noting the discrepancy in state funds supplied to local school districts for handicapped pupils and for gifted students ($162 million compared with $3.6 million), plaintiffs alleged that gifted students were being denied their right to be educated to the maximum level of their ability. Although the state circuit court dismissed the plaintiffs' action, it appears likely that other suits will be initiated challenging the disproportionate appropriation of educational funds to serve handicapped versus gifted children.

## CLASSIFICATIONS BASED ON HANDICAPS

Since handicapped children represent a vulnerable minority group, the treatment of these children has aroused much judicial and legislative concern. Courts have addressed the constitutional rights of handicapped children to attend school and to be classified accurately and instructed appropriately. Federal and state laws have further clarified the rights of handicapped students, and have provided financial assistance to school districts to help them meet the special needs of these pupils.

### CONSTITUTIONAL PROTECTIONS

No firm precedent has yet been established by the United States Supreme Court regarding the rights of handicapped children to a public education,[94] but several lower courts have delineated the safeguards afforded to such children under the Federal Constitution. The first noteworthy case was initiated in Pennsylvania and resulted in a consent agreement which stated that handicapped children could not be denied admission to public school programs or have their educational status changed without procedural due process of law.[95] The agreement further stipulated that each mentally retarded child must be placed in a free public program of education and training appropriate to the child's capacity.

*Mills v. Board of Education,* a Washington, D.C., case, followed the principle established in the Pennsylvania agreement and expanded the right to an appropriate public education beyond the mentally retarded to all other children alleged to be suffering from mental, behavioral, emotional, or physical deficiencies.[96] Moreover, the court in *Mills* held that public interest in conserving funds could not justify the denial of an education to a certain class of students. The court also ordered school officials to adhere to stringent due process procedures in pupil assignments, and stated that any change which would affect a student's instructional program for as much as two days had to be accompanied by some type of hearing to give parents an opportunity to contest the placement.

Litigation similar to the Pennsylvania and Washington, D.C., cases has been initiated in many states, and the basic right of each handicapped child to receive a public education has been upheld consistently by the courts.[97] The judiciary, however, has gone further than simply ensuring that children with disabilities are allowed to attend school, and has assessed whether classification procedures are accurate and educational programs are suitable to the students' needs.

In an illustrative 1977 case, a federal district court in Wisconsin held that handicapped children who were being denied a meaningful education at public expense were being deprived of their equal protection rights. The court issued specific orders (including timetables) for school officials to implement state laws pertaining to the identification of handicapped children and the provision of appropriate educational services for each child identified.[98] The same year, the Third Circuit Court of Appeals affirmed a lower court order requiring the Philadelphia school system to identify all learning disabled students in the school system.[99] While school officials argued that they were obligated by law to identify only the exceptional children who required special services, the court concluded that all learning disabled students had to be identified in order to determine which children needed special instruction. Furthermore, the appellate court agreed with the lower court's conclusion that the school district was required to provide appropriate educational services for handicapped children regardless of the level of state reimbursement for the additional costs.[100]

Other courts also have addressed the extent to which state agencies must bear the financial burden for special services for handicapped children. A Virginia federal district court invalidated a plan that only partially reimbursed parents for services for their handicapped children who were placed in private facilities, because the plan disadvantaged poor families.[101] Similarly, the North Dakota Supreme Court sustained the right of a handicapped child who was a ward of the state to have her tuition paid by the school district in which she had been living,[102] and the Colorado Supreme Court ruled that a school district was obligated to provide kindergarten programs for handicapped children if such opportunities were provided for nonhandicapped pupils.[103] In addition, courts have held that school districts must incur the full cost of transporting handicapped children to and from special schools.[104]

The judiciary has stipulated that school boards cannot use the defense of insufficient funds to excuse them from providing appropriate services for handicapped students [105] or from reimbursing parents for charges incurred in a private school placement of a handicapped child.[106] Furthermore, courts have held public school districts responsible for such private school placements, even if in a different state.[107]

However, parents can be denied reimbursement for tuition in a private institution if a suitable program for the child is available in the public school system.[108] In essence, handicapped children are entitled to an appropriate education at public expense, but parents cannot unilaterally decide that a private school placement is necessary and must be supported by the state. In an illustrative 1979 case, a Pennsylvania court denied a parents' petition for reimbursement for an out-of-state placement for their socially and emotionally disturbed child. Since the parents had enrolled the child in a Connecticut school on their own initiative and would not make the child available for an evaluation to determine if an appropriate placement could be made within Pennsylvania, the court ruled that the parents were not entitled to tuition reimbursement.[109]

## STATUTORY PROTECTIONS

As often happens, legislation has paralleled court decisions regarding the rights of handicapped children. Two pieces of federal legislation, in particular, appear destined to alter the roles of public school personnel. Section 504 of the Rehabilitation Act of 1973 prohibits the recipients of any federal financial assistance from discriminating against an otherwise qualified handicapped person solely because of the handicap.[110] Public Law 94-142, the Education for All Handicapped Children Act of 1975, provides federal funds to assist state and local education agencies in offering appropriate educational programs for handicapped children.[111] In essence, Section 504 is a civil rights law that stipulates what *cannot* be done in the treatment of handicapped individuals. On the other hand, Public Law 94-142 contains a blueprint for what *can* be done to upgrade educational opportunities for handicapped children.

Section 504 is more global than Public Law 94-142 and applies to educational and noneducational agencies receiving any type of federal assistance. It bars recipients of federal funds from discriminating against otherwise qualified handicapped persons in recruitment, selection, compensation, job assignment and classification, and fringe benefits. Furthermore, it requires that all new facilities be constructed for access by handicapped persons. It does not mandate that all existing facilities be remodeled, but all *programs* must be readily accessible to handicapped individuals. Section 504 also prohibits discrimination against handicapped persons in post-secondary education [112] and requires public school agencies to provide appropriate educational services for all handicapped children.[113] This last requirement is coordinated closely with the mandates of Public Law 94-142.

Public Law 94-142 focuses specifically on the state's obligation to provide a free, appropriate public education for all handicapped children and offers federal assistance in implementing the mandates. Among the major provisions of the law are the following:

1. States must institute a comprehensive program to identify all handicapped children within the state.
2. No handicapped child is to be excluded from an appropriate public education (zero reject).
3. Individualized educational programs must be developed for all handicapped children.
4. Policies and procedures must be established to safeguard due process rights of parents and children.
5. Handicapped children must be placed in the least restrictive educational setting, which means educating handicapped children with nonhandicapped children to the extent appropriate.
6. Nondiscriminatory tests and other materials must be used in evaluating a child's level of achievement for placement purposes.

7. Parents must have access to their child's records, and the confidentiality of such information must be respected.
8. Comprehensive personnel development programs, which include in-service training for regular and special education teachers and ancillary personnel, must be established.
9. One state agency must be accountable for ensuring that all provisions of the law are properly implemented by other agencies in the state serving handicapped children.

Public Law 94-142 is generating substantial litigation, and the scope of rights guaranteed by this law has not yet been clarified. In a major class action suit, a Mississippi federal district judge in 1979 issued a final consent decree outlining a comprehensive compliance plan that must be followed in order for the state to qualify for federal funds under the Act.[114] The decree includes specific criteria that must be adhered to in placing handicapped children in the least restrictive environment, developing individualized educational programs, and revamping the state's procedures for classifying handicapped students. In addition, each school district is required to identify children who have been misclassified and provide them with an opportunity for compensatory education. The decree also strengthens procedural safeguards for handicapped children and their parents, and mandates strict state monitoring of local school districts.

In a significant 1980 decision, the Third Circuit Court of Appeals affirmed the federal district court's conclusion that a Pennsylvania administrative policy establishing a limit of 180 days of instruction per year for all children violated Public Law 94-142.[115] The district court had invalidated the 180-day rule as interfering with the federally mandated goal of maximizing the self-sufficiency of each disabled child.[116] While the appeals court affirmed the district court's holding, it differed as to rationale. The appellate court did not interpret Public Law 94-142 as establishing a uniform goal (i.e., self-sufficiency) for all handicapped children. Instead, it reasoned that the Act places responsibility on the school to establish educational goals for each handicapped child and reasonable means to attain the goals. Accordingly, the appeals court concluded that the 180-day rule violated the Act by precluding development of appropriate programs for those handicapped children who might suffer substantial regression without extended services. If additional courts conclude that handicapped children are entitled to year-round programs, possibly students with other types of special needs will make similar demands. The final resolution of this issue could have significant fiscal implications for public education.

Conflicting rulings have been rendered as to whether the federal mandates require state education agencies to incur all *noneducational* costs associated with a private placement. A New Jersey court concluded that a school district was not obligated to support residential care for a severely retarded child because the child's placement was primarily for custodial rather than educational reasons.[117] In contrast, the federal district court for the District of Columbia held that the board of education was responsible for the total cost of a private placement, even though the child's problems were educational *and* noneducational in nature.[118] The court reasoned that the child's social, emotional, medical, and educational problems were so "intimately intertwined that realistically it is not possible for the court to perform the Solomon-like task of separating them." [119] The court ruled that the student's federal right to an appropriate educational placement required the school district to incur the full fiscal obligation.

Following the federal lead, most states have enacted statutes and agency regulations, similar to Public Law 94-142, that protect the rights of handicapped children. Pennsylvania law, for example, imposes a duty on district superintendents to identify all exceptional children and to obtain state approval of plans for the proper education and training of such children.[120] Special services, classes, and schools must be established in accordance with the plan in order for Pennsylvania school districts to receive state reimbursement for approved special education costs. Also representative of state mandates is the Florida statute, which stipulates that all school boards must "provide for an appropriate program of special instruction, facilities, and services for exceptional students as prescribed by the state board as acceptable." [121] Like most states, Florida authorizes school boards to make contractual arrangements with private schools in the event that public schools do not have the special facilities or personnel to provide an adequate education for certain exceptional students.

The federal and state mandates, in concert, require additional commitments from building administrators and teachers. No longer are special educators primarily accountable for the services provided for exceptional children. For example, the individualized educational programs (IEPs) must be designed jointly by the handicapped child's teacher, a staff member qualified in special education, the child's parents or guardian, and—if possible—the child. The written plan must include annual goals and short-term objectives, specification of the services that will be provided, and an evaluation schedule. The responsibility for assuring that these plans are established and revised at least annually rests on local school personnel.

Some educators are apprehensive that the IEP will be challenged as a legally enforceable contract, but to date no court has addressed this issue. It seems unlikely, however, that a court would hold school personnel accountable for achieving the objectives of an IEP. The framers of Public Law 94-142 have stated that the IEP is intended as a planning device, not as a legally binding document. Nonetheless, liability might result if teachers and administrators fail to conform to the federal mandates in developing IEPs for handicapped children and providing the appropriate services.

Another volatile issue is the administration of disciplinary procedures vis-à-vis handicapped children. In a Connecticut case, a federal district court ruled that a handicapped child could not be expelled for disciplinary reasons because of the irreparable injury that would occur as a result of being without any educational program.[122] Relying on Public Law 94-142, the court concluded that the student was entitled to an appropriate public education in the least restrictive environment and to procedural safeguards in connection with any placement changes. Recognizing that handicapped children are not immune from the disciplinary process, the court ruled that the procedures outlined in Public Law 94-142 for handling handicapped students with behavior problems must be followed in securing more suitable placements for such children.

Interpretation of what constitutes an "appropriate" program also has evoked controversy. Must handicapped children be provided an optimum program, designed to enable them to reach their full potential, or will a minimally adequate program satisfy legal mandates? In 1980, the Second Circuit Court of Appeals affirmed a New York federal district court's conclusion that a hearing impaired child must be provided with a sign language interpreter in order for her program to be considered appropriate.[123] Even though the child was making above average progress in the regular classroom without an interpreter, the district court reasoned that she was not performing as well academically as she could with special assistance. Accordingly, the court held that the child was entitled to a sign language interpreter to enable her to realize her potential commensurate with the opportunity provided for normal children. In affirming the district court's ruling, the appeals court cautioned that its decision was limited to this particular child and set of circumstances and was not intended to be used as authority beyond this case.

Legal questions also have been generated by the mandate that handicapped children must be placed in the least restrictive educational setting. This requirement means that handicapped students should be educated with nonhandicapped pupils to the maximum extent possible. Assignments to special schools or classes must be verified as necessary to meet the students' needs. Thus, initial grouping decisions no longer can become permanent placements; assessment of each child must be a dynamic process, including assurances that appropriate changes will be made in the child's instructional program. Parents have the right to challenge any proposed placement for their handicapped child to ensure that it is suitable and *in fact* the least restrictive alternative. Questions have been raised as to whether children must be placed in educational programs in their home community for the placement to satisfy the least restrictive mandate.[124] Concern also has been voiced that overzealous attempts to mainstream handicapped children with nonhandicapped students may result in the placement of some pupils in the regular classroom when their needs dictate a special class or program. Such erroneous placements could generate lawsuits on behalf of the misplaced child or on behalf of nonhandicapped pupils who allegedly are denied their fair share of teacher attention.

In addition to the substantial impact on the education of handicapped children, the federal and state legislation and court decisions on behalf of students with special needs have the potential to influence all public school programs. For example, advocates of nonhandicapped children's rights may assert that every pupil is entitled to an individualized educational program. Similarly, the procedural safeguards required to ensure appropriate placements for handicapped children may ultimately be sought to guarantee the accuracy of all educational assignments. As noted previously, the mandate that no single criterion can be used to determine the instructional program for a handicapped child may also cause changes in many public school grouping practices. Furthermore, since handicapped children are entitled to private school placements if appropriate programs are not available in the public school system, perhaps other students with special needs will begin asserting similar rights. Indeed, Public Law 94-142, hailed as the Bill of Rights for handicapped children,[125] could conceivably affect the educational opportunities of every child.

## CLASSIFICATIONS BASED ON ETHNIC BACKGROUND/NATIVE LANGUAGE

As indicated in the preceding section, courts and legislatures have directed attention to the *absence* of needed student classifications as well as to the existence of discriminatory classifications. In other words, the lack of special instruction for certain groups of children who cannot benefit from the mainstream educational program has been critically reviewed. Some of the legal activity dealing with such "functional exclusion" has focused on the rights of non-English-speaking students, who allegedly have been denied an adequate education because of the absence of remedial English instruction.

In the one case involving English-deficient children which has reached the Supreme Court, *Lau v. Nichols,* Chinese students asserted that the San Francisco public school program failed to provide for the needs of non-English-speaking students in violation of the equal protection clause of the Federal Constitution and Title VI of the Civil Rights Act of 1964.[126] Both the federal district court and the Ninth Circuit Court of Appeals rejected the pupils' claim. The appellate court acknowledged that each student brought to school different advantages and disadvantages "caused in part by social, economic and cultural backgrounds," and that some of these disadvantages could be overcome by special instructional programs. Nonetheless, the court reasoned that the provision of such special services, although desirable, was not constitutionally required.[127]

The United States Supreme Court, however, reversed the appellate court's ruling and held that the lack of sufficient remedial English instruction violated Section 601 of the Civil Rights Act of 1964. The Court concluded that equality of treatment was not realized merely by providing students with the same facilities, textbooks, teachers, and curriculum, and that requiring children to acquire English skills on their own before they could hope to make any progress in school made "a mockery of public education." [128] The Court emphasized that "basic English skills are at the very core of what these public schools teach," and, therefore, "students who do not understand English are effectively foreclosed from any meaningful education." [129]

The Supreme Court declined to address the constitutional issue in *Lau*, but several lower courts have relied on equal protection guarantees in ordering bilingual-bicultural education programs in school districts where discrimination against non-English-speaking children has been uncovered. For example, in 1972 the Fifth Circuit Court of Appeals affirmed the lower court's conclusion that the segregation of Mexican-American students in a Texas school district resulted in a *de jure* dual school system.[130] As part of the remedial decree, the federal court ordered a comprehensive bilingual program. In another Texas case, a federal district court similarly mandated the expansion of bilingual programs in order to provide equal educational opportunities for Mexican-American students.[131] It is noteworthy that in the latter case the court did not find the existence of *de jure* segregation, but still declared that the absence of an appropriate curriculum for bilingual children created an "inherently unequal" situation that placed a constitutional duty on school officials to provide for the unique needs of non-English-speaking students. Other federal courts have ordered school districts to provide special services for limited-English-speaking students, even if only a few students within the district have needed such assistance[132] and have required school officials to upgrade bilingual programs considered to be insufficient.[133] In 1975, the Fifth Circuit Court of Appeals stated that "it is now an unlawful education practice to fail to take appropriate action to overcome language barriers." [134]

The same year, however, the Tenth Circuit Court of Appeals held that the provision of bilingual education could not be a substitute for desegregating schools.[135] The appellate court ruled that Hispanic children in Denver had a constitutional right to desegregated schooling, but that the lower court had acted beyond constitutional requirements in ordering the implementation of a bilingual/bicultural education program for minority children. More recently, the Ninth Circuit Court of Appeals concluded that school districts do not have a duty under the Federal Constitution or civil rights laws to ensure that all courses, instructors, testing procedures, and instructional materials for English-deficient children are bicultural and bilingual.[136] The appellate court reasoned that the provision of compensatory programs to cure language deficiencies of non-English-speaking students satisfies the mandate announced in *Lau v. Nichols*. While courts have agreed that English-deficient children are entitled to special assistance, consensus has not been reached as to whether they are entitled to only remedial English instruction or instruction in their native language as well.

Federal and state legislative and administrative bodies have attempted to clarify the school's responsibility to assist English-deficient pupils. In 1968, Congress enacted the Bilingual Education Act amending Title VII of the Elementary and Secondary Education Act of 1965. This Act provided supplemental funding for school districts to establish programs to meet the special educational needs of low-income students with limited English-speaking ability.[137] The Bilingual Education Act of 1974 removed the criterion that children receiving such assistance had to be from low-income families and provided a more explicit definition of bilingual education as instruction in English and the child's native language to the extent necessary for the child to make effective progress.[138] Subsequently, in response to the *Lau* decision, HEW issued advisory guidelines, known as the *Lau Remedies,* to assist school districts in designing programs to meet the needs of English-deficient students. Finally, in 1980, the Department of Education proposed formal regulations under Title VI of the Civil Rights Act of 1964 to prevent discrimination based on national origin in elementary and secondary education. The proposed rules stipulate that "transitional" bilingual education programs must be provided for students with severe deficiencies in the English language.[139] Many states also have enacted legislation and/or administrative regulations pertaining to bilingual education. For example, Indiana law specifies that non-English-dominant students must be provided with bilingual-bicultural instruction designed to meet their language skill needs.[140]

Future legal activity may focus on the special needs of students who speak various English dialects in addition to students who speak foreign languages. A federal judge in Michigan ruled in 1979 that school districts must offer students who speak "black English" assistance in learning to use standard English.[141] The judge reasoned that the dialect used by many black children constituted a language barrier necessitating special consideration from teachers in order to enable the students to participate equally in instructional programs. Although dismissing the constitutional challenges, the judge held that the students' rights under the Equal Educational Opportunities Act of 1974 were violated because the education agencies failed to take appropriate action to overcome the students' language deficiencies. School officials were ordered to submit a plan for identifying children speaking black English and to design a program to offer special assistance to the students in acquiring standard English skills.

The legal mandates pertaining to English-deficient students, in conjunction with directives on behalf of handicapped children, raise several crucial issues regarding individual rights and the corresponding state duty to provide appropriate educational opportunities for all pupils. The mandates go beyond the mere right of every child to attend school. They address the suitability of the programs to the unique characteristics of pupils. In *Lau,* the Supreme Court implied that because education is state-imposed, the curriculum offered must be *appropriate* to the needs of the students in order to be legally acceptable. Possibly, other classes of children who cannot benefit from the mainstream instructional program, such as the culturally disadvantaged or the gifted, may begin capitalizing on the protections afforded to handicapped and non-English-speaking students in asserting their rights to a public school program designed to meet their unique needs.

## CONCLUSION

A basic purpose of public education is to enhance adult opportunities for all students, regardless of their innate characteristics. Accordingly, courts and legislatures have become increasingly assertive in guaranteeing that pupils have the chance to maximize their capabilities while in school. Arbitrary classification practices that disadvantage certain groups of children no longer will be tolerated.[142] On the other hand, valid classifications, applied in the best interests of students, are not being questioned. Indeed, legal mandates *require* the classification of certain pupils to ensure that they receive instruction appropriate to their needs. In exercising professional judgment pertaining to the classification of pupils, educators should be cognizant of the following generalizations drawn from recent judicial and legislative mandates:

1. The classification of pupils by race in public schools is unlawful.
2. Students cannot be segregated by sex in academic programs or schools unless there is a legitimate educational reason for maintaining sex segregation, and then only if comparable courses/ schools are available to both sexes.
3. Criteria for admission to programs or schools cannot be sex-based.
4. If a school district establishes an interscholastic athletic program, such opportunities must be made available to male and female athletes on an equal basis (i.e., either mixed-gender teams or comparable sex-segregated teams).
5. Students cannot be disadvantaged based on their marital status.
6. Any differential treatment of pregnant students must be justified by valid health or safety considerations.
7. Students can be classified by age, but such classifications must be substantiated as necessary to advance legitimate educational objectives.
8. Ability tracking schemes are permissible; however, any such schemes that result in the segregation of minority children will be carefully scrutinized by the courts to ensure that such practices are not a ploy to perpetuate discrimination.

9. If ability grouping is used, pupil assignments should be based on multiple criteria such as tests, teacher recommendations, and the socioeconomic background and adaptive behavior of the child.

10. Tests used to determine instructional placement must be administered in the student's native language.

11. Handicapped children are entitled to an appropriate public education in the least restrictive environment.

12. An individualized educational program (including goals and objectives, specification of the services to be provided, and an evaluation plan) must be developed for each handicapped child.

13. Due process procedures must be followed in changing a handicapped child's instructional assignment.

14. English-deficient children are entitled to compensatory instruction designed to overcome English language barriers.

## NOTES

1. Most states have similar antidiscrimination provisions. Connecticut law, for example, stipulates that "public schools shall be open to all children over five years of age without discrimination on account of race, color, sex, religion, or national origin . . .," Conn. Gen. Stat. § 10-15.

2. See Dunn v. Blumstein, 405 U.S. 330 (1972) (right to vote in state elections); Shapiro v. Thompson, 394 U.S. 618 (1969) (right to interstate travel); Skinner v. Oklahoma, 316 U.S. 535, 541 (1942) (right to procreation).

3. See Holt v. Shelton, 341 F. Supp. 821 (M.D. Tenn. 1972); Ordway v. Hargraves, 323 F. Supp. 1155 (D. Mass. 1971).

4. San Antonio Independent School Dist. v. Rodriguez, 411 U.S. 1 (1973).

5. See Graham v. Richardson, 403 U.S. 365 (1971) (alienage); Brown v. Board of Educ. of Topeka, 347 U.S. 483 (1954) (race); Oyama v. California, 332 U.S. 633 (1948) (national origin).

6. See San Antonio Independent School Dist. v. Rodriguez, 411 U.S. 1 (1973) (wealth); Frontiero v. Richardson, 411 U.S. 677 (1973) (sex); Gurmankin v. Costanzo, 411 F. Supp. 982 (E.D. Pa. 1976) aff'd 556 F.2d 184 (3d Cir. 1977) (handicaps).

7. Dunn v. Blumstein, 405 U.S. 330, 335 (1972).

8. See Bullock v. Carter, 405 U.S. 134, 145 (1972); Eisenstadt v. Baird, 405 U.S. 438, 452 (1972).

9. See John Hogan, "An Analysis of Selected Court Decisions Which Have Applied the Fourteenth Amendment to the Organization, Administration, and Programs of the Public Schools" (doctoral diss., University of California, 1972), pp. 127–29.

10. See Lau v. Nichols, 414 U.S. 563 (1974), text with note 126, infra; Mills v. Board of Educ., 348 F. Supp. 866 (D.D.C. 1972), text with note 96, infra.

11. 347 U.S. 483, 493 (1954).

12. *See* Dayton Bd. of Educ. v. Brinkman, 443 U.S. 526 (1979).
13. Keyes v. School Dist. No. 1, 313 F. Supp. 90 (D. Colo. 1970); *aff'd in part, rev'd in part,* 445 F.2d 990 (10th Cir. 1971), *modified and remanded,* 413 U.S. 189 (1973).
14. *See* Amos v. Board of School Directors of the City of Milwaukee, 408 F. Supp. 765 (E.D. Wis. 1976); Morgan v. Kerrigan, 509 F.2d 580 (1st Cir. 1974); Booker v. Special School Dist. No. 1, Minneapolis, Minn., 351 F. Supp. 799 (D. Minn. 1972); Soria v. Oxnard School Dist. Bd. of Trustees, 328 F. Supp. 155 (C.D. Cal. 1971); Davis v. School Dist. of Pontiac, 309 F. Supp. 734 (E.D. Mich. 1970); *aff'd* 443 F.2d 573 (6th Cir. 1971), *cert. denied,* 404 U.S. 913 (1971).
15. Washington v. Davis, 426 U.S. 229 (1976). *See* Board of Educ. of the City School Dist. of the City of New York v. Harris, 444 U.S. 130 (1979) for a discussion of the distinction between constitutional and statutory standards of review. In this case the Court noted that Congress has the authority to establish standards more protective of minority rights than constitutional minimums require.
16. *See* Milliken v. Bradley, 418 U.S. 717, 744–46 (1974).
17. *See* Milliken v. Bradley, 433 U.S. 267 (1977).
18. *See* Milliken v. Bradley, 418 U.S. 717 (1974).
19. *See* Dayton Bd. of Educ. v. Brinkman, 433 U.S. 406 (1977).
20. Pasadena City Bd. of Educ. v. Spangler, 427 U.S. 424 (1976).
21. *See* Bradley v. Milliken, 402 F. Supp. 1096,1113–39 (E.D. Mich. 1975). *See also* Evans v. Buchanan, 447 F. Supp. 982 (D. Del. 1978); Reed v. Rhodes, 455 F. Supp. 546, 569 (N.D. Ohio 1978).
22. *See* Hart v. Community School Bd. of Educ., New York School Dist. No. 21, 512 F.2d 37 (2d Cir. 1975); Smiley v. Vollert, 453 F. Supp. 463, 467 (S.D. Tex. 1978).
23. *See* Dayton Bd. of Educ. v. Brinkman, 443 U.S. 526 (1979); Columbus Bd. of Educ. v. Penick, 443 U.S. 449 (1979); Lemon v. Bossier Parish School Bd., 566 F.2d 985 (5th Cir. 1978); Reed v. Rhodes, 455 F. Supp. 546 (N.D. Ohio 1978).
24. Frontiero v. Richardson, 411 U.S. 677, 686 (1973) (Douglas, Brennan, White, and Marshall, J. J., plurality opinion).
25. *Id.,* quoting from Weber v. Aetna Casualty & Surety Co., 406 U.S. 164, 175 (1972).
26. *See* Craig v. Boren, 429 U.S. 190 (1976); Reed v. Reed, 404 U.S. 71 (1971).
27. Education Amendments of 1972, 20 U.S.C. § 1681 *et seq.* (1976). The Department of Education is empowered to terminate federal funds to institutions if charges of sex bias are substantiated. In 1979, the Supreme Court also ruled that individuals may initiate suits in federal court if their Title IX rights have been abridged, Cannon v. University of Chicago, 441 U.S. 677 (1979). Thus, aggrieved individuals do not have to rely on administrative remedies in seeking relief under this law. For a discussion of the application of Title IX to employees, *see* text with note 94, Chapter 4.
28. Brenden v. Independent School Dist., 477 F.2d 1292 (8th Cir. 1973).
29. *See* Bucha v. Illinois High School Ass'n, 351 F. Supp. 69 (N.D. Ill.

1972), in which the federal district court upheld the exclusion of two girls from the school's interscholastic swimming team on the basis of the state athletic association regulation barring coeducational competition. The court reasoned that the physical and psychological differences between the sexes were constitutionally sufficient reasons for prohibiting coeducational interscholastic competition among high school students.

30. *See* Morris v. Michigan State Bd. of Educ., 472 F.2d 1207 (6th Cir. 1973); Gilpin v. Kansas State High School Activities Ass'n, 377 F. Supp. 1233 (D. Kan. 1973); Reed v. Nebraska School Activities Ass'n, 341 F. Supp. 258 (D. Neb. 1972); Haas v. South Bend Community School Corporation, 289 N.E.2d 495 (Ind. 1972).

31. Ruman v. Eskew, 333 N.E.2d 138 (Ind. App. 1975). *See also* Ritacco v. Norwin School Dist., 361 F. Supp. 930 (W.D. Pa. 1973).

32. Morris v. Michigan State Bd. of Educ., 472 F.2d 1207 (6th Cir. 1973).

33. Darrin v. Gould, 540 P.2d 882 (Wash. 1975).

34. Pennsylvania v. Pennsylvania Interscholastic Athletic Ass'n, 334 A.2d 839 (Pa. 1975). The Pennsylvania ERA states: "Equality of rights under the law shall not be denied or abridged in the Commonwealth of Pennsylvania because of the sex of the individual," Pa. Const., art. 1, § 28.

35. Yellow Springs Exempted Village School Dist. Bd. of Educ. v. Ohio School Athletic Ass'n, 443 F. Supp. 752 (S.D. Ohio 1978).

36. *Id.* at 759. *See* 45 C.F.R. 86.41(a) (1978).

37. Leffel v. Wisconsin Interscholastic Athletic Ass'n, 444 F. Supp. 1117 (E.D. Wis. 1978). *See also* Hoover v. Meiklejohn, 430 F. Supp. 164 (D. Colo. 1977), in which the federal district court held that the state athletic association rule limiting participation on soccer teams to male students violated equal protection rights.

38. Cape v. Tennessee Secondary School Athletic Ass'n, 424 F. Supp. 732 (E.D. Tenn. 1976); *rev'd* 563 F.2d 793 (6th Cir. 1977).

39. Jones v. Oklahoma Secondary School Activities Ass'n, 453 F. Supp. 150 (W.D. Okla. 1977).

40. Dodson v. Arkansas Activities Ass'n, 468 F. Supp. 394 (E.D. Ark. 1979).

41. "Califano Approves Girls' Rules in High School Basketball," *Education Daily*, Vol. 12, No. 1, January 2, 1979, p. 1.

42. Gomes v. Rhode Island Interscholastic League, 469 F. Supp. 659 (D.R.I. 1979), *vacated as moot*, 604 F.2d 733 (1st Cir. 1979).

43. *Id.*, 604 F.2d 733.

44. Attorney General v. Massachusetts Interscholastic Athletic Ass'n, 393 N.E.2d 284 (Mass. 1979).

45. Petrie v. Illinois High School Ass'n, 394 N.E.2d 855 (Ill. App. 1979).

46. Compare Kirstein v. Rector and Visitors of the University of Virginia, 309 F. Supp. 184 (D. Va. 1970) with Williams v. McNair, 316 F. Supp. 134 (D.S.C. 1970), *aff'd per curiam*, 401 U.S. 951 (1971).

47. 532 F.2d 880 (3d Cir. 1976), *aff'd by an equally divided court*, 430 U.S. 703 (1977). The Equal Educational Opportunities Act of 1974, 20 U.S.C. § 1701 *et seq.* (1976), states that "all children enrolled in public schools are entitled to equal educational opportunity without regard to race, color, sex, or national origin."

48. *Id.*, 532 F.2d 886, quoting from Kahn v. Shevin, 416 U.S. 351, 356 (1974).

49. *Id.*, 532 F.2d 886.

50. *See* Della Casa v. Gaffney, No. 171673 (Cal. Super. Ct. 1973); Seward v. Della, No. 134173 (Cal. Super. Ct. 1973); Sanchez v. Baron, No. 69-C-1615 (E.D.N.Y. 1971). *See also* Susanne Martinez, "Sexism in Public Education: Litigation Issues," *Inequality in Education,* No. 18, October 1974, pp. 6–7.

51. *See* Hickey v. Black River Bd. of Educ., No. 73-889 (N.D. Ohio 1973).

52. *See* 45 C.F.R. § 86.34-36 (1978). An unresolved issue is whether sex-segregated physical education classes can be provided for students who object to coeducational classes on religious grounds. An Illinois federal court has upheld the right of students to be excused from participation in classes with students of the opposite sex dressed in "immodest attire." *See* Moody v. Cronin, 484 F. Supp. 270 (C.D. Ill. 1979); text with note 35, Chapter 10.

53. Title IX regulations also stipulate that differential admission criteria cannot be applied to male and female students. 45 C.F.R. § 86.35(b) (1978).

54. Bray v. Lee, 337 F. Supp. 934 (D. Mass. 1972).

55. Berkelman v. San Francisco Unified School Dist., 501 F.2d 1264 (9th Cir. 1974).

56. The proposed equal rights amendment (ERA) states in part that "equality of rights under the law shall not be denied or abridged by the United States or by any state on account of sex." As of October 1980, thirty-five states had ratified this proposed amendment. Thirty-eight states must ratify it by June 30, 1982, in order for the ERA to become the twenty-seventh amendment to the Federal Constitution.

57. State v. Marion County Bd. of Educ., 302 S.W.2d 57 (Tenn. 1957).

58. State *ex rel.* Baker v. Stevenson, 189 N.E.2d 181 (Ohio C.P. 1962). *See also* Board of Directors of Independent School Dist. of Waterloo v. Green, 259 Iowa 1260, 147 N.W.2d 854 (1967); Starkey v. Board of Educ. of Davis County School Dist., 14 Utah 2d 227, 381 P.2d 718 (1963).

59. Board of Educ. of Harrodsburg v. Bentley, 383 S.W.2d 677, 680 (Ky. App. 1964). *See also* Anderson v. Canyon Independent School Dist., 412 S.W.2d 387 (Tex. Civ. App. 1967).

60. Davis v. Meek, 344 F. Supp. 298, 301 (N.D. Ohio 1972). *See also* Moran v. School Dist. No. 7, 350 F. Supp. 1180, 1186-87 (D. Mont. 1972).

61. Holt v. Shelton, 341 F. Supp. 821 (M.D. Tenn. 1972).

62. *See* Beeson v. Kiowa County School Dist. RE-1, 567 P.2d 801 (Colo. App. 1977); Bell v. Lone Oak Independent School Dist., 507 S.W.2d 636, 641-42 (Tex. Civ. App. 1974). *See also* Hollon v. Mathis Independent School Dist., 358 F. Supp. 1269 (S.D. Tex. 1973), *vacated for mootness,* 491 F.2d 92 (5th Cir. 1974).

63. Alvin Independent School Dist. v. Cooper, 404 S.W.2d 76 (Tex. Civ. App. 1966). *See also* Perry v. Grenada Municipal Separate School Dist., 300 F. Supp. 748, 753 (N.D. Miss. 1969).

64. Ordway v. Hargraves, 323 F. Supp. 1155 (D. Mass. 1971).

65. 20 U.S.C. § 1681(a) (1976); 45 C.F.R. §§ 86.57, 86.21(c) (1978).

66. *See* Houston v. Prosser, 361 F. Supp. 295 (N.D. Ga. 1973), in which the federal district court sanctioned a school policy requiring teenage mothers to complete high school by enrolling in evening classes (comparable to the regular daytime program), but prohibited school officials from charging such students fees for textbooks and tuition. It should be noted that this ruling does not follow the prevailing precedent in so far as the court sanctioned the segregation of pregnant students in special programs based on the conclusion that married and pregnant students were more promiscuous.

67. *See* Gault v. Garrison, 569 F.2d 993 (7th Cir. 1977), *cert. denied*, 440 U.S. 945 (1979); Purdie v. University of Utah, 584 P.2d 831 (Utah 1978); Texas Women's Univ. v. Chayklintaste, 530 S.W.2d 927 (Tex. 1975). *See also* text with note 101, Chapter 4.

68. O'Leary v. Wisecup, 364 A.2d 770 (Pa. Commw. 1976). *See also* Zweifel v. Joint Dist. No. 1, Belleville, 251 N.W.2d 822 (Wis. 1977).

69. Hammond v. Marx, 406 F. Supp. 853 (D. Me. 1975).

70. Ackerman v. Rubin, 35 Misc. 2d 707, 231 N.Y.S.2d 112 (Sup. Ct., Bronx County, 1962).

71. *Id.* at 114.

72. 42 U.S.C. § 6101 *et seq.* (1976); 42 U.S.C.A. § 6101 *et seq.* (Supp. 1979).

73. 269 F. Supp. 401, 492 (1967), *aff'd sub nom.* Smuck v. Hobson, 408 F.2d 175 (D.C. Cir. 1969).

74. *Id.*, 269 F. Supp. 511.

75. Singleton v. Jackson Municipal Separate School Dist., 419 F.2d 1211, 1214 (5th Cir. 1969).

76. Moore v. Tangipahoa Parish School Bd., 304 F. Supp. 244 (E.D. La. 1969).

77. United States v. Gadsden County School Dist., 572 F.2d 1049 (5th Cir. 1978).

78. Smith v. Dallas County Bd. of Educ., 480 F. Supp. 1324 (S.D. Ala. 1979).

79. *See* Lemon v. Bossier Parish School Bd., 444 F.2d 1400 (5th Cir. 1971); Cuyahoga County Ass'n for Retarded Children and Adults v. Essex, 411 F. Supp. 46 (N.D. Ohio 1976); Stewart v. Phillips, No. 70-119-F (D. Mass. 1970). *See also* Paul Dimond, "The Constitutional Right to Education: The Quiet Revolution," *Hastings Law Journal*, Vol. 24, 1973, p. 1090.

80. Lebanks v. Spears, 60 F.R.D. 135 (E.D. La. 1973). *See also* Lebanks v. Spears, 417 F. Supp. 169 (E.D. La. 1976).

81. 343 F. Supp. 1306 (N.D. Cal. 1972), *aff'd* 502 F.2d 963 (9th Cir. 1974).

82. Larry P. v. Riles, 495 F. Supp. 926 (N.D. Cal. 1979). It should be noted that in July, 1980, a federal district judge in Chicago came to an opposite conclusion as to the constitutionality of using intelligence tests to place students in classes for the mentally retarded. After reviewing all test items, the judge concluded that the tests were not culturally biased or suspect. Parents in Action for Special Education v. Hannon, No. 74-C-3586 (N.D. Ill., July 7, 1980).

83. Diana v. State Bd. of Educ., No. C-70-37 RFP (N.D. Cal. 1970).

84. 426 U.S. 229 (1976). *See* text with note 7, Chapter 4.

85. P.L. 94-142, The Education for All Handicapped Children Act of 1975, 20 U.S.C. § 1401 *et seq.* (1976). *See* text with note 111, *infra.*

86. *See* 45 C.F.R. § 121a.532-34 (1978).

87. A related issue receiving current attention is the enactment of truth-in-testing laws, which require education agencies to provide students graded exams upon request and to release research results regarding test validity. New York's truth-in-testing law, effective January 1, 1980, has been challenged as infringing upon professional schools' property rights pertaining to student admissions standards.

88. 20 U.S.C. § 881 (1976).

89. *See* Gifted and Talented Children's Education Act of 1978, 20 U.S.C.A. § 3311 (Supp. 1979).

90. Central York School Dist. v. Pennsylvania, 399 A.2d 167 (Pa. Commw. 1979).

91. Conn. Gen. Stat. §§ 10-76a, 10-76d(d).

92. "Gifted Kids Need More Help, Lyon Says," *Education Daily*, Vol. 13, No. 31, February 13, 1980, pp. 1–2.

93. Irwin v. Board of Educ., Community Consolidated School Dist. No. 15, No. 79L49 (Ill. Cir. Ct., McKindry County, dismissed, June 1980).

94. The landmark school finance decision, San Antonio Independent School Dist. v. Rodriguez, 411 U.S. 1 (1973), lends support to the contention that the exclusion of selected children (i.e., handicapped) from public schools would not withstand constitutional scrutiny. Although stating that the right to an education is not an inherent fundamental right, the Court conceded that "some identifiable quantum of education" may be constitutionally protected. *Id.* at 36–37.

95. Pennsylvania Ass'n for Retarded Children v. Commonwealth, 343 F. Supp. 279, 302-303 (E.D. Pa. 1972).

96. 348 F. Supp. 866 (D.D.C. 1972).

97. *See* Mattie T. v. Holladay, No. DC-75-31-s (N.D. Miss. 1979); Hairston v. Drosick, 423 F. Supp. 180 (S.D. W.Va. 1976); O'Grady v. Centennial School Dist.; 401 A.2d 1388 (Pa. Commw. 1979); In the Matter of John Young, 377 N.Y.S.2d 429 (Family Ct., St. Lawrence County, 1975).

98. Panitch v. State of Wisconsin, 444 F. Supp. 320 (E. D. Wis. 1977).

99. Frederick L. v. Thomas, 419 F. Supp. 960 (E.D. Pa. 1976), *aff'd* 557 F.2d 373 (3d Cir. 1977).

100. *Id.*, 419 F. Supp. 974-75.

101. Kruse v. Campbell, 431 F. Supp. 180 (E.D. Va. 1977), *vacated and remanded*, 434 U.S. 808 (1977). While the federal district court invalidated the practice on constitutional as well as statutory grounds, the Supreme Court remanded the case for reconsideration solely under Section 504 of the Rehabilitation Act. Upon rehearing the case, the district court reversed its original ruling, No. 75-0622-R (E.D. Va. 1978), but the Virginia law subsequently was changed to provide full tuition reimbursement for handicapped children placed in private facilities.

102. *In re* G. H., 218 N.W.2d 441 (N.D. 1974).

103. Denver Ass'n of Retarded Children, Inc. v. School Dist. No. 1 of Denver, 535 P.2d 200 (Colo. 1975).

104. *See* In the Matter of James A. Stevenson, 385 N.Y.S.2d 477 (Family Ct., St. Lawrence County, 1976); In the Matter of John Young, 377 N.Y.S.2d 429 (Family Ct., St. Lawrence County, 1975).
105. *See* Lora v. Board of Educ. of the City of New York, 456 F. Supp. 1211 (E.D.N.Y. 1978); Mills v. Board of Educ., 348 F. Supp. 866 (D.D.C. 1972).
106. *See* Elliot v. Board of Educ. of City of Chicago, 380 N.E.2d 1137 (Ill. App. 1978); Meyer v. City of New York, 392 N.Y.S.2d 468 (App. Div. 1977); In the Matter of Saberg, 386 N.Y.S.2d 592 (Family Ct., Rockland County, 1976).
107. *See* In the Matter of Suzanne, 381 N.Y.S.2d 628 (Family Ct., Westchester County, 1976); In the Matter of Saberg, *id.*
108. *See* Moran v. Board of Directors of School Dist. of Kansas City, 584 S.W.2d 154 (Mo. App. 1979); Stemple v. Board of Educ. of Prince George's County, 464 F. Supp. 258 (D. Md. 1979); Lux v. Connecticut State Bd. of Educ., 386 A.2d 644 (Conn. C.P. 1977).
109. Welsch v. Commonwealth of Pennsylvania, 400 A.2d 234 (Pa. Commw. 1979).
110. Section 504 of the Rehabilitation Act of 1973, 29 U.S.C. § 794 (1976); Rehabilitation Act Amendments of 1974, 29 U.S.C. § 706 (1976).
111. The Education for All Handicapped Children Act of 1975, P.L. 94-142, 20 U.S.C. § 1401 *et seq.* (1976). *See* Michael Kindred et al., eds., *The Mentally Retarded Citizen and the Law* (New York: The Free Press, 1976).
112. In the first case to reach the United States Supreme Court involving Section 504 of the Rehabilitation Act of 1973, the Court ruled that an applicant with a severe hearing disability could be denied admission to a nurse's training program based on the rationale that such a handicap would prevent the applicant from performing adequately as a nurse. The Court concluded that educational institutions can use legitimate physical requirements for admission to certain programs. Furthermore, the Court held that education agencies are not required to make substantial modifications in their programs to allow disabled persons to participate. Southeastern Community College v. Davis, 442 U.S. 397 (1979). *See also* Camenisch v. University of Texas, 616 F.2d 127 (5th Cir. 1980), in which the Fifth Circuit Court of Appeals held that a deaf graduate student was entitled to an interpreter under Section 504, because he was an "otherwise qualified" handicapped person. The court further ruled that he was not required to exhaust administrative remedies before bringing suit to vindicate rights guaranteed under Section 504. For a discussion of these cases, *see* text with note 112, Chapter 4.
113. In 1980, a federal district court ruled that New Mexico could decline to participate in P.L. 94-142 funding, but nonetheless was obligated under Section 504 of the Rehabilitation Act to provide an appropriate level of support services and procedural safeguards for all handicapped children within the state. New Mexico Ass'n for Retarded Citizens v. New Mexico, No. 75-633-M (D.N.M. 1980).
114. Mattie T. v. Holladay, No. DC-75-31-s (N.D. Miss. 1979).
115. Armstrong v. Kline, 476 F. Supp. 583 (E.D. Pa. 1979), *modified and remanded*, 629 F.2d 269 (3d Cir. 1980).

116. *Id.*, 476 F. Supp. 583.
117. Guempel v. State, 387 A.2d 399 (N.J. Super. 1978).
118. North v. District of Columbia Bd. of Educ., 471 F. Supp. 136 (D.D.C. 1979).
119. *Id.* at 141. *See also* Smith v. Cumberland School Committee, 415 A.2d 168 (R.I. 1980).
120. 24 Pa. Cons. Stat. Ann. §§ 13-1371, 13-1372.
121. Fla. Stat. Ann. § 230.23(4)(m).
122. Stuart v. Nappi, 443 F. Supp. 1235 (D. Conn. 1978). *See also* Doe v. Kroger, 480 F. Supp. 225 (N.D. Ind. 1979), in which the federal court concluded that handicapped children may be expelled for disruptive behavior only if the reason for expulsion is unrelated to the handicapping condition; Southeast Warren Community School Dist. v. Department of Public Instruction, 285 N.W.2d 173 (Iowa 1979), in which the Iowa Supreme Court held that school districts can expel handicapped students, but special procedures are required.
123. Rowley v. Board of Educ. of the Hendrick Hudson Central School Dist., 483 F. Supp. 528 (S.D.N.Y. 1980), *aff'd* No. 80-7098 (2d. Cir., July 17, 1980).
124. *See* DeWalt v. Burkholder, No. 80-0014-A (E.D. Va., March 13, 1980); Bettencourt v. Rhodes, No. C77-12 (N.D. Ohio, September 14, 1977); Panitch v. Wisconsin, 390 F. Supp. 611 (E.D. Wis. 1974).
125. Leroy M. Goodman, "A Bill of Rights for the Handicapped," *American Education*, Vol. 12, No. 6, July 1976, p. 6.
126. 483 F.2d 791 (9th Cir. 1973), *rev'd* 414 U.S. 563 (1974).
127. *Id.*, 483 F.2d 798.
128. *Id.*, 414 U.S. 566. Section 601 of the Civil Rights Act of 1964, 42 U.S.C. § 2000d (1976) bans discrimination based "on the ground of race, color, or national origin" in "any program or activity receiving federal financial assistance."
129. *Id.*, 414 U.S. 566.
130. United States v. Texas, 342 F. Supp. 24 (E.D. Tex. 1971), *aff'd* 466 F.2d 518 (5th Cir. 1972).
131. Arvizu v. Waco Independent School Dist., 373 F. Supp. 1264 (W.D. Tex. 1973).
132. Otero v. Mesa County School Dist. No. 51, 408 F. Supp. 162 (D. Colo. 1975).
133. Rios v. Read, 73 F.R.D. 589 (E.D.N.Y. 1977).
134. Morales v. Shannon, 516 F.2d 411, 414-15 (5th Cir. 1975).
135. Keyes v. School Dist. No. 1, Denver, Colorado, 521 F.2d 465 (10th Cir. 1975). The appellate court remanded the case for a determination of the relief, if any, necessary to ensure that Hispanic and other minority children were provided the opportunity to acquire proficiency in the English language.
136. Guadalupe Organization, Inc. v. Tempe Elem. School Dist. No. 3, 587 F.2d 1022 (9th Cir. 1978). *See also* Serna v. Portales Municipal Schools, 351 F. Supp. 1279 (D.N.M. 1972), *aff'd* 499 F.2d 1147 (10th Cir. 1974).
137. Bilingual Education Act, 20 U.S.C. § 880b *et seq.* (1970).
138. 20 U.S.C. § 880b-1(a)(4)(A) (1976). Also the Equal Educational

Opportunity Act of 1974, 20 U.S.C. §1701 *et seq.* (1976), requires education agencies to take steps to overcome student language barriers that may impede equal participation in school programs.

139. *See Federal Register*, Vol. 45, No. 152, August 5, 1980. These regulations have created extensive controversy as to the responsibilities placed on school districts to provide bilingual instruction in addition to compensatory English instruction. Some professional associations have asserted that the Dept. of Education has acted beyond its scope of authority in prescribing *how* instruction must be offered to overcome English language deficiencies among pupils. *See* "Education Groups Say Bilingual Rules Subvert Local Control," *Education Daily*, Vol. 13, No. 172, September 3, 1980, p. 3; "Debate Intensifies on Bilingual Education," *Education Daily*, Vol. 13, No. 178, September 11, 1980, p. 1.

140. Ind. Code Ann. § 20-10.1-5.5-1.

141. Martin Luther King Junior Elementary School Children v. Ann Arbor School Dist. Bd., 473 F. Supp. 1371 (E.D. Mich. 1979).

142. In addition to the student classifications discussed in this chapter, children classified as illegal aliens have been the focus of litigation. In September 1980, Justice Powell vacated a Sixth Circuit Court of Appeals stay of the implementation of a federal district court order requiring Texas school districts to educate children of parents residing illegally in the state. In July 1980, the district court had ruled in seventeen consolidated cases that the Texas law excluding illegal alien children from free public schooling violated the fourteenth amendment. *See* Certain Named and Unnamed Non-citizen Children and their Parents v. Texas, No. A-179, 49 U.S.L.W. 3133 (September 9, 1980). *See also* Doe v. Plyler, 458 F. Supp. 569 (E.D. Tex. 1978).

# 10

# Students' First Amendment Rights

The first amendment to the United States Constitution affords pervasive rights to citizens, and the Supreme Court has recognized that the public school is an appropriate setting in which to instill a respect for these rights. In 1943, the Court declared that first amendment freedoms must receive "scrupulous protection" in schools "if we are not to strangle the free mind at its source and teach youth to discount important principles of our government as mere platitudes." [1]

While perhaps the most preciously guarded of individual liberties, these first amendment rights are not without limits. As Justice Oliver Holmes aptly noted, freedom of speech does not allow an individual to yell "fire" in a crowded theater if there is no fire. In the educational context, school officials can restrict the exercise of first amendment rights, but only if a legitimate school interest, such as the prevention of disruption, justifies the restriction. Students have challenged numerous public school policies and practices as placing arbitrary constraints on first amendment guarantees. This chapter focuses on judicial interpretations of students' rights to freedom of religion, speech, press, and assembly/association.

## RELIGIOUS GUARANTEES

Two distinct religious protections are included in the first amendment. The government is prohibited from either enacting legislation respecting the establishment of religion or interfering with an individual's right to exercise religious beliefs. Although these prohibitions originally were directed toward Congress, the Supreme Court has applied them to state governments through the fourteenth amendment. The Court has recognized that religious freedoms are among the liberties protected against arbitrary state action.[2]

Substantial litigation has been generated in an attempt to delineate the appropriate church-state relationship vis-à-vis education. Cases have dealt with first amendment implications of diverse topics such as state aid to parochial schools,[3] tax relief programs for parents of nonpublic school pupils,[4] lease arrangements between public and private schools,[5] governmental authority to regulate nonpublic schools,[6] religious activities and observances in public schools,[7] and curricular accommodations for religion in public education.[8] This section focuses on legal activity in the two areas that most directly affect public school pupils. Specifically, prohibitions against religious indoctrination by the state and religious challenges to secular school activities are examined.

## PROHIBITIONS AGAINST RELIGIOUS INDOCTRINATION BY THE STATE

With some regularity, courts have been called upon to review various public school policies and practices to ensure that students are protected from religious inculcation by the state. Historically, many public school activities reflected the tenets of the dominant religion, and such accommodations to religion were seldom questioned. After World War II, however, sentiments began to change, and courts exhibited greater interest in protecting the individual's right to free exercise of religious beliefs. The judiciary became particularly assertive in shielding public elementary and secondary school students from state-imposed religious inculcation because of their age and the fact that they comprise a captive audience, compelled to attend school.

For example, prayer and Bible reading in public schools have been declared unconstitutional.[9] Also, the observance of holy days and the display of religious symbols, such as the crucifix, have been invalidated in public schools. Furthermore, courts have ruled that religious clubs, devotional rather than academic, cannot meet on public school premises during lunch period or after school, unless the clubs rent space in the school building.[10] Such devotional activities need not be mandatory in order to abridge the first amendment. The Supreme Court has noted that whether or not religious observances in school are voluntary is irrelevant. When such activities are state-sanctioned, "the indirect coercive pressure upon religious minorities to conform to the prevailing officially approved religion is plain." [11]

The Supreme Court also has ruled that the practice of releasing students from regular school activities for religious education held on public school grounds violates the first amendment.[12] However, the Court has recognized that released time for such instruction held off public school property is permissible.[13] In sanctioning the legality of a statute permitting students to leave the public school to receive religious training, the Court noted in 1952 that the state should not advance religion but neither should it be hostile to the practice of religious beliefs.[14] More recently, the Supreme Court declined to review a Fourth Circuit Appellate Court decision sanctioning a "weekday religion program" in which students received religious instruction in a mobile unit parked on the edge of school property.[15] Based on the Supreme Court endorsement, most states have enacted laws permitting a limited amount of released time during public school hours for sectarian instruction conducted off school grounds. Courts have recognized, however, that instruction designed to reinforce religious beliefs must be disassociated from the public school and clearly cannot be the basis for academic credit.[16]

While it is unconstitutional to attempt to influence students' religious choices under the auspices of the public school, it is permissible to teach the Bible and other religious documents from a literary perspective and to explain various holy days, as long as one religion is not preferred over others. Also, teachers can present information about religion from a cultural or historical perspective if the instruction is not designed to inculcate students.[17] Essentially, courts have held that the practice of religion in public schools abridges the first amendment, but instruction about religion is permissible. Awareness of and exposure to various religions can be legitimate school objectives, whereas religious indoctrination cannot.

It would appear that school personnel stand on firm legal ground in teaching citizenship values such as honesty, responsibility, self-control, and respect for justice, law, and authority. These values, necessary to prepare students to function as adults in American society, can be disassociated from religion and thus do not raise any first amendment issues.[18] Also, seasonal decorations such as pine trees, wreaths, and colored eggs are usually considered permissible, as they have only incidental religious connotations.

The use of silent meditation periods in public schools generally has been upheld as constitutional. Some states have enacted statutes permitting or requiring such meditation periods. Indiana law, for example, stipulates that each public school teacher (if so directed by the governing body) must conduct a brief period of meditation at the opening of each school day.[19] Courts have sanctioned silent meditation periods if designed to reflect on the events of the day and not to advance religion. In Massachusetts, a federal district court upheld a state law providing that "a period of silence not to exceed one minute in duration shall be observed for meditation or prayer " [20]

The line between permissible and forbidden activities, however, is not always clear. For example, a Tennessee federal district court concluded that a Bible study course in public elementary schools violated first amendment rights because it served to advance the Christian religion, rather than to expand students' awareness of religion from a historical or literary perspective.[21] In contrast, the use of prayer during graduation ceremonies has been judicially sanctioned. A Virginia federal court concluded that there was no intent to indoctrinate students by using an invocation at the graduation exercise, and, therefore, this single event constituted a minimal first amendment infringement.[22] The court held that such a fleeting incident could not be equated with daily devotional activities in public schools.

The posting of the Ten Commandments in public school classrooms has been the source of recent first amendment litigation. In November 1980, the Supreme Court invalidated a Kentucky law that required copies of the Ten Commandments to be posted in every public school classroom upon receipt of voluntary contributions made to the state treasury for such purpose.[23] Previously, justices on the Kentucky Supreme Court had divided evenly as to the constitutionality of the law, thereby affirming the lower court's endorsement of the statute. The lower court had reasoned that the Ten Commandments contain a code of conduct fundamental to western civilization which is appropriate for school children to learn regardless of their specific religious beliefs. However, the Supreme Court disagreed with this rationale, and in a five to four decision struck down the law as advancing religion. Since several of the commandments outline religious duties toward God, the majority reasoned that the Kentucky law could not be defended as secular.

The legality of religious holiday observances in public schools also has generated recent controversy. In 1979, a South Dakota federal judge endorsed a school board policy that permitted the singing of Christmas carols such as "Silent Night" in school assemblies. The following year, the Eighth Circuit Court of Appeals affirmed the decision, and the Supreme Court declined to review the case.[24] The challenged board policy stipulated that one of the school district's educational goals was to "advance students' knowledge and appreciation of the role that our religious heritage has played in the social, cultural, and historical development of civilization." [25] The policy authorized the observance of holidays with both a secular and religious basis, including the use of religious music, art, literature, and drama and the temporary display of religious symbols. The judiciary considered the policy and its implementation to be constitutionally permissible.

Although courts usually have disallowed the distribution of religious literature in public schools,[26] in 1979 the United States Supreme Court declined to review a Florida case in which lower courts departed somewhat from this posture. The case involved a first amendment challenge to (1) a Florida statute that instructed educators to instill "Christian virtues" in public school children, (2) a school board policy requiring "inspirational" Bible reading and prayer, and (3) board guidelines allowing the distribution of religious literature at designated places in public schools.[27] The trial court had dismissed the petition for injunctive and declaratory relief, concluding that the students had not proven that any school practices pursuant to the statute and policies had resulted in injury to them. The Fifth Circuit Court of Appeals held that the policy requiring Bible reading and prayer in public schools violated the first amendment. However, the appeals court affirmed, by an equally divided vote, the district court's dismissal of the challenge to the state statute requiring the teaching of "Christian virtues" and the board guidelines pertaining to the distribution of religious literature. Since the Supreme Court declined to review the case, the contested law and policy were left in force after a decade of litigation.

It appears likely that state legislatures and school boards will continue to enact statutes and policies that strain the wall of separation between church and state. There is even some sentiment in Congress in favor of enacting federal legislation—and a constitutional amendment if necessary—permitting Bible reading in public schools. Recently, several courts have assumed a more permissive posture toward religion in public education than was common a decade ago. Since the composition of the United States Supreme Court is substantially different from what it was in 1963 when Bible reading was barred from public schools, clarification is needed from the current Court regarding the types of religious activities that are constitutionally permissible in American public schools.

## RELIGIOUS CHALLENGES TO SECULAR ACTIVITIES

Given the range of the public school's mission and the diversity among religious convictions, it is not surprising that many school practices have been challenged as offending one or more religious groups. Consequently, courts have been called upon to balance the interests involved and to resolve such conflicts. The Supreme Court has recognized that "the state has no legitimate interest in protecting any or all religions from views distasteful to them." [28] Secular programs that may conflict with some religious convictions, however, should not be confused with state-sanctioned *devotional* activities, which have been deemed impermissible. When secular activities have been challenged as offensive to certain dogmas, courts often have exempted the particular children from participation. But courts have not banned the secular activity from the public school curriculum, whereas they have barred purely devotional activities.

For example, in 1943 the Supreme Court held that students could not be compelled to salute the American flag and pledge their allegiance if such practices offended their religious or philosophical beliefs.[29] The Court, however, did not invalidate the continuation of these observances in public schools. Rather, it weighed the individual and state interests involved in mandatory participation, and concluded that students were entitled to be excused from such activities. In rendering the decision, Justice Jackson stated for the Court:

> If there is any fixed star in our constitutional constellation, it is that no official, high or petty, can prescribe what shall be orthodox in politics, nationalism, religion, or other matters of opinion or force citizens to confess by word or act their faith therein. If there are any circumstances which permit an exception, they do not now occur to us.[30]

Subsequently, courts have ruled that students cannot be required to stand at attention during the pledge, because such a required observance amounts to explicit expression.[31]

Curricular offerings, as well as school observances, have been challenged on religious grounds. Statutes in some states specify that students can be exempted from certain curricular offerings because of their sectarian beliefs. For example, in Indiana, any person who objects on religious grounds to the state-required hygiene course is entitled to be excused (without penalty) from receiving medical instruction or instruction in disease prevention.[32] Courts also have addressed students' rights under the Federal Constitution to specific exemptions for religious reasons. Students have been excused from participating in folk dancing [33] and from wearing a specified outfit in physical education class [34] on first amendment grounds. In 1979, an Illinois federal district court declared that students could not be required to participate in coeducational physical education classes if the presence of members of the opposite sex dressed in "immodest attire" offended their religious beliefs.[35] The court noted that school officials could excuse the specific students or provide them with special classes or individualized instruction.

In balancing the public and private interests at stake, some courts have been less sympathetic when parents have asked that their children be excused from school activities, particularly if the requested exemption has involved academic classes or requirements. In an illustrative New Hampshire case, parents were unsuccessful in challenging the school's instructional use of audiovisual equipment that offended their religious dogma.[36] The federal district court held that the children could not be excused from class when such equipment was used as part of regular instructional activities, but they could be excused when the use was for entertainment only.

Parents also have been unsuccessful in attempts to mold the public school curriculum to the tenets of a particular religion. Nonetheless, such efforts continue to create legal controversies. For example, the teaching of evolution has been a popular target. In 1968, the United States Supreme Court seemingly settled the legality of the right to teach evolution by invalidating an Arkansas statute that banned instruction regarding Darwin's theory.[37] However, the more recent controversy has focused on the issue of whether advocates of the biblical theory of creation have a right to demand that this viewpoint be presented along with other theories of creation. In 1975, the Sixth Circuit Court of Appeals struck down a Tennessee statute that required the teaching of the biblical version whenever the theory of evolution was discussed.[38] Two years later, a trial court in Indiana invalidated action by the state textbook commission that allowed school districts to adopt a biology textbook presenting creation only from the biblical point of view.[39] While it would appear permissible to expose public school students to the biblical theory, recent decisions indicate that such instruction cannot be required and cannot be the only theory of creation presented.

The topic of sex education also has regularly evoked lawsuits initiated under first amendment religious guarantees, and most parental objections to the inclusion of sex education in the curriculum have not prevailed. Courts in states such as New Jersey, Hawaii, Michigan, and California have upheld sex education instruction in public schools as justified by the overriding public interest in teaching students important health information.[40] Although the legality of teaching sex education has been uniformly endorsed, such instruction usually has not been considered a mandatory part of the school curriculum.

In general, secular activities and instructional offerings in public schools need not be altered to accommodate religious beliefs. Indeed, the Supreme Court has recognized that the curriculum *must not* reflect the preferences of one or all religions. Even though courts have upheld students' rights to be excused from certain activities for religious reasons, pupils can be compelled to fulfill academic requirements.

# FREEDOM OF SPEECH AND EXPRESSION

While the religious freedoms enumerated in the first amendment have generated educational litigation during much of the twentieth century, only recently have students' constitutional rights to freedom of speech and expression been judicially recognized. It was not until 1969 that the United States Supreme Court rendered the landmark decision *Tinker v. Des Moines Independent School District,* thus initiating a new era in students' rights. The court declared that "students in school as well as out of school are 'persons' under our Constitution. They are possessed of fundamental rights which the state must respect." [41]

## APPLICATION OF THE TINKER PRINCIPLE

In *Tinker,* three students were suspended from school for wearing armbands to protest the Vietnam War. The school officials did not attempt to prohibit the wearing of all symbols, but instead chose to ban the expression of one particular opinion. Concluding that school officials punished the students for the expression of an opinion that was not accompanied by any disorder or disturbance, the Supreme Court ruled that "undifferentiated fear or apprehension of disturbance is not enough to overcome the right to freedom of expression." [42] Furthermore, the court declared that school officials must have "more than a mere desire to avoid discomfort and unpleasantness that always accompany an unpopular viewpoint" in order to justify the curtailment of student expression.[43]

In rendering the *Tinker* decision, the Supreme Court reiterated statements made in an earlier circuit court ruling, *Burnside v. Byars*.[44] In this case, the Fifth Circuit Court of Appeals held that a student may express opinions on controversial issues in the classroom, cafeteria, playing field, or any other place, as long as the exercise of such rights does "not materially and substantially interfere with the requirements of appropriate discipline in the operation of the school" or collide with the rights of others.[45]

Although some educators feared that the holdings in *Burnside* and *Tinker* were designed to constrict school officials' power to control student misconduct, this was not the intent and has not been the result of these decisions. In both cases, the courts emphasized that educators have the authority and *duty* to maintain discipline in schools. School officials simply must consider students' constitutional rights as they exert their control. A comparison of *Burnside* with *Blackwell v. Issaquena County Board of Education* [46] provides some insight as to what constitutes a valid regulation of students' rights to free expression.

In *Burnside,* the appellate court invalidated a regulation that prohibited students from wearing freedom buttons while attending school. The court concluded that the wearing of these buttons did not hamper the school in carrying out its regular schedule of activities, nor were the rights of other students impaired. Indeed, only a mild state of curiosity was evident among the students. Noting that the right to communicate a matter of vital public concern is protected by the first amendment, the court held that the students were merely exercising this right by wearing buttons to express an idea.[47]

On the same day that the Fifth Circuit Appellate Court endorsed the students' rights to wear freedom buttons in *Burnside,* it denied students this form of expression in *Blackwell*. The reason for this apparent reversal was that in *Blackwell* the button wearers created disturbances within the school by harassing students who did not take part in the expression. Following the *Blackwell* rationale, in 1970 the Sixth Circuit Court of Appeals concluded that a rule banning the wearing of freedom buttons was lawful because it was reasonably related to the prevention of disruption.[48] In this case, the particular school rule had been enforced consistently and uniformly for a number of years, conditions not present in *Burnside* and *Tinker*.[49]

It appears, therefore, that courts will sanction regulations that place constraints on students' freedom of verbal and nonverbal expression, but only in situations where disruption reasonably can be predicted as a result of the expression. Courts have recognized that this expectation of disruption must be based on "fact, not intuition" [50] and that regulations impairing students' rights to free expression must be necessary to advance legitimate state interests "lest students' imaginations, intellects, and wills be unduly stifled or chilled." [51]

## EXPRESSION CONSIDERED DISRUPTIVE

School officials are faced with the difficult task of determining what forms of student expression are sufficiently disruptive to justify prohibitions against them. The law is clear in allowing students to be punished *after the fact* if their behavior interferes with the educational process, but the issuance of *prior restraints* on expression places a greater burden of justification on school authorities. Nonetheless, courts have recognized that certain types of expression can be prohibited.

The judiciary has sanctioned regulations banning the use of "fighting words" in public schools. Courts have differentiated speech that agitates and exhorts from speech that "is a mere doctrinal justification of a thought or idea," leaving an opportunity for calm and reasonable discussion.[52] Speech intended to elicit immediate disruptive action clearly can be prohibited,[53] whereas student criticism of school regulations is generally considered to be protected speech.[54]

In addition to expression that threatens violence, courts have recognized that walkouts or boycotts,[55] sit-ins,[56] and excessive noise [57] can—under certain circumstances—constitute a material or substantial disruption, and thus justifiably can be curtailed. In 1972, the Eighth Circuit Court of Appeals held that students who disrupted a school assembly by walking out were properly suspended.[58] Similarly, student protests involving conduct such as blocking hallways or damaging property have been considered beyond the reach of first amendment protections. Policies governing demonstrations, however, should be couched in terms of time, place, and manner restrictions to convey to students that they have the right to express their ideas under nondisruptive circumstances.

Vague wording of a regulation pertaining to demonstrations may result in a judicial declaration that the conduct cannot be punished because the demonstrators did not know in advance precisely what behavior was prohibited. Regulations banning "misconduct" or "crimes of a serious nature" have been invalidated as overbroad, and thus not capable of supporting the punishment of sit-in protesters.[59] Furthermore, the assertion that a demonstration hampered school officials in performing their regular duties has been considered an inadequate basis for disciplining students involved in a peaceful protest.[60] However, courts have recognized that if demonstrations caused students to miss class or disrupted the progress of classes, the protesters could be punished for interfering with essential school activities.[61]

Excessive noise is the most difficult category of disruptive expression with which to deal, since it is often pure speech. Nonetheless, excessive noise has been recognized as disruptive in situations where it has interfered with classes or work environments. The Supreme Court has endorsed a noise ordinance prohibiting "loud and raucous" noise [62] and a city regulation prohibiting noise near a school that impedes school functions.[63] School authorities have generally been supported in prohibiting noise or speech accompanied by the intent to disrupt classes or official duties, since the existence of such an intent has negated the assertion that the noise was pure communication.

It seems inevitable that courts will continue to be called upon to balance the interests involved when students' rights to free expression collide with educators' duty to maintain an orderly school. Courts are very protective of students' rights, given the length of time they spend in school and the fact that most individuals are first introduced to free expression rights and responsibilities in the public school setting. The Supreme Court has noted that "teachers and students must always remain free to inquire, to study and evaluate, [and] to gain new maturity and understanding." [64] The *Tinker* decision provides the basic guideline for educators to follow in evaluating student expression, and under this mandate students' first amendment rights are subject to certain constraints. Disruptive expression can be prohibited, and school authorities still have "comprehensive authority . . . to prescribe and control conduct in the schools" so as to maintain an environment conducive to learning.[65] The Supreme Court has noted that first amendment protections must be applied "in light of the special circumstances of the school." [66]

# FREEDOM OF PRESS:
# STUDENT PUBLICATIONS

Recently, student publications have generated substantial controversy in public schools. Courts frequently have been asked to determine whether school officials have the power to suppress student literature or punish its distributors on the basis of the publication's content.

## PRIOR REVIEW REGULATIONS

Many of the controversies have focused on school policies requiring official approval prior to the distribution of student publications. The Supreme Court has stated that "any prior restraint of expression comes to this Court with a 'heavy presumption' against its constitutional validity." [67] The burden of proof is placed on those who wish to suppress free expression, not on those who seek to exercise that right. Consequently, courts have been extremely sensitive to any prior approval of student publications that serves to curtail first amendment freedoms.

A few courts have invalidated all types of prior review of student literature as an unconstitutional restraint on free expression. In 1972, the Seventh Circuit Court of Appeals held that Chicago school officials could not require prior approval of the content of student publications or prevent distribution of the material.[68] The court recognized, however, that school authorities could regulate the *manner* of distribution and could punish students if the distributed materials were obscene or libelous or caused a disruption. More recently, the California Supreme Court interpreted the state law pertaining to free expression rights of students as not authorizing school districts to (1) establish systems of prior restraint with respect to prohibited categories of expression, or (2) prevent the distribution of student literature through administrative censorship of its content.[69] The court did acknowledge that once distribution had begun, school officials could intervene if the material was obscene, libelous, or inflammatory, and could impose sanctions on the students responsible for distributing such literature.

In contrast to the preceding opinions, most courts have approved the principle of prior review applied to student publications, but have placed the burden of justifying such policies on school officials. Many rules pertaining to prior approval have been successfully challenged because of defects in the policies or their application. Courts have invalidated school regulations if the procedures for the prior review have not been clearly articulated,[70] and have noted that "where the boundaries between prohibited and permissible conduct are ambiguous, we cannot assume that the curtailment of free expression is minimized." [71]

Generally, courts have held that "narrow, objective and reasonable standards" are essential in any prior approval scheme.[72] In an illustrative case, the Second Circuit Court of Appeals invalidated procedures for prior submission of student literature because the policy failed to specify when review was to take place and to whom and how the material was to be submitted.[73] Similarly, in 1971 the Fourth Circuit Court of Appeals struck down regulations requiring prior review of student publications because written criteria were not available for judging the material.[74]

Conversely, a tightly controlled scheme for prior submission of literature was upheld by the Fifth Circuit Court of Appeals because the regulations were specific and consistently applied.[75] More recently, the same court reiterated that where there is a well-defined system of prior submission and a student flagrantly and consciously disregards the policy, such conduct is not protected under the *Tinker* mandate.[76]

## PERMISSIBLE AND IMPERMISSIBLE CONTENT

There are several judicially recognized exceptions to the right of high school students to distribute literature at school. The distribution of printed material that fosters disruption of the educational process or peril to the health or safety of students can be curtailed. In 1980, the Fourth Circuit Court of Appeals ruled that school administrators acted within their authority when they banned further distribution on school property of an underground student publication that contained an advertisement for drug paraphernalia.[77] The appeals court emphasized that the literature was not subjected to pre-distribution approval; copies were impounded *after* distribution began. The school regulation authorizing the principal to halt the distribution of any publication encouraging actions that endanger the health or safety of students was not found to be unconstitutionally vague. In addition, the court concluded that school officials did not have to establish that the suppressed publication would substantially disrupt school activities in order for the ban to be upheld. The court further noted that the school district's appeals procedures for students to contest the confiscation of literture were adequate and not unduly lengthy.

The judiciary also has recognized that obscene material is not protected by the first amendment.[78] Yet, the law concerning obscenity has been in a state of flux in recent years. In *Miller v. California,* which did not involve a school situation, the United States Supreme Court attempted to distinguish obscene material from material that would receive first amendment protection by using the following test:

> (1) whether "the average person, applying contemporary community standards" would find that the work, taken as a whole, appeals to the prurient interest; . . . (2) whether the work depicts or describes, in a patently offensive way, sexual conduct, specifically defined by the applicable state law; and (3) whether the work, taken as a whole, lacks serious literary, artistic, political or scientific value.[79] [Citations omitted.]

The *Miller* standard, however, has not clarified the concept of obscenity as applied to student publications. Debate continues as to whether school systems can enforce obscenity standards in schools that are different from those in society at large. Some courts have noted that material permissible for distribution to adults is not necessarily appropriate for distribution to children: "The concept of obscenity or of unprotected matter may vary according to the group to whom the questionable material is directed or from whom it is quarantined." [80] Hence, a student publication may be judged by community standards in determining what is obscene, but it is unclear whether such an assessment must follow the *Miller* guidelines. Although it might appear that student literature should be subject to more stringent criteria, in several cases the use of profanity and vulgarisms in student publications has not been considered obscene.[81]

In a West Virginia case, a federal court invalidated a publication policy because the words "decency, taste, obscenity, and libelous" were not precisely defined.[82] Calling the publication policy "a monument to vagueness," the court concluded that the regulation provided "no guidelines or criteria by which such levels of accuracy, taste and decency can be ascertained by either the author of literature or the reviewing principal." [83] In addition, the court held that the policy was deficient in that it lacked adequate procedures for review of the materials in question.

In 1974, the United States Supreme Court declined the opportunity to settle many of the legal issues pertaining to first amendment protection of student literature. This case, *Board of School Commissioners v. Jacobs,* involved a challenge by students to an Indianapolis school code allowing suppression of literature that "produces or is likely to produce a significant disruption of the normal educational processes" or is "obscene to minors." [84] The Seventh Circuit Court of Appeals ruled in favor of the students on the grounds that the disruption provision of the policy was unconstitutionally vague and that the controversial literature, which contained a few earthy words relating to bodily functions and sexual intercourse, was not obscene to high school pupils. On appeal, the United States Supreme Court delivered an unsigned opinion, noting that all of the students involved had graduated from high school and therefore the issues had become moot as far as the original plaintiffs were concerned. Justice Douglas, dissenting, argued that the Court should have ruled on the merits of the case because the requirements of a class action had been met. Furthermore, he admonished the Court majority for leaving the important issues raised in this case for some future resolution, thus permitting the school board to "continue its enforcement, for an indefinite period of time, of regulations which have been held facially unconstitutional by both of the courts below." [85]

Judicial ambiguity also has surrounded the regulation of libelous material in student literature. Like obscenity, defamatory statements that are made with malice and expose others to public shame or ridicule have been considered outside of the protective arm of the first amendment.[86] Nonetheless, regulations prohibiting libelous material have been voided in situations where the policies have been vague or overbroad.[87] In a California case in which such regulations were invalidated, a federal court held that school authorities were not empowered to prevent the distribution of "potentially libelous" material by imposing prior restraints.[88] However, the court noted that once distribution had begun, school officials could curtail dissemination of libelous content and impose sanctions on students responsible for the material.

While obscene, libelous, or inflammatory content in student publications can be prohibited, the fact that articles criticize school officials has been deemed an unjustifiable reason to suppress literature.[89] In an illustrative case, the Seventh Circuit Court of Appeals upheld students' rights to criticize school personnel and policies in a mimeographed paper containing editorials, poetry, and reviews pertaining to the school administration and urging students to reject "propaganda."[90] The content included charges against the principal and an attack on the school's attendance requirements. Relying on *Tinker,* the court held that disciplinary action against the students responsible for the material unconstitutionally impaired protected rights because there was no evidence that the publication would create a disruption. Other courts have reiterated that school authorities cannot ban student literature simply to choke off criticism of themselves or school policies.[91]

Courts also have ruled that the mere discussion of controversial issues cannot be barred from student publications.[92] A policy that allows school authorities discretion in determining which content may create a material or substantial disruption is not sufficient to convey notice to students as to what specific content will be prohibited.[93] During the 1970s, courts recognized that material dealing with the Vietnam War, marijuana, or birth control information was not too controversial for high school students.[94]

In 1978, however, the United States Supreme Court refused to hear an appeal of a second circuit ruling in which the appellate court upheld school officials in prohibiting the high school newspaper editor from questioning students on their feelings about sex, contraception, homosexuality, masturbation, and the extent of their sexual experience.[95] In this case, *Trachtman v. Anker,* the appeals court deferred to the school authorities' judgment that the survey could endanger the emotional health of some immature students. The court distinguished this factual situation from the one presented in *Gambino v. Fairfax County School Board,* where the Fourth Circuit Court of Appeals ruled that students' constitutional rights were violated by the censorship of a school newspaper article dealing with student attitudes toward contraception.[96] In *Gambino,* the court concluded that the paper was created as a vehicle for student expression, and thus articles could not be censored merely because they offended school officials. Since the survey of student attitudes toward birth control had already been completed in *Gambino,* only the exercise of expression was at issue. In contrast, the activity of conducting the survey itself was being prohibited in *Anker.* The Second Circuit Appellate Court emphasized that the first amendment does not protect the "right to importune others to respond to questions when there is reason to believe that such importuning may result in harmful consequences."[97]

## SCHOOL-SPONSORED PUBLICATIONS

The judiciary has recognized that constitutional protections apply to school-sponsored publications as well as to nonschool literature. If the publication was originally created as a free speech forum, removal of financial or other school board support can be construed as an unlawful effort to stifle free expression. For example, in a New York case, students challenged the authority of the school principal to impound copies of a school-affiliated literary magazine based on his judgment that some of the content was obscene.[98] One of the articles used four-letter words and referred to a movie scene where a couple "fell into bed." The federal district court concluded that the content of the magazine was protected by first amendment guarantees because it contained "no extended narrative . . . constituting a predominant appeal to prurient interest" and because it was not "patently offensive . . . as evidenced by comparable material appearing in respected national periodicals and literature contained in the high school library."[99] Therefore, the court ruled that nondisruptive distribution of the magazine on school property must be allowed. However, the court noted that school officials did have the right to stamp each copy to disclaim responsibility for its content.

In 1979, the same court upheld a high school principal's authority to prevent distribution of an issue of the school newspaper because its content would create a substantial risk of disruption to school activities.[100] The controversial publication contained a libelous attack on a student government officer and a threat of violence to the players on the school lacrosse team. The court concluded that the principal's interest in protecting students from harm provided a justifiable basis for barring distribution of the literature. Moreover, the court noted that the school board's authority to prevent distribution of material that is libelous, obscene, disruptive of school activities, or violative of the rights of others is not lessened simply because the board has not adopted written policies requiring prior review of student publications.

Boards of education are not totally powerless to regulate student literature, nor are they obligated to support such publications. School officials can determine the goals of a school-sponsored paper, its advertising policies, and criteria for staff selection. If a student paper is published as part of a journalism class taken for credit, school authorities may even be able to justify restricting articles to assigned topics. School personnel, however, must bear the burden of proof in substantiating that the publication is solely an instructional tool and not a free speech forum for students. Courts have noted that a governmental body "is not necessarily the unfettered master of all it creates."[101] Thus, the content of a school-sponsored paper that is established as a medium for student expression cannot be regulated more closely than a nonsponsored paper. Mere school affiliation does not remove student literature from first amendment protection.[102] Any policy governing the content of student publications must have clearly drawn standards and procedures that permit a speedy determination of whether the material meets those standards.

## TIME, PLACE, AND MANNER REGULATIONS

Even though courts often have invalidated policies involving prior censorship of student publications, the judiciary has endorsed reasonable policies regulating the time, place, and manner of distribution.[103] Courts have concluded that such time, place, and manner restrictions are justified in order to ensure that the distribution of student publications does not infringe upon other school activities. Accordingly, courts have upheld bans on literature distribution near the doors of classrooms while class is in session, near building exits during fire drills, and on stairways when classes are changing.[104]

Time, place, and manner regulations, however, must be reasonable and must be uniformly applied to all forms of literature. School officials must inform students specifically as to when, how, and where they may distribute materials. Moreover, literature distribution cannot be relegated to remote times or places either inside or outside the school building.[105] Also, the regulations must not inhibit any person's right to accept or reject literature that is distributed in accordance with the rules. School officials must be able to substantiate the reasonableness of any time, place, and manner restrictions, because vague or ambiguous regulations can curtail student expression as much as a blanket policy prohibiting literature distribution.

Although the distribution of student publications at school can be reasonably regulated, restrictions cannot be placed on the distribution of such literature off school grounds. In a 1979 decision, the Second Circuit Court of Appeals concluded that school officials overstepped their authority by disciplining high school students who published a satirical magazine in their homes and sold it at a local store.[106] While not addressing the question of whether distribution of the "vulgar" publication at school was permissible, the court prohibited school officials from punishing the student publishers for its off-campus distribution. The court concluded that to rule otherwise would subject students to school-imposed punishments for watching X-rated movies on cable television in their own homes.

Since the Supreme Court has declined to deliver an opinion in a case involving student publications, school authorities must seek guidance from decisions rendered by their respective federal circuit courts of appeal. In general, educators would be wise to ensure that any restriction placed on the distribution of student literature is absolutely necessary to maintain a proper learning environment. School personnel must be able to justify all policies and practices that interfere with students' exercise of constitutionally protected freedoms of speech or press.

## FREEDOM OF ASSEMBLY AND ASSOCIATION

Included among first amendment freedoms are the rights to assemble peaceably and to petition the government for redress of grievances. In the school setting, this generally means that groups of students can hold meetings and distribute petitions as long as these activities do not materially or substantially impede the educational process (e.g., interrupt classes). School authorities may, however, control the time and place of student meetings and the circulation of student petitions in order to minimize safety hazards and to preserve order in the school.

### STUDENT CLUBS

Related to the right of peaceful assembly is the right to freedom of association. While freedom of association is not specifically included among first amendment protections, the Supreme Court has recognized that this right is "implicit in the freedoms of speech, assembly, and petition." [107] Adults have received consistent judicial protection in organizing social and political groups that promote unpopular and undemocratic causes. However, student clubs in public schools traditionally have not been afforded similar protection.

Pupils have unsuccessfully asserted that the right to association shields student-initiated social organizations or secret societies.[108] Courts have upheld school officials' rights to deny recognition to such clubs and to prohibit student membership in secret societies. Some states, by statute, forbid student participation in a club that sustains itself by selecting new members "on the basis of the decision of its membership rather than upon the free choice of any pupil in the school who is qualified by the rules of the school to fill the special aims of the organization." [109] The judiciary has endorsed the notion that secret societies "tend to engender an undemocratic spirit of caste, to promote cliques, and to foster a contempt for school authority." [110] Various punishments, ranging from suspension to denial of participation in extracurricular activities, have been upheld as penalties for membership in secret societies.[111]

In a typical case, a regulation of a California school district prohibited student membership in any fraternity, sorority, or nonschool club perpetuating its membership by the decision of its own members.[112] A student challenged the rule, claiming that a specific club was created to meet the objectives of "literature, charity and scholarship." However, the appeals court concluded that despite its stated objectives, the club was a secret society in that new members were "rushed" each semester and then chosen through a secret voting process. Also, in Fort Worth, Texas, a civil appeals court upheld a school board regulation requiring parents of all students entering high school to certify that their children would not join a secret society.[113] The court reasoned that the regulation was not an unconstitutional invasion of parents' rights to rear their children.

In contrast to bans pertaining to secret societies, prohibitions against student organizations that have open membership may be more vulnerable to first amendment challenges.[114] In Michigan, high school students successfully attacked a school board policy forbidding schools to recognize student organizations that advocated controversial ideas or addressed only one side of an issue.[115] Two groups, the Committee to End Stress and the Young Socialist Alliance, were not officially recognized (and therefore were denied the use of school facilities) because the principal determined that these clubs violated the board policy. The federal district court ruled that the policy impaired the students' protected rights under the first, fifth, and fourteenth amendments, and accordingly held that the groups were entitled to official recognition. The court indicated that school authorities would have to present clear evidence that the clubs would produce a disruption to the educational process in order to deny recognition to selected student organizations.

School personnel should also be cognizant of the United States Supreme Court decision *Healy v. James,* in which college authorities were not allowed to deny recognition to a student political organization merely because they disagreed with the group's philosophy.[116] Justice Powell stated for the Court majority that "denial of official recognition, without justification, to college organizations" abridges students' constitutional right of association.[117] The Court concluded that the proposed student organization did not present a substantial threat of disruption to the educational process, and that school officials did not carry their "heavy burden" of justifying the refusal of recognition, which was in effect "a form of prior restraint." [118] Of course, there are differences between the recognition of groups on college campuses and the recognition of student clubs in high schools. Nonetheless, any prohibition against selected student organizations with open membership should be supported by evidence that the clubs would materially and substantially disrupt the operation of the school or impair the rights of other students.[119] It seems likely that in the future courts will delve more deeply into the justification for restrictions placed on student organizations in public schools.

## SPEAKERS AND ASSEMBLIES

Freedom of association also has been used as the basis for student challenges to bans against particular speakers and assemblies in public schools. Generally, the students have prevailed if they have shown that school officials acted arbitrarily or discriminated against certain groups. Although boards of education have the authority to bar all outside speakers from schools, controversies have arisen when only selected speakers have been afforded access to school forums. Courts have held that school officials cannot discriminate among speakers or censor their ideas. However, speakers can be limited to certain times and places approved by school personnel, and specific speakers can be barred if a disruption to educational activities can be reasonably forecast by their presence.

In an illustrative New Hampshire case, students attacked the actions of school authorities in prohibiting the vice-presidential candidate of the Socialist Workers Party from speaking at the high school, while a number of the "major" candidates were afforded such an opportunity.[120] The federal court held that once a school elects to provide a forum for outside speakers, it must do so in a nondiscriminatory manner and may not censor ideas either directly or by barring certain speakers. The court declared that the right to receive information and ideas is included in first amendment protections.

In an Oregon case, a federal district court also invalidated a school board's order that barred political speakers from the high school. Concluding that the order violated the first amendment, the court stated:

> The board's only apparent reason for issuing the order which suppressed protected speech was to placate angry residents and taxpayers. The first amendment forbids this; neither fear of voter reaction nor personal disagreement with views to be expressed justifies a suppression of free expression, at least in the absence of any reasonable fear of material and substantial interference with the educational process.[121]

Furthermore, the court held that the school board action discriminated against political speakers (because other types of speakers were not banned from the high school) and against teachers of politically oriented subjects (because other teachers were not prohibited from using outside speakers in their classrooms). The court concluded that the board acted unlawfully in permitting individuals with views palatable to the board to speak but refusing the same privilege to individuals with less readily digestible views.[122]

While students' rights to freedom of association and assembly have not generated as much litigation as have their rights to freedom of speech and press, school personnel should be sensitive to potential lawsuits in this area. Any restriction on students' rights to associate, whether pertaining to the formation of student clubs or to the opportunity to hear controversial speakers, must be justified on legitimate educational grounds and must not discriminate against any particular groups.

## CONCLUSION

During the past decade, courts consistently have reiterated that children's first amendment rights must be respected in educational settings. In 1975, the Fourth Circuit Court of Appeals captured the general judicial sentiment in the following statement:

We have both compassion and understanding of the difficulties facing school administrators, but we cannot permit those conditions to suppress the first amendment rights of individual students.[123]

Such personal liberties, however, can be restricted if necessary to ensure the general welfare of the school. Courts have recognized that students' first amendment rights at times must be modified or curtailed by school rules "reasonably designed to adjust those rights to the needs of the school environment." [124] Although the body of law interpreting first amendment rights of students is continually evolving, the following generalizations seem accurately to portray the current posture of the courts.

1. Devotional activities such as Bible reading, prayer, and the observance of holy days in public schools violate students' rights to freedom of religion.
2. Students may be released from public schools to attend religious instruction held off school grounds if state statutes authorize such released time programs.
3. Teachers may explain various religious holidays (as long as one religion is not preferred) and may use seasonal decorations that have incidental religious connotations.
4. Religious documents (e.g., the Bible) and religious music can be included in the public school curriculum as long as the objective is to inform and not to inculcate students.
5. Silent meditation periods are permissible if designed as reflection periods and disassociated from religion.
6. Citizenship values (e.g., honesty, responsibility, self-control) can be taught in public schools from a nonreligious standpoint.
7. Students cannot be compelled to salute the American flag or pledge their allegiance to the flag if they are opposed to such acts on religious or philosophical grounds.
8. While school officials may excuse students from certain secular activities that offend their religious beliefs, secular instruction and materials must not be tailored to the preferences of particular religious sects.
9. School personnel cannot deny students' rights to free speech or symbolic expression unless a material interference with or substantial disruption of the educational process can be reasonably forecast from the exercise of these rights.
10. Expression that agitates ("fighting words"), boycotts, sit-ins, and excessive noise can, under certain circumstances, constitute disruptive expression that justifiably can be curtailed.
11. Any regulation prohibiting a certain form of student expression must be specific, publicized to students and parents, and uniformly applied without discrimination.

12. In most jurisdictions, school authorities can establish regulations pertaining to prior review of student literature, but such rules must specify the procedures for review and the type of material that is prohibited.

13. Distribution of student literature at school can be curtailed if the material is obscene, libelous, or inflammatory, or encourages actions that endanger the health or safety of students.

14. Student literature distribution at school cannot be prohibited simply because the content is controversial, offensive to school personnel, or critical of school policies.

15. Schools are not obligated to support student newspapers, but once such sponsorship is established, arbitrary prior restraints cannot be imposed to control the content.

16. The time, place, and manner of student literature distribution at school can be regulated by reasonable policies to ensure that such distribution does not interfere with school activities.

17. School authorities cannot punish students for the content of literature that is published and distributed off school grounds.

18. School authorities can forbid student membership in secret societies and can punish students for joining such clubs.

19. Selected student organizations with open membership cannot be denied official recognition simply because they espouse unpopular ideas; any denial of recognition must be based on evidence that the organization would impede the educational process.

20. If a school elects to provide a forum for outside speakers, it must do so in a nondiscriminatory manner.

## NOTES

1. West Virginia Bd. of Educ. v. Barnette, 319 U.S. 624, 637 (1943).
2. *See* Cantwell v. Connecticut, 310 U.S. 296 (1940).
3. *See* Committee for Public Educ. and Religious Liberty v. Regan, 100 S. Ct. 840 (1980); Wolman v. Walter, 433 U.S. 229 (1977); Meek v. Pittenger, 421 U.S. 349 (1975); Committee for Public Educ. and Religious Liberty v. Nyquist, 413 U.S. 756 (1973); Lemon v. Kurtzman, 403 U.S. 602 (1971); Board of Educ. of Central School Dist. v. Allen, 392 U.S. 236 (1968); Everson v. Board of Educ., 330 U.S. 1 (1947).
4. *See* Byrne v. Public Funds for Public Schools, 590 F.2d 514 (3d Cir. 1979), *aff'd* 442 U.S. 907 (1979).
5. *See* Americans United for Separation of Church and State v. Porter, 485 F. Supp. 432 (W.D. Mich. 1980).
6. *See* Kentucky State Bd. for Elementary and Secondary Educ. v. Rudasill, 589 S.W.2d 877 (Ky. 1979), *cert. denied*, 100 S. Ct. 2158 (1980).
7. *See* Meltzer v. Board of Public Instruction of Orange County, Florida,

577 F.2d 311 (5th Cir. 1978), *cert. denied,* 439 U.S. 1089 (1979); Florey v. Sioux Falls School Dist. 49-5, 464 F. Supp. 911 (D.S.D. 1979), *aff'd* 619 F.2d 1311 (8th Cir. 1980).

8. *See* Moody v. Cronin, 484 F. Supp. 270 (C.D. Ill. 1979); Davis v. Page, 385 F. Supp. 395 (D.N.H. 1974), *cert. denied,* 49 U.S.L.W. 3351 (November 10, 1980).

9. *See* School Dist. of Abington Township v. Schempp, Murray v. Curlett, 374 U.S. 203 (1963); Engel v. Vitale, 370 U.S. 421 (1962); Collins v. Chandler Unified School Dist., 470 F. Supp. 959 (D. Ariz. 1979). Courts have ruled that teachers can be dismissed for conducting such devotional activities in state-supported schools. *See* Lynch v. Indiana State Univ. Bd. of Trustees, 378 N.E.2d 900 (Ind. App. 1978), in which an Indiana appeals court upheld the dismissal of a professor for reading the Bible at the beginning of his classes.

10. *See* Brandon v. Board of Educ. of Guilderland, 487 F. Supp. 1219 (N.D.N.Y. 1980); Trietley v. Board of Educ. of the City of Buffalo, 409 N.Y.S.2d 912 (App. Div. 1978); Johnson v. Huntington Beach Union High School Dist., 68 Cal. App. 3d 1, 137 Cal. Rptr. 43 (Cal. App. 1977). It should be noted that courts have taken a different view toward student religious clubs meeting on college campuses in state-owned buildings due to the fact that college students are less impressionable and they reside on campus. *See* Chess v. Widmar, 480 F. Supp. 907 (W.D. Mo. 1979), *rev'd* No. 80-1048 (8th Cir., August 4, 1980); Keegan v. University of Delaware, 349 A.2d 14 (Del. Super. 1975).

11. Engel v. Vitale, 370 U.S. 421, 431 (1962).

12. McCollum v. Bd. of Educ., 333 U.S. 203 (1948).

13. Zorach v. Clauson, 343 U.S. 306 (1952).

14. *Id.* at 314–15.

15. Smith v. Smith, 391 F. Supp. 443 (W.D. Va. 1975), *rev'd* 523 F.2d 121 (4th Cir. 1975), *cert. denied,* 423 U.S. 1073 (1976).

16. *See* Lanner v. Wimmer, 463 F. Supp. 867 (D. Utah 1978).

17. *See* School Dist. of Abington Township v. Schempp, Murray v. Curlett, 374 U.S. 203, 225 (1963).

18. *See* Jesse H. Choper, "Religion in the Public Schools: A Proposed Constitutional Standard," *Minnesota Law Review,* Vol. 47, 1963, pp. 377–379.

19. Ind. Code Ann. § 20-10.1-7-11.

20. Gaines v. Anderson, 421 F. Supp. 337 (D. Mass. 1976). It should be noted that while silent meditation periods have been judicially sanctioned, attempts to legislate voluntary prayer periods with student leaders have been invalidated. *See* Kent v. Commissioners of Educ., 402 N.E.2d 1340 (Mass. 1980). The teaching of transcendental meditation in public schools also has been challenged on first amendment grounds. The Third Circuit Court of Appeals ruled that the teaching of transcendental meditation as an elective course in five New Jersey high schools violated the first amendment because the course had a primary effect of advancing religious concepts. *See* Malnak v. Yogi, 592 F.2d 197 (3d Cir. 1979).

21. Wiley v. Franklin, 468 F. Supp. 133 (E.D. Tenn. 1979).

22. Grossberg v. Deusevio, 380 F. Supp. 285 (E.D. Va. 1974). *See also* Weist v. Mount Lebanon School Dist., 320 A.2d 363 (Pa. 1974), *cert. denied*, 419 U.S. 967 (1974).
23. Stone v. Graham, 599 S.W.2d 157 (Ky. 1980), *rev'd* 101 S. Ct. 192 (1980). *See also* Ring v. Grand Fork Public School Dist., 483 F. Supp. 272 (D.N.D. 1980).
24. Florey v. Sioux Falls School Dist. 49-5, 464 F. Supp. 911 (D.S.D. 1979), *aff'd* 619 F.2d 1311 (8th Cir. 1980), *cert. denied*, 49 U.S.L.W. 3351 (November 10, 1980).
25. *Id,* 464 F. Supp. 918.
26. *See* Hernandez v. Hanson, 430 F. Supp. 1154 (D. Neb. 1977); Goodwin v. Cross County School Dist., 394 F. Supp. 417 (E.D. Ark. 1973); Tudor v. Board of Educ., 100 A.2d 857 (N.J. 1953), *cert. denied*, 348 U.S. 816 (1954).
27. Meltzer v. Board of Public Instruction of Orange County, Florida, 577 F.2d 311 (5th Cir. 1978), *cert. denied*, 439 U.S. 1089 (1979). Prior to review of this case by the full appellate court, a three-judge panel had concluded that all three contested provisions violated the first amendment, 548 F.2d 559 (5th Cir. 1977).
28. Epperson v. Arkansas, 393 U.S. 97, 107 (1968), quoting from Joseph Burstyn, Inc. v. Wilson, 343 U.S. 495, 505 (1952).
29. West Virginia Bd. of Educ. v. Barnett, 319 U.S. 624 (1943).
30. *Id.* at 642.
31. *See* Lipp v. Morris, 579 F.2d 834 (3d Cir. 1978); Goetz v. Ansell, 477 F.2d 636 (2d Cir. 1973).
32. Ind. Code Ann. § 20-10.1-4-7.
33. Hardwick v. Board of School Trustees, 54 Cal. App. 696, 205 P. 49 (1921).
34. Mitchell v. McCall, 273 Ala. 604, 143 So. 2d 629 (1962). *See also* Spence v. Bailey, 465 F.2d 797 (6th Cir. 1972) (student excused from mandatory R.O.T.C. course on religious grounds).
35. Moody v. Cronin, 484 F. Supp. 270 (C.D. Ill. 1979).
36. Davis v. Page, 385 F. Supp. 395 (D.N.H. 1974).
37. Epperson v. Arkansas, 393 U.S. 97, 107 (1968).
38. Daniel v. Walters, 515 F.2d 485 (6th Cir. 1975).
39. State of Indiana v. Campbell, No. 5577-0139 (Ind. Super., Marion County, April 14, 1977).
40. *See* Citizens for Parental Rights v. San Mateo County Bd. of Educ., 124 Cal. Rptr. 68 (Cal. App. 1975); Hobolth v. Greenway, 52 Mich. App. 682, 218 N.W.2d 98 (Mich. 1974); Valent v. New Jersey State Bd. of Educ., 114 N.J. Super. 63, 274 A.2d 832 (1971); Medeiros v. Kiyosaki, 478 P.2d 314 (Hawaii 1970).
41. 393 U.S. 503, 511 (1969).
42. *Id.* at 508.
43. *Id.* at 509.
44. 363 F.2d 744 (5th Cir. 1966).
45. *Id.* at 749.
46. 363 F.2d 749 (5th Cir. 1966).

47. 363 F.2d 744, 747-49 (5th Cir. 1966).

48. Guzick v. Drebus, 431 F.2d 594 (1970), *cert. denied*, 401 U.S. 948 (1971).

49. Conflicting opinions have been rendered in cases involving the wearing of insignia that might be offensive to some students. In Melton v. Young, 465 F.2d 1332 (6th Cir. 1972), *cert. denied*, 411 U.S. 951 (1973), and Smith v. St. Tammany Parish School Bd., 448 F.2d 414 (5th Cir. 1971), which involved situations with known racial tensions, courts upheld regulations prohibiting students from wearing confederate flags. However, in Augustus v. School Bd. of Escambia County, 361 F. Supp. 383 (N.D. Fla. 1973), *rev'd* 507 F.2d 152 (5th Cir. 1975), and Banks v. Muncie Community Schools, 433 F.2d 292 (7th Cir. 1970), courts upheld students' rights to wear insignia that might be offensive to a significant portion of the student bodies.

50. *See* Butts v. Dallas Independent School Dist., 306 F. Supp. 488 (N.D. Tex. 1969), *rev'd* 436 F.2d 728 (5th Cir. 1971).

51. Scoville v. Board of Educ. of Joliet, 425 F.2d 10, 14 (7th Cir. 1970). In 1980, a federal district court ruled that the right to free expression entitled a homosexual student to select another male as his escort for the senior prom. Fricke v. Lynch, 491 F. Supp. 381 (D.R.I. 1980).

52. Stacy v. Williams, 306 F. Supp. 963, 972 (N.D. Miss. 1969).

53. *See* Siegel v. Regents of University of California, 308 F. Supp. 832 (N.D. Cal. 1970).

54. *See* Hatter v. Los Angeles City High School Dist., 310 F. Supp. 1309 (C.D. Cal. 1970), *rev'd on other grounds*, 452 F.2d 673 (9th Cir. 1971).

55. *See* Tate v. Board of Educ., 453 F.2d 975 (8th Cir. 1972).

56. *See* Herman v. University of South Carolina, 457 F.2d 902 (4th Cir. 1972); Farrell v. Joel, 437 F.2d 160 (2d Cir. 1971); Gebert v. Hoffman, 336 F. Supp. 694 (E.D. Pa. 1972); Buttny v. Smiley, 281 F. Supp. 280, 286-87 (D. Colo. 1968).

57. *See* McAlpine v. Reese, 309 F. Supp. 136 (E.D. Mich. 1970).

58. Tate v. Board of Educ., 453 F.2d 975 (8th Cir. 1972).

59. *See* Rasche v. Board of Trustees of Univ. of Illinois, 353 F. Supp. 973 (N.D. Ill. 1972).

60. *See* Gebert v. Hoffman, 336 F. Supp. 694 (E.D. Pa. 1972).

61. *Id.*

62. Kovacs v. Cooper, 336 U.S. 77 (1949).

63. Grayned v. City of Rockford, 408 U.S. 104 (1972). *See also* Hill v. Lewis, 323 F. Supp. 55 (E.D.N.C. 1971); McAlpine v. Reese, 309 F. Supp. 136 (E.D. Mich. 1970).

64. Sweezy v. New Hampshire, 354 U.S. 234, 250 (1957). *See* Shelton v. Tucker, 364 U.S. 479, 487 (1960); West Virginia Bd. of Educ. v. Barnette, 319 U.S. 624, 637 (1943). *See also* Chapter 8, for a discussion of curriculum censorship cases in which students have asserted a first amendment right to have access to controversial materials.

65. 393 U.S. 503, 506-07 (1969).

66. *Id.* at 506.

67. Carroll v. President and Commissioners of Princess Anne, 393 U.S. 175,

181 (1968). *See also* New York Times Co. v. United States, 403 U.S. 713 (1971).

68. Fujishima v. Board of Educ., 460 F.2d 1355 (7th Cir. 1972).
69. Bright v. Los Angeles Unified School Dist., 134 Cal. Rptr. 639 (1976).
70. *See* Baughman v. Freienmuth, 478 F.2d 1345, 1348 (4th Cir. 1973); Shanley v. Northeast Independent School Dist., 462 F.2d 960, 969 (5th Cir. 1972); Quarterman v. Byrd, 453 F.2d 54, 57-59 (4th Cir. 1971); Eisner v. Stamford Bd. of Educ., 440 F.2d 803 (2d Cir. 1971).
71. Jacobs v. Board of School Comm'rs, 490 F.2d 601, 604, 609 (7th Cir. 1973), *vacated as moot*, 420 U.S. 128 (1975).
72. *See* Baughman v. Freienmuth, 478 F.2d 1345, 1350 (4th Cir. 1973).
73. Eisner v. Stamford Bd. of Educ., 440 F.2d 803, 805-808 (2d Cir. 1971).
74. Quarterman v. Byrd, 453 F.2d 54 (4th Cir. 1971).
75. Speake v. Grantham, 317 F. Supp. 1253 (S.D. Miss. 1970), *aff'd per curiam*, 440 F.2d 1351 (5th Cir. 1971).
76. Sullivan v. Houston Independent School Dist., 475 F.2d 1071 (5th Cir. 1973).
77. Williams v. Spencer, 622 F.2d 1200 (4th Cir. 1980). *See also* Norton v. Discipline Committee of East Tennessee State University, 419 F.2d 195, 197 (6th Cir. 1969), *cert. denied*, 399 U.S. 906 (1970), in which the appellate court upheld disciplinary action against college students who distributed a publication that encouraged classmates to participate in a demonstration.
78. Chaplinsky v. New Hampshire, 315 U.S. 568, 571-72 (1942).
79. 413 U.S. 15, 24 (1973).
80. Bookcase, Inc. v. Broderick, 18 N.Y.2d 71, 218 N.E.2d 668, 671 (N.Y. 1966).
81. *See* Papish v. Board of Curators, 410 U.S. 667 (1973); Vail v. Board of Educ. of Portsmouth School Dist., 354 F. Supp. 592, 599 (D.N.H. 1973).
82. Liebner v. Sharbaugh, 429 F. Supp. 744 (E.D. Va. 1977).
83. *Id.* at 748.
84. 490 F.2d 601 (7th Cir. 1973), *vacated as moot*, 420 U.S. 128 (1975).
85. *Id.* at 134 (Douglas, J., dissenting).
86. *See* Nitzberg v. Parks, 525 F.2d 378, 381 n. 3 (4th Cir. 1975).
87. *See* Nitzberg v. Parks, *id.*; Scelfo v. Rutgers University, 116 N.J. Super. 403, 282 A.2d 445 (1971); Vought v. Van Buren Public Schools, 306 F. Supp. 1388 (E.D. Mich. 1969).
88. Bright v. Los Angeles Unified School Dist., 134 Cal. Rptr. 639, 646-47 (1976).
89. *See* Sullivan v. Houston Independent School Dist., 307 F. Supp. 1328, 1341 (S.D. Tex. 1969); Norton v. Discipline Committee of East Tennessee State University, 419 F.2d 195, 198 (6th Cir. 1969).
90. Scoville v. Board of Educ. of Joliet, 425 F.2d 10 (7th Cir. 1970).
91. *See* Baughman v. Freienmuth, 478 F.2d 1345 (4th Cir. 1973); Pliscou v. Holtville Unified School Dist., 411 F. Supp. 842 (S.D. Cal. 1976).
92. *See* Shanley v. Northeast Independent School Dist., 462 F.2d 960 (5th Cir. 1972).

93. *See* Nitzberg v. Parks, 525 F.2d 378 (4th Cir. 1975).
94. *See* Gambino v. Fairfax County School Bd., 429 F. Supp. 731 (E.D. Va. 1977); Jacobs v. Board of School Comm'rs, 490 F.2d 601 (7th Cir. 1973); Koppell v. Levine, 347 F. Supp. 456 (E.D.N.Y. 1972).
95. Trachtman v. Anker, 563 F.2d 512 (2d Cir. 1977), *cert. denied*, 435 U.S. 925 (1978).
96. 429 F. Supp. 731 (E.D. Va. 1977), *aff'd* 564 F.2d 157 (4th Cir. 1977).
97. Trachtman v. Anker, 563 F.2d 512, 520 (2d Cir. 1977).
98. Koppell v. Levine, 347 F. Supp. 456 (E.D.N.Y. 1972).
99. *Id.* at 459.
100. Frasca v. Andrews, 463 F. Supp. 1043 (E.D.N.Y. 1979).
101. *See* Trujillo v. Love, 322 F. Supp. 1266, 1270 (D. Colo. 1971).
102. *See* Reineke v. Cobb County School Dist., 484 F. Supp. 1252 (N.D. Ga. 1980); Trujillo, *id.*; Antonelli v. Hammond, 308 F. Supp. 1329 (D. Mass. 1970); Zucker v. Panitz, 299 F. Supp. 102 (S.D.N.Y. 1969).
103. *See* Shanley v. Northeast Independent School Dist., 462 F.2d 960 (5th Cir. 1972); Riseman v. School Comm. of Quincy, 439 F.2d 148 (1st Cir. 1971).
104. *See* Fujishima v. Board of Educ., 460 F.2d 1355 (7th Cir. 1972).
105. *See* Vail v. Board of Educ. of Portsmouth School Dist., 354 F. Supp. 592 (D.N.H. 1973), in which a rule was invalidated that banned all distribution of literature within 200 feet of the school.
106. Thomas v. Board of Educ., Granville Central School Dist., 607 F.2d 1043 (2d Cir. 1979), *cert. denied*, 100 S. Ct. 1034 (1980).
107. Healy v. James, 408 U.S. 169, 181 (1972).
108. In opposition to the prevailing view, a Missouri appeals court upheld students' rights to belong to secret societies in 1922, Wright v. Board of Educ., 246 S.W. 43 (Mo. App. 1922). The court concluded that the St. Louis school board regulation forbidding student membership in secret organizations was not authorized by the state legislature, and that student conduct out of school hours could not be regulated unless it was substantiated that it would clearly interfere with school discipline.
109. Ill. Rev. Stat., ch. 122, § 31-1.
110. Bradford v. Board of Educ., 121 P. 929 (Cal. App. 1912). *See also* Burkitt v. School Dist. No. 1, Multnomah County, 246 P.2d 566 (Ore. 1952).
111. *See* Passel v. Fort Worth Independent School Dist., 453 S.W.2d 888 (Tex. Civ. App. 1970); Holroyd v. Eibling, 116 Ohio App. 440, 188 N.E.2d 797 (1962).
112. Robinson v. Sacramento City Unified School Dist., 53 Cal. Rptr. 781 (Cal. App. 1966).
113. Passel v. Fort Worth Independent School Dist., 453 S.W.2d 888 (Tex. Civ. App. 1970).
114. *See* Edward L. Winn, "Legal Control of Student Extracurricular Activities," *School Law Bulletin*, Vol. VII, No. 3, July 1976, p. 4. *See also* Hughes v. Caddo Parish School Bd., 57 F. Supp. 508 (W.D. La. 1944), *aff'd* 323 U.S. 685 (1945).
115. Dixon v. Beresh, 361 F. Supp. 253 (E.D. Mich. 1973).
116. 408 U.S. 169 (1972).

117. *Id.* at 181.
118. *Id.* at 184.
119. *See* Winn, "Legal Control of Student Extracurricular Activities," p. 5.
120. Vail v. Board of Educ. of Portsmouth, 354 F. Supp. 592, 596 (D.N.H. 1973).
121. Wilson v. Chancellor, 418 F. Supp. 1358, 1364 (D. Ore. 1976). *See* text with note 50, Chapter 3.
122. *Id. See also* National Socialist White People's Party v. Ringers, 473 F.2d 1010 (4th Cir. 1973), in which the appeals court held that a school board could not arbitrarily refuse to rent the high school auditorium to a particular group when the board previously had made the auditorium available for wide public use.
123. Nitzberg v. Parks, 525 F.2d 378, 384 (4th Cir. 1975).
124. Quarterman v. Byrd, 453 F.2d 54, 57-58 (4th Cir. 1971).

# 11

# Student Discipline

One of the most persistent and troublesome problems confronting educators is student misconduct. According to the annual Gallup Poll of public attitudes toward education, the lack of appropriate school discipline has been the primary concern among citizens for eleven of the past twelve years.[1] In this chapter, the various strategies employed to address such disciplinary problems are examined from a legal perspective. The analysis focuses on the development of conduct regulations, the imposition of sanctions for noncompliance, and the procedures required in the administration of pupil punishments.

The law is clear in authorizing the state and its agencies to establish and enforce reasonable conduct codes in order to protect the rights of students and school districts and to ensure school environments conducive to learning. Historically, courts exercised limited review of student disciplinary regulations, and pupils were seldom successful in challenging policies governing their behavior. In 1923, the Arkansas Supreme Court upheld the expulsion of a student who wore talcum powder on her face in violation of a school rule forbidding pupils to wear transparent hosiery, low-necked dresses, face paint, or cosmetics.[2] In another early case, the Michigan Supreme Court endorsed the suspension of a female high school student for smoking and riding in a car with a young man.[3] In these and similar cases, courts were reluctant to interfere with the judgment of school officials because public education was considered to be a privilege bestowed by the state.[4]

While there has been a quantum leap from the posture espoused during the first third of the twentieth century to the active protection of students' rights characterized by cases such as *Tinker v. Des Moines,*[5] the judicial developments of the latter sixties and seventies have not eroded educators' rights or their responsibilities. Reasonable disciplinary regulations, even those infringing on students' protected liberties, have been upheld if justified by a "legitimate state interest." [6] Educators have not only the authority but also the *duty* to maintain discipline in public schools. While rules made at any level cannot conflict with higher authorities (e.g., constitutional and statutory provisions), building administrators and teachers retain a great deal of latitude in establishing and enforcing conduct codes that are necessary for instructional activities to take place. In the subsequent sections of this chapter, educators' prerogatives and students' rights are explored in connection with the following topics: punishment in general, expulsions and suspensions, disciplinary transfers, corporal punishment, academic sanctions, regulation of pupil appearance, and search and seizure.

## PUNISHMENT IN GENERAL

In determining the legality of a given punishment, courts initially assess the validity of the conduct regulation that allegedly has been breached. In 1885, the Wisconsin Supreme Court discussed the criteria by which such conduct rules should be judged.

> The rules and regulations made must be reasonable and proper . . . for the government, good order, and efficiency of the schools, such as will best advance the pupils in their studies, tend to their education and mental improvement, and promote their interest and welfare. But the rules and regulations must relate to these objects.[7]

Disciplinary policies often have been challenged as unconstitutionally vague. Policies prohibiting "improper conduct" and behavior "inimical to the best interests of the school" have been invalidated because they have not specified the nature of the impermissible conduct.[8] Courts have recognized, however, that disciplinary regulations do not have to satisfy the stringent criteria of specificity required in criminal statutes.[9] Less detail has been required in regulations dealing with activities that are clearly disruptive, such as behavior interfering with the right of access to school buildings.[10]

In addition to reviewing the validity of the conduct regulation upon which a specific punishment is based, courts evaluate the nature and extent of the penalty imposed in relation to the gravity of the offense. In deciding whether a given punishment is appropriate, courts also consider the age, sex, mental condition, and past behavior of the student.[11] Punishments such as the denial of privileges, suspension, expulsion, corporal punishment, and detention after school have been judicially sanctioned.

Any of these punishments, however, could be considered unreasonable under a specific set of circumstances. Consequently, courts study each unique factual situation. They do not evaluate the validity of student punishments in the abstract.

Lawsuits challenging disciplinary practices often have focused on the procedures followed in administering punishments, rather than on the substance of disciplinary rules or the nature of the sanctions imposed. Implicit in all judicial declarations regarding school discipline is the notion that severe penalties require more formal hearings, while minor punishments necessitate only minimal due process. Nonetheless, any disciplinary action should be accompanied by some procedure to ensure the rudiments of fundamental fairness and to prevent mistakes in the disciplinary process. The Fifth Circuit Court of Appeals has recognized that "the quantum and quality of procedural due process to be afforded a student varies with the seriousness of the punishment to be imposed." [12]

Although school boards have discretionary authority pertaining to student disciplinary matters, they cannot place students' protected rights at the mercy of the collective bargaining process. In an illustrative case, the Erie, Pennsylvania teachers' organization secured a contract that provided an inadequate procedure for student disciplinary cases.[13] Teachers were authorized to remove any disruptive child from the classroom and send the student to another teacher. The receiving teacher also had the right to reject the disruptive student, and in such instances the child was not to be readmitted to school until a special committee had met and determined what action should be taken. In a consent agreement, this procedure was invalidated as depriving students of their constitutional right to due process.

In addition to prohibiting boards of education from bargaining away students' protected rights, courts have prohibited school authorities from punishing students because of the acts of others, such as their parents. In 1974, for example, the Fifth Circuit Court of Appeals held that two children could not be suspended indefinitely from school simply because their mother struck the assistant principal.[14] In reaching its conclusion, the appellate court noted that a fundamental principle of justice is that personal guilt must be present before an individual can be punished.[15]

The judiciary also has recognized that punishments imposed for student conduct *off school grounds* must be supported by evidence that the student behavior outside of school has a detrimental impact on the well-being of other pupils, teachers, or school activities. In an early case, the Connecticut Supreme Court held that "the misconduct of pupils outside of school hours and school property may be regulated by rules established by the school authorities if such conduct directly relates to and affects the management of the school and its efficiency." [16] Courts have upheld sanctions imposed on students for fighting after school,[17] using insulting language to a teacher on the way home from school,[18] and making an offensive remark about a teacher to a group of students at a shopping center.[19] However, courts have prohibited school authorities from punishing students for misbehavior off school grounds if pupils have not been informed that such conduct would result in sanctions[20] or if the misbehavior has had no direct relationship to the welfare of the school.[21]

School personnel should be careful not to place *unnecessary* constraints on student behavior. In developing disciplinary policies, all possible means of achieving the desired outcomes should be explored, and means that are least restrictive of students' personal freedoms should be selected. Once it is ascertained that a certain conduct regulation is necessary, the rule should be clearly written so that it is not open to multiple interpretations. Each regulation should include the rationale for enacting the rule as well as penalties for infractions. Some commentators have suggested that students should be required to sign a form indicating that they have read the conduct regulations.[22] With such documentation, pupils would be unable to plead ignorance of the rules as a defense for their misconduct.

In general, educators would be wise to adhere to the following guidelines.

1. Any conduct regulation adopted should be necessary in order to carry out the school's educational mission; rules should not be designed merely to satisfy preferences of school board members, administrators, or teachers.
2. The rules should be publicized to students and their parents.
3. The rules should be specific and clearly stated so that students know which behaviors are prohibited.
4. The regulations should not infringe on constitutionally protected rights unless there is an overriding public interest to justify the infringement, such as a threat to the safety of other students.
5. A rule should not be "ex post facto"; it should not be promulgated to prevent a specific activity that school officials know is being planned or has already occurred.
6. The regulations should be consistently enforced and uniformly applied to all students without discrimination.
7. Punishments should be appropriate to the offense, taking into consideration the child's age, sex, mental condition, and past behavior.
8. Some procedural safeguards should accompany the administration of all punishments; the formality of the procedures should be in accord with the severity of the punishment.

In designing and enforcing pupil conduct codes, it is important for school personnel to keep in mind the distinction between students' substantive and procedural rights. If a disciplinary regulation or the administration of punishment violates substantive rights (e.g., freedom of expression), the regulation cannot be enforced nor the punishment imposed. However, if only procedural rights are impaired, the punishment eventually can be administered after the student has been provided a proper hearing.

## EXPULSIONS AND SUSPENSIONS

Expulsions and suspensions are among the disciplinary measures most widely used to control student behavior. Uniformly courts have upheld educators' authority to use expulsions and suspensions as punishments, but due process is required to ensure that students are afforded fair and impartial treatment.

### EXPULSIONS

State laws and/or school board regulations usually are quite specific regarding the grounds for expulsions (i.e., the denial of school attendance for a period in excess of ten days[23]). Such grounds are not limited to occurrences during school hours, but generally include infractions on school property immediately before or after school or at any time the school is being used for a school-related activity. Also, expulsions can result from infractions occurring en route to or from school or during school functions held off school premises. While specific grounds vary from state to state, the following infractions are typically considered legitimate grounds for expulsion, as long as the offense occurs while the student is under the jurisdiction of the school:

1. using or encouraging others to use violence, force, noise, coercion, or comparable conduct that interferes with school purposes;
2. stealing or vandalizing valuable school or private property or repeatedly damaging or stealing school or private property of small value;
3. causing or attempting to cause physical injury to a school employee or student;
4. possessing a weapon;
5. knowingly possessing, using, or transmitting intoxicants of any kind (with the exception of prescriptions from authorized physicians);
6. failing repeatedly to comply with reasonable directives of school personnel; and
7. engaging in criminal activity or other behavior forbidden by the laws of the state.[24]

State statutes specify limitations on the length of student expulsions.

Generally, a student cannot be expelled beyond the end of the current academic year unless the expulsion takes place near the close of the term. A teacher or administrator may initiate expulsion proceedings, but only the school board itself can expel a pupil. Although the details of required procedures must be gleaned from state statutes and school board regulations, courts have held that students facing expulsion from school are guaranteed at least minimum due process under the fourteenth amendment. The judiciary has recognized that the following safeguards are constitutionally required:

1. written notice of the charges, the intention to expel, and the place, time, and circumstances of the hearing, with sufficient time for a defense to be prepared;[25]
2. a full and fair hearing before an impartial adjudicator;[26]
3. the right to legal counsel or some other adult representation;[27]
4. the opportunity to present witnesses or evidence;[28]
5. the opportunity to cross-examine opposing witnesses;[29] and
6. some type of written record demonstrating that the decision was based on the evidence presented at the hearing.[30]

State laws and school board regulations often provide students confronting expulsion with more elaborate procedural safeguards than the constitutional protections noted above. Once such expulsion procedures are established, courts will require that they be followed. In a 1979 Texas case, an expulsion decision was invalidated because the student did not have proper notice that his behavior would result in expulsion and the applicable school policy was not followed in making the expulsion decision.[31] The student was expelled for possession of marijuana in his car (parked off school grounds), but the school regulation did not stipulate that such behavior off school property would constitute grounds for expulsion. Furthermore, the school district policy on expulsion specified that other means of correcting a student's misbehavior had to be employed before expulsion could be recommended. Since there was no evidence that any other disciplinary measures were used, the Texas civil appeals court ordered reinstatement of the student.

## SUSPENSIONS

Suspensions are frequently used to punish students for violating school rules and standards of behavior when the infractions are not of sufficient magnitude to warrant expulsion. Suspensions include the short-term denial of school attendance as well as the denial of participation in regular courses and activities (in-school suspensions). Most legal controversies have focused on out-of-school suspensions, but the same principles of law apply to any disciplinary action that separates the student from the regular instructional program for a short period of time.

In contrast to the detailed statutory provisions pertaining to expulsions, state laws traditionally have been silent concerning procedures that must be followed in suspending students from a class or school. As a result, there has been little consistency in standards from one jurisdiction to the next. Prior to 1975, lower courts differed widely in interpreting whether fourteenth amendment procedural protections applied to student suspensions. One federal district court upheld a thirty-day suspension of a student without a hearing, while another court declared that a student's educational status could not be changed for even two days without procedural due process.[32] Standards across the nation ranged on a continuum between these extremes. Finally, in 1975 the United States Supreme Court provided substantial clarification regarding the constitutional rights of students confronting short-term suspensions.

In this case, *Goss v. Lopez*, the Supreme Court majority held that minimum due process must be provided before a student is suspended for even a short period of time.[33] Recognizing that a student's state-created property right to an education is protected by the fourteenth amendment, the Court ruled that such a right cannot be impaired unless the student is afforded notice of the charges and an opportunity to refute them. The Court stated that in routine circumstances the hearing must precede suspension,while in an emergency it must be held as soon as practicable.

In *Goss* the Supreme Court also emphasized the potentially damaging effects that the disciplinary process can have on a student's reputation and permanent record.

School authorities here suspended appellees from school for periods of up to ten days based on charges of misconduct. If sustained and recorded, those charges could seriously damage the students' standing with their fellow pupils and their teachers as well as interfere with later opportunities for higher education and employment.[34]

The Court majority strongly suggested, but did not make explicit, that its holding applied to *all* short-term suspensions, including those of only one class period. Consequently, many school boards have instituted policies that require informal procedures for every brief suspension and more formal procedures for longer suspensions. In the absence of greater specificity in state statutes or administrative regulations, students facing short-term suspensions have a constitutional right to the following protections:

1. oral or written notification of the nature of the violation and the intended punishment;
2. an opportunity for the pupil to refute the charges before an objective decision maker (such a discussion may immediately follow the alleged rule infraction); and

3. an explanation of the evidence upon which the disciplinarian is relying.[35]

The requirement of an impartial decision maker does not infer that an administrator or teacher who is familiar with the facts cannot serve in this capacity. The decision maker simply must judge the situation fairly and on the basis of valid evidence.

Although the Supreme Court has recognized the possibility of "unusual situations" which would require "something more than the rudimentary procedures" outlined in *Goss*, it has given little guidance as to what these unusual circumstances might be. The only suggestion offered in *Goss* was that a disciplinarian should adopt a more formal procedure in instances involving factual disputes "and arguments about cause and effect." [36] Perhaps repeated individual suspensions that accumulate to more than ten days also would constitute an "unusual situation," necessitating additional procedures. Similarly, suspensions during exam week or involving very serious charges against the student might require more formal due process.[37]

## REMEDIES FOR UNLAWFUL SUSPENSIONS OR EXPULSIONS

There are several remedies available to students who are unlawfully suspended or expelled from public school. Courts have ordered school districts to reinstate students without penalty to grades[38] and have required school records to be expunged of any reference to the illegal suspension or expulsion.[39] Also, in *Wood v. Strickland*, the Supreme Court stated that school officials could be held liable for monetary damages under the Civil Rights Act of 1871[40] if they arbitrarily violated students' protected rights in disciplinary proceedings.[41] The Court declared that ignorance of the law could not be used as a valid defense to shield school officials from liability if they should have known that their actions would impair "clearly established" rights of students. Under the *Wood* proclamation, a showing of malice is not always required in order to prove that the actions of school officials were taken in bad faith.[42] However, a mere mistake in carrying out duties does not render school authorities liable. The Court also recognized in *Wood* that educators are not charged with predicting the future direction of constitutional law.

Other courts have reiterated the potential liability of school officials in connection with student disciplinary proceedings, but to date students have not been as successful as teachers in obtaining actual monetary awards for constitutional violations.[43] Courts have been reluctant to delineate students' "clearly established" rights, the impairment of which would warrant compensatory damages. In an illustrative case involving the exclusion of students from a soccer team because of their hair length, the Third Circuit Court of Appeals dismissed the claim for damages, concluding that the right of students to wear their hair at a chosen length was not "clearly established law," since circuit courts were almost evenly divided on the question and the Supreme Court had not addressed the issue.[44]

In 1978, the Supreme Court placed restrictions on the amount of damages that could be awarded to students in instances involving impairment of due process rights. In *Carey v. Piphus*, the Court declared that students who were suspended without a hearing, but were not otherwise injured, could recover only nominal damages (not to exceed one dollar).[45] This case involved two Chicago students who had been suspended without hearings for violating school regulations. They brought suit against the school district for a total of $8,000 in damages for the alleged abridgment of their constitutional rights. The federal district court ruled that the students' rights to procedural due process had been impaired by the suspensions without hearings, and that the school authorities could not use as a defense the assertion that they were acting in good faith. Yet the court refused to award damages because of the lack of evidence of actual injury to the students. The Seventh Circuit Court of Appeals disagreed, holding that the students were entitled to monetary damages and equitable and declaratory relief. The appeals court concluded that the district court erred in disallowing punitive damages for due process violations and special damages to compensate for the value of the school days missed.[46] The United States Supreme Court, however, reversed the appellate court decision, ruling that substantial damages could be recovered only if the suspensions were unjustified. Accordingly, the case was remanded for the district court to determine whether the students would have been suspended if correct procedures had been followed.

While this decision may appear to have strengthened the position of school boards in exercising discretion in disciplinary proceedings, the Supreme Court indicated that students *might* be entitled to substantial damages if suspensions are proven to be unwarranted. Consequently, the extent to which school officials may be held liable for unlawful suspensions or expulsions remains somewhat unclear.[47] Nonetheless, educators should take every precaution to afford fair and impartial treatment to students. School personnel would be wise to provide at least an informal hearing if in doubt as to whether a particular situation necessitates due process. Liability never results from the provision of too much due process, whereas punitive damages possibly could be assessed in situations involving inadequate procedures that result in unjustified suspensions or expulsions.

Although constitutional and statutory due process requirements do not mandate that a specific procedure be adhered to in every situation, courts will carefully study the record to ensure that any procedural deficiencies do not impede the student's efforts to present a full defense.[48] School personnel, however, should not feel that their authority to discipline students has been curtailed by the judiciary. As noted in *Goss*, courts "have imposed requirements which are, if anything, less than a fair-minded principal would impose upon himself to avoid unfair suspensions." [49]

## DISCIPLINARY TRANSFERS

Closely related to suspensions are involuntary student transfers for disciplinary reasons. Legal challenges to the use of disciplinary transfers have focused primarily on the adequacy of the procedures followed. Recognizing that students do not have an inherent right to attend a given school, courts nonetheless have held that pupils facing involuntary reassignment are entitled to a hearing if such transfers are occasioned by alleged misbehavior.

For example, a New Jersey superior court ruled that a hearing was required before a pupil could be relegated to home instruction because of misconduct occurring off school premises after school hours. [50] The court noted that school officials had the authority to suspend the student, and to assign him to homebound instruction, if it were determined at a proper hearing that he was dangerous to himself or others. The court declared, however, that the student could not be denied the right to attend school without first being given an opportunity to present a full defense regarding the incident precipitating the disciplinary action. Similarly, a New York court held that a pupil could not be assigned to homebound instruction for disruptive behavior and truancy without procedural due process. [51] The court rejected the assertion that the student was merely being afforded alternative education, and equated the assignment to homebound instruction with a suspension from school.

Courts also have held that disciplinary transfers to special schools or programs necessitate some type of procedural safeguards to ensure that the students are not being relegated to inferior programs. The judiciary has required due process prior to reassigning a student to a school for habitual truants or to a program for pupils with behavior problems. [52] Transfer policies allowing the receiving program or school to refuse to admit the child also have been disallowed. [53]

In 1977, a Pennsylvania federal district court ruled that "lateral transfers" for disciplinary reasons affected personal interests of sufficient magnitude to require due process procedures. [54] Even though such transfers involved comparable schools, the court reasoned that a disciplinary transfer carried with it a stigma, and thus implicated a protected liberty right. Noting that the transfer of a pupil "during a school year from a familiar school to a strange and possibly more distant school would be a terrifying experience for many children of normal sensibilities," the court concluded that such transfers were more drastic punishments than suspensions, and thus necessitated due process. [55] As to the nature of the procedures required, the court held that the student and parents must be given notice of the proposed transfer and that a prompt informal hearing before the school principal must be provided. The court stipulated that if parents were still dissatisfied with the arrangement after the informal meeting, they had to be given the opportunity to contest the transfer recommendation at a more formal hearing, with the option of being represented by legal counsel.

## CORPORAL PUNISHMENT

Corporal punishment is defined as chastisement inflicted on the body in order to modify behavior. Corporal punishment in American public schools has evoked litigation for several decades, and historically it has been the most frequently challenged type of student punishment. Courts generally have assumed that teachers acted reasonably in using corporal punishment and have placed the burden on the aggrieved students to prove otherwise. In evaluating the reasonableness of a teacher's actions in a given situation, courts have assessed the child's age, maturity, and past behavior; the nature of the offense; the instrument used; whether there was evidence of any lasting harm to the child; and the motivation of the person inflicting the punishment.[56] Corporal punishment accompanied by malice or anger has been deemed unlawful.[57]

### FEDERAL CONSTITUTIONAL ISSUES

Although there had been much activity in lower courts, the United States Supreme Court repeatedly declined to address the legality of corporal punishment under the Federal Constitution until 1975. In *Baker v. Owen*, the high court affirmed a ruling in which a North Carolina federal court sanctioned a teacher's use of corporal punishment over parental objections.[58] The federal district court concluded that the use of reasonable corporal punishment did not constitute "cruel and unusual punishment" under the eighth amendment, and that parental consent was not necessary before using this disciplinary technique. However, the North Carolina court did stipulate that the following procedural safeguards must accompany the administration of corporal punishment:

1. Students must be informed as to what behaviors will occasion a spanking.
2. School officials must try other disciplinary measures before resorting to corporal punishment.
3. The use of corporal punishment must be witnessed by another staff member.

4. Written reasons for the punishment must be provided to parents upon request.

Since the United States Supreme Court affirmed the district court decision in *Baker* without delivering a written opinion, the high court left some ambiguity as to its stance on the issue until two years later, when it again reviewed a case pertaining to corporal punishment. In *Ingraham v. Wright* the Supreme Court majority stated that the use of corporal punishment in schools does not violate the eighth amendment, nor does it violate fourteenth amendment due process guarantees.[59] In essence, the Court majority concluded that cases dealing with corporal punishment should be handled by state courts under provisions of state laws, since no federal constitutional issues are involved. The majority distinguished corporal punishment from a suspension by noting that the denial of school attendance is a more severe penalty, and thus necessitates procedural requisites. Furthermore, the majority reasoned that the purpose of corporal punishment would be diluted if elaborate procedures had to be followed prior to using this disciplinary measure. The Court emphasized that state remedies are available, such as suits in assault and battery, if students are excessively or arbitrarily punished by school personnel. Hence, the Court majority concluded that the procedures outlined by the federal court in *Baker v. Owen*, although desirable, are not required under the Federal Constitution.

## STATE LAWS AND SCHOOL BOARD POLICIES

While the Supreme Court has announced that the administration of corporal punishment in public schools does not raise any issues of constitutional magnitude, the use of such punishment may conflict with state statutes or local administrative regulations. Some states prohibit corporal punishment by law,[60] and many school boards have regulations that place explicit conditions on the use of this form of discipline. In contrast, a few states, such as Virginia, by law empower school personnel to use corporal punishment. Local school boards cannot prohibit corporal punishment if a state law specifically authorizes educators to use this disciplinary technique.[61] In states without statutory language to the contrary, corporal punishment is permissible, but local boards may develop policies restricting or banning its use.

Teachers can be discharged for violating state laws or board policies regulating corporal punishment. Several courts have upheld dismissals based on insubordination for failure to comply with reasonable school board requirements in administering corporal punishment.[62] In a typical case, a New York teacher was dismissed because he violated board policy by using corporal punishment after having been warned repeatedly to cease.[63] Teachers also have been dismissed under the statutory cause of "cruelty" for improper use of physical force with students. In Illinois, a tenured teacher was dismissed on this ground for using a cattle prod in punishing students.[64] A Pennsylvania teacher was dismissed for "cruelty" because she threw a student against the blackboard and then pulled him upright by his hair.[65]

A California case involving the use of corporal punishment is illustrative of the relationship between state law and school board policies in governing the administration of student punishment.[66] An amendment to the California Education Code permitted the use of corporal punishment, but stipulated that it could not be administered without prior written approval of the pupil's parent or guardian. Furthermore, boards of education were required to inform parents that corporal punishment would not be used without their consent. Pursuant to the amendment, school officials in a district mailed letters to parents of children enrolled in four fundamental schools, requesting that they grant written permission for school personnel to use corporal punishment with their children or accept a transfer of their children to schools without an emphasis on strict discipline. Some parents refused to sign the permission forms and challenged the board's action as creating an unlawful prerequisite to enrolling their children in the fundamental schools. The California appeals court upheld the parents, noting that the school district acted beyond its authority by setting additional terms that conflicted with state statutory guarantees. The court ruled that the state law was clear in stipulating that corporal punishment could not be applied to a student in any school without written parental consent. Accordingly, the court held that the school district was obligated to operate its fundamental schools within the ambit of the law. The legal principle enunciated in this case can be applied to other jurisdictions as well; school boards have discretion in establishing policies regulating the use of corporal punishment, but all such policies must be consistent with state laws.

In the absence of statutory or board restrictions, there are other legal means available to challenge the use of unreasonable corporal punishment in public schools. Teachers can be charged with criminal assault and battery which might result in the imposition of a fine and/or imprisonment. Civil assault and battery suits for monetary damages also can be initiated against school personnel. For example, a Louisiana appeals court awarded a student $1,000 for pain, suffering, and humiliation associated with an excessive and unreasonable whipping administered by a teacher.[67]

Educators should use caution in administering corporal punishment since its improper use can result in dismissal, monetary damages, and even imprisonment.[68] Corporal punishment should never be administered with malice, and the use of excessive force should be avoided. Teachers would be wise to keep a record of incidents involving corporal punishment and to adhere to the minimum procedures outlined by the federal court in

*Baker v. Owen*[69] as legal safeguards in the event that their actions are challenged. Moreover, teachers should become familiar with relevant state laws and school board policies before attempting to use corporal punishment in their classrooms.

## ACADEMIC SANCTIONS

It is indisputable that school authorities have the right to use academic sanctions for poor academic performance. Consistently, courts have been reluctant to substitute their judgment for that of educators in assessing students' academic accomplishments. Failing grades, denial of credit, academic probation, retention, and expulsion from particular programs have been upheld as legitimate means of dealing with poor academic performance.[70] In 1965, the Vermont Federal District Court stated:

> In matters of scholarship, the school authorities are uniquely qualified by training and experience to judge the qualifications of a student, and efficiency of instruction depends in no small degree upon the school faculty's freedom from interference from other noneducational tribunals. It is only when the school authorities abuse this discretion that a court may interfere with their decision . . . .[71]

While courts usually have granted broad discretionary powers to school personnel in establishing academic standards,[72] there has been less agreement regarding the use of grade reductions or academic sanctions as punishments for student misbehavior and/or absences. More complex legal issues are raised in connection with the use of academic penalties for nonacademic reasons.

Generally, courts have ruled that academic course credit or high school diplomas cannot be withheld solely for disciplinary reasons. As early as 1921, the Supreme Court of Iowa held that students who had completed all academic requirements had the right to receive a high school diploma even though they refused to wear the graduation caps during the ceremony.[73] The court ruled that the school board was obligated to issue a diploma to a pupil who had satisfactorily completed the prescribed course of study and who was otherwise qualified to graduate from high school.[74]

Courts have issued conflicting decisions regarding the legality of denying a student the right to participate in graduation ceremonies as a disciplinary measure. A New York appeals court held that a student could not be denied such participation on disciplinary grounds,[75] whereas a North Carolina federal district court held that a student could be denied the privilege of participating in the graduation ceremony as a penalty for misconduct.[76] In the latter case, the federal court concluded that the student was not deprived of any property right, since he did receive his high school diploma even though he was not allowed to take part in the ceremony.

Recently, many school boards have begun using academic sanctions for student absenteeism, and some of these practices have generated legal challenges. Two Illinois appeals courts have rendered conflicting opinions on the legality of lowering pupils' grades for truancy. In a 1976 case, a student claimed that protected rights were impaired by a school regulation stipulating that grades would be lowered one letter grade per class for an unexcused absence.[77] In defending the rule, school officials asserted that it was the most appropriate punishment for the serious problem of truancy. It was also argued that students could not perform satisfactorily in their classwork if they were absent, as grades reflected class participation in addition to other standards of performance. The appeals court was not persuaded by the student's argument that grades should reflect only scholastic achievement, and therefore concluded that the regulation was reasonable.

> We do not find the reduction in plaintiff's grades by one letter grade for a period of one quarter of the year in three subjects in consequence of two days of truancy to be so harsh as to deprive him of substantive due process.[78]

In contrast, two years later an Illinois appeals court invalidated a school board's attempt to impose academic sanctions for truancy. The plaintiff student's grades were reduced in three classes because of an unexcused absence, even though the pupil brought a written explanation from her mother the following day.[79] The court ruled that such arbitrary grade reduction penalties were not related to valid discipline objectives. Noting the importance of grades to future educational and employment opportunities, the court stated that a school board has the authority to enact disciplinary regulations but does not have the power to use academic sanctions for these purposes.

In an earlier decision, a Kentucky appeals court voided a regulation whereby grades were reduced because of unexcused absences resulting from student suspensions.[80] The school board policy stated that work missed because of unexcused absences could not be made up, and that five points would be deducted for every unexcused absence from each class during the grading period. The court held that the use of suspensions or expulsions for misconduct was permissible, but the lowering of grades as a punitive measure was not.

In 1978, a Colorado appeals court also addressed the legality of imposing academic sanctions for absenteeism.[81] The contested school board policy stipulated that any student who missed more than seven days during a semester would not receive academic credit for the courses taken.

Under the regulation, it was irrelevant whether the absences were because of illness, family problems, or any other reasons. Two students, who were denied academic credit because of the accumulation of more than seven absences in a semester, filed suit challenging the policy as inconsistent with state statutory provisions. The court invalidated the regulation, holding that the school board had exceeded its authority in enacting such a policy. The court concluded that days missed because of suspensions and expulsions, as well as excused absences, could not be used as a basis for reducing grades.

The use of academic penalties as punishment for student conduct unrelated to academic performance remains open to challenge on several constitutional grounds. Such practices also may be vulnerable under provisions of the Family Educational Rights and Privacy Act, which guarantee parents the right to challenge inaccurate or misleading information in student records.[82] Nonetheless, the use of grade reductions as sanctions for truancy and student misconduct is prevalent at the current time. Even if the Supreme Court should finally declare that grades need *not* reflect only academic performance, any regulation stipulating that grades will be lowered for nonacademic reasons should be reasonable and related to a legitimate school purpose. Furthermore, the rules should be made known to all students through the school's official student handbook or some similar means.[83]

## REGULATION OF STUDENT APPEARANCE

Fads and fashions in hairstyles and clothing regularly have evoked litigation as educators have attempted to exert some control over pupil appearance. Courts have been called upon to balance students' interests in selecting their attire and hair length against school authorities' interests in preventing disruptions to the school environment.

### PUPIL HAIRSTYLE

Judicial action during the late 1960s and early 1970s focused primarily on school regulations governing the length of male students' hair. The United States Supreme Court consistently has refused to enter the student haircut controversy,[84] and federal circuit courts of appeal have reached different conclusions in assessing the legality of such regulations.

In the fifth, sixth, ninth, and tenth circuits, appellate courts have upheld grooming policies pertaining to pupil hairstyle.[85] In sanctioning a hair length restriction, the Fifth Circuit Court of Appeals concluded from testimony that the wearing of long hair by male students created some disturbances during school hours. Therefore, the requirement that hair be trimmed as a prerequisite to enrollment was not considered arbitrary or unreasonable.[86] The court concluded that the compelling state interest in maintaining an effective and efficient school system justified the interference with students' freedom to govern their appearance. Several years later, the same court announced that within the "plain meaning" of the Federal Constitution there is no personal right to wear hair at any chosen length in public schools.[87] Relying on the fifth circuit precedent, in 1978 a Florida appeals court upheld the suspension of a male student because he refused to conform to the school board policy requiring students to be clean shaven.[88] Concluding that no fundamental freedom was implicated, the court held that the school policy must simply be reasonably related to the accomplishment of a permissible objective.

In contrast, the first, fourth, seventh, and eighth circuit courts of appeal have declared that hair length regulations impair students' constitutional rights. These courts have based their conclusions on the first amendment freedom of symbolic expression, the fourteenth amendment right to personal liberty, or the right to privacy included in the ninth amendment "unenumerated rights." [89] For example, in 1969, the Seventh Circuit Court of Appeals ruled that school personnel failed to produce evidence of an overriding interest that would justify impairing students' rights to select their hairstyle, which "is an ingredient of personal freedom protected by the United States Constitution." [90] It was not established that any distraction occurred as a result of male students wearing long hair, or that academic performance of male students with long hair was inferior to that of their short-haired peers. The following year, the First Circuit Court of Appeals held that a male student's right to wear shoulder-length hair was a protected liberty under the fourteenth amendment. The court stated:

> We do not believe that mere unattractiveness in the eyes of some parents, teachers or students, short of uncleanliness, can justify the proscription. Nor . . . does such compelled conformity to conventional standards of appearance seem a justifiable part of the educational process.[91]

In situations where school officials have offered valid health or safety reasons for grooming regulations, usually the policies have been upheld. In an illustrative case, the Third Circuit Court of Appeals concluded that a school board acted properly in requiring a student to cut his hair because the student's long, unclean hair was a health hazard in the school cafeteria.[92] Similarly, regulations requiring hair nets, shower caps, and other hair restraints designed to protect students from injury or to promote sanitation have been judicially upheld, as long as such regulations have been narrowly drawn.[93] Opposing decisions have been rendered regarding the issue of whether hair length restrictions are appropriate for athletic team members as necessary safety precautions.[94] It also is unclear whether school authorities can place hairstyle restrictions on members of the school band.[95] However, a federal court in Ohio noted that long-haired male students could not be denied band participation if long-haired female students were not excluded.[96]

In a Maine case, a federal district court concluded that school authorities had the right to regulate student appearance if hairstyle or other unusual appearance interfered with the rights of others.[97] Accordingly, a vocational school's regulation barring beards and long hair on students was upheld as being necessary in order to create a positive image for potential employers visiting the school for recruitment purposes. The court reasoned that the legitimate goal of enhancing job opportunities for graduates justified the restrictions placed on student appearance.

A controversial issue has been whether different hair length restrictions can be applied to male and female students. Until 1979 many school districts assumed that Title IX of the Education Amendments of 1972 (prohibiting sex discrimination in educational programs receiving federal funds) did not apply to differential standards in grooming codes. In November 1979, however, it was announced that the Office of Civil Rights would enforce Title IX regulations barring sex discrimination in grooming codes.[98] Thus, it would appear that school districts must justify the necessity for any restrictions on student appearance that are applied only to one sex.

## PUPIL ATTIRE

Although hairstyle continues to elicit some litigation, generally the issue of public school students' hair length has subsided as a major educational concern. Undoubtedly, other fads pertaining to student grooming will generate legal challenges as students continue to assert a right to govern their own appearance. Possibly, cases involving pupil attire (or lack thereof) will replace the haircut controversies during the next decade. Some courts have concluded that the decision to wear clothes of one's own choosing is, like the hairstyle decision, a constitutional right guaranteed by the fourteenth amendment.[99] Courts have invalidated school rules prohibiting female students from wearing slacks, prohibiting tie-dyed clothing, and requiring male students to wear socks.[100]

The legality of school regulations forbidding students to wear blue jeans has generated conflicting court rulings. In a New Hampshire case, the federal district court held that such a regulation impaired students' rights under the fourteenth amendment.[101] The court concluded that school officials did not present a legitimate educational rationale for interfering with the students' freedom to select their clothing as long as the attire was neat and clean. In contrast, the Supreme Court of Kentucky ruled that a dress code provision forbidding female students from wearing blue jeans did not impair any constitutional guarantees.[102]

In some jurisdictions, courts have distinguished dress codes from hair regulations because clothes, unlike hair length, can be changed after school. Even in situations where students' rights to govern their appearance have been upheld, the judiciary has noted that attire can be regulated if immodest and/or disruptive. The federal district court in New Hampshire elaborated on the school's authority to exclude students who are unsanitary or scantily clad.

> Good hygiene and the health of the other pupils require that dirty clothes of any nature, whether they be dress clothes or dungarees, should be prohibited. Nor does the Court see anything unconstitutional in a school board prohibiting scantily clad students because it is obvious that the lack of proper covering, particularly with female students, might tend to distract other pupils and be disruptive of the educational process and school discipline.[103]

Although circuit appellate courts differ in their interpretations of constitutional protections regarding grooming regulations, school officials would be wise to ensure that there is an overriding state interest before instituting a restrictive grooming or dress code. Generally, educators should adhere to the *Tinker* guideline in designing regulations pertaining to student appearance: If specific hairstyles or attire can be related to a disruption of the educational process, then restrictions will be upheld by courts. Also, policies designed to protect the health and safety of students usually will be endorsed.

## SEARCH AND SEIZURE

Search and seizure cases involving public schools have increased in recent years, and the majority of these cases have resulted from the confiscation of some type of drugs. Students have asserted that warrantless searches conducted by school officials impair their rights guaranteed by the fourth amendment to the Federal Constitution. This amendment protects individuals against arbitrary searches by requiring state agents to obtain a warrant based on probable cause prior to conducting a search.[104] Probable cause is legally defined as reasonable grounds of suspicion, supported by sufficient evidence, to warrant a cautious person to believe that the individual is guilty of the offense charged.[105] In the school context, most legal challenges have arisen when school authorities have submitted the fruits of warrantless searches to the police for use as evidence against students in juvenile or criminal proceedings.

Since fourth amendment protections apply only to searches conducted by agents of the state, a fundamental question in education cases is whether school authorities function as private individuals or as state officers. Unfortunately, courts have not spoken in unison on this issue. Some courts have concluded that school personnel are private persons for fourth amendment purposes and, therefore, authorized to conduct warrantless searches in schools.[106] A California appeals court declared in 1969 that school authorities conducting searches on school property are not acting as government officials, and consequently the fourth amendment is not applicable.[107] In 1974, a Pennsylvania court similarly ruled that school authorities are private citizens and thus not constrained by fourth amendment limitations pertaining to search and seizure.[108]

Other courts have considered school personnel to be state agents, but have ruled that the doctrine of *in loco parentis* (in place of parent) relaxes fourth amendment restrictions. A Delaware court, while rejecting the assertion that school administrators were private citizens, held that their *in loco parentis* status was nonetheless controlling in justifying a warrantless search.[109] Similarly, the Supreme Court of Georgia noted that school officials were government officers "subject to some fourth amendment limitations," but ruled that school administrators must be empowered to make and enforce reasonable school disciplinary rules.[110] The court concluded that secondary school students do not have the maturity of adult citizens and thus are subject to the control of school authorities in situations involving reasonable searches. In 1979, a Florida appeals court held that the doctrine of *in loco parentis* justifies and requires relaxation of constitutional limitations relating to search and seizure.[111] These courts have reasoned that the fourth amendment does not prohibit school personnel from conducting a warrantless search as long as it is based on reasonable suspicion that contraband disruptive to the school is hidden on the person or private property. Furthermore, the contraband uncovered has been considered admissible evidence in judicial proceedings against the students.

In contrast to the preceding cases, some courts have held that school authorities are governmental agents under the fourth amendment, and that the *in loco parentis* doctrine cannot be used to justify warrantless school searches. For example, the Supreme Court of Louisiana declared that school officials are state agents subject to fourth amendment limitations in searching students.[112] A federal district court in Illinois also concluded that "the *in loco parentis* authority of a school official cannot transcend constitutional rights." [113]

Basically, the following options have been available to courts in applying the fourth amendment to school searches: (1) the fourth amendment does not apply because school officials function as private citizens; (2) the fourth amendment does apply, but the doctrine of *in loco parentis* lowers the standard in determining the reasonableness of a search; or (3) the fourth amendment applies, and probable cause is required before conducting a search.[114] While traditionally courts followed the first option in reviewing school search and seizure cases, recent decisions have favored the second approach, and a few courts have adopted the logic that school officials must be held to the same fourth amendment standards as police officials.

## LOCKER SEARCHES

Courts generally have made a distinction between locker searches and personal searches of students, and have exempted reasonable locker searches from fourth amendment protections. Among the unique characteristics affecting locker searches is the fact that lockers are school property and are not owned by students. Courts have held that school authorities have the right to inspect lockers to protect the general welfare of the student body.[115] The judiciary, however, has not given school personnel blanket approval to make indiscriminate locker searches; any search must be based on reasonable suspicion that contraband disruptive to the educational process will be uncovered. If the purpose of the search is to gather criminal evidence, a search warrant is required.[116]

In 1969, the Kansas Supreme Court maintained that it is a proper function of school personnel to inspect the lockers under their control and to prevent the use of lockers in illicit ways or for illegal purposes. The court concluded that the right of inspection is inherent in the power vested in school authorities, and that it must be retained and exercised to ensure appropriate management of schools.[117] Previously, the New York Court of Appeals, noting that students were fully aware that school officials possessed the combinations of their lockers, stated that students had exclusive possession of their lockers against other students but not against teachers and administrators.[118] Furthermore, the court reasoned that not only did school personnel have a right to inspect lockers, but this right became a *duty* when suspicion arose that something potentially disruptive to the school was secreted in a locker.

## PERSONAL SEARCHES

The law is not as clear on personal searches of students by teachers and administrators as it is on locker searches. Until the Supreme Court delivers an opinion in this area, diversity among lower court interpretations seems likely to persist. Courts that have upheld warrantless personal searches in schools have not consistently defined what constitutes a "reasonable" search. In making such a determination of "reasonableness," courts have assessed the student's age, prior behavior, and school record; the prevalence and seriousness of the problem in the school to which the search is directed; the necessity to make the search without delay; and the probative value and reliability of the information used as a justification for the search.[119]

It should be emphasized that students may waive any entitlement to fourth amendment protection by volunteering material to school officials. Thus, in some instances a search can be avoided if school authorities ask students to submit the secreted contraband and the pupils comply. In an illustrative Louisiana case, an assistant principal received information that

nt was in possession of marijuana and accordingly escorted the
his office for questioning.[120] The student denied having drugs and
refused to be searched. The assistant principal informed the student that
if he did not turn over the contraband, the sheriff's office would be contacted to secure a warrant and conduct the search. The student then turned
over a bag of marijuana to the school officials and was subsequently
adjudicated a delinquent for possession of drugs in violation of state law.
The student asserted that his detention in the assistant principal's office
constituted an arrest and that the seizure of the marijuana was illegal. The
Louisiana appeals court disagreed. Although noting that school authorities
were subject to fourth amendment restrictions, the court concluded that no
search was actually conducted in this situation. The court reasoned that
since the student presented the contraband without undue coercion, a
search warrant was not necessary.

Some courts have upheld warrantless personal searches conducted by
school officials if there are reasonable grounds to believe that such action
is necessary to maintain school order and discipline. In 1977, the Washington Supreme Court espoused this rationale in upholding a personal
search of two students by the high school principal and vice-principal, who
were acting on information from the chief of police.[121] Amphetamines were
found on the students, the police were called, and both students were
placed under arrest. Subsequently, the police discovered that one of the
students had two bags of marijuana. The court rejected the assertion that
the school searches were invalid because they were instigated by police
officials, reasoning that school authorities have the right to follow up a
"tip" from any informant, including the police. The court concluded that
the search without delay was necessary to maintain school order and was
not initiated with the intent to gather evidence for criminal conviction of
the students.

The following year, a New York court also upheld the submission of
illegal contraband uncovered in a warrantless school search as evidence
against a student.[122] A school official had been informed that the pupil had
a revolver and accordingly questioned the student. When the student refused to be searched and put his hand in his pocket, he was grabbed and
his hand was slowly withdrawn by the school official. The pupil was holding
an operable pistol which was confiscated and turned over to the police.
The court ruled that the school official acted appropriately upon reasonable suspicion, and that the fruits of the search could be submitted as
evidence in judicial proceedings.

In contrast, other courts have ruled in favor of plaintiff students who
have challenged the reasonableness of personal searches. In a Louisiana
case, a physical education instructor searched the wallet of one of his
pupils because of the student's suspicious actions.[123] The wallet had been
left in the instructor's office for safe keeping while the student participated
in a class. When the wallet was opened, the instructor found a plastic bag

that contained a leafy substance. Believing the substance to be
the instructor called the school drug coordinator and the prin
concurred with the assessment. The material was turned over
authorities, and subsequently the student was convicted of pos.
marijuana. The student asserted that the conviction was based c  ... unlawful search. The Louisiana Supreme Court agreed, reasoning that public
school principals and instructors are government agents within the purview
of the fourth amendment's prohibition against unreasonable searches and
seizures. The court concluded that a search without a warrant is constitutional only if it falls within one of the specifically established and well-
delineated exceptions, which do not include a search of a student's personal effects on school grounds by school personnel. Therefore, the court
held that the fruits of such a search could not be submitted as evidence
against the student.[124] The United States Supreme Court declined to review
this case, thus leaving the Louisiana Supreme Court decision intact.

In a 1976 Illinois case, students challenged a search in which nothing
unlawful was discovered.[125] The defendant school principal had received a
telephone call which led him to suspect that the thirteen-year-old plaintiff
and two other students possessed illegal drugs. The principal was then
advised by the superintendent to call the police, which he did. When the
police arrived, each of the students was searched by the school nurse and
the school psychologist, and no drugs were found. Subsequently, suit was
brought against three school officials and two policemen, alleging that in
the course of the search the students' civil rights were violated. The court
held that the search conducted by school officials who were in contact with
the police was not justified by an overriding state interest in maintaining
the order, discipline, safety, and education of the students in the school.
The court noted that school officials are generally considered to be private
persons in the absence of police participation. However, the court emphasized that the existence of police involvement prior to the search changed
the standard for assessing the reasonableness of the conduct. In such instances, the court concluded that there must be probable cause for arrest
in order to justify a search.[126]

The next year, a search of an entire elementary class in New York
was contested as violating the children's protected rights under the Civil
Rights Act of 1871.[127] The search was initiated because of the allegation
that three dollars had been stolen from one of the children in the classroom. All children were forced to strip down to their undergarments, but
the missing money was never found. The federal district court concluded
that the guarantees of the fourth amendment did apply in this situation,
and that school authorities could be liable under the Civil Rights Act of
1871 if it was established that the search violated the students' constitutional rights. However, the court noted that a showing of probable cause
was not necessary in order to uphold the search as reasonable. The court
stated that in determining the reasonableness of the search, it must "weigh

the danger of the conduct, evidence of which is sought, against the students' right of privacy and the need to protect them from the humiliation and psychological harms associated with such a search." [128] Emphasizing that it was aware of the dilemma confronting school personnel, the court nonetheless concluded that the search was unreasonable in view of the students' age, the extent of the search, and the "relatively slight danger" of the conduct involved.[129] Although finding a violation of constitutional rights, the court did not award compensatory or punitive damages. Relying on *Wood v. Strickland*,[130] the court stated that the plantiffs failed to substantiate that the school officials' actions were not taken in good faith.

Cases initiated by students who are subjected to searches in which nothing unlawful is uncovered may proliferate during the next decade. Whereas traditionally students were not motivated to bring a suit unless attempting to suppress the use of certain evidence against them in judicial proceedings, now students and their parents are more sophisticated in employing civil rights statutes to challenge abridgments of their protected rights.

In an illustrative New York case, a female high school student sought and received monetary damages in connection with an unreasonable search.[131] A teacher found the student alone in a room during a fire drill and searched her book bag based on mere suspicion that the student "might" have stolen some unidentified object. Due to the student's subsequent suspicious actions she was taken to the dean's office, where she was forced to undress and submit to a search conducted by female security guards. A New York federal district judge ruled that the school personnel did not have sufficient grounds to justify the search, and therefore were liable for impairing the student's protected rights to privacy and to remain free from unreasonable searches. Accordingly, the student was awarded $7,500 in damages to compensate for the emotional trauma associated with the incident.

In 1979, the Second Circuit Court of Appeals affirmed the lower court decision and declared that strip searches must be based on probable cause that a crime has been committed.[132] For the first time a federal appellate court made a distinction between standards applicable to strip searches and those applicable to body searches. Noting that reasonable suspicion of a crime could justify searches of students' pockets and outer garments, the court concluded that strip searches must be based on the more stringent fourth amendment standard.

As issue that has received recent publicity is whether drug-detecting dogs can be used to assist school officials in establishing reasonable grounds for searching students. In 1980, the Seventh Circuit Court of Appeals affirmed an Indiana federal district court ruling that a school-wide inspection of classrooms, conducted with the assistance of the local police department and volunteer canine units trained in drug detection, did not violate any protected rights of students.[133] The lower court noted the severity of the drug problem in the schools involved and concluded that the inspection was justified in order to maintain a safe, orderly, and healthy educational environment. Although police officials were present, the court emphasized that an agreement had been made that no arrests would occur as a result of finding drugs on any student. Since a search was not performed until a dog gave an "alert," the court held that a warrant was not required by the mere presence of a drug-detecting dog and its trainer for five minutes in each classroom. The court further concluded that the dog "alerts" established reasonable cause to believe that drugs were secreted, and therefore provided legitimate grounds for searches of students' outer garments.

However, a nude search, based on a continued dog alert after a student had emptied her pockets, was held to violate fourth amendment rights. Thus, the Seventh Circuit Court of Appeals joined the Second Circuit Appellate Court in requiring greater justification for strip searches. While not specifically stating that probable cause would be necessary before conducting a nude search, such "an intrusion into an individual's basic justifiable expectation of privacy," based only on a dog alert, was held to violate protected rights.[134] Furthermore, the appellate court rejected the contention that the school personnel were protected against liability by good faith immunity. The court declared that the nude search of a thirteen-year-old child was "not only unlawful but outrageous under 'settled indisputable principles of law'." [135] Concluding that the school officials did not act in good faith or even within the "bounds of reason," the appeals court ruled that the victim of the nude search was entitled to seek damages.

Some legal commentators have argued that all personal searches of public school students should be based on the same standard that is applied to searches of adults by police officials—that is, probable cause. Most courts have not been inclined to require a showing of probable cause in school searches, but there is some indication that courts in the future may favor this more stringent standard, particularly in situations involving strip searches.

## Suggestions for School Personnel

While many legal issues involving search and seizure in schools remain unsettled, school personnel generally can protect themselves from a successful legal challenge by adhering to the following guidelines.

1. If police officials are conducting a search in the school, either with or without the school's involvement, school authorities should ensure that a search warrant is obtained.

2. Students and parents should be informed at the beginning of the school term of the procedures for conducting locker searches and personal searches.
3. Before school personnel conduct a search, the student should be asked to turn over the contraband, as such voluntary submission of material can eliminate the necessity for a search.
4. The authorized person conducting a search should have another staff member present who can verify the procedures used in the search.
5. School personnel should refrain from using strip searches or mass searches of groups of students.
6. Any search should be based on at least "reasonable belief" or "suspicion" that the student is in possession of contraband that may be disruptive to the educational process.

## CONCLUSION

In 1969, Justice Black noted that "school discipline, like parental discipline, is an integral and important part of training our children to be good citizens—better citizens." [136] Accordingly, school personnel have been empowered with the authority and the duty to regulate pupil behavior in order to protect the interests of the student body and the school. Reasonable sanctions can be imposed if students do not adhere to legitimate conduct regulations.

Courts, however, no longer will permit the promulgation of arbitrary disciplinary procedures that impair students' protected rights. The judiciary is not hesitant to enjoin the actions of school personnel, and even to assess punitive damages if warranted. Courts will evaluate the legality of challenged disciplinary regulations and the sufficiency of the evidence establishing that the rules have been violated. Mere intuition that the process of education will be impeded unless a specific rule is enforced cannot justify a regulation that infringes upon students' rights. Courts will ensure, if educators do not, that rules of conduct are reasonable and that punishments are appropriate.

Although the law pertaining to certain aspects of student discipline remains in a state of flux, judicial decisions support the following generalizations.

1. School authorities must be able to substantiate that any disciplinary regulation enacted is reasonable and necessary for the management of the school or for the welfare of pupils and school employees.
2. All regulations should be stated in precise terms and disseminated to students and parents.

3. Punishments for rule infractions should be appropriate for the offense and the characteristics of the offender (e.g., age, mental condition, prior behavior).
4. Some type of due process should be afforded to students prior to the imposition of punishments. For minor penalties, an informal hearing suffices; for serious punishments, more formal procedures are required (e.g., notification of parents, representation by counsel, opportunity to cross-examine witnesses).
5. A grievance procedure should be established for students to use in contesting disciplinary regulations or the administration of punishments.
6. Students can be punished for misbehavior occurring off school grounds if the conduct directly relates to the welfare of the school.
7. Suspensions and expulsions are legitimate punishments if accompanied by appropriate procedural safeguards and not arbitrarily imposed.
8. The transfer of students to different classes, programs, or schools for disciplinary reasons must be accompanied by due process procedures.
9. Reasonable corporal punishment can be used as a disciplinary technique as long as state laws and board regulations are followed.
10. Academic sanctions should not be used to punish students for nonacademic conduct unless the pupil behavior can be directly related to academic performance.
11. Policies regulating student appearance that are necessary for health or safety reasons or to prevent a disruption to the educational process can be enforced.
12. School personnel can search students' lockers or personal effects for educational purposes and upon reasonable suspicion that the students are in possession of contraband that will disrupt the school.
13. Students cannot be punished for the acts of others (e.g., their parents).
14. If students are unlawfully punished, they are entitled to be restored (without penalty) to their status prior to the imposition of the punishment and to have their records expunged of any reference to the illegal punishment.
15. School officials can be held liable for compensatory damages if unlawful punishments result in substantial injury to the students involved (e.g., unwarranted suspensions from school); however, only nominal damages, not to exceed one dollar, can be assessed against school officials for the abridgment of students' procedural rights (e.g., the denial of an adequate hearing).

# NOTES

1. *See* George Gallup, "The Twelfth Annual Gallup Poll of the Public's Attitudes Toward the Public Schools," *Phi Delta Kappan*, Vol. 62, No. 1, September 1980, p. 34.
2. Pugsley v. Sellmeyer, 158 Ark. 247, 250 S.W. 538 (1923). *See also* Jones v. Day, 127 Miss. 136, 89 So. 906 (1921).
3. Tanton v. McKenney, 226 Mich. 545, 197 N.W. 510 (1924).
4. *See* Mark Yudof, "Student Discipline in Texas Schools," *Journal of Law and Education*, Vol. 3, No. 2, 1974, p. 223.
5. 393 U.S. 503 (1969). *See* text with note 41, Chapter 10, for a discussion of this case.
6. Richards v. Thurston, 424 F.2d 1281, 1284 (1st Cir. 1970). *See also* "Note, Public Secondary Education: Judicial Protection of Student Individuality," *Southern California Law Review*, Vol. 42, 1969, p. 130.
7. State *ex rel.* Bowe v. Board of Educ. of City of Fond du Lac, 63 Wis. 234, 23 N.W. 102-103 (1885).
8. *See* Mitchell v. King, 169 Conn. 140, 363 A.2d 68 (1975); Soglin v. Kauffman, 418 F.2d 163 (7th Cir. 1969).
9. *See* Murray v. West Baton Rouge Parish School Bd., 472 F.2d 438 (5th Cir. 1973); Sword v. Fox, 446 F.2d 1091 (4th Cir. 1971).
10. *See* Sill v. Pennsylvania State Univ., 462 F.2d 463 (3d Cir. 1972).
11. *See* People v. Mummert, 183 Misc. 243, 50 N.Y.S.2d 699 (Nassau County Ct. 1944).
12. Pervis v. LaMarque Independent Dist., 466 F.2d 1054, 1057 (5th Cir. 1972).
13. Jordan v. School Dist. of the City of Erie, Pennsylvania (Jordan I), 548 F.2d 117 (3d Cir. 1977); Jordan II, 583 F.2d 91 (3d Cir. 1978); Jordan III, 615 F.2d 85 (3d Cir. 1980).
14. St. Ann v. Palisi, 495 F.2d 423, 426 (5th Cir. 1974).
15. Courts also have been called upon to assess the school's authority to punish students for damaging school property. While students can be punished for willful and wanton acts of vandalism, the judiciary has invalidated disciplinary action against pupils for careless destruction of school property, reasoning that carelessness is a common fault of children. *See* State v. Vanderbilt, 116 Ind. 11, 18 N.E. 266, 267 (1888); Holman v. School Trustees of Avon, 77 Mich. 605, 43 N.W. 996 (1889).
16. O'Rourke v. Walker, 102 Conn. 130 (1925).
17. Hutton v. State, 23 Tex. App. 386, 5 S.W. 122 (1887).
18. Lander v. Seaver, 32 Vt. 114 (1859).
19. Fenton v. Stear, 423 F. Supp. 767 (W.D. Pa. 1976).
20. *See* Galveston Independent School Dist. v. Boothe, 590 S.W.2d 553 (Tex. Civ. App. 1979); text with note 31, *infra.*
21. *See* Thomas v. Board of Educ., Granville Central School Dist., 607 F.2d 1043 (2d Cir. 1979), *cert. denied*, 100 S. Ct. 1034 (1980); text with note 106, Chapter 10.
22. *See* Eugene Connors, *Student Discipline and the Law* (Bloomington, Ind.: Phi Delta Kappa, 1979).
23. It should be noted that the definition of an expulsion varies from state

to state. While generally expulsions are considered the denial of school attendance in excess of ten days, in some states, such as Indiana, an expulsion is defined as the denial of school attendance in excess of five days. Ind. Code Ann. § 20-8.1-1-10.

24. *See* Ind. Code Ann. §20-8.1-5-5.

25. *See* Pervis v. LaMarque Independent School Dist., 466 F.2d 1054 (5th Cir. 1972); Dunn v. Tyler Independent School Dist., 460 F.2d 137, 144 (5th Cir. 1972); Wasson v. Trowbridge, 382 F.2d 807, 812 (2d Cir. 1967); Vail v. Board of Educ. of Portsmouth, 354 F. Supp. 592 (D.N.H. 1973); Fielder v. Board of Educ., 346 F. Supp. 722, 730 (D. Neb. 1972); Givens v. Poe, 346 F. Supp. 202, 209 (W.D.N.C. 1972); DeJesus v. Penberthy, 344 F. Supp. 70 (D. Conn. 1972); Pierce v. School Comm. of New Bedford, 322 F. Supp. 957 (D. Mass. 1971); Davis v. Ann Arbor Public Schools, 313 F. Supp. 1217 (E.D. Mich. 1970); Lafferty v. Carter, 310 F. Supp. 465 (W.D. Wis. 1970).

26. *See* Andrews v. Knowlton, 509 F.2d 898 (2d Cir. 1975); Murray v. West Baton Rouge Parish School Bd., 472 F.2d 438, 443 (5th Cir. 1973); Sill v. Penn State Univ., 462 F.2d 463, 469–70 (3d Cir. 1972); Lance v. Thompson, 432 F.2d 767 (5th Cir. 1970); Herman v. University of South Carolina, 341 F. Supp. 226, 232–34 (D.S.C. 1971), *aff'd* 457 F.2d 902 (4th Cir. 1972).

27. *See* Black Coalition v. Portland School Dist. No. 1, 484 F.2d 1040, 1045 (9th Cir. 1973); Fielder v. Board of Educ. of Winnebago, 346 F. Supp. 722, 724 n. 1, 730-31 (D. Neb. 1972).

28. *See* Jones v. State Bd. of Educ., 279 F. Supp. 190 (M.D. Tenn. 1968), *aff'd* 407 F.2d 834 (6th Cir. 1969), *cert. dismissed as improvidently granted*, 397 U.S. 31 (1970); Esteban v. Central Missouri State College, 277 F. Supp. 649 (W.D. Mo. 1967), *approved* 415 F.2d 1077 (8th Cir. 1969), *cert. denied*, 398 U.S. 965 (1970).

29. *See* Dillon v. Pulaski County Special School Dist., 594 F.2d 699 (8th Cir. 1979); DeJesus v. Penberthy, 344 F. Supp. 70 (D. Conn. 1972); Buttny v. Smiley, 281 F. Supp. 280 (D. Colo. 1968); Esteban, *id.*

30. *See* Marzette v. McPhee, 294 F. Supp. 562, 567 (W.D. Wis. 1968); Esteban, *id. See also* "Student Discipline: Suspension and Expulsion," *A Legal Memorandum* (Reston, Va.: National Association of Secondary School Principals, June 1975), pp. 6–7.

31. Galveston Independent School Dist. v. Boothe, 590 S.W.2d 553 (Tex. Civ. App. 1979).

32. Compare Hernandez v. School Dist. No. 1, Denver, 315 F. Supp. 289 (D. Colo. 1970) with Mills v. Board of Educ. of District of Columbia, 348 F. Supp. 866 (D.D.C. 1972).

33. 419 U.S. 565 (1975).

34. *Id.* at 574–75.

35. *See* "Student Discipline: Suspension and Expulsion," p. 7.

36. Goss v. Lopez, 419 U.S. 565, 583–84 (1975).

37. For a discussion of other possible "unusual situations," *see* P.M. Lines, "Procedural Due Process," *Constitutional Rights of Students* (Cambridge, Mass.: Center for Law and Education, 1976), p. 226.

38. *See* Papish v. Board of Curators of Univ. of Missouri, 410 U.S. 667, 671 (1973); Shanley v. Northeast Independent School Dist., 462 F.2d

960, 975 (5th Cir. 1972); Trujillo v. Love, 322 F. Supp. 1266, 1271 (D. Colo. 1971).

39. *See* Goss v. Lopez, 419 U.S. 565 (1975); Hatter v. Los Angeles City High School Dist., 452 F.2d 673 (9th Cir. 1971); Breen v. Kahl, 296 F. Supp. 702, 710 (W.D. Wis. 1969), *aff'd* 419 F.2d 1034 (7th Cir. 1969), *cert. denied*, 398 U.S. 937 (1970).

40. Section 1983 of the Civil Rights Act of 1871, 42 U.S.C.§ 1983 (1976), states: "Every person who, under color of any statute, ordinance, regulation, custom, or usage, of any State or Territory, subjects, or causes to be subjected, any citizen of the United States or other person within the jurisdiction thereof to the deprivation of any rights, privileges, or immunities, secured by the Constitution and laws, shall be liable to the party injured in an action at law, suit in equity, or other proper proceeding for redress."

41. 420 U.S. 308 (1975).

42. *Id.* at 320–27.

43. *See* Thonene v. Jenkins, 517 F.2d 3 (4th Cir. 1975); Boyd v. Smith, 353 F. Supp. 844 (N.D. Ind. 1973). *See* generally Chapters 3, 4, and 5.

44. Zeller v. Donegal School Dist. Bd. of Educ., 517 F.2d 600, 609 (3d Cir. 1975).

45. 545 F.2d 30 (7th Cir. 1976), *rev'd and remanded*, 435 U.S. 247 (1978).

46. *Id.*, 545 F.2d 30, 32.

47. *See* Monell v. Department of Social Services of the City of New York, 436 U.S. 658 (1978), in which the Supreme Court ruled that cities and school boards, as well as individuals, can be sued for civil rights violations; Owen v. City of Independence, Missouri, 100 S. Ct. 1398 (1980), in which the Supreme Court held that government agencies are not protected by good faith immunity. *See* text with note 133, Chapter 3, for a discussion of these cases.

48. *See* Lines, "Procedural Due Process," p. 253; "Student Discipline: Suspension and Expulsion," p. 7.

49. Goss v. Lopez, 419 U.S. 565, 583 (1975).

50. R. R. v. Board of Educ. of Shore Regional High School Dist., 263 A.2d 180 (N.J. Super. 1970).

51. Johnson v. Board of Educ., Union Free School Dist. No. 6, Manhasset, 393 N.Y.S.2d 510 (Sup. Ct., Nassau County, 1977).

52. *See* Chicago Bd. of Educ. v. Terrile, 361 N.E.2d 778 (Ill. App. 1977) (due process required before transferring a student to a school for habitual truants); Betts v. Board of Educ. of Chicago, 466 F.2d 629, 633 (7th Cir. 1972) (due process required before transferring a student to a continuation school as a disciplinary measure).

53. *See* Jordan v. School Dist. of the City of Erie, Pennsylvania, 615 F.2d 85 (3d Cir. 1980); text with note 13, *supra.*

54. Everett v. Marcase, 426 F. Supp. 397 (E.D. Pa. 1977). *See also* Hobson v. Bailey, 309 F. Supp. 1393 (W.D. Tenn. 1970).

55. Everett v. Marcase, *id.* at 400.

56. *See* Suits v. Glover, 260 Ala. 449, 71 So. 2d 49 (1954); Calway v. Williamson, 130 Conn. 575, 36 A.2d 377 (1944); People v. Mummert, 183 Misc. 243, 50 N.Y.S.2d 699 (Nassau County Ct. 1944).

57. *See* People *ex rel.* Hogan v. Newton, 185 Misc. 405, 56 N.Y.S.2d 779 (White Plains City Ct. 1945); Berry v. Arnold School Dist., 199 Ark. 1118, 137 S.W.2d 256 (1940).

58. 395 F. Supp. 294 (M.D.N.C. 1975), *aff'd* 423 U.S. 907 (1975).

59. 525 F.2d 909 (5th Cir. 1976), *aff'd* 430 U.S. 651 (1977). It should be noted that in June 1980, the Fourth Circuit Court of Appeals ruled that a child has a constitutional right to "bodily security" against severe corporal punishment. The appeals court reasoned that *Ingraham v. Wright* barred federal litigation of *procedural* due process issues in connection with corporal punishment but did not address the *substantive* due process right to physical safety which is the "most fundamental aspect of personal security." The appellate court concluded that there may be circumstances, independent of an allegation of cruel and unusual punishment, whereby the administration of corporal punishment is subject to litigation under 42 U.S.C. § 1983 for the impairment of substantive due process rights. Hall v. Tawney, 621 F.2d 607 (4th Cir. 1980).

60. For example, New Jersey and Massachusetts prohibit corporal punishment by statute, and Maryland prohibits its use by action of the state board of education.

61. *See* Conner, *Student Discipline and the Law*, p. 11.

62. *See* Harris v. Commonwealth, 372 A.2d 953 (Pa. Commw. 1977); Welch v. Board of Educ. of Bement Community School Dist. No. 5, 358 N.E.2d 1364 (Ill. App. 1977).

63. Jerry v. Board of Educ. of the City School Dist. of the City of Syracuse, 376 N.Y.S.2d 737 (App. Div. 1975). *See* text with note 119, Chapter 5.

64. Rolando v. School Directors of Dist. No. 125, 44 Ill. App. 3d 658, 358 N.E.2d 945 (1976).

65. Landi v. West Chester Area School Dist., 353 A.2d 895 (Pa. Commw. 1976).

66. Burton v. Pasadena City Bd. of Educ., 139 Cal. Rptr. 383 (Cal. App. 1977).

67. Johnson v. Horace Mann Mutual Ins. Co., 241 So. 2d 588 (La. App. 1970). *See* text with note 67, Chapter 7.

68. For a discussion of recommended guidelines, *see* Robert Simpson and Paul O. Dee, "Usual but Not Cruel: Policy Guidelines on Corporal Punishment," *NOLPE School Law Journal*, Vol. 7, No. 2, 1977, pp. 183–193.

69. 395 F. Supp. 294 (M.D.N.C. 1975). *See* text with note 58, *supra.*

70. *See* Fiacco v. Santee, 421 N.Y.S.2d 431 (App. Div. 1979); Barnard v. Inhabitants of Shelburne, 216 Mass. 19, 102 N.E. 1095 (1913).

71. Connelly v. University of Vermont and State Agricultural College, 244 F. Supp. 156, 160 (D. Vt. 1965).

72. In Horowitz v. Board of Curators of the University of Missouri, 538 F.2d 1317 (8th Cir. 1976), *rev'd* 435 U.S. 78 (1978), the United States Supreme Court reiterated that school authorities can establish and enforce academic standards. In this case, a medical student who was dismissed without notice of the charges or a formal hearing alleged that her constitutional rights were violated. However, the high court concluded that neither the student's liberty nor property interests were impaired by the academic dismissal without a hearing.

73. Valentine v. Independent School Dist. of Casey, 191 Iowa 1100, 183 N.W. 434 (1921).

74. *See* Spence v. Bailey, 465 F.2d 797 (6th Cir. 1972), in which the appellate court ruled that a school board's denial of a diploma to a student who refused to take a required officer's training course impaired his rights protected by the first amendment.

75. Ladson v. Board of Educ. of Union Free School Dist. No. 9, 323 N.Y.S.2d 545 (Sup. Ct., Nassau County, 1971).

76. Fowler v. Williamson, 448 F. Supp. 497 (W.D.N.C. 1978). There have also been a few challenges to school board policies prohibiting students from participating in graduation activities if they have completed graduation requirements in less than the normal four years. *See* Clark v. Board of Educ., Hamilton Local School Dist., 51 Ohio Misc. 71, 367 N.E.2d 69 (1977), in which the Ohio Supreme Court held that public school officials could not deny an early graduate the right to participate in graduation ceremonies.

77. Knight v. Board of Educ. of Tri-Point Community Unit School Dist., 348 N.E.2d 299 (Ill. App. 1976).

78. *Id.* at 303.

79. Hamer v. Board of Educ. of Township High School Dist. No. 113, 383 N.E.2d 231 (Ill. App. 1978).

80. Dorsey v. Bale, 521 S.W.2d 76 (Ky. App. 1975).

81. Gutierrez v. School Dist. R-1, Otero County, 585 P.2d 935 (Colo. 1978).

82. 20 U.S.C. 1232g (1976). *See* text with note 94, Chapter 8.

83. *See* "Grade Reduction, Academic Dismissal and the Courts," *A Legal Memorandum* (Reston, Va.: National Association of Secondary School Principals, October 1977).

84. The Supreme Court did uphold a grooming regulation for policemen in Kelley v. Johnson, 425 U.S. 238 (1976). *See* text with note 120, Chapter 3.

85. *See* Ferrell v. Dallas Independent School Dist., 392 F.2d 697 (5th Cir. 1968), *cert. denied*, 393 U.S. 856 (1968); Jackson v. Dorrier, 424 F.2d 213 (6th Cir. 1970), *cert. denied*, 400 U.S. 850 (1970); Olff v. East Side Union High School Dist., 445 F.2d 932 (9th Cir. 1971), *cert. denied*, 404 U.S. 1042 (1972); Freeman v. Flake, 448 F.2d 258 (10th Cir. 1971), *cert. denied*, 405 U.S. 1032 (1972).

86. Ferrell v. Dallas Independent School Dist., *id.*

87. Karr v. Schmidt, 460 F.2d 609, 613 (5th Cir. 1972), *cert. denied*, 409 U.S. 989 (1972).

88. Ferrara v. Hendry County School Bd., 362 So. 2d 371 (Fla. App. 1978). *See also* Stevenson v. Board of Educ. of Wheeler County, Georgia, 426 F.2d 1154 (5th Cir. 1970), in which the Fifth Circuit Court of Appeals upheld a school policy requiring students to be clean shaven in the interests of maintaining school discipline.

89. *See* Richards v. Thurston, 424 F.2d 1281 (1st Cir. 1970); Massie v. Henry, 455 F.2d 779 (4th Cir. 1972); Breen v. Kahl, 419 F.2d 1034 (7th Cir. 1969), *cert. denied*, 398 U.S. 937 (1970); Bishop v. Colaw, 450 F.2d 1069 (8th Cir. 1971). In the third federal circuit, decisions have been rendered in favor of both the student and the school board.

*See* Gere v. Stanley, 453 F.2d 205 (3d Cir. 1971) (upholding hair regulation); Stull v. School Bd. of Western Beaver Jr.-Sr. High School, 459 F.2d 339 (3d Cir. 1972) (upholding students' rights to govern their own appearance).

90. Breen, *id.* at 1036.

91. Richards v. Thurston, 424 F.2d 1281, 1286 (1st Cir. 1970).

92. Gere v. Stanley, 453 F.2d 205 (3d Cir. 1971).

93. *See* Ronald Elberger, *The Rights of Public High School Students in Indiana* (Indianapolis, Ind.: Indiana Civil Liberties Union, 1974), p. 4.

94. *See* Neuhaus v. Torrey, 310 F. Supp. 192 (N.D. Cal. 1970) (upheld grooming regulations for student athletes); Dunham v. Pulsifer, 312 F. Supp. 411 (D. Vt., 1970) (invalidating grooming code for student athletes); text with note 84, Chapter 8.

95. Compare Dostert v. Berthold Public School Dist. No. 54, 391 F. Supp. 876 (D.N.D. 1975), with Corley v. Daunhauer, 312 F. Supp. 811 (E.D. Ark. 1970).

96. Cordova v. Chonko, 315 F. Supp. 953 (N.D. Ohio 1970).

97. Farrell v. Smith, 310 F. Supp. 732 (D. Me. 1970). *See also* Bishop v. Cermenaro, 355 F. Supp. 1269 (D. Mass. 1973).

98. *See* "School Groups Differ Over HEW Move on School Dress Codes," *Education Daily*, Vol. 12, No. 224, November 21, 1979, p. 1.

99. *See* Bannister v. Paradis, 316 F. Supp. 185 (D.N.H. 1970).

100. *See* Johnson v. Joint School Dist. No. 60, Bingham County, 508 P.2d 547 (Idaho 1973); Wallace v. Ford, 346 F. Supp. 156 (E.D. Ark. 1972); Press v. Pasadena Independent School Dist., 326 F. Supp. 550 (S.D. Tex. 1971); Scott v. Board of Educ., Union Free School Dist. No. 17, 61 Misc. 2d 333, 305 N.Y.S.2d 601 (Sup. Ct., Nassau County, 1969).

101. Bannister v. Paradis, 316 F. Supp. 185 (D.N.H. 1970).

102. Dunkerson v. Russell, 502 S.W.2d 64 (Ky. 1973).

103. Bannister v. Paradis, 316 F. Supp. 185, 188-89 (D.N.H. 1970). *See also* Westley v. Rossi, 305 F. Supp. 706, 714 (D. Minn. 1969).

104. *See* Camara v. Municipal Court, 387 U.S. 523 (1967).

105. *See* Shore v. United States, 49 F.2d 519 (D.C. Cir. 1931).

106. *See In re* W., 29 Cal. App. 3d 777, 105 Cal. Rptr. 775 (1973); People v. Stewart, 63 Misc. 2d 601, 605, 313 N.Y.S.2d 253, 257 (Crim. Ct. of City of New York, 1970); Mercer v. State, 450 S.W.2d 715 (Tex. Civ. App. 1970).

107. *In re* Donaldson, 269 Cal. App. 2d 509, 75 Cal. Rptr. 220 (1969).

108. Commonwealth v. Dingfelt, 227 Pa. Super. 380, 323 A.2d 145 (1974).

109. State v. Baccino, 282 A.2d 869 (Del. Super. 1971).

110. State v. Young, 132 Ga. App. 790, 209 S.E.2d 96, 98 (1974).

111. State v. F.W.E., 360 So. 2d 148 (Fla. App. 1978). *See also* People v. Singletary, 333 N.E.2d 369 (N.Y. 1975).

112. State v. Mora, 307 So. 2d 317 (La. 1975), *cert. denied*, 429 U.S. 1004 (1976). *See* text with note 123, *infra. See also* People v. Scott D., 358 N.Y.S.2d 403, 406 (N.Y. 1974); State v. Walker, 528 P.2d 113 (Ore. App. 1974); People v. Bowers, 72 Misc. 2d 800, 803, 339 N.Y.S.2d 783, 787 (Crim. Ct. of City of New York, Kings County, 1973); *In re* G.C., 121 N.J. Super. 108, 115-17, 296 A.2d 102, 106-07 (1972).

113. Picha v. Wielgos, 410 F. Supp. 1214, 1218 (N.D. Ill. 1976). *See* text with note 125, *infra*.
114. *See* L. L. v. Circuit Court of Washington County, 280 N.W.2d 343 (Wis. App. 1979), for a discussion of various options in applying the fourth amendment to school searches.
115. *See In re* Donaldson, 269 Cal. App. 2d 509, 510 (1969).
116. *See* Piazzola v. Watkins. 442 F. 2d 284, 289-90 (5th Cir. 1971); Moore v. Student Affairs Comm. of Troy State Univ., 284 F. Supp. 725, 730-31 (M.D. Ala. 1968).
117. State v. Stein, 203 Kan. 638, 639, 456 P.2d 1, 2 (1969).
118. People v. Overton, 283 N.Y.S.2d 22, 229 N.E.2d 596 (N.Y. 1967).
119. *See* Bilbrey v. Brown, 481 F. Supp. 26 (D. Ore. 1979); State v. McKinnon, 558 P.2d 781 (Wash. 1977); People v. Scott D., 358 N.Y.S.2d 403, 408 (N.Y. 1974); People v. Cohen, 57 Misc. 2d 366, 292 N.Y.S.2d 706 (Dist. Ct., Nassau County, 1968); People v. Kelly, 195 Cal. App. 2d 669, 16 Cal. Rptr. 177 (1961).
120. State in Interest of Feazell, 360 So. 2d 907 (La. App. 1978).
121. State v. McKinnon, 558 P.2d 781 (Wash. 1977).
122. Matter of Ronald B., 401 N.Y.S.2d 544 (App. Div. 1978).
123. State v. Mora, 307 So. 2d 317 (La. 1975), *cert. denied*, 429 U.S. 1004 (1976).
124. *Id.*, 307 So. 2d 318.
125. Picha v. Wielgos, 410 F. Supp. 1214 (N.D. Ill. 1976).
126. *See also* Potts v. Wright, 357 F. Supp. 215 (E.D. Pa. 1973), in which a Pennsylvania federal district court declared that school officials could be found liable under the Civil Rights Act of 1871 if (1) they participated with police in taking actions that would cause plaintiffs to succumb to unlawful searches, or (2) there was an understanding between school officials and police to deny students their constitutional rights.
127. Bellnier v. Lund, 438 F. Supp. 47 (N.D.N.Y. 1977).
128. *Id.* at 53.
129. *Id.* at 54.
130. 420 U.S. 308 (1975). *See* text with note 41, *supra*.
131. M. M. v. Anker, 477 F. Supp. 837 (E.D.N.Y. 1979), *aff'd* 607 F.2d 588 (2d Cir. 1979).
132 *Id.*, 607 F.2d 589.
133. Doe v. Renfrow, 475 F. Supp. 1012 (N.D. Ind. 1979), *aff'd and remanded* for determination of damages, 631 F.2d 91 (7th Cir. 1980). It should be noted that in September 1980, a Texas federal district court reached an opposite conclusion as to the legality of searching students based on the "alert" of drug-detecting dogs. The court held that items seized as a result of such unconstitutional searches could not be used as grounds for subjecting the students to disciplinary actions. Jones v. Latexo Independent School Dist., No. TY-80-219-CA (E.D. Tex., September 3, 1980).
134. Doe v. Renfrow, 475 F. Supp. 1024.
135. *Id.*, 631 F.2d 92-93.
136. Tinker v. Des Moines Independent School Dist., 393 U.S. 503, 524 (1969) (Black, J., dissenting).

# 12

# Conclusion: Summary of Legal Generalizations

During the past three decades, courts increasingly have influenced the operation of schools by interpreting statutory and constitutional mandates as they apply to public school students and teachers. Similarly, legislative bodies at both state and national levels have become assertive in enacting laws to protect individuals' rights in school settings. Citizens are becoming more knowledgeable in using legal tools to challenge arbitrary school practices, and taxpayers are demanding greater accountability from public education agencies. No longer are school personnel shielded from the critical eyes of legislators or justices, and there are indications that legal intervention in public education will continue to escalate.

In the preceding chapters, principles of law have been presented as they apply to specific aspects of teachers' and students' rights and responsibilities. Constitutional and statutory provisions, in conjunction with judicial decisions, have been analyzed in an attempt to depict the current status of the law. Many diverse topics have been explored, some with clearly established legal precedents and others where the law is still evolving.

The most difficult situations confronting school personnel are those where specific legislative or judicial guidelines are lacking. In such circumstances, educators must make judgments based on their professional training and general knowledge of the law as it applies to education. The following broad generalizations, synthesized from the preceding chapters, are presented here to offer assistance to educators as they make such determinations in their daily school activities.

## GENERALIZATIONS

**The legal control of public education resides with the state as one of its sovereign powers.** Courts consistently have held that state legislatures possess plenary power in establishing and operating public schools; this power is restricted only by federal and state constitutional mandates. In attempting to follow the law, school personnel must keep in mind the scope of the state's authority to regulate educational activities. If courts have prohibited a given school practice under the Federal Constitution (e.g., racial discrimination, religious indoctrination), the state or its agents cannot enact laws or policies that conflict with the constitutional mandate unless justified by a compelling governmental interest. On the other hand, if the Constitution has been interpreted as permitting a certain activity (e.g., corporal punishment, public sector collective bargaining), states retain wide discretion in either restricting or expanding the practice.

For example, while the Supreme Court has rejected the assertion that probationary teachers have an inherent federal right to due process in situations of contract nonrenewals, state legislatures have the authority to create such a right under state law. Similarly, the Supreme Court has declared that the administration of corporal punishment in public schools does not raise any federal constitutional issues. Nonetheless, individual state legislatures can prohibit corporal punishment in public schools or require that certain procedures accompany its use.

Unless constitutional rights are at stake, courts defer to the will of legislative bodies in determining educational matters. State legislatures have the authority to create and redesign school districts, to collect and distribute educational funds, and to determine teacher qualifications and curricular offerings. With such pervasive control vested in the states, a thorough understanding of the operation of an educational system can be acquired only by examining the individual state's statutes, administrative regulations, and judicial decisions interpreting such provisions. The existence of fifty separate state systems of public schools has produced wide divergence in operational practices that affect teachers and students.

Parameters for the employment of teachers are delineated through either statute or state board of education regulations. For example, all states require that a teacher possess a valid teaching certificate based on satisfaction of certain minimum qualifications. Additionally, tenure laws define the permanency of the employer/employee relationship with respect to conditions of employment. Furthermore, the dismissal process for all teachers, tenured and nontenured, is circumscribed by state law and enforced by the judiciary. The scope of teachers' rights to engage in collective bargaining is also defined by state statute.

Like conditions of teacher employment, conditions of school attendance for students are specified in state law. Every state has enacted a compulsory attendance statute to ensure an educated citizenry. These laws are applicable to all children, with only a few legally recognized exceptions. In addition to mandating school attendance, states also have the authority to dictate courses of study and to select textbooks and instructional materials. Courts will not invalidate such decisions unless constitutional rights are abridged. Comparable reasoning also is applied by courts in upholding the state's power to establish graduation requirements, including the use of minimum competency tests as prerequisites to graduation. Courts have recognized that the establishment of academic standards is within the ambit of the states' legal authority.

It is a widely held misconception that local school boards control public education in this nation; local boards hold only those discretionary powers conferred by state law. Depending on the state, a local board's discretionary authority may be quite broad, narrowly defined by statutory guidelines, or somewhere in between these extremes. Nonetheless, school board regulations enacted pursuant to statutory authority are legally binding on employees and students. Hence, it is imperative for educators to become familiar with their respective state education laws, as well as local school board regulations enacted to implement the laws.

**All school policies and practices that impinge upon protected personal freedoms must be substantiated as necessary to carry out the educational mission of the school.** While the state and its agents have broad authority to regulate public schools, policies that impair federal constitutional rights must be justified by an overriding public interest. This generalization applies to any condition placed on employment or school attendance or any regulation of teachers' or students' activities. Although both school attendance and public employment were traditionally considered privileges bestowed upon individuals at the will of the state, this sentiment has changed during the past two decades. The Supreme Court has recognized that teachers and students do not shed their constitutional rights at the schoolhouse door. The state controls education, but this power must be exercised within the confines of the Federal Constitution.

For example, any constraints on teachers' academic freedom or rights to privacy must be substantiated as necessary for the proper functioning of the school. Also, if teachers are dismissed or disciplined for exercising protected rights, such as freedom of speech, school authorities must be able to establish that the specific behavior impaired teaching effectiveness or impeded the operation of the school. Furthermore, there must be valid educational objectives to justify prerequisites to employment, such as residency requirements or loyalty oaths.

Likewise, any condition attached to students' school attendance must be related to legitimate school purposes. Student disciplinary regulations that restrict appearance, speech, literature distribution, and so forth, also must be proven necessary to fulfill the school's educational mission. Unless student behavior will result in a material or substantial disruption of the school or interfere with the rights of others, it should not be curtailed.

If there are reasonable means of attaining the school's purposes that are less restrictive of individual freedoms, courts will require that such alternatives be pursued. However, personal rights can be abridged if such action is justified by an overriding public interest. As an illustration, a student's right to exercise free speech can be curtailed if the expression would lead to a disruption of the educational process. Similarly, in some instances courts have concluded that the *in loco parentis* (in place of parent) status of school personnel can justify relaxation of fourth amendment prohibitions against warrantless searches in schools. Also, teachers' rights to academic freedom can be impaired in the interest of maintaining a proper school environment.

Any interference with such rights, however, must be proven necessary—and not merely convenient—for the operation of the school. Courts recently have scrutinized carefully the rationale supporting educational practices. In balancing public and private interests, courts weigh the importance of the protected personal right against the governmental need to restrict its exercise. For example, courts have reasoned that there is no overriding public interest to justify compelling students to salute the American flag and pledge their allegiance if such observances conflict with religious or philosophical beliefs. In contrast, mandatory vaccination against communicable diseases has been upheld as a prerequisite to school attendance, even if opposition to immunization is based on religious grounds. Courts have reasoned that the overriding public interest in safeguarding the health of all students justifies such a requirement.

Every regulation that impairs individual rights, whether at the school district, school building, or classroom level, should be reviewed periodically to ensure that it is based on valid educational considerations and is essential to fulfilling the school's mission. Such regulations also should be clearly stated and well publicized so that all individuals understand the basis for the rules and the penalties for infractions.

**School policies and practices must not disadvantage selected employees or students.** The inherent personal right to remain free from governmental discrimination has been emphasized throughout this book. State action that draws distinctions on the basis of a suspect classification, such as race, has been evaluated with strict judicial scrutiny. In school desegregation cases, courts have charged school officials with an affirmative duty to take whatever steps are necessary to overcome the lingering effects of past discrimination. Similarly, racial discrimination associated with student grouping practices, testing methods, or suspension procedures, as well as with employee hiring or promotion practices, has been disallowed. However, neutral policies, uniformly applied, are not necessarily unconstitutional even though they have a disparate impact on minorities. For example, prerequisites to employment, such as tests that disqualify a disproportionate number of minority applicants, have been upheld as long as their use is based on nondiscriminatory objectives and is accompanied by racially neutral motives. Also, the assignment of a disproportionate number of minority students to certain instructional classes is permissible if such placements are based on legitimate educational criteria that are applied in the best interests of students.

In addition to racial classifications, other bases for distinguishing among employees and students have been invalidated if such classifications have disadvantaged individuals. Federal civil rights laws, in conjunction with state statutes, have reinforced constitutional protections afforded to various segments of society that traditionally have suffered discrimination. Indeed, the judiciary has recognized that legislative bodies are empowered to go beyond constitutional minimums in protecting citizens from discriminatory practices. Accordingly, laws have been enacted that place specific responsibilities on employers to ensure that employees are not disadvantaged on the basis of sex, age, religion, national origin, or handicaps. If it can be substantiated that such distinctions are the grounds for withholding benefits from certain individuals, school officials can be held liable for compensatory damages.

Also, federal and state mandates stipulate that students cannot be denied school attendance or otherwise disadvantaged based on characteristics such as sex, handicaps, national origin, marriage, or pregnancy. Eligibility for certain activities, such as participation on interscholastic athletic teams, cannot be denied to a certain class of students, such as females. In addition, disciplinary procedures that disproportionately disadvantage identified groups of students are vulnerable to legal challenge. Educators should be certain that all school policies are applied in a nondiscriminatory manner.

Courts will scrutinize grouping practices to ensure that they do not impede students' rights to equal educational opportunities. Nondiscrimination, however, does not necessitate the identical treatment of all pupils. Students can be classified based on their unique needs, but any differential treatment must be justified in terms of more appropriately serving the pupils. For example, students with learning disabilities can be provided with special services designed to address their deficiencies. In fact, judicial rulings and federal and state laws have placed an *obligation* on school districts to provide special services to meet the needs of handicapped and non-English-speaking students. Other children, such as the gifted and culturally disadvantaged, are beginning to assert a similar right to instructional accommodations for their unique needs.

**Due process is required before students or teachers may be deprived of protected liberty or property rights.** Due process is a basic tenet of the United States system of justice—the foundation of fundamental fairness. The fourteenth amendment, which has been used widely in educational litigation, stipulates that state action cannot deprive a person of life, liberty, or property without due process of law. This notion of due process has been an underlying theme in the discussion of teachers' and students' rights throughout this book. The nature of due process required is contingent upon the interest at stake and the procedures outlined in applicable state laws. Many state legislatures have been quite specific about the procedures that must be followed before an individual's protected rights may be impaired.

In the absence of greater statutory specificity, courts have held that under constitutional guarantees teachers cannot be discharged or disciplined without procedural requisites if property or liberty rights are implicated. A property claim to due process can be established by tenure status or contractual agreement or by action of the employer that creates a valid expectation of reemployment. A liberty right to due process can be asserted if the employer's action impairs the teacher's status in the community or opportunity to obtain other employment.

At a minimum, due process requires notice of the charges and a hearing before an impartial decision maker. The provision of due process does not imply that a teacher will not be dismissed or that sanctions will not be imposed. It simply means that the teacher must be given the opportunity to refute the charges and that the decision must be made fairly and supported by evidence.

Students, as well as teachers, have due process rights. Students have a state-created property right to attend school that cannot be denied without procedural requisites. If this right to attend school is withdrawn for disciplinary reasons, or if a student's instructional program is altered, due process is required. The nature of the proceedings depends on the deprivation involved, with more serious impairments necessitating more formal proceedings. Federal and state laws have become increasingly explicit in affording procedural protections to students in academic placement decisions as well as in disciplinary matters. Consequently, educators should ensure that some type of due process is provided before a student's educational status is altered in any fashion.

Inherent in the notion of due process is the assumption that all individuals have a right to a hearing if state action impinges on personal freedoms. Such a hearing need not be elaborate in every situation; an informal conversation can suffice under many circumstances. The crucial element is for all interested parties to have an opportunity to air their views. Often an informal hearing can serve to clarify issues and facilitate a mutual agreement, thus eliminating the need for more formal proceedings.

**Educators are expected to act reasonably and to anticipate potentially adverse consequences of their actions.** Educators hold themselves out as having certain knowledge and skills by the nature of their special training and certification. Accordingly, they are expected to exercise sound professional judgment in their daily activities. Reasonable actions in one situation may be viewed as unreasonable under other conditions. For example, in administering pupil punishments, teachers are expected to consider the student's age, mental condition, and past behavior as well as the specific circumstances surrounding the rule infraction. The failure to exercise reasonable judgment can result in dismissal, or possibly financial liability for impairing students' rights.

Teachers are also expected to make reasonable decisions pertaining to the academic program. Materials and methodology should be appropriate for the age of the students and the educational objectives. If students are grouped for instructional purposes, teachers are expected to base such decisions on legitimate educational considerations and to anticipate negative consequences that the grouping practices might have on selected students.

Also, teachers are held accountable for reasonable actions in supervising students, providing appropriate instructions, maintaining equipment in proper repair, and warning students of any known dangers. A teacher must exercise a standard of care commensurate with the duty to protect students from unreasonable risks of harm. Personal liability can be assessed for negligence if a teacher should have foreseen that an event could precipitate a pupil injury. Educators also are expected to exercise sound judgment in personal activities that affect their professional roles. In their private lives teachers and other school personnel are held to a higher level of discretion than the general public, since they serve as role models for students.

## CONCLUSION

One objective of this book, noted in the introduction, has been to alleviate fears of educators who feel that the scales of justice have been tipped against them. It is hoped that this objective has been achieved. Courts and legislatures have not imposed on school personnel any requirements that fair-minded educators would not impose on themselves. *Reasonable policies and practices based on legitimate educational objectives consistently have been sanctioned by the courts.* If anything, legislative and judicial mandates have clarified and supported the *authority* as well as the *duty* of school personnel to make and enforce regulations that are necessary to operate schools and to maintain a proper educational environment.

However, courts have invalidated school practices and policies if they have been clearly arbitrary, unrelated to educational objectives, or in violation of protected individual rights without an overriding justification. Since reform is usually easier to implement when designed from within than when externally imposed, educators should become more assertive in identifying and altering those practices that have the potential to generate legal intervention. Furthermore, school personnel should stay abreast of legal developments, since the Supreme Court has announced that ignorance of the law cannot be used as a defense for violating individuals' clearly established rights.

In addition to understanding basic legal rights and responsibilities, educators are expected to transmit this knowledge to students. Pupils also need to understand their constitutional and statutory rights, the balancing of interests that takes place in legislative and judicial forums, and the rationale for legal enactments, including school regulations. Only with increased awareness of fundamental legal principles can all individuals involved in the educational process develop a greater respect for the law and the responsibilities that accompany legal rights.

# Glossary

*Absolute privilege:* protection from liability for communication made in the performance of public service or the administration of justice.

*Appeal:* a petition to a higher court to alter the decision of a lower court.

*Appellate court:* a tribunal having jurisdiction to review decisions on appeal from inferior courts.

*Arbitration:* a process whereby an impartial third party, chosen by both parties in a dispute, makes a final determination regarding a contested issue.

*Assault:* the placing of another in fear of bodily harm.

*Battery:* the unlawful touching of another with intent to harm.

*Certiorari:* a writ of review whereby an action is removed from an inferior court to an appellate court for additional proceedings.

*Civil action:* a judicial proceeding to redress an infringement of individual civil rights, in contrast to a criminal action brought by the state to redress public wrongs.

*Civil right:* a personal right that accompanies citizenship.

*Class action suit:* a judicial proceeding brought on behalf of a number of persons similarly situated.

*Common law:* a body of rules and principles derived from usage or from judicial decisions enforcing such usage.

*Concurring opinion:* a statement by a judge or judges, separate from the majority opinion, that endorses the result of the decision but expresses some disagreement with the reasoning of the majority.

*Consent decree:* an agreement, sanctioned by a court, that is binding on the consenting parties.

*Consideration:* something of value given or promised for the purpose of forming a contract.

*Contract:* an agreement between two or more competent parties that creates, alters, or dissolves a legal relationship.

*Criminal action:* a judicial proceeding brought by the state against a person charged with a public offense.

*Damages:* an award made to an individual because of a legal wrong.

*Declaratory relief:* a judicial declaration of the rights of the plaintiff without an assessment of damages against the defendant.

*De facto segregation:* separation of the races that exists but does not result from action of the state or its agents.

*Defamation:* false and intentional communication that injures a person's character or reputation.

*Defendant:* the party against whom a court action is brought.

*De jure segregation:* separation of the races by law or by action of the state or its agents.

*De minimis:* something that is insignificant, not worthy of judicial review.

*Dictum:* a statement made by a judge in delivering an opinion that does not relate directly to the issue being decided and does not embody the sentiment of the court.

*Discretionary power:* authority that involves the exercise of judgment.

*Dissenting opinion:* a statement by a judge or judges who disagree with the decision of the majority of the justices in a case.

*Due process:* the fundamental right to notice of charges and an opportunity to rebut the charges before a fair tribunal if life, liberty, or property rights are at stake.

*Fact finding:* a process whereby a third party investigates an impasse in the negotiation process to determine the facts, identify the issues, and make a recommendation for settlement.

*Governmental function:* an activity performed in discharging official duties of a state or municipal agency.

*Governmental immunity:* the common law doctrine that governmental agencies cannot be held liable for the negligent acts of their officers, agents, or employees.

*Impasse:* a deadlock in the negotiation process in which parties are unable to resolve an issue without assistance of a third party.

*Injunction:* a writ issued by a court prohibiting a defendant from acting in a prescribed manner.

*In loco parentis:* in place of parent; charged with rights and duties of a parent.

*Liability:* an obligation one is bound by law to discharge.

*Mediation:* the process by which a neutral third party serving as an intermediary attempts to persuade disagreeing parties to settle their dispute.

*Ministerial duty:* an act that does not involve discretion and must be carried out in a manner specified by legal authority.

*Negligence:* the failure to exercise the degree of care that a reasonably prudent person would exercise under similar conditions.

*Plaintiff:* the party initiating a judicial action.

*Plenary power:* full, complete, absolute power.

*Precedent:* a judicial decision serving as authority for subsequent cases involving similar questions of law.

*Prima facie:* a fact presumed to be true unless disproven by contrary evidence.

*Probable cause:* reasonable grounds, supported by sufficient evidence, to warrant a cautious person to believe that the individual is guilty of the offense charged.

*Proprietary function:* an activity (often for profit) performed by a state or municipal agency that could as easily be performed by a private corporation.

*Qualified privilege:* protection from liability for communication made in good faith, for proper reasons, and to appropriate parties.

*Remand:* to send a case back to the original court for additional proceedings.

*Respondeat superior:* a legal doctrine whereby the master is responsible for acts of the servant (a governmental unit is liable for acts of its employees).

*Stare decisis:* to abide by decided cases; to adhere to precedent.

*Statute:* an act by the legislative branch of government expressing its will and constituting the law of the state.

*Tenure:* a statutory right that confers permanent employment on teachers, protecting them from dismissal except for adequate cause.

*Tort:* a civil wrong, independent of contract, for which a remedy in damages is sought.

*Ultra vires:* beyond the scope of authority of the corporate body.

*Vacate:* to set aside; to render a judgment void.

*Verdict:* a decision of a jury on questions submitted for trial.

# Index

Ability grouping (*see* Classification of pupils)
Academic freedom (*see also* Censorship)
    community objections to classroom materials, 47–48
    discussion of controversial topics, 47–48
    removal of classroom and library materials, 48–49, 195–197
    selection of textbooks, 47, 195
    use of controversial materials, 46, 47–48
Academic sanctions
    academic performance, 296
    misconduct, 296–297
    truancy, 296–297
Accidents (*see* Tort liability)
Admissions standards (*see* Classification of pupils)
Affirmative action (*see* Discrimination in employment)
Age (*see also* Classification of pupils)
    Age Discrimination Act, 95–96, 229–231
    discrimination in employment, 94–97

Agency shop
    definition of, 152
    legality of, 152–153
Appearance
    dress codes for teachers, 62–64
    pupil attire, 300–301
    pupil hairstyle, 298–300
Assault and battery charges in connection with corporal punishment, 178–179
Association
    loyalty oaths, 49–51
    outside speakers, 47, 272–273
    political activity, 52–56
    student clubs, 271–272
    subversive activities, 51–52
    union membership, 52
Athletics (*see* Extracurricular activities)
Attorneys' fees, recovery of, 134–135

Bargaining (*see* Collective bargaining)
Bible
    Bible study courses, 257–258
    distribution of religious literature, 258–259

objective study of, 257
reading of, 256
Bilingual/bicultural education
black English, 243
federal legislation and regulations, 243–244
right to bilingual/bicultural programs, 241–244
Boards of education
local, 5–7
state, 3–4
Buckley Amendment (*see* Family Educational Rights and Privacy Act)

Case law
in general, 12–13
rules of judicial review, 13–14
Censorship (*see also* Academic freedom)
removal of classroom and library materials, 48–49, 195–197
selection of textbooks, 47, 195
Certification (*see* Employment)
Chief state school officer, duties of, 4
Church-state relations (*see* Religion)
Civil Rights Act of 1871
applications of, 64–66
definition of, 12
liability of school officials, 64–65, 290–292, 305–306
Civil Rights Act of 1964
Title VI, 83–84, 241–242
Title VII
race, 76–79, 81–86
religion, 58–59
sex, 78–79, 86–93
Class size, scope of negotiations, 156–157
Classification of pupils
ability
gifted and talented students, 234–235

special education placements, 232–233
tracking schemes, 231–232
age
admission to programs, 229–231
condition of participation in extracurricular activities, 205
ethnic background/native language
non-English-speaking students, 241–244
students speaking black English, 243
handicaps (*see* Handicapped students)
marital status
denial of school attendance, 228
participation in extracurricular activities, 228
pregnancy
denial of school attendance, 228–229
differential treatment, 228–229
race (*see* Desegregation)
sex (*see also* Title IX of the Education Amendments of 1972)
admission criteria, 227
high school athletics, 222–225
sex-segregated programs and schools, 225–227
Collective bargaining
agency shop, 152–153
Executive Order 10988, 147
first amendment protection, 147, 153–154
good faith bargaining, 150
impasse procedures
arbitration, 151
fact-finding, 151
mediation, 151

injunctions, 146, 160
labor relations boards, 149–150
National Labor Relations Act,
    146–147
Norris LaGuardia Act, 146
private versus public sector,
    145–147
rights of nonunion teachers,
    152–153
scope of negotiations
    class size, 156–157
    due process protections for
        probationary teachers, 158
    governmental policy, 155–156
    grievance procedures, 158
    reduction in force, 157
    school calendar, 157
    student disciplinary proce-
        dures, 285
    teacher evaluation, 157
    work day, 157
state legislation, 149–151
strikes, 159–161
unfair labor practices, 150–151
Competency testing
    litigation, 202
    state legislation, 201–203
Compulsory attendance
    age requirements, 229–231
    attempts to evade, 191–192
    equivalent instruction, 190
    exceptions, 190–191
Constitutional law in general, 7–8
Contracts (see Employment)
Controversial issues (see Academic
    freedom; Censorship)
Corporal punishment (see Dis-
    cipline)
Courts (see Judicial system)
Curriculum (see also Censorship)
    federal constitutional con-
        straints, 194, 259–260
    parental objections, 193–194
    religious conflicts, 259–261
    sex education, 194–195, 261
    state requirements, 193

Defamation, 180–181
Desegregation, 219–221
Discipline (see also Academic
    sanctions; Search and sei-
    zure)
    conduct off school grounds,
        285–286
    corporal punishment
        criteria for reasonableness,
            293
        definition of, 293
        dismissal of teachers for in-
            appropriate use, 127–128,
            294–295
        federal constitutional issues,
            293–294
        school board policies, 294–
            295
        state laws, 294–295
        state remedies for inappro-
            priate use, 295
    expulsions
        due process safeguards, 288
        grounds, 287
        remedies for unlawful expul-
            sions, 290–292
    guidelines for regulations, 286
    in general, 284–287
    suspensions
        due process requirements,
            289–290
        remedies for unlawful suspen-
            sions, 290–292
    transfers, 292–293
Discrimination against students
    (see Classification of
    pupils)
Discrimination in employment
    age
        criteria for evaluation, 96
        mandatory retirement ages,
            94–96
        promotions, transfers, and
            discharges, 96–97
    handicaps

Section 504, Rehabilitation
    Act of 1973, 97–99
race
    reverse discrimination, 83–86
    selection and hiring practices,
        76–79
    staff reductions, 79–83
sex
    compensation, 92
    judicial standards of review,
        87
    pregnancy-related policies,
        86–90
    promotion, 91–92
    retirement programs, 90–91
    Title IX, 93–94
Dismissal (*see* Teacher dismissal)
Dress (*see* Appearance)
Due process procedural require-
        ments
    dismissal of teachers
        evidence, 113–114
        in general, 108–109
        hearing, 111–113
        notice, 110–111
        summary, 114
    punishment of pupils (*see* Dis-
        cipline)

Education for All Handicapped
    Children Act of 1975, 237–
    238
Educational malpractice, 199–
    201
Employment (*see also* Teacher
        dismissal)
    assignment, 24–26
    certification
        citizenship, 23
        examination, 22
        loyalty oaths, 22–23
        professional preparation, 22
        revocation, 23–24
    contracts
        basic elements, 26–27
        termination, 27

outside employment, 33–34
reduction in force, 30–32
residency requirements, 32–33
summary of terms and condi-
        tions, 34–35
tenure
    award of, 28–30
    collective negotiations issue,
        158
    dismissal for cause, 118–133
    guarantees, 28
    purpose, 28
    types of contracts, 28
Equal educational opportunities
    (*see* Classification of
        pupils)
Equal employment opportunity
    (*see* Discrimination in em-
        ployment)
Equal protection clause, 217–
    218
Evaluation
    student (*see* Instruction)
    teacher, 157
Evolution, teaching of, 194
Exceptional children (*see* Handi-
        capped students; Gifted
        students)
Expulsion (*see* Discipline)
Extracurricular activities
    athletics
        classifications based on mar-
            riage, 228
        classifications based on sex,
            222–225
        eligibility requirements, 205
        grooming regulations, 206
        handicapped students, 206
        residency requirements, 204–
            205
        training regulations, 203–204
    definition of, 203
    right to participate, 203

Family Educational Rights and
    Privacy Act, 207–208

Federal Constitution
in general, 7-8
major provisions affecting
public schools, 8-10
Field trips, liability for negligence,
172-173
Flag, salute to, 57, 259-260
Freedom of expression (*see also*
Academic freedom; Student
publications)
balancing of interests, 40-41, 44
criticism of school administration, 40, 268
disruptive expression, 263-264
expression of views on public
issues, 40, 268
private expression to superiors,
43-44
symbolic expression, 41, 261-
262
teacher transfers, 41, 43
*Tinker* principle, 261-263
Freedom of religion (*see* Religion)

Gifted students
Gifted and Talented Children's
Education Act of 1978, 234
state legislation, 234-235
Governmental immunity (*see* Immunity; Tort liability)
Grades (*see* Academic sanctions)
Grievance procedures
definition of, 158
topic of collective negotiations,
158

Hairstyle (*see* Appearance)
Handicapped students
appropriate education programs, 240
disciplinary procedures, 239-240
Education for All Handicapped
Children Act of 1975, 208,
237-239
extended school year programs,
238

fiscal support of programs, 235-
236, 238-239
individualized educational programs, 239
least restrictive environment,
240
participation on athletic teams,
206
placement, 232-233
right to education, 235-236
Section 504 of the Rehabilitation Act of 1973, 237
tuition reimbursement, 236
Homosexuality
basis for teacher dismissal, 125-
126
right to privacy, 61-62

Immorality
cause for teacher dismissal, 122-
126
private conduct, 60-62
Immunity
application to municipalities,
65-67
eleventh amendment immunity,
66-67
good faith defense, 64-65, 290-
291
governmental immunity for tort
actions, 174-175
Immunization (*see* Vaccination)
In loco parentis
application of doctrine, 302
definition of, 302
Incompetency (*see* Teacher dismissal)
Injuries (*see* Tort liability)
Instruction (*see also* Academic
freedom; Censorship)
academic achievement
competency testing, 201-203
educational malpractice, 199-
201
curricular requirements, 193-
194

prescribed textbooks, 195–197
required fees for textbooks and
    courses, 197–198
Insubordination (*see* Teacher dis-
    missal)

Judicial system
    federal courts, 14–15
        courts of appeal, 14–15
        district courts, 14
        United States Supreme Court,
            15
    general role, 12–13
    state courts, 14

Labor relations (*see* Collective
    bargaining)
Labor unions, right to organize,
    147
Legislative power, definition of,
    2–3
Liability (*see* Immunity; Tort liabil-
    ity)
Local boards of education, powers
    of, 5–7
Loyalty oaths (*see* Association)

Malpractice (*see* Educational mal-
    practice)
Married students (*see* Classifica-
    tion of pupils)
Ministerial functions, definition
    of, 6

Negligence (*see* Tort liability)
Negotiations (*see* Collective bar-
    gaining)
Nonpublic schools (*see* Private
    schools)

Parents
    accommodation of religious
        beliefs in curriculum, 260–
        261
    compulsory attendance man-
        dates, 189–193

reimbursement for private
    placement of handicapped
    children, 236
right to govern children's educa-
    tion, 189–190, 193–194
Placement of pupils (*see* Classifi-
    cation of pupils)
Political activity
    circulation of petitions, 53
    participation in political cam-
        paigns, 52–55
    patronage dismissals, 53–54
    political speakers, 47, 272–273
Prayer (*see* Religion)
Pregnancy (*see also* Classification
    of pupils)
    disability programs, 87–89
    dismissal of teachers for im-
        morality, 124–125
    leave of absence, 88–89
    unwed teachers, 61, 124–125
Privacy (*see also* Teacher dismis-
    sal; Student records)
    sexual conduct of teachers, 60–
        62
        homosexuality, 61–62
        living arrangements, 60
        pregnancies out of wedlock,
            61
Private schools
    placement of handicapped stu-
        dents, 236
    right to exist, 190
    state regulation, 190
Publications (*see* Student publica-
    tions)

Race (*see* Desegregation; Discrim-
    ination in employment)
Reduction in force
    cause for dismissal, 30, 132–133
    statutory provisions, 30–32
    topic of negotiations, 157
Religion
    Bible reading, 256

conflict with compulsory school
    attendance laws, 191–192
conflict with curricular offer-
    ings, 259–261
curriculum exemptions, 194,
    259–261
discrimination in employment,
    58–59
distribution of literature, 258–
    259
flag salute ceremony, 57, 259–
    260
meditation, 257
observance of holy days, 256
posting of Ten Commandments,
    258
prayer, 256
proselytizing in school, 56
released time for instruction,
    256–257
religious garb, 57–58
religious symbols, 256
Residency requirements
    condition of employment, 32–
        33
    extracurricular activities, 205–
        206
Retirement (see Discrimination in
    employment)
Reverse discrimination (see Dis-
    crimination in employment)

Safe place statutes, 174
School calendar, scope of negotia-
    tions, 157
Search and seizure
    drug-detecting dogs, 306–307
    fourth amendment, 301–307
    guidelines, 307–308
    in loco parentis doctrine, 302
    locker searches, 303
    personal searches, 303–307
    police involvement, 304, 305,
        306–307
    strip searches, 305–306
Secret societies, 271

Section 504 of the Rehabilitation
    Act of 1973
    litigation, 97–99
    provisions, 97, 237
Sex discrimination (see Classifica-
    tion of pupils; Discrimina-
    tion in employment)
Sex education, 194, 261
Slander (see Tort liability)
Special education (see Classifica-
    tion of pupils; Gifted stu-
    dents; Handicapped stu-
    dents)
Speech (see Freedom of expres-
    sion)
State boards of education
    general authority, 3–4
    membership, 3
State departments of education,
    functions of, 4–5
State legislatures, general powers
    of, 2–3
Statistics in discrimination cases,
    79
Strikes (see Collective bargaining)
Student achievement (see Instruc-
    tion)
Student clubs
    political, 272
    religious, 256
    secret societies, 271
Student publications
    controversial issues, 268
    disruptive material, 266–268
    distribution off school grounds,
        270
    libelous material, 267–268
    obscene material, 266–267
    prior review regulations, 265–
        266
    school-sponsored, 269–270
    time, place, and manner regula-
        tions, 270
Student records (see also Educa-
    tion for All Handicapped
    Children Act)

Family Educational Rights and
    Privacy Act, 207
guidelines, 207–208
Suspension (*see* Discipline)

Teacher dismissal
causes
    immorality, 122–126
    incompetency, 120–122
    insubordination, 126–129
    other, 129–132
    reduction in force, 30–32,
        132–133
    statutory provisions in gen-
        eral, 118–120
    summary, 133
definition of, 107
due process
    defined, 108
    liberty interest, 108, 114–118
    nontenured teachers' rights,
        114–118
    procedural requirements in
        discharge, 109–114
    property interest, 108, 114–
        118
remedies for wrongful
    attorneys' fees, 134–135
    civil rights legislation, 64–66
    damages, 133–134
    reinstatement, 134
Tenure (*see* Employment)
Testing procedures (*see also* Com-
    petency testing; Classifica-
    tion of pupils)
    prerequisite to employment, 22
Textbooks (*see* Instruction)
Title VI of the Civil Rights Act
    (*see* Civil Rights Act of 1964)
Title VII of the Civil Rights Act
    (*see* Civil Rights Act of 1964)
Title IX of the Education Amend-
    ments of 1972
    employees, 93–94
    students
        exclusion of females from

athletic teams, 222–224
    exclusion of males from
        athletic teams, 225
    sex-based admission criteria,
        227
    sex-based rules in sports, 224
    sex-segregated classes, 226
Tort liability
    assault and battery, 178–179
    categories of actions, 167
    defamation, 180–181
    definition of, 167
    liability insurance, 181
    negligence (*see also* Educational
        malpractice)
        breach of duty, 168–170
        defenses, 173–177
        defined, 168
        elements identified, 168
        failure to exercise reasonable
            care, 171–173
    workers' compensation, 179–
        180
Tracking schemes (*see* Classifica-
    tion of pupils)
Transfer
    students
        disciplinary, 292–293
        extracurricular requirements,
            204–205
    teacher disciplinary, 41, 43
Truancy
    academic sanctions, 296–298
    compulsory attendance, 189–
        190, 191–192
    liability of school personnel, 170
Tuition
    private school placements, 236
    public school courses, 198

Unions (*see* Collective bargaining)

Vaccination, as prerequisite to
    school attendance, 192–193

Work day, scope of negotiations,
    157